Praise for *Living Co*ntradiction

Drawing from a great wealth of research and the even greater v rience, Sean Warren and Stephen Bigger have written som deconstructs the thorny issues endemic in the British educatior tive and achievable remedies for them.

Cha...

A fascinating insight into teaching and education – I can personally identify with so many of the aspects discussed. What is clear throughout is that relationships in teaching are crucial: they underpin and determine the behaviour of students in our schools, whether we agree that this should be the case or not.

I would recommend *Living Contradiction* to anyone entering or already in the education profession.

Clare Gammons, Head Teacher, Cambian Wisbech School

Living Contradiction is a fascinating, honest examination of that genuine contradiction faced by teachers in reconciling the effort made to encourage young people towards independent critical thinking, with the simultaneous sense of responsibility to instruct and insist on a particular behaviour.

The authors' methodology is robust, providing a full discussion and acknowledgement of the benefits and constraints of autobiography in an academic research project, and offers thought-provoking insight into the use of the immediacy of blogging as a tool to record or diarise, and share, immediate experience. *Living Contradiction* also offers an interesting evaluation of the role of educational theorists set against the realities of teachers' experience on the front line in schools, where years of academic research are set against the need to respond to a behaviour in a matter of minutes.

Suzie Grogan, author of *Shell Shocked Britain*

Living Contradiction is the book that I wish I had had when I embarked on a career as a teacher.

The 'living contradiction' that is its starting point is painfully familiar to everyone who has stood in a classroom and wondered how they had ended up this way, with the energy-sapping task of keeping order becoming an end in itself. We had thought it was a precondition for learning, and we craved the respect of pupils and colleagues, but we had sacrificed the excitement that brought us into the profession.

Warren and Bigger's book breaks out of this sterile dilemma: discipline versus self-expression, strength versus weakness. Warren is no naive idealist, and is well aware that teachers continue to be accountable to a regime that insists on measurable, quantitative, and sometimes trivial outcomes. The breaking of familiar patterns is challenging for him, for colleagues, and for pupils. It is a rocky ride for everyone, but also an exemplary exercise in practice-based research. Armed with insights from educationalists and a rigorous methodology that enables him to analyse and interpret the results of his new approach, and fortified by a constant, questioning dialogue with Stephen Bigger, Sean Warren succeeds in changing the dynamic in his classroom – a hard-won achievement and a thrilling one.

This is not an arid book – all teachers will recognise the day-to-day dilemmas, confrontations, and compromises recounted here with honesty and wit. But it is inspirational: here is someone who has had the courage to believe in his students, in himself, and in the power of education.

Ann Miller, University Fellow, University of Leicester

Living Contradiction is an intelligent, sensitive, and socially situated antidote to the macho, authoritarian 'what works' publications in education that cocksurely proselytise about what needs to be done to improve teaching and learning.

In conceptualising teaching as a moral and ethical practice, Warren and Bigger seek to illuminate and confront some of the complexities involved in dealing with the thorny issues of behaviour and discipline in schools. But rather than providing spurious, short term solutions, *Living Contradiction* takes the reader on a journey of critical reflection and self-learning as the authentic experience of Warren's professional life is openly interrogated. The richness, sensitivity, and depth of thought with which this book examines matters relating to behaviour and discipline in schools makes it very unique from many other publications.

Dr Matt O'Leary, Reader in Education, Birmingham City University

Warren and Bigger's account is deeply human and is a model example of how to turn a piece of academic research (a PhD in this case) into a beautifully written, highly readable, and truly inspirational book.

Living Contradiction is a book for now which addresses the urgency for a radical reassessment of what schooling should mean. Some of the source material – particularly the extracts from pupils' diaries – are frankly shocking, and illustrate an alarming lack of respect afforded to pupils' human rights and dignity. Not all schools are the same, of course, but all who are involved in the education of our young people will find here a fascinating and inspiring journey that grapples with the real issues of schooling.

I'm certain that many teachers will find *Living Contradiction* deeply relevant and truly inspirational.

Dr Geoff Teece, Honorary Research Fellow,
University of Exeter Graduate School of Education

What I like most about *Living Contradiction* is its collaborative nature and its honesty. Sean Warren and Stephen Bigger exemplify a collaborative educational relationship: the book shows how Bigger shared his understandings of critical theory, encouraging Warren to see that autobiographical writings could produce a valid and academically legitimate contribution to educational knowledge in the generation of a living educational theory. The honesty is in Warren's educational journey, which will captivate your imagination and resonate with your own experiences of the imposition of institutional power relations.

I believe that *Living Contradiction* will be of great value on initial and continuing professional development programmes in education, and to all professionals in a wide range of workplace contexts who are facing their own contradictions in living their values as fully as they can.

Jack Whitehead, Visiting Professor of Education, University of Cumbria

Warren and Bigger present a highly engaging account of a teacher's journey from an approach founded in authoritarianism to one founded in respect and care: moving from discipline imposed by teachers, to developing pupils' self-discipline that is the result of self-learning. The move from compliance and confrontation to cooperation and care is compelling in its challenge to readers to review their professional practice and relationships.

Underpinned by research and personal reflection, *Living Contradiction* is a powerful challenge to the ways in which schools work.

Dr Richard Woolley, Head, Centre for Education and Inclusion,
Deputy Head (Research), Institute of Education, University of Worcester

Living Contradiction

A Teacher's Examination of Tension and Disruption in Schools, in Classrooms and in Self

Sean Warren and Stephen Bigger

Crown House Publishing Limited
www.crownhouse.co.uk

First published by
Crown House Publishing Limited
Crown Buildings, Bancyfelin, Carmarthen, Wales, SA33 5ND, UK
www.crownhouse.co.uk

and

Crown House Publishing Company LLC
PO Box 2223, Williston, VT 05495, USA
www.crownhousepublishing.com

First published 2017.

British Library Cataloguing-in-Publication Data

A catalogue entry for this book is available from the British Library.

Print ISBN 978-178583177-5
Mobi ISBN 978-178583263-5
ePub ISBN 978-178583264-2
ePDF ISBN 978-178583265-9

LCCN 2017948367

Printed and bound in the UK by
TJ International, Padstow, Cornwall

Acknowledgements

Sean: The content of this book spans my entire life. The process of articulation began nine years ago.

Acknowledging the family and friends who have made contributions for the full duration of my 50 plus years, I send my love and thanks.

For those teachers and classmates who walked with me during my school days, I give a thumbs up and a smile. I know you are all much older now, but in my memories you all look the same today as you did all those moons ago. In spite of the hardships, for me, it remains a blessed time.

For the colleagues and pupils who have shared some of my professional journey over the past three decades, I extend a handshake – and for others a hug. Making specific contributions to my research – Jon A, for generously sharing his intellectual property, and Graeme S, my faculty leader – take your pick, boys – too late, a hug it is!

For my doctorate supervisors, Richard Woolley, John Visser, and of course my co-author, Stephen, I give my sincere gratitude. To those 'critical friends' who read the thesis – a substantial piece of work which provides the foundation for this book – I offer a 'cheers'. (Brian H, John B, and Tim WM – really appreciated it.) Both Stephen and I wish to say thank you to Emma T, our copy editor at Crown House, for her thorough review of our first draft.

Tying together many of these threads is my wonderful wife, Julia: a loyal friend, a fellow teacher, and my chief proofreader, she has been my anchor throughout. And finally, to our beautiful children: Emma, Libby, and Chad, for the many sacrifices they have made during a prolonged period of research and writing. Daddy is all done now.

Stephen: Dedicated to the memory of my parents and of the many other relatives and friends we have sadly lost.

Contents

Acknowledgements ..... *i*
Prologue: Sean ..... *v*
Preface: Stephen ..... *ix*

Introduction: The Background to the Book 1
1. A Sense of 7
2. Autobiographical Research 17
   Reflexivity 21

Part I. Power *Over* **27**
3. Subscribing to Authoritarianism 29
   An Authoritarian School 32
   The Situation 36
   Sanctions 36
   Internal Isolation Unit 38
   Training Colleagues 43
   Staff Disempowerment 47
   Inner Emotions 48
   Outbursts 50
4. Conceptions of Good and Bad 55
   Fear and Blame 59
   The Significant Minority 63
   Rules 66
5. A Consideration of Curriculum 69
   What Is Education For? 71
   The Politicisation of Learning 72
   Positive School Relationships: Critical Pedagogy 75
   Resistance to Authoritarianism 77
   Promoting Well-Being: Schooling and Mental Health 78

Part II. Methodological Considerations **81**
6. Knowledge and Values 83
   Application to Research in Education and Schooling 84
   Evidence and Evidence-Based Research in Education 86
7. Quality As Measured 89

A Number 91
Accountability 93
A Directed Profession 94
Site of Struggle 96
Positioning 99
My Contextual Settings 100
8. Quality As Experienced 103
Subjective Knowledge 104
Living Logics 106
9. Complexity 109
Interactions 109
Conceptual Fudge 110
Complex Adaptive Systems 111
'Is' Not 'Ought' 114
Clocks or Clouds? 116

Part III. Degrees of Resistance: Low Level Disruptions 119

10. Variance 121
Positionality 123
11. Weather Forecast 127
'Can' Not 'Do' 128
Conduct Offers Up Clues 129
Possibility of Localised Showers 131
An Assumption of Quality 132
12. Testing and Challenging Boundaries 137
Rain Cloud Behaviour 138
Crossing the Line 139
Staff Language Conveying Disruptive Incidents 141
Undeterred 142
Theorising Through a Complexity Lens 144
The Significance of Timings 146
13. Recognising Boundaries 149
The 'Means Business' Teacher 153
The 'Scary' Teacher 154
Commentary 154
14. Indistinct Boundaries 157
The Ineffective Teacher 159

15. In-Group/Out-Group 163
Territory 164
Disregard 165
16. Professional Identity 171
Split-Self 171
Self-laceration 172
Sub-identities 173

Part IV. Power *With* **177**

17. Classroom Climate 179
Initial Forming Phase 183
Reinforcing Cues During the Re-forming Process 185
'With-it-ness' 189
Collective Responsibility 191
Classroom Climate Questionnaire 192
Secure, Significant, and Valued 193
18. Dark Clouds 197
Hidden Goals 197
Solitary Rain Cloud 201
19. Stormy Weather 209
Analysis of Games 214
Reflexive Turmoil 217
20. React or Respond: Examining the Patterns 219
React 220
Dominating 222
21. Core Gimmicks 225
The Socialised Self, School, and Teachers 227
Exposure 230
Parental Figures 232
Exposed Again 234
22. Transitions 239
Product 239
Servant 241
Agent 244
Authoritative Presence 246
23. Social Dynamics 249
Self-organisation 250

Isolates 253

24. The Teaching and Learning Interaction 257

Reconceptualising 'Disorder' 259

Lesson Observation Model 261

Archetypal Friday Period 5 264

Capturing the Edge of Chaos 266

Part V. Working with Colleagues 271

25. Affirmation and the Potential for Continuing Professional Development 273

Established Teacher 273

NQTs 274

Trainee 276

26. A Salutary Reminder: Colleagues and Pupils 279

Harried 279

A Mere Contribution 283

Epilogue 285

Appendix A: FIRO Theory 291

Appendix B: Temple Index of Functional Fluency (TIFF) Descriptors 293

Appendix C: Professional Development 295

References 301

Prologue

Sean

In 1981, I was coming to the end of my compulsory education, and about to embark on the world of work – I was yet to realise that it would lead to a career in teaching. When I belatedly chose to become a teacher, I was largely oblivious to politics, educational history, theory, or policy. A desire to work with children and to help them achieve motivated me. I was totally unaware that the vocation I had chosen would cause me to compromise and distort these noble but simplistic intentions. I had no inkling that through steadfast adherence to institutional standards and expectations, I would lose something of myself in the process.

In the same year, 1981, Berlak and Berlak conducted a study producing insights which I remained ignorant of for over 30 years. Whilst preparing to leave classroom teaching to write up the findings from my own research, I read their work for the first time and smiled. Unbeknownst to me, they had foretold (and affirmed) the validity of investigating the deep sense of incongruity which had come to define my experience of operating in the English education system. In the Berlaks' terms, I had been brooding over the *dilemmas* of schooling:

> The authors describe dilemmas as representing contradictions that reside in the situation, in the individual, and in the larger society – as they are played out in one form of institutional life: schooling. These dilemmas focus on the fluidity and the reflexivity of the social process that are encapsulated in daily encounters between teachers and children. The practitioner's exchanges are not to be seen as disconnected, contradictory, discrete, or situational, but a complex pattern of behaviours which are joined together through consciousness.
>
> A participant in the Berlaks' research (Mr Scott), provides a hint of his continuing internal conversations, as he deliberates over the apparent thoughtful choices he is making. He concludes: "I have yet to come to terms with myself," as he distinguishes between the 'act' and the person. It is evident that he has some degree of awareness of a wide range of contradictory social experiences and social forces, past and contemporary – both in his classroom, his school, and beyond in the wider community. He has internalised these contradictions (in his personal and social history, and in his present circumstances) and they are now 'within' him, a part of his generalised other, informing his outward responses.

> The writers suggest that an awareness of how these forces come to bear on our conditions means that we are capable of altering our behaviour patterns and/or act with others to alter our circumstances – to become steadfast in our efforts to transform.
>
> They conclude that the purpose of enquiry for teachers is to enable us to partake in reflective action. Engaging in this process requires participants to look again and recognise that what they have been taking for granted about classroom life, the origins of schooling activities, and the ensuing consequences upon children and society are all problematic. (adapted from Berlak and Berlak 2002: 8–10)

Turbulent change defines the past three decades in education, yet the dilemmas (or contradictions) remain as pertinent today as they ever were, perhaps even more so, as schools negotiate market forces, incessant political intervention, media platforms, and that old chestnut – pupil behaviour. Think of the teaching profession, and increasingly there are concerns about stress, recruitment, and retention. The Children's Society report (Pople et al. 2015) informs readers that children in England are amongst the unhappiest in the world. These, I argue, are clear symptoms: they substantiate an apparent tension in schools in light of the relentless demand for us to be ever more rigorous in the pursuit of quantifiable effectiveness, lest we be judged as failing.

Dilemmas reside in the lived experiences of practitioners, and, as I will show, may even be detected by discerning pupils as they protest against the nature of teacher–pupil encounters and query the legitimacy of the institutional status quo. Schooling is distinguished from education. On the surface, the situations I describe in this book are familiar and routine, yet the exchanges I experienced were rich and complex, often representing sites of struggle. The concepts of *tension* and *disruption* in the title relate to school systems and classroom interactions, but I also came to discover how these concepts could play out from deep within a teacher's psyche. These are the realms that I interrogated as a practitioner-researcher.

I believe this perturbing state – this condition – to be endemic. For me it was subliminal, obscured, undefined. Nias (1989: 65) describes teachers as living with tension, dilemma, and contradiction, and concludes, "those who claim that they can be themselves in and through work … are signalling that they have learned to live not just with stress but with paradox". Unfortunately, I came to a point in my career when I could not. Looking beyond paradox, my sense of dissonance intensified as I came to better appreciate the hypocrisy engrained within the school system; it had infiltrated my professional identity, it was inherent within me, and it was apparent in my practice.

It is my privilege to take the baton from Mr Scott all these years on, and to offer an array of perspectives to probe his predicament, for it is one with which I began to identify. As I sought "to come to terms with myself", I came to recognise myself as a *living* contradiction. Significantly, I want to convey both the profound and subtle implications as I critique my contribution as a teacher and as an authority figure. And yet, it is important to declare that my attention extends beyond these formal roles. Implicit in the text is the thought, the possibility, that I am being a man in our society with all that entails – the anger, the appeal of strength and assertion of will, an inclination to resort to violence to deal with threat. Negotiating issues of masculinity, identity, and status as a child and an adult, in the family and the workplace, I acknowledge that this might be an 'everyman's' tale but it is not everyone's story. I ponder whether my experiences would have the same resonance with a female teacher, or indeed male colleagues who don't identify with the power dynamic I convey. Regardless of gender, my fervent hope is that this book might encourage some brave colleagues to run the next leg. Whilst this book is written with teachers in mind, I am aware that there is growing interest amongst practitioners about the use of evidence to inform practice. I want to illustrate how the research process has the capacity to shine a discerning light on the classroom elements we find important and troublesome. The holistic coverage incorporates and shifts between perspectives I classify as 'I' and 'them' – 'we' and 'us'. The interests I explore in my work include the exchange of teaching and learning interactions, and low level disruptions. These provide context to examine *my* dilemmas. The scene in which I unravel my concern is a typical secondary school in the UK; the broad setting is the education system, whose current constitution was established as I was about to start my professional career at the end of the 1980s.

Preface

Stephen

I remember in 1987, when working in teacher education, the assembled education staff at Westminster College, Oxford being firmly told by Secretary of State for Education Kenneth Baker, who had helicoptered in for that purpose, that the education service was in a parlous state and that the new national curriculum, national testing, league tables, and a new inspection service would solve all the problems and turn everything around. The finger was pointed at left-wing educators and politicians, and explicitly at John Dewey's influence. The grass roots development of bodies such as the Inner London Education Authority and the Schools Council were being swept away and centralised policies imposed. His 30 minute speech has defined the three decades that followed, whatever the colour of the government. Of course, this centralising policy did not solve all the problems. Even defining the national curriculum was, and is, difficult and at times bitterly contested, not least concerning the place of Britain in history. To a crowded, subject based curriculum was added cross-curricular themes to answer criticisms of the limitations of focusing only on academic subjects. That the planners were pouring a gallon into a pint pot has always been a major criticism. Amongst the many issues was the differentiation between what is taught (content) and how it is taught (pedagogy and developmental learning).

In 1988, national projects called Compacts began to encourage secondary schools to up their game. It was a grass roots scheme, imported in 1987 from Boston, Massachusetts, and it was financially cheap. Year 11 pupils were set Compact Goals, which were crystallised as excellent attendance and punctuality, demonstrating personal qualities, coursework completion, and participation in work related activities. Mentors from local businesses went into the schools regularly to help and support. I was seconded to a leadership role in Birmingham Compact (1992–1994). The schools were self-selecting, in the sense that head teachers had to be keen and feel their staff would be enthusiastic about it. The inner city school catchments were deprived, but most were vibrant schools which we had regularly used for teaching practice placements. Each school had a three year programme in which staff committed themselves to working in motivational ways, mentors from industry offered classroom based support, and Year 11 pupils were rewarded with a formal certificate for achieving Compact Goals (see Bigger 1996 and 2000). Enough to say here that the programme achieved very significant results in the schools' examination results for the majority of pupils. The percentage ending Year 11 with five GCSEs (all grades) rose from 30% up to 70% or 80% in many of the schools, showing that pupils became increasingly engaged with their studies. This was an example of how positive pedagogy greatly enhances achievement. The project was killed by league tables: these forced schools to focus on raising a few grade Ds to Cs rather than motivating *all* pupils. It was a privilege to work alongside 21 inner city comprehensive schools, even if it meant signing thousands of certificates.

I was responsible for education PhDs at the University of Worcester when Sean came in to discuss his project. By now a well-respected religious education teacher responsible for behaviour and discipline, he wished to explore this area in order to disseminate good practice to others. In the ensuing discussion, it became clear that there were issues of power and authority that needed further thought. As a consequence, he began asking the broad question, "Is it possible to build good positive relationships with pupils without sacrificing order and discipline?" and more specifically, "Could we find ways to support pupils to become more self-disciplined without compromising their education?"

To achieve this, habits of a lifetime needed to be reassessed. Where issues had once been resolved by authoritarian means (through a demand, instruction, or reproof), new strategies were needed. This formed the basis of a part-time action research project which formed the basis of his PhD, and now this book. The supervision relationship included using a research diary in blog format allowing frequent discussions of experiences and findings, all of which helped to articulate issues and theories. I explain this process in more detail elsewhere (Bigger 2009a).

These thoughts formed the melting pot from which this book is the end product. It has been, in a real sense, Sean's journey, but a journey taken with interested and willing co-travellers. Our conversations are reflected in most pages of the book.

I will end with some thoughts on teaching, learning, and schooling. Firstly, these are not the same thing. Schooling can take place without much learning. Teaching does not necessarily end with learning. Learning is not always positive: pupils can learn not to care and not to achieve. That these three can work well together to enhance the experience of pupils is the belief that has inspired this book. It is depressing that the issues which a century ago inspired John Dewey to develop a pedagogy of hands-on experience are still problematic today. The curriculum has become a stagnant testing regime. I remember a 6-year-old Chinese-American girl weeping through her (American) maths SAT, and would not be surprised if now, in middle age, she has difficulties with maths as a consequence. A curriculum and pedagogy which fails to motivate and enthuse has failed pupils. There are many questions to be asked about current credentialist and accountability policies in schools; this book invites further thought on how a school can benefit its pupils by creating an environment where they feel respected and enthused.

At the end of the 19th century, Dewey set out a pedagogic creed to help pupils develop into the creative thinkers, producers, and inventors needed for the following century (see McDermott 1981: 442–454). This creed emphasised five 'articles':

1. Learning should enhance understanding of and for social life.
2. Schools are social institutions and should represent society at its best, and be an embryo society in which children participate in disciplined ways.
3. The curriculum should relate to the social experiences of the pupils.
4. Children learn best through activity, developing good habits of action, and thought.
5. Education is shared social consciousness. Teachers are engaged in the formation of the proper social life.

Thus, learning should be hands on, engaging pupils with real experiences. Pedagogy should be judged on the way it motivates and energises learners. It should make pupils more critically aware. It should induct young people into lifelong learning and encourage democracy, not compliance and blind obedience. In Dewey's view, schooling is not a preparation for future life: the jobs these young people will end up doing may not exist at the time of their schooling. School learning has to be a thing in itself, a form of present enrichment rather than training for something uncertain. Now the 20th century has turned into the 21st we need to update this broad credo in detail. The curriculum and pedagogy need to become socially enriching again. This vision was Kenneth Baker's bête noire, and its opposite now holds schooling in its grip, except where teachers subvert the usual mediocrity with creative pedagogy. Dewey was one of many voices seeking to explore real learning. Others will help us to articulate ideas later in the book.

Introduction

The Background to the Book

Stephen

When prominent politicians call for tougher discipline in schools, requiring pupils to respect and even fear their teachers, they encourage advocates of zero tolerance and champions of Assertive Discipline to quash any disruption to learning and to use punishment or 'consequences' as a key weapon. The latest manifestation is encompassed in the phrase 'no excuses'. Pupils have on occasions found themselves described in the media and some popular books through emotive and derogatory terms, such as 'yobs' and 'buggers'. Pupils belong to a family, most will be future parents, and all are people whom we hope will enrich society in the future. They have to be in school for well over a decade, whether they like it or not. Schools and teachers have the power to make their stay profitable, ideally enjoyable, or something to be endured; likewise, pupils have the power to make or break teachers. I believe that when adults are entrusted to contribute to these formative years, there is a straight choice between suppression and empowerment. Sean's research shows that in certain and testing circumstances the choice feels anything but straightforward.

Values are in vogue in education stated in school policies across the land. They are a list of what the school wants people to think about them – that they are caring, effective, and ethical. Of course, the values they state may not be the values they operate. Institutions cannot be regarded as ethical just because they say they are. This book explores some ethical implications for pedagogy and school management, rooting educational processes in positive relationships between teachers and pupils.

Conventional notions of teacher professionalism and effectiveness can compromise the very best of intentions amidst the reality of classroom life. Even with experienced and successful teachers, the elusive subtleties of power, responsibility, pressure, and stress shape their expectations of what they are tasked to do. The pressure and expectations for firm classroom control can lead to disciplinarian and authoritarian assumptions. Beyond the advocated techniques and advice espoused in training materials and by high profile 'behaviour experts' via social media, implicit strategies – such as shouting, belittling, shaming, and sarcasm – are resorted to much too easily. Some staff are even able to impose their will by their very presence. In other words, a 'good' teacher, conceived by many serving and aspiring teachers, as well as many children and parents, is an authoritarian who can *control* children. Sean's research shows that for some pupils who are familiar with this power relationship, it is underlying fear which masquerades as respect. Unfortunately, fear breeds subversion and rebellion, with pupils constantly testing boundaries to get away with whatever they can – if not with the strict teachers, then with others who seem fair game. In certain circumstances, this diversion from learning includes even the normally compliant or 'good' student. Perhaps this is best illustrated when the authority of a supply or substitute teacher is collectively undermined or dismissed. As power is selectively contested, the classroom chemistry is thus infused with variable expressions of subtle resistance and explicit conflict, rather than the development of a learning relationship. This is described in greater detail in Part III.

Sean's description of the process of personally altering his established approach to discipline and teaching derived, he realised, from sustained professional conditioning which he calls 'living contradiction' – that is, he realised that what was required of him professionally was in contradiction to his personal aspirations and values. His absorption of these implicit expectations could be traced back to his childhood,[1] and subsequently reinforced daily, term on term, year on year, within the school environment. When in charge of others, he described himself not as a tyrant but as someone firmly in control whose views and will were paramount – he had learned to dominate, and his methods were affirmed by colleagues, observers, pupils, and parents alike. Class control was largely by diktat, with rules clearly set by the establishment and policed by staff. Sean gradually became responsible for whole school discipline, organising detentions and the broader paraphernalia of discipline. His efforts were valued by the school and praised as outstanding by Ofsted and most pupils were responsive.

The articulation of Sean's sense of disquiet over a prolonged period, and his subsequent search for a different way forward through research, finds a historical parallel which illuminates his gradual shift with regard to discipline. Until the 1970s, corporal punishment was considered normal and any teacher who opposed it was out of step. I was caned once, for no great crime. I remember my last head teacher caning 40 boys in one morning. After corporal punishment was banned, that situation changed (Conroy and de Ruyter 2008). Sean may feel out of step now, but may not be in 20 years' time.

Today, pupil discipline is very high on the national agenda for education. Ofsted have reported continuously on low level disruption as a serious cause of pupil under-achievement. Some newspapers have demonised young

1 Sean's research contained autobiographical reflexivity. He discovered many ghosts that needed to be laid to rest from his own difficult schooling and experiences of bullying relationships. He theorised this through the literature on reflexivity, emphasising 'the living I', focusing on his own life performance through action research, and living theory. This methodology is expanded on in Chapters 2 and 8.

people and demanded tougher measures. Some schools, and increasingly academies free of local authority constraints, operating under zero tolerance policies have demanded that some pupils be expelled as a matter of course once procedures have been followed or exhausted. The very idea of questioning whether the relational and educational experiences offered might have contributed to the pupil's objectionable behaviour is rare. Discipline is presented as something *done* to a child, not a strength that they are *encouraged to develop*. We reverse that here. A school's mission should be to encourage self-discipline, not to enforce and police an imposed disciplinary code. This book develops an alternative way which places self-learning first. We seek to show that this is not a threat to either academic standards or school behaviour; rather, it is the current behaviourist and authoritarian strategies which damage and impede the development of the young person.

This state of affairs was the product of an education system which was unreflective and assumed its own truth and validity. It held the pupil liable for the problem without considering that it may be the adults – in the form of decision makers and enforcers – who were the source of much of the disruption. Sean began his PhD at the peak of his career as head of discipline, wishing to explore and disseminate authoritarian strategies. The subsequent period of reflection and questioning challenged his beliefs, attitudes, and values as an educator. He realised that he habitually compromised his personal values in the name of professionalism and effectiveness, dissociating personal values and aspirations from the teaching task. Claiming to be teaching pupils to think for themselves and to be self-disciplined, the professional reality was telling pupils to do as they were told. This further defines the notion of 'living contradiction', of living a life based on a lie. It was not the real Sean who was teaching, rather the authoritarian mask and persona he had created as he absorbed external notions of effectiveness.

This book describes the turbulent intellectual and professional process of redesigning pedagogy around the aspirations of self-learning and self-discipline, amidst the reality of pupils' challenging behaviour. There was a danger of a significant minority of pupils perceiving the new non-authoritarianism as a sign of weakness, especially when such a strategy was the exception rather than the rule in the school. This prompted Sean to shine a light on his doubts, insecurities, and engrained defensive habits as he tried to find effective ways to fill the void.

Another way of negotiating this time of transition was to bring the pupils along for the journey, explaining the new thinking and offering them a vision of self-determination. Over a three year period, pupils were progressively given more ownership of their learning. Teachers need to have authority, and there are circumstances where pupils might be unsafe if this were not so. But having authority is not the same as being authoritarian. It is a dangerous polarity to see teachers as either authoritarian or lax, and classes as either ordered or disorderly. Pupils learn from discussing, considering, and reviewing their experiences. Integral to the process of learning are opportunities for dialogue, expressing opinion balanced with listening to others. Naturally there were challenges, anxieties, and temptations to resort back to quick-fix authoritarian strategies. Sean sought to find harmony between control and care and to negotiate the difference between compliance and cooperation.

Acknowledging that being on-task and learning are not the same thing, he tried to develop an approach which gave pupils more opportunities for autonomy. Of course there were occasions when the best strategy was for the teacher to lead and direct – for example, when teaching novice learners or presenting unfamiliar content. The challenge was to ensure that pupils didn't become over-dependent. It was affirmed that some did not have the capacity or resilience to cope immediately with independence if their previous schooling had not encouraged it. Sean had to find ways of nurturing learning habits whilst also delivering subject content. In the interim, he had to find effective ways to deal with some pupils' passive obstinacy as well as their active ploys to deflect their deficiencies or lack of engagement. It was clear that behaviour and learning held a reciprocal relationship – one influencing the other – therefore both aspects had to be addressed through his research. In building a classroom climate defined by his commitment to be respectful, fair, responsible, and trustful, the pupils were invited to use this as a model and to develop greater self-discipline. The approach negates the default practice of viewing any deviance from established norms as warranting punishment – a predetermined response sugar-coated in school policies and redefined in 'consequences' posters.

In addition, how children are taught has moral and human rights implications, so we would wish the book to contribute to these fields too. This includes areas such as dialogic education and education for democracy. There is today a global campaign to ensure that children are schooled, in some cases against a background of no schooling – for example, we have seen a campaign to allow girls in particular to be schooled, focusing around Malala Yousafzai. It seems perverse then to suggest that schools harm children, as John Holt once did in his book *How Children Fail* (1982 [1964]), which has led to a major home schooling programme in the United States. Questions need to be asked about education and schooling, amongst which are questions about potential abuse and harm, as Charles Dickens once did. There is literature today on well-being and happiness which are both relevant to school values and vision. Pupils who are stressed are unlikely to be achieving their full potential. Schools with stressed staff are unlikely to be effective either. Being driven by quantitative outcomes (i.e. league tables) dictates strategies, destroys creativity, and hampers pedagogical freedom.

Pupils enter school with a range of experiences and problems perhaps unknown to their teachers. There may well be a way to switch them on to social awareness and confidence. I recall one boy who said very little, until it was discovered that rugby football was his passion. Another boy was hyperactive and uncooperative until a stuffed barn owl was placed in front of him, which he spent hours drawing. A girl was the despair of her teachers until a story gave her an imaginary mentor in her head, with whom she had inner conversations when stress arose. After being threatened by expulsion, she received a good behaviour prize a year later. Teaching is an art. Problems have to be identified, solutions have to be imagined. Above all, teaching and learning is a dialogue which encapsulates social awareness and engagement.

This book was initiated by a simple question: how do pupils feel about the *authoritative* stance adopted?[2] Of course, Sean didn't use this term; instead he tried to live the values which qualify the phrase, and through research provided a platform for pupils to comment freely, and without reprimand, on their experience of learning in his classroom. Probing the assumption that pupils view *authoritarianism* as normal, he sought to challenge learned behaviour either to conform or exploit – depending on the perceived effectiveness and competence of the adult. Personal reflection began at this point. Is authority something someone has, or do they learn to acquire it – perhaps through a training course, a book, or online advice? Is it defined by someone being consistent? Is that the same as being strict? Authoritarianism is a persona which works with some and not with others. With some, compliance with task directives suppresses initiative and imagination, undermining the learning process. With others, resistance sets the learner up for conflict with the teacher.

We drew on critical pedagogy which encourages social critique (Darder et al. 2009; Giroux 2011). These essays cover three decades: of these we point especially to 'Rethinking education as the practice of freedom: Paulo Freire and the promise of critical pedagogy' (Giroux 2011: 152–166) and Pauline Lipman's 'Beyond accountability: towards schools that create new people for a new way of life' (in Darder et al. 2009: 364–383). Giroux, following Freire, presents pedagogy as a social and political awareness-raising enterprise – that is, encouraging pupils to become active contributors rather than passive consumers, understanding their rights and responsibilities within a democratic community. By this we mean not so much the limited right to vote every few years, but involvement in a community that discusses needs and actions constantly to achieve fair and just solutions. This is John Dewey's social involvement on a democratic school. Dewey is the enemy of systems

2 It is important to distinguish between *authoritative* and *authoritarian*. For Freire (2005), authoritative means exercising authority which is based on expertise; authoritarian implies an emphasis on power to control (Porter 2006).

schooling and a promoter of process education – pragmatism in action. These perspectives are explored further in Chapter 5.

Sean's work took place in a rural secondary school which, like other schools in the UK, has been incessantly responsive to government initiatives and Ofsted's impending shadow. The school became a converter academy in 2011. A bastion of the system he diligently served, he had no intention of questioning its validity or indeed that his own 'successful' methodology should be placed under scrutiny. Having become aware of critical theorists to engage with external perspectives, Sean drew on a range of 'lenses' (Brookfield 2008) to challenge him to critically examine his assumptions. In particular, Michel Foucault's (1977) portrayal of power as something which circulates and is exercised through everyday rituals and interactions was illuminating and intellectually stimulating. Application of the French social theorist's work provided a fresh perspective to interpret common phenomena. A liminal process, with all its insecurities, moving towards an uncertain future, helped Sean to explore alternative pedagogies.

We will address issues of methodology in Part II. These initial comments set up our later discussion of research which reflects on personal experience. We may have been trained to be 'objective' and avoid the use of the personal pronoun 'I'. This hides the fact that, even in laboratory research, the researcher makes personal choices about all aspects of the research. The reader may not be aware that the results presented have been selected for helpfulness. If a researcher observes a phenomenon, their understanding and interpretation rely on their personal experiences. Their comments will reflect probably flawed understandings.

So first person research using the pronoun 'I' is a serious enterprise which has to avoid bias and presuppositions. Researching human experiences requires respondents to tell their story and a researcher to interpret it. Grounded theory started this way, researching how dying people felt. Ethnography is in this tradition – a researcher interviewing the people involved and observing what they do. Autobiographical research was an offshoot. Donald Schön emphasised reflective practice. Reflection in the workplace became popular (see Chapter 2). If we reflect at work, we need to write it down and discuss it, so autobiography has a context. Soon the new field of autoethnography arrived, when researchers studied aspects of their own life experiences, reflecting on incidents, attitudes, and relationships (Denzin 2013). We try in this book to apply rigour to this process.

Chapter 1

A Sense of ...

Sean

In September 2014 Ofsted published a report entitled, *Below the Radar: Low-Level Disruption in the Country's Classrooms*. It alludes to conduct which, although evident, has an elusive quality which is both pervasive and detrimental to learning in schools. Going beyond the rhetoric typically found in school policies and brochures regarding discipline and standards, it seeks to draw attention to the reality of what is happening in Britain's classrooms. Its findings and conclusions will be placed under scrutiny within the fabric of this book. Here, I borrow the analogy of radar for a moment and extend it. I apply it, not to children whose behaviour is evidently disruptive – for they attract ample coverage in these pages – but to high achieving, diligent, and conscientious pupils who, I argue, perfectly epitomise another cohort existing beneath the school's radar. These are represented by 'Sarah', a 14-year-old who articulated her experiences of having to tolerate the dilemmas of schooling which acted to constrain her. Her diary formed part of my action research; I offer some extracts below.

To provide some context, in the previous year the school Sarah attended had been graded by Ofsted as 'outstanding' for "the effectiveness of care, guidance and support". The school's report quoted one parent: "Both my children went to small primary schools. I was both surprised and delighted at how personal X School is despite its size. *Children are treated as individuals*" (emphasis added).

This is a school which espouses the very best for its pupils and strives incessantly to move from, using Ofsted's terms, 'good' to 'outstanding' to qualify its overall effectiveness to existing and prospective parents. Sarah's account does not serve to minimise or dismiss the guidance and support many hard-working, caring professionals demonstrate on a daily basis throughout the year; neither is it an opportunist platform from which to moan and criticise apparent injustices. The significance of Sarah's account, for me, was that she wrote it as a pupil and I reviewed it as a researcher. I then read it as a dad (two of my own children attended the same school, and Sarah's account tallied with their experiences).

> From the first day of Year 9 I knew this was going to be a tough year. In fact, from the first five minutes of Year 9, just from seeing my timetable, I knew it was going to be a tough year. Reading through my list of subjects and teachers, my first worry was about the 'choices' I had

ended up with … I had somehow managed to give up all the DT subjects, art, food, and I couldn't see drama on my timetable – one of my favourite subjects. There was one teacher, who I hadn't heard great things about, who I had five times a week. I was quite depressed about it all to begin with before I even knew how bad the lessons would be!

Our new uniform policy is now fully in action, including the no more than 3 inches above the knee skirt policy, or detention. If your uniform doesn't meet requirements you are sent to the head's office and given a detention and a card to inform teachers that you have already received your punishment for the day. This morning, during PSHE, my house leader walked into my form and said to me, "Is your skirt long enough?" then she ordered me to stand up, with my whole form watching and listening. I had to stand up by myself as she judged my almost knee-length skirt. Obviously trying not to back down from her initial accusations she said, "*Only* just. No, I mean it, only just. In fact if I made you kneel on the floor I don't think it would fit the requirements. Don't test me: I've done it before." I was shocked and embarrassed that on the first day back from the holiday, before even saying good morning, she ordered me around in front of a whole class, almost like a dog.

A few days later I was *sat down* in maths when my male teacher walked up to me and said, "Have you got a card for that skirt?" I looked up at him, surprised, and replied, "What? No … I'm sat down – that makes it look shorter!" He said, "OK, then stand up." Still shocked, I stood up and my skirt went down by at least 4 inches. He apologised and walked away. I was very concerned that he had been looking at my skirt in the first place! I find it incredibly pervy! Around school, male staff walk down corridors staring at our skirts (bums and legs). It's horrible but there's no one we can talk to as the head and deputy head are both 'starers'.

There are so many issues with the new uniform – I was wearing a light pink hairband which I was told to remove or be sent to the head's office … Strict uniform is said to improve behaviour, but this week it has caused so many issues, made me feel exhausted and unhappy, and led to me being constantly ordered around and controlled by adults I don't particularly like.

For the last two days, I have been really struggling with science as our (pregnant) teacher has been off school, so we have had a cover teacher. In the past, we have had cover lessons in science which have been completely random and nothing to do with the topic we are learning about, and when our teacher has come back she has been really surprised that we didn't get the actual work, and it has been a waste of time. We had the same issue yesterday – we were in the middle of a unit on oxygen in the atmosphere, and were told by our normal teacher that we would be writing an equipment list for the experiment we were midway through. When the cover teacher gave us our work, it turned out to be a completely random practical on acids and alkalis – we have already done that topic this year! I had no idea what to do as I said to the teacher that it was different to what we were expecting to be doing and she was very dismissive saying, "Well, this is what I've been given, so do it." We wrote two full A4 pages yesterday, and then today we had her again. She clearly had limited work left for us, as our task for the lesson was to copy out the entire PowerPoint. I don't see why this was of use to us … It just wasted my ink!

Today I was in one of my lessons, busy packing away my things, when the head teacher brought about 15 visitors (Year 5 prospective parents) and started talking to me, with them all listening. For the first time this year (it is mid-June) he asked me, "Have you enjoyed science this year?" But sadly, I was left on the spot in front of 15 visitors waiting for my answer. So I said yes. What else could I have said? What I wanted to say was, "Well, it's not that good, but I quite like the teacher so it qualifies as my best lesson. It's the only lesson I can stand. I hate school. [Turning to the parents] Don't send your children here! They will lose all enthusiasm for learning! Adults will treat them like numbers, completely ignoring the fact that they are humans too. If the school has their way, they will lose every spark of individuality, and become compliant sheep, with no opinion or personality. Don't believe their figures and stories. Don't listen to the visitor answers most people will say. It's all lies! Get out of here while you can!" But I couldn't. Or wouldn't. That's probably why he asked me – he knew I would give him a visitor appropriate answer. A visitor appropriate, untruthful, 'I want to be a prefect' answer.

Today one of my friends had a cover teacher for her German lesson, who is rapidly gaining a really bad reputation around school. She set them the work and then my friend was talking (I think they were supposed to be silent) so, without warning, she was sent outside the class. A few other people were sent out, and a member of the SLT was summoned (one who can be really nasty). He stood shouting in their faces (actually in their faces), then when my friend said something he said, "YOU ARE NOT ALLOWED TO JUDGE A TEACHER – YOU ARE ONLY 14! I HAVE THINGS IN MY FREEZER THAT ARE OLDER THAN YOU!" He really upset her – what he said is actually against her human rights. Just because of our age, our opinions are invalid?

> I feel like the message we are constantly being given is that we are nothing. We are not important. It is our job to sit down, shut up, and do whatever the adults tell us. Because they are adults. Gone are those primary school philosophy lessons (If a teacher told you to jump off a building, would you do it?). The message I am being given all day, every day, is that of course you would have to jump off that building – a teacher told you.
>
> With no consultations whatsoever, we have now been informed that we must all buy a new, standard school skirt by next September. No choice in the matter. This announcement comes just four weeks after we were all told to buy a new skirt to fit with last month's new skirt policy. What!? But there is nothing we can do about it. We're only children.

Haim Ginott (1972: 15) writes:

> I have come to a frightening conclusion. I am the decisive element in the classroom. It is my personal approach that creates the climate. It is my daily mood that makes the weather. As a teacher I possess tremendous power to make a child's life miserable or joyous. I can be a tool of torture or an instrument of inspiration. I can humiliate or humor, hurt or heal. In all situations, it is my response that decides whether a crisis will be escalated or de-escalated, a child humanized or de-humanized.

I am a teacher, Sarah could plausibly be my daughter, and I could so easily have been any of the adults she describes. In fact, searching for an appropriate term, I plead guilty as charged. Having lost my 'non-contact' time I have been a frustrated cover teacher; I have been that public face of the school; I have been that disciplinarian coming to the aid of a colleague; and I have checked 101 uniforms. Yet, I would claim that, in my defence – and with hand on heart – I have only ever wanted what was best for my pupils. I would do anything to guide and support them.[1] I was in many respects a model professional – the type of teacher politicians might champion: someone who is trustworthy, hard-working, strong on discipline, and gets good results. I missed only a handful of days over a 20 year teaching career and I had not been absent for a solitary day in the last six years. This despite enduring my fair share of all the illnesses which are par for the course for a teacher – even if I felt off-colour, I didn't want the pupils to miss their lesson, and I didn't want a colleague to have to cover for me. My head teacher once

1 It is important for me to state that I recognise some of the characters in Sarah's account, and can vouch for them as being decent people.

wrote: "Governors congratulate you ... No one could ask for a more professional or dedicated colleague."

So, it is not that I was an ogre; it is not that I was unprofessional. Yet, in my role as a teacher and authority figure, there is no doubt in my mind that I have actively suppressed children, like Sarah, without giving it a second thought. In fact, my approach was often held up to colleagues and trainee teachers as an exemplar of good practice. I am fully aware that 'suppressed' is a controversial term and requires further exploration in order to justify its usage. I will do so in due course. My subsequent PhD action research records a reflexive account of a progressive realisation that each of the indistinctive names which appeared on my register list at the beginning of each new school year represented more than a grade, a reputation, or even a pupil. Each young *person* is someone's child. The point is even more acute as I pause to consider the deep and incessant desire for my own children to do well in life. Obvious to say, isn't it? But it was a perspective which was largely lost on me as I organised and directed the sporadic cohorts of 25 to 30 non-descript uniforms on an hourly basis.

The literature provided some stimulating concepts which would help me to look beyond obstructive behaviour and challenge my propensity to judge and label. Cannella's (1999) concept of 'other' and Buber's (1958 [1937]) work on I and thou reconceptualised my view of the individuals with whom I regularly shared time and space. I discovered Victor Turner's notion of liminality (see Turner 1969; Bigger 2009b) which describes a state where one is neither here nor there – betwixt and between. I conceived that this was applicable to the adolescents I taught. Having progressed to the top of the primary school hierarchy, they then revert to being bottom of the pile upon entering Year 7. They arrive in secondary school as children and leave as young adults. A comparison of any pupil's Year 7 and Year 11/13 photos illustrates that the transformation is profound. I came to better appreciate their vulnerability as they negotiated this liminal state in the intervening years: the onset of puberty, the forming of an identity amongst peers, the testing of boundaries in the act of becoming a young man or woman. My reflections, which I expand on later, revealed that some teachers can represent a buffer for those who feel powerless and insignificant. Regardless of what is measured, there is clearly more to school than acquiring knowledge and gaining certificates.

This book charts a process of consciousness, not an epiphany event. Insights emerged from various sources – from observation, from pupil feedback, from theory, from the literature, from a study of research methodology, from an exploration of my own history. These form a thread throughout this book. Each contributed perspectives which challenged me to question who I was and to scrutinise what I had become in my role as an authority figure. As I have mentioned, if there is one phrase which encapsulated this enquiry it was Jack Whitehead's (2006) 'living contradiction': the realisation that my practice was habitually incongruent with my espoused values. That these values derive from my Christian commitment, with its ethical implications, makes instances of inaptness even more acute. The task of realigning my philosophy with my conduct, whilst continuing to operate amidst the reality of classroom life, represents the crux of my research and consequently this book. It does not advocate an uncritical shift from 'authoritarian' to 'liberal', nor 'traditional' to 'progressive';[2] it does not seek to convict or accuse colleagues who, like me, have come to 'live for the job'. School life is far too complex to present polarised dichotomies and simply suggest a shift; it is far too demanding to just tell and direct. Charlie Taylor's behaviour checklist (DfE 2011a) hardly scratches the surface! Instead, I invite readers to be discerning, to engage with my narrative and sift, for there is no prescribed formula to photocopy and stick on the wall.

During the research period, I had to strike an accord between the pragmatic requirements stipulated by my professional role, and an ideal I held which championed greater democracy in *my* classroom. I examined the apparent diametrical states of chaos and order to frame my conception of group dynamics and inform the ebb and flow of pedagogical interactions. I placed assumptions about order under further scrutiny to contemplate the distinction between compliance and cooperation. As a teacher, I had to constantly negotiate between control and care, between being tough and being kind. These terms needn't be read as divergent opposites – as good or bad, right or wrong, strong or weak. Experienced teachers will recognise that *all* of these operational stances can be appropriate responses, depending on the situation. The underlying distinction is concerned with whether those involved (pupils and teacher) benefit or suffer. This distinction can be obscured within the busyness of the classroom, so an examination of the ethical intent is required. It is this level of critical self-analysis which intrigued me as I engaged with tools which converted these abstract concepts into plain, common sense terms to decipher my underlying patterns of behaviour.

The subtlety of ever-shifting perspectives is perhaps best illustrated by this well-known optical illusion.[3]

2 One of the 'critical friends' for my action research has children at the school. As a parent who subscribes wholeheartedly to 'traditional school standards', his responses called attention to a requirement for my explanations to be grounded in common language so as not to be misinterpreted. (He assumed I was advocating a liberal approach devoid of boundaries in response to my querying of dominating control.)

3 I did contemplate substituting the image for Jekyll and Hyde, but the comparison was too overt. I didn't want to convey the idea of a change of character, just a subtle change of perspective.

Throughout the process of my research, the *composed/responsive* image represented, for me, the times when my actions were consistent with my values. From this composed responsive stance I was able to, or at least aimed to, for example, address disruption to learning without reverting to dominance to enforce obedience, or conversely without provoking challenge or resistance from the pupils. However, in reality such perspectives are fluid and susceptible to change. For instance, when variables such as illness, tiredness, or the pressures of time are added to the equation, it can be all too easy for the veiled *superior/reactive* 'old' character to emerge and reassert itself, shaping (and distorting) the situation. In this state, I had a tendency to believe I was 'right' – that I knew better. I adopted an adversarial 'me or you' stance and had a propensity to communicate warnings, threats, and punishments. I struggled internally not to resort back to my default psyche, for s*he* was always present in the background, immersed in my thoughts and emotions, so I was tempted to revert to quick-fix, dominating strategies because I could – and they 'worked'. I suspect that the distinction was not always readily apparent to others as I tried to resist. However, on those occasions when I struggled, the more observant pupils might have detected an alteration in my tone or body language revealing an underlying urge to control, to impose myself to the detriment of others.

I came to describe this predisposition as being akin to wearing a mask or even a cast, the original layer of which could be traced back to my difficult formative years. The metaphor of 'cast' represents the depth of my allegiance to dominance, and it shaped the defensive mask I habitually donned when in role. Through my research, I probed beyond my habits to inspect underlying beliefs and repressed fears. An examination of the origins of the professional persona I had come to embrace proved to be personal and sensitive. Aware that ontology – that is, the study of one's being – is subjective, I have sought to show how feelings can become knowledge through reflexive thought. Such knowledge enabled me to comprehend the attitude which had come to define me as an authority figure – 'my way or the highway' and 'my way' gets results!

In fact, if I were to offer a simple phrase which encompassed, and seemingly justified, my professional approach, it would be, 'it worked'. Applied to pupil behaviour, my way quickly established – and ensured – order and compliance. Applied to teaching, I gravitated towards making things predictable: to be in charge, to be wary of uncertainty, of disorder. As I will show, the paradigm of control that I had absorbed came initially, in part, from my own teachers when I was a pupil and was reaffirmed when I copied more experienced colleagues. At the beginning of my journey working with children, aged 18, I observed a model who would become my template. It came through a part-time job at a primary school play centre in Tower Hamlets, East London. The infants and juniors took no notice of me on my first day and I had to be rescued by the woman in charge. I stood back mildly embarrassed as she shouted loudly at them to bring about their complete obedience. It seemed that my noble intention to support children required a more pragmatic approach if I was not to flounder. I quickly learned techniques – or a way of 'being' – that achieved the desired outcome: order! I got very good at it. Eventually I developed a tacit knowledge which was judged by those in authority to be effective. Who was I to question, for the evidence was plain and simple: 'it worked' – the kids did what they were told!

There is a self-evident necessity for degrees of organisation, structure, and direction to be part of the equation when hundreds of children gather together in a school environment. Going beyond that, I am now inclined to ponder different questions when I hear the seemingly valid argument, 'it works'. I have come to ask, "For whom?" and more recently, "At what cost?"[4] The questions I have come to ask seem to me to be conspicuous in their absence from much public debate.

During a period of incessant change in the educational world, and an explosion of contradictory and incomplete information bombarding me, I did not have the time, inclination, energy, or indeed capacity to dissect all the ideas embedded in educational journals. I was, instead, susceptible to media headlines which so easily convinced me. Whilst I was teaching, these also came in the form of private franchises presenting the latest silver bullet or through more official sources in the form of national strategies. I now recognise these marketed franchises as fads which became infused into my daily practice. My susceptibility to absorb, for example, Lee and Marlene Canter's Assertive Discipline or the alluring mantra of learning styles, impacted chiefly on those pupils subject to my teaching.

I now find the use of erroneous evidence claims by those entrusted to govern particularly disturbing, as their decisions and agendas have a profound effect on whole generations of learners. It is all too easy to become a passive recipient of highly publicised findings, too easy to be seduced by the latest buzzwords which pave the way for commercial and political gain. I was experienced and established, yet insular and naive, unaware of an arrangement where: "a strong mutually beneficial relationship appears to exist between the communities of policy makers and higher education researchers (whose ranks are largely made up by social science researchers) which often manifests in ways that are beneficial to both parties, such as continued funding for specialist research centres and the increased prestige of policy makers" (Whitehead and McNiff 2006: 18).

My co-author, Stephen, takes us behind the scenes in Chapter 6. It is worth stating that I hold no particular political affiliations. I believe that teachers, as a profession, are putty in the hands of the unscrupulous: those who have

4 Prompted by Ross Ashcroft's interview with Ian Gilbert (see Gilbert 2015).

become versed in being economical with the truth. I found the uncritical acceptance of selective forms of evidence and knowledge to be part of the problem. The broad theme of 'being played' acts as a thread for the entire book, as I argue that the subtleties of ideology, power, and discourse infuse the system to pervade the psyche of its custodians. I present my tale as an exemplar for this controversial assertion.

The scope of my research – to figure out the nature of concealed levers influencing my performance – was comprehensive. Charting my conditioning about how school works, I suggest I was a *product* of the system, becoming familiar with its expectations and rituals from age 5; out of necessity I became (belatedly) a *successful product* of the system. Having initially left school with one CSE pass, the requirement to gain qualifications ensured that I stopped resisting and came to absorb the implicit messages, thus enabling me to proceed to teacher training.

In my formative years as an educator, I concede that I was a *servant* of the system: I jumped through every hoop and upheld customs and rules without hesitation. There, I was susceptible to absorbing all sorts of messages from internal and external sources which affirmed and directed my evolving practice. I was described as a 'rough diamond' in my first Ofsted inspection in 1994. Upon promotions, I reflect how I became an *agent* of the system. There, in addition to exerting control over the children, I began to heavily influence colleagues and, significantly, I came to dominate myself through perfectionist traits and a skewed notion of what it meant to be a diligent professional. Immersed in the job, I was increasingly mindful of responsibilities which my position(s) brought, and of an expanding reputation I felt compelled to maintain. Every internal and external observation of my lessons in the eight years preceding my doctorate was judged to be 'outstanding'. This led to invitations to speak at national conferences. Recognition led to me absorbing even more unrealistic expectations.

Most of my thoughts were projected towards future events, which left me with minimal energy to operate with liberty in the present – I was constantly preoccupied with targets and deadlines. However, rather than causing concern, these traits became redefined and were 'approved' by external criteria because my efforts equated to the top standards. Of course, this thread – pupil, trainee, teacher – represents only one aspect of my life. My evolving identity was also informed by my experiences as a son, brother, friend, employee, husband, parent, and so on, which all fed into, and contributed to, my enactment of the role – which latterly came to define me in my own mind – that of authority figure. Rather than continuing to presume that I was lord over my domain, I came to conceive both pupils and adults as mere pawns disputing the semblance of power afforded to us by the institution. But I was wearing blinkers; essentially, in the grand scheme of things, I was a mere foot soldier. John Dewey rebuffed this notion as long ago as 1895:

"[The teacher] is not like a private soldier in an army, expected merely to obey, or like a cog in a wheel, expected merely to respond to and transmit external energy: he must be an intelligent medium of action" (quoted in Goldstein 2014: 1).

And thus I engaged in action research. Throughout this book, I share my struggles and my doubts as I tried to find a better and more fulfilling way to relate to and educate the children who are placed, by the quirk of timetabling, in my charge. For many years – even at the height of my responsibilities in school – I continued to be oblivious to the politics and rationale behind educational policies, and unaware of the origins of the infatuation with data which determined normality for me in the classroom. Once I became qualified, I simply learned to play the cards I had been dealt: I am the adult; I am the teacher; I am responsible and accountable; learn to do as I say. I became very good at it. As I established a reputation and was afforded status, I developed a way of being which ensured I had a 'strong hand'. The hand remained largely unexamined as I became established within the profession.

Chapter 2

Autobiographical Research

Stephen

Brookfield (1995: 31) argues:

> Our autobiographies as learners and teachers represent one of the most important sources of insight into teaching to which we have access. Yet in much talk and writing about teaching, personal experience is dismissed and demeaned as merely anecdotal – in other words as hopelessly subjective and impressionistic. It is true, of course, that at one level, all experience is inherently idiosyncratic.

This sets up our dilemma: autobiographies have value, but they also have dangers. When teachers begin to think about their teaching careers, they put themselves in a position of asking strategic questions and challenging their assumptions. The fashion through the 1980s was the reflective practitioner, referring to learning models suggested by Donald Schön and his colleagues (Argyris and Schön 1975). A teacher comes into an academic continuing professional development (CPD) course at master's or doctoral level with a working lifetime of experience. It is what they do with that experience which concerns us here. Teachers could assume that more of the same is appropriate, that they have nothing to learn, that their instinctive performance is adequate. Such a person could scarcely benefit from a course requiring reflection. What is needed is the preparedness to ask some sharp questions about how we have approached the task in hand. Each question gives some content to a query about whether things could have been done better. Thus, willingness to interrogate one's experience is essential.

A second point is ensuring that self-reflective comments speak to others outside the situation. Why should we trust that what a person says about themselves is a valid representation? How can their thoughts be validated by others and so become persuasive to readers and listeners? Bullough and Pinnegar (2001: 17) point out: "authentic voice is a necessary but not sufficient condition for the scholarly standing of a biographical self-study". They offer 14 guidelines for trustworthiness and rigour, all underpinned by reflexivity rooted in context: "Self-study points to a simple truth, that to study a practice is simultaneously to study self: a study of self-in-relation to other." We need to recognise the limitations of the autobiographical voice. A detail remembered will depend on the level of understanding of the issue at the time. If we misperceive and misunderstand an event, our memory of it will enshrine the misunderstanding. Just to have remembered something does not imply it is wholly true. When a family tries to piece together the events of a lifetime, different members recall different things, and remember them differently, partly because they knew and understood things differently when they happened. The police and courts are aware of the limitations of eye witness testimony, and that different eye witnesses will describe an event differently. Just having been in a school 35 years ago does not privilege the information claimed.

To verify memories, a family talking together will remind each other of events and people, offer alternative assessments, correct and nudge memories. So, autobiographical research is a social and communal enterprise, with the various people involved talking about the past together, and individuals discussing their findings with others to reach a joint assessment of its significance. An autobiography is not a statement of true fact, but a version of something held in memory, a point of view for discussion from which some confirmation might result.

Action research has developed over the past half century. It starts with a personal story and after reflection a deliberate set of actions to solve a problem. It is often a group enterprise as the action involves a number of colleagues – participative research carried out by a group. Kurt Lewin (1951) developed research on group experiential learning which developed into action research. Although one person might initiate and lead, in a real sense it is a cooperative project. Action research is social research – research on and with a community. Sean had an idea that control in a classroom could be created as a joint enterprise rather than imposed; as Brookfield (2008) states, 'power with' rather than 'power over' makes the purpose of the research clear to all concerned.

So, Sean's faculty colleagues and the pupils needed to be aware of what was intended, and their general consent obtained. Much of it was, of course, normal teaching and learning so there was not a great deal to opt out from.[1] For some pupils, they were new and had not known Sean before; for others, the change of attitude and strategy might be puzzling if not explained. Pupils' views were part of the mix of voices heard in the project. It may be that they had concerns not fully understood. For example, the new order gave them more freedom to make choices and decisions, but some may have preferred to be told what to do. Pupil voice was thus a valuable – and necessary – balancer.

1 Permissions were sought and obtained both through the school's ethics policy (via the head teacher) and in negotiation with classes and individual pupils. The children had to be in Sean's class, but he always left it open whether they completed the end of module evaluation or did other useful work. The evaluations were always planned as educational activities to round off a section of learning. It was always made explicit when these would be used for his research.

Other staff may have noticed a difference in attitude in the new reasoned approach. This was perhaps best illustrated when Sean was required to tutor a Year 11 group as they came towards the end of their compulsory schooling. Representing possibly the most overtly demonstrative expression of inner change, for the first time a familiar practice he had witnessed hundreds of times caused him discomfort. Whereas his 16-year-old charges were compelled to take off their coats and shoes upon entering the theatre for assembly, the staff retained their full attire. Whilst the budding men and women were required to sit in straight lines on the grubby floor, the staff (some of whom were on teaching practice and were therefore only a few years older) stood on the periphery or sat on chairs. Unprompted, Sean took off his shoes and sat with his group on the dirty floor. He found it uncomfortable and undignified. Much of the 20 minute token message was drowned out by the drone of the heaters at the back of the hall. This became his established response over the last few weeks of term. Most colleagues in the room missed the gesture, although one or two did a double take when they spotted him sitting there. However, the action was not lost on a couple of prominent girls who were amazed at the sign of solidarity. Sean learned that actions can speak louder than words in winning over young people.

His request to the head teacher that the Year 11s ought to have chairs was accompanied by the suggestion that the senior leadership team (SLT) might try sitting on the floor without shoes before deliberating. The offer was not taken up. He was nonetheless amazed when his head of faculty and two other colleagues followed suit and stood in their socks during assemblies. Two of the three have since left the school, but I understand the last man standing still makes the gesture some four years on. Sean, the strict disciplinarian, became untenable in this new mindset, and ultimately it led to his resignation from the school (and from teaching), as he was more and more opposed to the demands being forced upon him. His new mindset of reasoned and considered approaches to discipline had attractions for other staff, some of whom tried to emulate him under his mentorship. However, all was not straightforward. His methods were not simplistic tips for teachers but a principled stance stemming from a great deal of reading and reflection. Nevertheless, these other staff voices were brought into the evaluation mix.

In addition, his ideas and experiences were discussed with a diverse group of 'critical friends', which encouraged him to express his ideas clearly and meet their misunderstandings. His research notebooks were public in the sense that his supervision team could log in and comment every night and every week. This gave no place to hide, enshrining mistakes as well as successes. The reflection was public, not private.

There is a tricky question here: can autobiographical reflection, whether of the past or the present, be held to be trustworthy as research? A great deal of qualitative research uses life story or life history as its method. Usually this is by interviews, probably several in number, conducted by other people. The interviewer is a potential source of bias, but the variety of voices prevents the drawing of generalisations from a single experience. The autobiographic writer needs to inject a number of critical voices to achieve a similar balance. We are not necessarily the best judge of our own capabilities, actions, and intentions, and we may have tendencies to be over-critical, or under-critical, trying to show ourselves in a good light. That Sean has discussed the issues and judgements with others offers the reader the promise of greater balance, a kind of social verification, that the judgements have made sense to others. Often, autobiography is channelled through an outsider (i.e. the interviewer) and we have similar issues about whether that channel can be trusted. In both cases it is helpful not to claim generalisation, but to invite others, readers, to draw on their own experiences as they consider the issues raised.

Another solution is to avoid simplistic statements by the breadth of reading – for example, in educational psychology and social philosophy. This helps to structure the type of questions we use to interrogate experience, asking questions about justice, power, effectiveness, motivation, and so on. The more penetrating the questions, the better the quality of the result.

Autoethnography is a relatively new area of endeavour, using personal stories for research purposes (Denzin 2013). First-person reflexivity is now commonplace. The *Handbook of Autoethnography* (Holman Jones et al. 2013) has collected studies with an emphasis on accounts from a personal perspective to help construct knowledge and understanding which demonstrates trustworthiness. There are of course dangers when relying on personal experiences and memories, but then there are dangers in all research paradigms. Memory is a fragile thing, easily forgotten and twisted. That a personal account is corroborated is to be desired, but even where other witnesses are lacking, lack of corroboration is not an indication against trustworthiness. Sean was influenced by living theory (Whitehead and McNiff 2006) which has championed personal reflexivity. Sean's personal reflection on the past (autobiography) was combined with reflexivity[2] on his current work carried out in discussion with others (autoethnography). These recording and analytical methods fed into an action research scheme through which he made and evaluated major changes in his personal and pedagogical practices over a three year period.

---

2 See further Donna Qualley (1997: 11–14): I believe the most educative experiences – in Dewey's sense, the ones that deepen or transform thinking and lead to learning and further enquiry – are reflexive as well as reflective. The line between these processes is shaky, however, especially when the other is an individual's 'other self' or 'past life'.

The autoethnographic angle observes and records daily life and work minutely, including conversations and interviews with other participants. Field notes for observers are relatively straightforward, but in participant research the researcher is too busy teaching and managing to keep a minute-by-minute log. The decision was therefore made in the early stages to construct field notes electronically using commercial blog technology (see Bigger 2009a for details). It could be accessed in school or at home, so could include jottings as well as evaluative writing. The blog was set to be visible only to Sean and his supervisors. The intention was to write notes daily each evening to capture the details for the future. There is an immediacy about social media which lessens the task, especially when writing for a known audience. After a tiring day, writing a diary is a chore, but there are practical benefits to getting tensions out of the system. Sean's experience is documented (anonymously) in Bigger (2009a: 3):

> I had never had cause to contribute to a blog before my supervisor established one on my behalf. Immediately I felt it legitimised my need to share embryonic thoughts negating the awkwardness of bothering my supervisors yet again. The blog has provided an excellent sounding board for me to reflect on the initial steps of my journey. Many of my contributions did not require or invite feedback yet it still served the purpose of clarifying confused territory. Timely and insightful replies and contributions from my supervisors have served to pre-empt our personal meetings enabling them to quickly establish a flow from which to explore a focussed agenda. Apart from the easy access and a comprehensive record afforded by the blog I consider its fundamental purpose has been to allow me to feel that if I have something to say. I have a platform from which to be heard (even if I end up answering it myself).

As Sean's main supervisor, I tried to make some response each evening, providing immediate feedback, maybe short and encouraging, maybe more substantial if appropriate. I evaluate this process in the epilogue.

Reflexivity

Sean

My autobiographical study actively probed the information I gleaned from my students. I could justifiably point towards data conveying my pupils' personal and combined evaluation throughout the research period, which indicated their behaviour to be more cooperative and less disruptive than comparative performance in other classes. More so, I believe they experienced something approaching democracy. They were increasingly able to make choices about how they learned and who to work with, and they were provided with a platform to comment anonymously on their experience. That some individuals chose to criticise, without fear of admonishment or reprisal, is a privilege currently denied my own children (who vent their frustration about school on arriving home). Within a safe psychological environment, my students were appreciated for who they were as young people – and then encouraged, supported, and respected for what they could do as learners. However, I did not neglect teaching essential subject content, I did not sacrifice order, and my research did not impinge negatively on pupils' achievement in my lessons: I was observed eight times during the three year research period and was judged 'outstanding' on each occasion.

I have used the term 'emancipation' in my work in association with the concepts of improvement, effectiveness, and educational values. Although my intention was to extend this quality to my pupils, in truth, I had first to experience it for myself. My reading of critical theory left me feeling as though I'd been 'had', cheated. I had spent a career, conflicts and all, as a puppet dancing to someone else's tune – a hired gun if you like. If that was to represent my professional shift in philosophy, my experience of personal emancipation was equally as significant.

My personal story, which underpins my career, is dominated by a deprived background which left me simultaneously dominant over siblings, angry and resistant with target teachers but compliant with others, and vulnerable to intimidation from older boys. Central to this confusing state of affairs is the pervading figure of my dad who left me, the eldest of five children, when I was 5 years old. Perhaps most poignantly, I take heed of Illsley Clarke's work on developmental stages commonly attributed to age (Illsley Clarke and Dawson 1998). She names traits which suggest that a specific stage of growing up might need to be revisited if it was not appropriately assimilated at the time. She cites issues around identity confusion, signified by the need to define the self by a job, needing to be in a position of power, feeling driven to achieve, frequently comparing the self to others and needing to come off better, and wanting or expecting magical solutions or effects – all these chime with my established performance as a teacher. It is pertinent to record that these traits are attributed to stage 4, categorised as 'identity and power', which occurs around the ages of 3 to 6 – the period during which my dad disappeared and I was left to inadequately take on the mantle of leader and the man of the house.

During the research period, I revisited all the significant sites from my childhood. I went back to my old primary school and was taken back in an instant by the still familiar smells. I wandered through my old secondary school, disoriented by the low ceilings due to its conversion to upmarket flats. I experienced something akin to a spiritual happening as I eventually stumbled upon the old school staircase which had been preserved. Here I stood quietly for a good while in the company of the very bricks who were witness to my life as I passed this way decades before.

Later I stood on the rubble of the derelict estate which had once been my home, and then I returned to places I had revisited many times in my thoughts and dreams. Standing on the sites which housed my experiences of being a victim in the face of older, stronger kids, I comforted the young Sean. Now a strong, competent man, I audibly spoke to the frightened child I knew in some capacity still existed, and assured him that all would be and did turn out OK. There was no longer any need to fear; if any of those bullies were ever somehow to return I would be more than capable of dealing with them. In essence, through the reflexive activities afforded by my research, I experienced healing and release. Combined, the acquisition of critical consciousness and self-awareness enabled me to expose the foundations of this phrase 'living contradiction', so enabling me to address its manifestations entrenched in my persona as an authority figure.

I initially considered 'control' to be good, then I became suspicious of it and assumed it to be bad. Engagement with Susannah Temple's (1999) Functional Fluency taught me that control is value free. Only when it is enacted through behaviour does it take on the capacity to cause others (and ourselves) benefit or suffering. The same can be said for a knife: its wielding can either prepare life-sustaining food or be used to extinguish life. I learned that control's positive contribution comes through structuring (rather than dominating) and that it must strike a balance with ethical care. Situations and circumstances may cause control or care to take prominence on occasion, but essentially for an authoritative adult they exist in a general state of equipoise. I made a commitment to this and increasingly recognised the signs indicating that I was in need of rebalancing.

I can only offer tentative generalisations, for my work was restricted to action research in one school. On one level my journey is unique, although I hope the principles, processes, and tools – and more so, my conviction not to blindly contribute to an unethical status quo – might encourage others to tread the same path. I am particularly mindful of staff of my generation, and wonder if even considering a 'different' way is far too inconvenient amidst the culture and status which reaffirms itself on a daily basis. I have learned, however, that such hope is not folly, for my work articulated the experience of one of my key critical friends. Since then he has embarked on new educational ventures with renewed vigour. I am also encouraged that my research colleagues offered evidence that, even without a commitment to a philosophical rethink, aspects of my approach enhanced their capacity to be effective teachers for the benefit of their pupils.

I am not sure if my work offers *the* answers, although that was never my explicit intention. I would gain great satisfaction from the thought that my project has at least made colleagues more aware of pertinent questions around order, power, and ethics which rarely get asked. I am also keen to critique assumptions about the nature of research and evidence affecting the decisions and practice of colleagues. In Part II, I will present a methodology which acknowledges the contribution of dominant forms of evidence, and state my determination to no longer be constrained by it. I wish for colleagues to be equipped, or at least informed, that their own unique classroom experiences and explanations can make a valid contribution to knowledge – to be knowledge creators. Regardless of how informative, entertaining, and affirming the latest conference may have been, no matter how stimulating the debate amongst the galvanised grass root participants on Twitter, I have to keep returning to *my* reality: the process of dissecting what is happening with *my* docile Year 10 group on a Monday morning or *my* lively Year 9 bunch every Friday afternoon. I want to interrogate *my* dilemmas.

In concluding, I need to return to my compass: how do I want my own children to gain from their experience of education? I want them to leave school as capable, competent young adults who feel able to contribute positively to their community and to wider society. I want them to be self-aware as well as critically aware; not to be intimidated by others who are privileged due to inherent wealth, connections, or power; not to be afraid of those who mask their insecurities at others' expense; to be dutifully respectful of adults, of course, though not unquestionably yielding due to status or age (a string of high profile abuse cases in the media demonstrate the danger of blind obedience when this power dynamic is in play). I want my children to have experienced democracy, to have developed their own voice and articulated it with skill and conviction (ideally in the face of injustice). Of course, this is not the sole preserve of school, and I recognise the responsibility for me and my wife to set the foundations.

However, the system demands my children's school attendance and attention for the duration of their formative years. So what type of education do my children need to experience in order to become equipped to be more than a number in the masses? Is it within my rights to protest at the prospect that my kids might be, in Giroux's (2011) words, reduced to "cheerful robots" through a transmission model which fills children with information and skills deemed by select others to be useful to them and society? I am all too aware of the diet of compliance and targets which has progressively diminished the irrepressible curiosity and energy they had since they moved from the nurtured environment of home to take their place on the first of numerous class lists. Yet I sense that in particular lessons, with particular teachers, it periodically re-emerges – so all is not lost. Engagement, interest, and assurance are still possible for my children, and millions like them, but this seems to be subject to the whims of timetabling. My research work encourages staff to be one of those precious teachers to whom my children gladly pledge allegiance; those individuals who make a difference, who are significant in the lives of the children who pass through the system, and who are remembered fondly when they look back on their schooling; those who have contributed to them becoming a young adult.

What will my research achieve? It is difficult to predict until it is placed in the public arena. Even then, who is to know what the implications might be for individual readers? However, what it has already achieved cannot be disputed. It enabled an ordinary teacher to write a new and exciting final few chapters in his career. My desire is to help colleagues, whether indirectly through their academic engagement with my work, or directly through consultation and coaching. Essentially, I want to equip them to help children like me – I most certainly would have qualified for the pupil premium. At a recent reunion with childhood mates to mark our fiftieth birthdays, one confided that as kids, I was the poorest person he knew. It was sobering to hear it from someone else, even after all these years. Most of all, I hope that my original status as the product of a deprived and dysfunctional background motivates others to refuse to accept their lot in life.

Part I

Power *Over*

Chapter 3

Subscribing to Authoritarianism

Sean

It was late September/early October 2014. I was visiting a primary school, waiting to speak to the class teacher of the lad I was working with. It was breaktime, and the double glazing dulled the noise and energy emitting from the playground. The teaching assistant was busy preparing for the activity which awaited the Year 6 class when they returned after the sound of the bell. We casually engaged in conversation about education in general, then something quite specific.

The teaching assistant repeated a statistic to me just hours after I had first heard it in the morning media. She stated with some conviction that "the equivalent of 38 days of teaching was lost per year" due to low level disruption. The statistic emanated from Ofsted's *Below the Radar* report (2014: 5). The report had stimulated my interest for it emerged some months after I had finally submitted my research, and weeks before I was due to defend my thesis through the viva voce. I wondered if the examiners would catch wind of it and ask for my opinion, hence I analysed it with some intent to position my study in relation to it. In summary, the publication could have been written as a template for my unexamined perspectives prior to study; but now, six years on, it represented a skeleton to me, a narrative with some substance but devoid of flesh, critical insight, or depth. I was naturally interested to read what was reported, for the notion of low level disruptions encapsulated much of my work and research over the last few decades, but equally I was as intrigued by what was left unsaid. It was this facet which came to enable me not only to probe beyond observable behaviour, techniques, and functional systems to appreciate something of the complexity, but also to expose the inadequacy of simplistic, reductionist, quick-fix 'solutions'. I admit, on the face of it, not an easy position to defend when you find something that 'works' in the face of pupil resistance and challenge – whether it be the crutch of a 'consequences' system, arbitrarily administering detentions, or even looking mean and scary. Believe me, I know – I was that man!

If the teaching assistant had ventured past the headlines to read the full report, her opinion would have been further reinforced. Reflecting on our discussion, the publication's selective anecdotes from staff and parents resembled her portrayal of classroom life and mirrored her daily frustrations of trying to get the pupils to concentrate on work.

So very seductive and convincing. I have acknowledged my own susceptibility in the past to uncritically accept headlines and embrace fads. My reading of the literature provided the term 'discourse' to remind me, or rather alert me, to probe beneath the surface. Ball (2013: loc. 334) provides a working definition: "discourse is the conditions under which certain statements are considered to be truth". Regulative discourse relates to a school's values and beliefs – for example, in relation to discipline and how 'misbehaviour' is understood and dealt with. Within schools, Bernstein (2000) suggests two types of pedagogic discourse: regulative and instructional. *Below the Radar* advanced concerns, if not fear, around both – one was impacting negatively on the other and schools needed to sort it.

The 'equivalent to 38 days of teaching lost' statement certainly caught my attention. Now, hopefully a little more discerning, I noticed that the summative figure was calculated from a baseline figure which states, "pupils are *potentially* losing up to an hour of learning each day in English schools" (Ofsted 2014: 4; emphasis added). Very convenient to scale up and transform it into an eye-catching headline. Yet, generalising a small sample to *potentially* apply to all English schools,[1] the calculation resonated with literature I had found which had been used previously to provide supporting 'evidence' for Lee Canter's Assertive Discipline. I mention this because I recall purchasing the video set, adding its prescribed techniques to my armoury, and accepting its philosophical assertion that the adult is unequivocally in charge as affirmation for my existing approach.

"Can Assertive Discipline improve learning?" asked Canter back in 1988, as a prelude to citing proponent McCormack's (1989) study of off-task behaviour during reading instruction. The resounding affirmative answer is presented through a statistic which equates to a headline figure of 'five hours of teaching time saved per month'. The unequivocal conclusion is derived from a creative calculation: "Classrooms using Assertive Discipline had 5 per cent more on-task time than classrooms not using the program" (Canter 1988: 79–80). "That's 15 minutes per day, 75 minutes per week, 5 hours per month more time teachers have to teach and all students have to learn" (Canter 1988: 73). The summative figure omits any consideration of complex variables inherent in classrooms and assumes the attained statistic to be an indisputable constant with widespread application.

Initially, it was the official endorsement of this 'no nonsense' model by the Labour government in the white paper *Excellence in Schools* (DfEE 1997) which ensured its prominence in my literature review. A multi-million pound US franchise, Assertive Discipline has since been criticised in the United

1 Nearly 3,000 schools and academies from a pool of over 24,300.

States and subsequently in the UK. Rigoni and Walford (1998) express concern that there was no indication that the government had engaged in an extensive debate, particularly in light of criticisms of the method over the preceding decade. The power of a statistic in a headline seems to negate subsequent questions about reliability and validity. As I illustrate in due course, the requirement to keep abreast of the literature confirmed that the subsequent coalition and Conservative governments were also well versed in using selected reports to substantiate their ideology and policies. Interestingly, this type of calculation was also applied to the copying down of objectives. Debra Kidd (2014) estimates somewhere in the region of 32.5 hours a year is consumed by this practice. It was not reported so widely.

With playtime still in full swing, my teaching assistant companion continued to state categorically that 'behaviour is getting worse'. I sympathised with the view, and in the not too distant past would probably have engaged in the swapping of war stories to substantiate the assertion. As it was, my review of the literature had informed me that back in 1989 the Elton Report had stated that the government could provide no definitive answer to the question of whether discipline in schools was getting worse. Likewise, in 2011, the House of Commons Education Committee were unable to offer "any evidence-based or objective judgment on either the state of behaviour in schools today or whether there has been an improvement over time" (HCEC 2011: 3). I quietly recalled Hayden (2011) making reference to disturbances at Winchester Public School as far back as 1818 in order to illustrate that students' misbehaviour is far from a new phenomenon.

In conversation, as now in print, I will refrain from contradicting, minimising, or undermining the debilitating effect of disruptive behaviour on those charged with curbing it. For all its limitations, I consider the concerns raised in *Below the Radar* to be valid. As I illustrate in later chapters, in my own experience, one class, one clique, or even one child can have a disproportionately negative effect on one's sense of competence, let alone class learning. Thus, it seems apt that the Ofsted report should offer the lay reader direction and guidance on what might be done. And, indeed it does, citing the concepts of high expectations and consistency as pillars to the systematic approaches enshrined in school behaviour policies; naturally, the inappropriate wearing of uniform is presented as symptomatic of standards. The section entitled 'where schools are getting it right' identifies establishing "a positive climate for learning" on one hand (Ofsted 2014: 6), and staff implementing the behaviour policy "rigorously" on the other (ibid.: 24). Consulting a dictionary, I was interested to note that the adjective for rigorous is characterised by "rigidly severe or harsh, as people, rules, or discipline", and triggers synonyms such as strict, tough, hard, inflexible, draconian, uncompromising, demanding, and, of course, authoritarian when applied to a belief or system. I am sure the meaning here is more to do with being thorough, careful, and diligent, though I believe it is worth considering the subtlety of connotations.

The notion of sanctions and rewards represent the advocated approach. The language used is consequences and misdemeanours which are logged on behaviour systems to record evidence of schools' intolerance of 'bad behaviour'. These then form part of the skeleton I referred to – a functional framework. As I will qualify below, I recognise it well. If Ofsted or the Department for Education needed a champion to implement these strategies, I could have been that bloke. On the school's behalf, I implemented a consequential sanction system; I isolated the most disruptive students – I even worked with them one to one on intervention approaches; I volunteered to be involved in every detention; I trained the staff; I demanded consistency; I patrolled the corridors; and I had the undiluted support of the head teacher.

This unique role as lead teacher for behaviour, extending over four years, brought to the surface a lifetime of subliminal messages which had come to shape my professional identity. The reflexive enquiry afforded by action research enabled me to articulate what I had become as I donned the persona of an authority figure on a daily basis over many years. My study shines a discerning light on the detrimental impact on the psyche of the adult charged with quelling disruption and with being consistent in adhering to a behaviour policy. My brief conversation with my teaching assistant companion reminded me of a bygone propensity to uncritically soak up ideological and political memes. Aligned with formative influences, instilled way before I had even thought of becoming a teacher, I had somehow absorbed a discourse of crime and punishment to frame my conception of children: if you are 'bad', expect to be punished. By the turn of the millennium I was a reputable teacher with an established way of being in the classroom. I was apparently successful and effective. The perfect candidate, it seemed, for a role beyond the confines of my own classroom.

An Authoritarian School

In 2003 an exciting job opportunity came my way. At that point in my career I'd had experience of working periodically in places such as Papua New Guinea, Romania, and the United States, and I'd had a stint of working as a supply teacher for six months after graduating. I was now settled into my fourth school in the UK. Seven years previously, I had changed from PE to RE and had attained my second degree in the process. As I approached the interview I was confident. I was already known to the panel at the local education authority, for I was an advanced skills teacher as well as an established head of department. The post which had caught my attention required the successful candidate to deliver and disseminate the government's national strategy for behaviour and attendance to the county's secondary and special schools. In truth, had I been asked, I would have struggled to qualify my approach on a philosophical or theoretical level. Instead, I convinced them that I was a worthy candidate because my references and my pragmatic answers affirmed that whatever it was I did 'worked'.

I had progressively come to utilise a combination of authoritarian tips, techniques, strategies, tricks of the trade, and habits to complement personality, status, and reputation to ensure order. I had constructed my own personal theory which was shaped by experience. Young (1992) calls this approach "technical eclecticism", where one has a tendency to utilise one organising theory and borrow supplementary methods from other theories. Despite acknowledging the merits of Bill Rogers' (2002) positive behaviour leadership model, which advocates shared rights and responsibilities for both students and staff, my practice was dominated by adherence to behaviourist theories, including Canter's much vaunted Assertive Discipline. The literature informed me that the endorsement of 'implicit' or 'tacit' theories ensures that much teacher action becomes the product of custom, habit, coercion, and ideology, which acts to unconsciously constrain performance. In the hectic nature of the school day, these factors did not cross my mind.

Whilst the Department for Education and Skills' presentation slides (2003) espoused "values, principles and beliefs that inform an inclusive whole school policy", the implicit messages I absorbed from the national strategy's regional director were the importance of tangible results through the establishment of discipline and order. I was not afforded the luxury of listening and building relationships, for the early and concise directive was to 'get your foot in the door'. The last time I had heard that phrase was when I sold double glazing as a 17-year-old. The intensive year which followed my appointment as a behaviour and attendance consultant affirmed that my established quick-fix approach – through assertiveness and sanctions – was the dimension most colleagues I encountered seemed to desire.

Prior to an Ofsted inspection in 2004, I returned to my school to take on the role of lead teacher for behaviour. Due to a rogue and significant minority of pupils in Year 10, it was imperative that we developed a consistent behaviour policy. My strategy was greatly influenced by a contemporary flagship school for embedded organisational 'good practice'. Ninestiles School, a high profile state school in Birmingham, was praised for a zero tolerance stance on misbehaviour. Their discipline for learning policy stated: "Students must follow staff instructions first time round. This is the foundation of good behaviour, making sure students do what they're told with no quibbling. Without this basic principle, which puts staff in charge, chaos ensues" (see de Waal 2009). I had a template for organisational 'effectiveness' to guide my work. I now had to get staff to replicate what I did so they too could be 'in charge' – just as the Ninestiles document declared.

The concept of authority is used as the link between the institution of school and the teacher as its custodian. Most apt for my purposes was Súilleabháin's (1983) definition: he speaks of *de jure* authority, in which the authority of teachers is bestowed by parents and society. Contributions from parents to the *Below the Radar* report (Ofsted 2014) substantiate this acceptance, this expectation (or in some cases insistence), that the teacher takes rightful charge. "Using the word 'authority' in the *de jure* sense is making the normative claim that some individual has a right to rule" (Steutel and Spiecker 2000: 326). Although unaware of these specific works at the time, Canter's (1988) Assertive Discipline legitimised my evolving operational approach. It was whilst on secondment at the local authority that I had purchased his books and videos. Essentially "a no nonsense approach to setting and consistently enforcing classroom rules" (Brown 1983: 175), Assertive Discipline defines successful classrooms as those that are under firm teacher control (Swinson 1990). Looking back, it is as if this high profile and prominent approach had given me permission to carry on down the path I was travelling. Although Bill Rogers' work offered alternative signposts, Canter's route cut to the chase. Increasingly, especially when feeling under pressure, Assertive Discipline was the strategy I instinctively reverted to when pupils defied my will and provoked my emotions, thus I paid mere lip service to more reasoned strategies, even though I espoused them to others in training. The former got results – quickly. I now had the essential ingredients, and the trust and support of the head teacher, to get down to work.

A consequence (or C) system and accompanying rules set the framework for halting, as the serving deputy head teacher termed it, "the deterioration of standards in the school". I concluded that strong systems acted as a deterrent. Naturally, positive behaviour, praise, and reward were part of the rhetoric. Although the consequences were designed to primarily address the antics of a significant minority, of course they implicated the amenable and the majority. I did not give it a second thought as I reasoned that the measures presented a common shared language, encouraged consistency, and were for the benefit of all. My simplistic, essentially behaviourist, belief was that if the pupils were tempted to become distracted, the threat of consequences was enough for them to cease their course of action. If they were not cooperative with staff, then they would at least be compliant so as not to escalate the consequences. The limitations of this deterrent, however, quickly became apparent as, for some pupils, the system merely interrupted their activities, only to have them resume in another time and/or place.

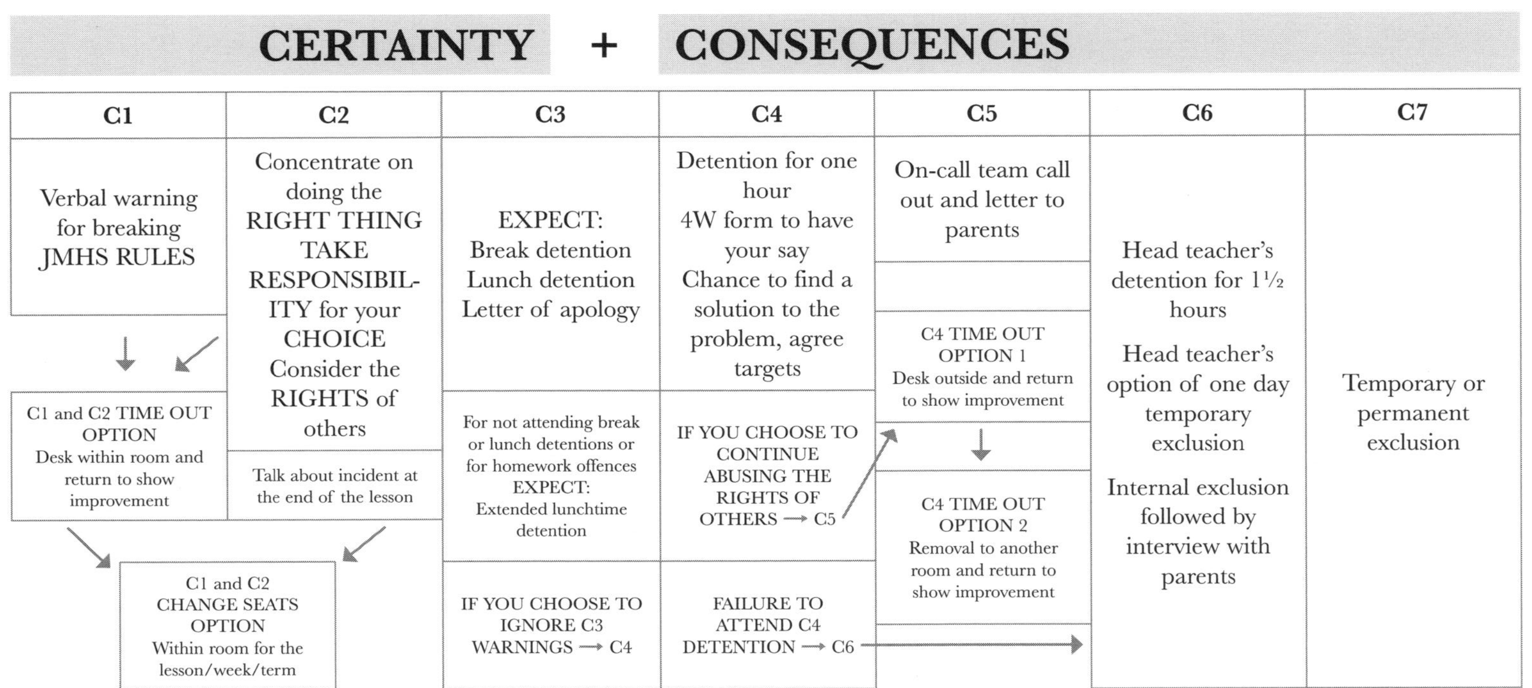

Figure 3.1. The consequence system

The Situation

Affirming my conviction to subdue the 'hard core', data revealed that this significant minority of students dominated detention lists and typically exhibited a range of low level disruptive behaviour alongside more wilful defiance and challenge. This habitually involved certain pupils and was more prevalent with certain staff. Key and consistent terms used in referrals are recorded as: failure to settle, distracted (off-task), distracting others, ignoring instructions, undermining and being disrespectful to staff, interruptions, defiance, and argumentative. School data highlights that the three highest offenders in Year 8 were boys who had accumulated a shared total of 51 detentions between January and March. Subject teachers' progress reports, issued in January, had alerted the school to impending difficulties, flagging up a combined 27 areas for concern. One boy in Year 9 was issued 39 sanctions in the same period. Each of the Year 8 students was eventually expelled from the school. The Year 9 boy was transferred to a special school. In the meantime, my self-appointed role was to meet each and every challenge they exhibited head on. This conviction was noted by the head teacher in a private letter in 2006: "I have also greatly appreciated the way you have tackled difficult incidents, never turning a blind eye even when it would have been easier to do so."

My strategic response was twofold: equipping staff through professional development and relieving them of responsibility for taking detentions. I would become their 'enforcer'. To underline this noble and well-intended gesture, I subsequently developed and ran an isolation unit. Over the four year period, the challenge to quell disruption became intoxicating, although the psychological cost of maintaining this level of performance was concealed from colleagues who applauded my efforts. In truth, this was because of the corrosion of my sense of perspective. The suggestion that the procedures I had put into place might be detrimental to myself, my colleagues, and the children I claimed to serve was obscured, at this stage, even to me.

Sanctions

Initially, upon taking over the inconsistent detention system, I identified a central room close to the hub of the school. I volunteered and then committed to taking, or being involved in, every school detention for the next four years. The third and fourth years were on a daily basis. The lunchtime provision compelled attendance for one hour. It was arranged in response to the escalating demand for consequences to be administered to a hard core of pupils, especially from the Year 10 cohort, whose propensity to skip after-school detentions was clogging up the system. I arranged for the leadership team members, including the head teacher, to assemble a team to assist me.

If the students failed to attend, colleagues went to search for them. This process became ever more efficient as targeted pupils were collected from lessons prior to lunchtime, and walkie-talkies/CCTV aided communication and surveillance.

Under the banner of 'standards', I stipulated that complete obedience was required during detentions. It was during these sessions that I adhered to the concept of zero tolerance. Upon entering, the children were met with a sign which spelled out and reinforced expectations. Protocols and rituals were quickly established without any scope for discussion. Coats were removed upon arrival, bags were assigned to be beneath their desks, and the pupils were strategically seated. This was to break up alliances and avert sight lines to each other; the environment was ordered and silent. Quantz et al.'s (2011) text on the non-rational impact of ritual on broader school performance and educational identity provides rich insight into understanding the patterns apparent within schooling. During these periods of confinement, I wished to convey – verbally and non-verbally – that the 'detainees' were to assume the role of docile subordinates.

An observed outcome of pupils' conduct in detentions and subsequent isolation was usually, and somewhat surprisingly, total conformity with the stated requirements. However, it often felt as if it was on a knife edge, especially on days when the mix of individual students was potentially toxic. I recall very clearly the cloak I donned whenever I approached the room. It was one of protection and bravado which suppressed any inkling of anxiety. I psychologically adopted a bullish mask of confidence, assurance, and assertiveness. It manifested in my walk and my stance; it exuded from my persona. Quantz et al. (2011: 37) recognise such preparation as ritual formalised as symbolic performance: we "carefully imbue our self, our identity, our claims to power … we are in the best position to perform our roles in the manner we wish others to perceive us or in the manner we assume others expect of us."

Added significance of these protective traits, in which one constructs and projects a persona, comes from Philip Zimbardo. His research suggested that situational forces, communicated predominately through symbols and rituals, are powerful mechanisms for altering one's identity in accordance to contextual stimuli. The pliability of human nature was revealed as research subjects adopted specified roles differentiated by power. For example, the arbitrary separation of volunteers into 'guards' and 'prisoners' to simulate prison conditions was initially symbolised by uniforms, until escalation of negative attributes rendered the project untenable. Echoes of the contrasting roles assumed in detentions resonate.

As with Milgram's obedience experiments (1974), the Stanford prison study (Haney et al. 1973; Zimbardo et al. 2000; Zimbardo 2007) found that the tendency for those in charge to over-assert the authority invested in them was inconsistent with their personality profiles. The studies revealed an abdication of personal responsibility, as participants deferred to duties in obedience to the 'system' they represented. As Zimbardo et al. (2000: 1) reflect, 'good' people can act in ways contrary to their previous character "within the context of socially approved roles, rules, and norms, a legitimizing ideology, and institutional support that transcends individual agency". My continued exposure to these combined elements established a way of 'being' whilst in role, which was contrary to the values I espoused.

Internal Isolation Unit

To extend the provision for temporary 'incarceration' I established the internal isolation unit. This facility hosted habitual offenders for two full days a week. Its primary rationale, expressed in documentation at the time, stated that it "should not be viewed as a short, sharp shock but experienced as a prolonged inconvenience the student does not want to repeat". In addition, and significantly for the school's data, it functioned as an alternative to external exclusion.

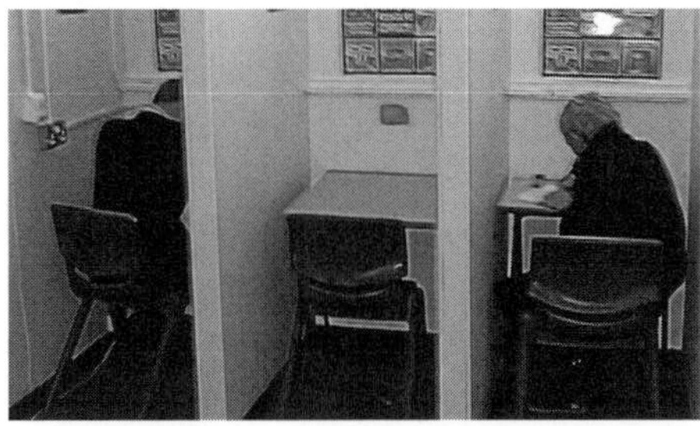

Figure 3.2a and b. Compliance in the session before break resulted in pupils progressing from one set of booths to the next

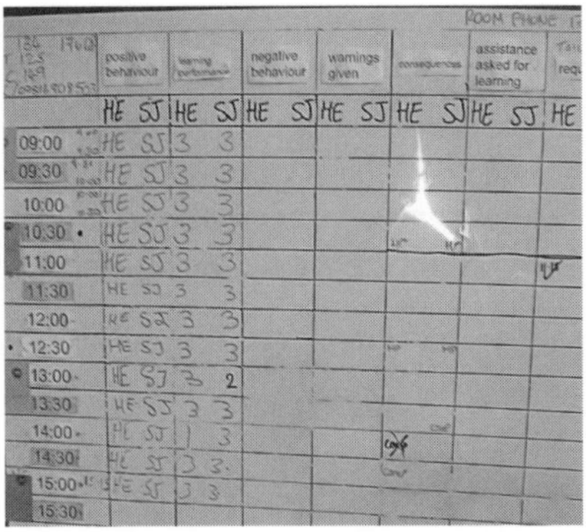

Figure 3.2c. Each and every interaction is monitored and contributes to a score every 30 minutes, leading to positive or negative consequences

Figure 3.2d. Successive 'green 3s' represent the carrot (or incentive) to earn a place on the third station in the afternoon session, which is symbolically closer to the exit

Constructed in a converted storage space, the internal isolation unit functioned primarily as an extension of the detention. The unit catered for 38 pupils during the year. Several attendees were siblings. Selection was determined by behaviour, irrespective of educational need. The pupils were allocated places in groups of two or three. The unit represented a tangible example of the unexamined confusion which defined my state of mind at the time. I did not perceive any philosophical contradiction between practice, which instilled complete obedience, and the intervention approaches we sought to implement, which espoused trust. On reflection, the construction of the internal isolation unit pre-empted the crossroads I was to approach upon commencement of my action research.

Using an array of computer programmes to diagnose the social, emotional, and cognitive capacities of pupils in the internal isolation unit, some common themes emerged. Often eliciting single figure percentages, the categories 'confidence in learning', 'perceived learning capacity', and 'self-regard as a learner' consistently drew the lowest scores. Perhaps unsurprisingly, PASS (Pupil Attitudes to School and Self) data affirmed that being 'unprepared for learning' had become a habitual ploy for many of the respondents.[2] The Year 9 boy who accumulated 39 detentions in a short period before he left us, produced the following PASS profile:

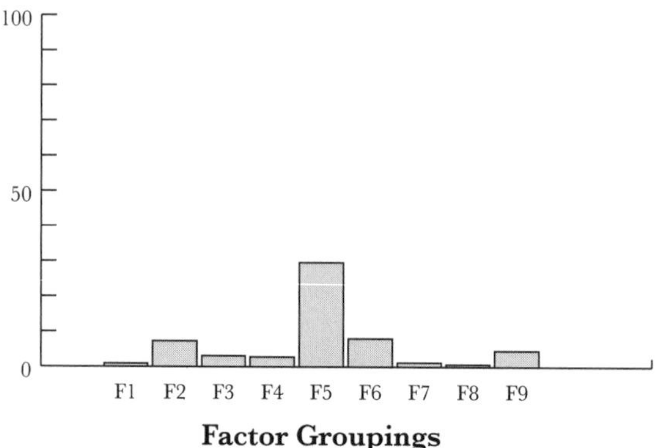

Figure 3.3. Pupil percentile scores

Notes: The higher the percentile score, the more positive the pupil attitude/self-perception. Factor 1: Feelings about school – 0.9; Factor 2: Perceived learning capability – 7.3; Factor 3: Self-regard as a learner – 3.1; Factor 4: Preparedness for learning – 2.8; Factor 5: Attitudes to teachers – 29.6; Factor 6: General work ethic – 8.0; Factor 7: Confidence in learning – 1.2; Factor 8: Attitude to attendance – 0.7; Factor 9: Response to curriculum demands – 4.6

Many of the children revealed poor eating and sleeping habits. This tended to be conveyed during informal chats whilst the rest of the school were in lessons. It became apparent that some pupils had learned to navigate around impending circumstances which may have exposed their sense of incompetence. My analysis of a Year 9 male concluded:

> One aspect of the group norm behaviour is to meet up so arriving late, being under-equipped and under-prepared for learning. Subsequent power struggles and servicing divert from the learning process and allow him to exist in the classroom as someone significant rather than someone who is constantly failing. He fails, but on his own terms!

2 The standardised tool poses 50 statements which invite a response on a four point rating scale – see http://www.gl-assessment.co.uk/products/pass-pupil-attitudes-self-and-school.

No matter what insights we thought we had gleaned, a perennial problem remained. Intervention was only half of the battle: the real issue centred on reintegration back into classrooms where the habitual behaviours tended to resurface unabated. The trend is illustrated through the following extract in which my colleague in the internal isolation unit witnessed a glimpse of B's (Year 9) reintegration period:

> A 24 minute observation (9.20–9.44) in Ms X's maths lesson clarified the reality of B's performance. He was on-task for approximately six minutes which meant he was off-task for 75% of the sample observation. He shouted out on 27 occasions including demanding the teacher attended to him, "Come 'ere and help me." He spent time rummaging through his bag, spent much of his time doodling on his page, and actively sought an audience for his antics. He was observed looking around trying to get the attention of other students. At one point he got out of his seat for three minutes to engage with K. This was done with a deliberate show of whistling as he strolled across by windows kicking the wall. IO summarised his 24 minute performance as aggressive and confrontational behaviour which engaged the teacher and HLTA frequently.

My response was to up the ante. I worked with the IT department to develop a mechanism where I could gather intelligence on a significant minority of pupils. Behaviour Spotlight (or Weasel Watch as it was initially termed) was akin to spying. Regardless, the rationale presented to staff justified its use and all were invited to contribute upon accessing a link on SIMS.

Identifying behaviour which is normally under the radar

What is Behaviour Spotlight?

Dear colleagues:

A few minutes of investment …

As you are well aware, some of our students have a tendency to bend the truth and play the 'denial' or 'blame' card when confronted about their conduct. In order that we deal in 'reality', it would be greatly beneficial if we have a comprehensive picture of everything that student does in the week leading up to the intervention. At present, such a student can have four teachers speak to him individually and then moving him on without the misdemeanours amounting to much. We will be concentrating on a single student at any one time (although the period of observation may be more than a week in fact) to stop the behaviour slipping below the radar.

> So, please contribute towards giving this specified child a 'truth tablet' by adding to the list below by clicking on the 'New' button and filling in the form.
>
> You can select which student to view by clicking on the drop-down list to the right of the 'Title' column and selecting the appropriate student to filter on. The list will contain all students under the spotlight, allowing you to view historical behaviour.
>
> It is vital for these types of students to realise teachers communicate with each other and that their conduct is being noticed and recorded, e.g. comment on lateness, uniform, jewellery, peer group associates, backchat – basically, anything and everything to build up a picture over and beyond normal sanctions.

Two of the first students I selected were Year 8 boys who I will call Alan and Jack. I taught both of these boys in their first week at the school. Both stood out for me, so much so that I can still remember which seats they sat in five years on. There was something self-assured about them. Alan was big for his age and this came through in his dominating influence on others. For some impressionable lads this meant joining in or going along with his antics; for the majority of the others a sense of wariness was evident. Jack was more subdued – he liked to watch. Both boys seemed to have school 'sussed'; the experience of leaving primary school in order to work out the boundaries represented by different teachers seemed like an opportunity that Alan, in particular, couldn't pass up. Jack was initially with us for a short while before he left to join another secondary school, only to return towards the end of the year. By the time the boys were in Year 8, the prior testing of boundaries had informed them when and where they could resist and even challenge. This would eventually escalate to include most members of staff, until exclusion and 'negotiated moves' came to represent the only logical boundary open to the school.

My records show that many staff contributed to Behaviour Spotlight, recording incidents and observations in great detail. It was apparent that these two individuals left a trail of destruction around the school. The descriptions make for tough reading, and a sense of impotence and frustration exudes from the staff accounts. Ominously, the catalogue seems to affirm that much of the boys' previous conduct appeared on record as isolated incidents – that is, only when it contravened rules and was recorded in accordance with the consequences system. I had suspected that the application of prescribed sanctions was arbitrary. The boys seemed to be acutely aware that there was no mechanism to square the circle, so they became adept at playing the system and setting one member of staff off against another. Two extracts from Behaviour Spotlight serve to illustrate:

> **02/06** P3 (Mr X): Alan turned up 6 minutes late with … (Y7) and said he had been released late by Mr A from detention. This was checked and found to be untrue. Alan demonstrated low level disruption during the lesson and reached a C2 for repeated interruptions.
>
> **11/06** lunch (Mr Y): Jack did not attend C4 detention AGAIN. Had to be found by Mr C. Jack agreed and said he was going but then ran away. Saw Jack at 1.55, he was with WJ who seemed to be acting as his lawyer. Initial questioning extracted a completely contradictory account from Mr C's. Further questioning established Mr C's version was probably closer to the truth.

Not only did hard core students such as Alan and Jack reinforce my conviction that a draconian approach was justified, but these records also illuminated the clear and apparent inconsistency between staff which our habitual offenders took great glee in exploiting. Staff development was on the agenda.

Training Colleagues

Even though my own practice became increasingly draconian, many of the ideas I espoused when training others were more philosophical.

●

Using Bill Rogers' idea, which he had shared during a training event at my previous school in 1998, I presented a single black dot on a white sheet of paper and asked the group to describe what they saw. Predictably the focus homed in on the dot rather than the expansive white space around it. I spoke of our habitual tendencies to ignore the majority and focus most of our energies and a disproportionate amount of time on the minority. The realisation that a faulty perspective could lead to a class being mislabelled hit home for a senior male member of staff. Despite his body language, which represented that of the archetypal sceptic of new-fangled theories and ideas throughout the training session, the next day a bottle of wine awaited me in my pigeon hole with a note attached:

> Sean – thanks again for yesterday morning. I had the best lesson I've ever had with 8AB lesson 5 as a direct result of looking at my own feelings and attitudes towards the class. I saw the white space and not the black dot; for there are some wonderful students in the group – all of them if you look right! Thanks again.

This idea would expand to represent the composition of a typical class. It would encompass the categories of light and dark greys before coming to be associated with the metaphor of weather during my research (this is explained further in Chapter 11).

The head teacher also conveyed his gratitude for my continued and sincere efforts:

> Governors congratulate you … particularly the high quality training programme on behaviour management you provided for all teachers. We also appreciate the work you do on a day-to-day basis in promoting high standards of behaviour throughout the school.

Unbeknownst to the head teacher or the governors, offering guidance and advice sometimes seemed inadequate as individual colleagues, both male and female, exhibited the depth of their distress through sobbing. My genuine empathy and sympathy with some vied with the increasing frustration and sense of disapproval I felt towards others, as I sought to regulate the conduct of colleagues, despite micro circumstances clearly being beyond my control.

My records include a document that I sent to the SLT when my determination to direct staff, in the name of consistency and standards, became official. Logical and full of apparent common sense, pre-dating similar rhetoric from Michael Gove, it serves to encapsulate the single minded, well-meaning, self-righteous conviction that *I* knew best. I reread it and wonder to what extent I was somehow complicit in Sarah's experience of our school (Chapter 1):

> The key factor in making our Behaviour for Learning initiatives 'bite' is the role of our staff. Some seem to be waiting for signs that the

students are changing or getting 'better' but this is like putting the cart before the horse. The rules, the policy, the sanctions system, etc. are impotent without the investment of our staff. I propose that we need to backtrack over whole school agreements and make a commitment that all colleagues are fulfilling their professional obligations. For some, the emphasis, as with observing students, ought to be on noticing those who do their duty, are following the policy to the best of their ability – colleagues in the maths department spring to mind. For others, perhaps an initial enquiry as to whether they understand or agree with basic requirements. Either way, we must at some point move from "we would like you to …", to "this is part of your job and *responsibility*".

The area of the policy I am talking about is not necessarily classroom management, the implementation of that is complex and requires training and is dependent on teachers' self-esteem. I am referring to the *basics* that were introduced two terms ago:

- Students having corridor passes.
- Uniform passes for specified period and call to parents.
- Students not sent on errands in twos and threes.
- Staff recording latecomers and the following up trends.
- Jewellery policy enforced.
- Dismissal of classes in an orderly manner.
- Keeping classes until the bell sounds (not maths and English).
- Assemblies finishing on time.
- Staff being on time for duties etc.

These vital 'signs' have a profound, implicit effect on the climate of the school and are foundational for more complex initiatives to flourish in coming terms and years. I am also concerned about the implicit messages given in tutorials that contradict and undermine the behaviour expectations and standards in subject classes (though that isn't for now!).

Although there is evidence of progress in some of these areas, it is clear that there are numerous occasions when staff are ignoring these basics. In short they are abdicating their commitment and responsibility to the school and their colleagues. Because we are professionals it seems there is an assumption that staff will fulfil their responsibilities, even if there is a resignation that some will be more diligent than others.

> I would like to suggest that the success of the behaviour programme and our intention of becoming an 'excellent' school are being *undermined* by this persistent, low level unprofessional behaviour. We do not ask staff to do these basics out of goodwill, this is what they get paid for; it is their job. It is their *responsibility*! Every time students are let out early it undermines colleagues who fulfil the agreement – furthermore, others are left with groups waiting outside their teaching area whilst they are still teaching. Every time students are out of class in pairs another teacher has to ignore or confront them, forcing them to make a decision as to whether to intervene or not, often under a pressing time constraint. Staff should not have to be *compromised* because of colleagues' thoughtlessness and unprofessional habits and decisions.
>
> Weak excuses from staff, such as "I've run out of passes" or "I've misplaced ..." without doing something about it, is becoming unacceptable and akin to students with their homework excuses! And so I could go on illustrating how instances of unprofessional behaviour and the ignoring of agreed policy is compromising many staff who have to deal with the consequences of colleagues failing to take primary responsibility for the students in their immediate care. Because we have had this running for *two terms* I cannot see how it will be delivered consistently without direct intervention. In fact, I believe the reverse to be true: the standards will continue to be compromised until we are back to where we started.
>
> I would like to propose a focus where such incidents are actively noticed and the responsible person is made *accountable*. I am not proposing a 'police state', for at the beginning of this communication I acknowledged the need to explore underlying reasons for staff non-compliance. However, there still needs to come a time where "we would like you to ..." becomes an insistent "this is what you are responsible for and paid to do".
>
> I believe that time is fast approaching if we are to build on solid foundations. We have made a start, now we need to *persevere* if we are to instil standards and expectations in our lower school – for they will soon progress to become our upper school.

So there!

A 'solution', implemented by an influential member of the SLT after I had relinquished my strategic role, was to insist that all staff wear official school high visibility waistcoats when on duty. Illustrative of Foucault's (1977) discourse about disciplinary apparatus and self-surveillance, I recorded how I became conscious of its veracity:

> On duty – bright fluorescent jackets for all staff. The duty team leader saw I was where I was meant to be – from a distance. Secure in that knowledge I found myself looking out for other staff who should also be on duty. Felt like a policeman – 'supervising the supervisors'.

Foucault describes such instances of self-regulation as the most important component of disciplinary power, for it is cheap, efficient, and negates the need for coercive means. As Brookfield (2008: 135) writes: "a single gaze [ensures] those being surveyed are aware that at any time they may be subject to invisible scrutiny".

Devoid of critical insights about the subtle nature of power, when in post my response to inconsistencies was indeed to coerce. I readily channelled my frustration by becoming increasingly obsessive about ensuring that staff abided by agreed standards and procedures. I became perturbed by any child being out of class without a corridor pass. In the name of consistency, I frequently escorted children back to the offending teacher in full view of their class. I would deliberately seek to catch colleagues out, confronting them if they allowed their class to leave before the bell. I would wander the school and question any pupil who had been sent out of class or was found in the corridors. It was clear to me that, despite training, staff remained inconsistent in their application of the policy I had constructed and implemented.

The school's recent Ofsted report had affirmed the problem I was determined to address: "Some teachers are not yet using the sanctions outlined in the recently revised behaviour policy as consistently as they should." As Roach's submission to the House of Commons Education Committee cautions, "having a policy and what happens in practice are two very different things" (HCEC 2011: 26). I did not have the awareness to enquire why this might be.

Staff Disempowerment

It is only in retrospect that I reconsider the detrimental impact of my decision to personally administer the consequences of disruptive behaviour on behalf of staff. I now realise that the daily reinforcement of my authority through sanctions may, in the eyes of pupils, especially 'detainees', have heightened the contrast between those teachers deemed worthy of compliance and those waiting back in the classrooms, deemed as unworthy. As one habitual offender commented when reflecting back on his time as a pupil attending detentions, I (and select others) were able to "keep him in line" due to his "respect" for us. Two other young men I quizzed during a chance meeting in the local supermarket, attributed their compliance to the perception that "the teacher knows me" and the requirement for the teacher to be "important ... up there".

The issue had previously been raised in a consultation with middle leaders regarding their participation in detentions. The summary report reads: "We have many talented and established staff whose influence is not being utilised. Some staff have used the phrase 'disempowered' ... simply passing issues on acts to dissociate some staff with the consequences/solutions." I acknowledged it but, it seems, persistently carried on. Ultra-professional, yet abrupt in equal measure, I wore a mask which had the propensity to sometimes slip.

Inner Emotions

My inner turbulence manifested in different forms. The burden of self-expectation and sustaining my assigned status was a heavy one. I did not make this state apparent to others, but instead continued to operate through the veneer of a model practitioner and disciplinarian.

In 2004 I was head of department, an advanced skills teacher one day a week, still the county's behaviour and attendance consultant one day a week, and lead teacher for the school's response to behavioural issues. My classroom performance became increasingly subject to the diverse roles I held concurrently, often resulting in a feeling that teaching was getting in the way of my job. However, I was still capable of performing to a high standard in my capacity as a religious education teacher. An Ofsted inspection in the autumn term of 2004 saw me observed four times with four different year groups. The recognition of my performance was recorded in a card from the head teacher: "To teach four out of four excellent lessons is a superb achievement of which you should be very proud."

Unfortunately, the sentiment does not come close to appreciating the cost associated with the external expectations I had come to internalise. It does not portray the psychological state I endured the evening before an inspection – a state so acute I could not remember the access code to my computer. Mildly panicking, I phoned a colleague to enquire if there was any other way to gain admission to the device I used daily. But there was no intimation of that anxiety as I stood with a staffroom full of colleagues on the Monday morning ready to be introduced to the inspection team. I gave no hint of the relief upon learning that my subject inspector would not join the team until later that day, because my morning lessons were anything but excellent.

Those conveying sincere congratulations were oblivious to the main reason why my lessons were so successful: they were the product of me regularly rehearsing the content upon waking in the middle of the night until I fell asleep exhausted just before the alarm clock was due to go off. My delivery was near faultless as a result of excessive mental rehearsal. The perfectionist trait was absent earlier on in my career, but it was now a prerequisite to my operational role. I felt nothing other than relief that I had achieved the grades expected of the school's advanced skills teacher. Ball's (2003: 221) article, 'The teacher's soul and the terrors of performativity', now resonates: "A kind of values schizophrenia is experienced by individual teachers where commitment, judgement and authenticity within practice are sacrificed for impression and performance." Although lessons became subsidiary in importance, my perfectionism could not tolerate performances which slipped below 'very good', despite increasingly limited time to prepare. This is significant in recognising the strain under which I consistently performed, and therefore provides a perspective for my outbursts when I perceived a pupil was trying to sabotage my lesson.

Brookfield's (2008) application of Gramsci's (1971) concept of hegemony to education provides an insightful revelation. Hegemony (on a political level) refers to pervasive ideas which sustain the self-interests of those who have power over the education system, thus ensuring it runs efficiently and profitably. Althusser (1971) makes reference to the repressive state apparatus which supports the natural, preordained state of institutions, such as schools, and works in their best interests. Discussion of capitalism and inequality as part of this broad canvas was part of my literature review. A consideration of how the concept might be relevant to my condition was profound and resulted in my decision to amend my study's initial proposal (to articulate why I was apparently so effective and how to pass it on). Brookfield unerringly names a core aspect of my experience within the institution of education. He explains how hegemony leads to one taking pride in apparently selfless devotion; a perverse pride in exhaustion; learning to love servitude; and a willingness to sacrifice mental and physical health to the cause of student learning or institutional good. Hegemony manipulates, as dedication and hard work come to equate to an obligation to "squeeze two or three jobs into the space where one would fit comfortably" (Brookfield 2008: 103) and "a state of burnout becomes a sign of commitment to your vocation" (ibid.: 102). Doerr (2009), building on the insights of Varenne (2007), argues that acknowledgement of ignorance is a productive moment that pushes one to ponder what one might do with a previously unnoticed object in one's environment.

Hegemony alerts us to the process in which we learn to embrace a system of beliefs and practices which ends up harming us; ideology is embedded and lived out on a daily basis; hegemony, subtle and elusive, saturates (Williams 1977). I recognised that my embracement of this concept constantly left me feeling as though I was on the brink, and yet I took pride in my level of commitment. Increasingly intolerant of those who fell short of my standards, emotional outbursts were indicative of the inner tension I bore.

Outbursts

Although not apparent when subject to observation, up until the beginning of 2009 I had a tendency to explode with anger to incidents of challenge. In addition, I would all too easily employ traits which would undermine the confidence of the children such as sarcasm and thoughtless comment. Sylvester (2011) associates such conduct with bullying, which is defined by Olweus (1993) as repeated, intentional, and within the context of an unequal power relationship. Whether administered knowingly or unintentionally, I now recognise the validity of this characterisation. Absurdly, it was to my surprise that older and past students would reveal to me how 'scared' they were of me during my lessons when they were younger – before they got to know me better. These elements naturally remained obscured from all external assessments of my performance.

An entry into my reflexive research diary in October 2010 provides an introspective review of the ploys I utilised to relieve my inner pressure:

> I didn't seem to have the psychological shortcomings I associated with stress although a related aspect of the condition, anger, was very much part of my 'performance' as an authority figure. Genuine or feigned, the emotion had become an established part of my armoury. Evidently, on reflection, this was perceived, indeed experienced, as strength for it embodied my power and eliminated any inkling of weakness in my psyche. Whilst it would manifest in incidents of tension and conflict, I would only make tenuous, momentary links to stress as my assertion through outburst would always serve to reassert my dominance. Momentary loss of self-control worked to my advantage. Beyond this trait, when things were as I liked them, ordered with the pupils patently self-controlled in my presence – compliant – I was widely perceived to be a 'good bloke'. I was 'strict but fair' – 'but kids wouldn't want to mess with me'. My very presence upon entering a room could bring chaos to a hushed silence – I was someone who could control the 'kids'! I was yet to question the validity of this ability or 'success'.

One such incident which illustrates my capacity to act angrily involved a Year 10 pupil who had joined the school from Birmingham. His profile warned of a troubled past and he soon became acquainted with the like-minded students we already had on roll. Swann et al. (1992) recognise the propensity to gravitate towards people who affirm one's self-identity as a fundamental feature of social interaction. Upon confronting his antics within the group, I found to my extreme irritation that, having been denied experience of me in his younger years, he seemed immune to my status and reputation. His open defiance in front of his peers was not something I was prepared to tolerate in my position as lead teacher for behaviour. I arranged for the deputy head to collect him from his form base and escort him to my office. They arrived with the boy clearly smug. Standing in the doorway I turned and with an open palm hit the door with such force that it slammed into the filing cabinet behind it. Barely containing my 'rage', I spelt out in no uncertain terms what would happen if he dared try his luck with me again. The desired effect was instant. He was reduced to a shocked and compliant pupil. Upon leaving I reverted back and winked at the deputy, who it seems was also convinced that my 'performance' was for real. Although in control on this occasion, I reflect that the source of these feelings came from issues around power. I deliberately sought out the pupil with his peers the next day; they observed a transformed exchange from the previous day. My reputation was restored.

On another occasion, the same door was witness to the goading I was subjected to from a Year 8 boy. This time my anger was not feigned and the open hand became a fist as I turned from the student and punched a hole clean through the door. Obedience was immediate. The incident added to my reputation, and I spotted the lad bringing his mate back to the site to show them evidence of my fury. A strategically placed poster concealed the hole for several years after the incident. The student was eventually expelled and news came back that he had ended up hitting a teacher at his new school. It is with some discomfort that I deliberate whether I contributed in any way to that event. When it came to confrontation, the mindset I had developed extinguished any inkling of being scared of disruptive pupils.

The period depicted in this chapter captures something of the practice and mentality of an experienced, effective teacher with multiple responsibilities. It represents my professional identity; it conveys my use (and, at times, abuse) of power as an adult entrusted with the growth and well-being of other people's children. The inner threats emerge in the form of feeling incompetent; being unprepared; being less than excellent; not being able to control the situation, others (students and staff who affected my role and performance), and my teaching space (when other teachers had use of it); and, most of all, not being able to control myself in the face of confrontation.

Kitching (2009) argues that the concept of emotional labour indicates that teachers – who are perceived to be moral/caring agents, experts, and purveyors of social control/social efficiency – not only have to present a certain emotional front, but they must also act as role models. This 'front' is a key part of their role. I experienced an internal discrepancy between authentic emotion in the form of frustration and anger, and inauthentic performance in front of observers. I could have been (and frequently was) one of those teachers Sarah referred to – those who welcome in the head teacher and parents/guests to show off the school at its best. I now recognise the discontinuity between the script that my professional role demanded and what I felt. I am acutely aware of the facade I habitually performed under when other adults were present.

This chapter has provided a rationale for the dissonance I experienced and a description of my professional bid to suppress others in the name of standards. I have provided a glimpse of the inner turmoil which, for the most part, was kept at bay and directed towards an ever-increasing need to control others. However, to ensure balance, it is important that I state that these isolated incidents do *not* represent a constant or a norm. I could justifiably claim that thousands of children enjoyed learning in my lessons and that I had good relationships with them. But, of course, the vast majority of lessons were constructed on my terms. It was very rare for anyone to step out of line, let alone deliberately take me on.

I am intent on probing beyond the headline flashes of emotion to draw attention to the incessant, underlying feelings of dominance that exuded from my general persona; in short, my default psyche when enacting the role of a prominent authority figure or my professional identity. The mental state of those on the front line – that is, the cost of having to subscribe to generic, systemic solutions, regardless of whether they are wrapped up in affirmative terms such as consistency, standards, or Behaviour for Learning – is seemingly not contemplated when advanced by publications such as Ofsted's *Below the Radar* (2014). The suggestions it selects in response to the question, "What can be done better?" could represent a running commentary on many of the initiatives and approaches I implemented. So, I am stating that there is a potential cost to assuming the role of an authority figure, whether it be to the teacher's sense of well-being, sense of self, or in the nature of relationships. But I am not arguing that there is not a cost to well-being and relationships, let alone learning, if disruptive children are left to rule the roost – perish the thought.

My action research was mindful of Zembylas' (2003) investigation into how teachers' emotions contribute to professional identity. I concur with his view that instances in which emotion becomes focal have the capacity to become sites of resistance and self-transformation. However, it is reasonable to ask whether the uniqueness of my experience can really be applicable to others who operate within the classroom. Woods and Carlyle's (2002) study examines the notion of identity passage during a time of stress. Exploring how extreme, negative emotions involved at all stages of psychological pressure are socially structured, they offer exemplars from teachers' accounts. I recognise aspects which speak of losing all ontological security:

> "I didn't feel like myself at all. I couldn't recognise myself." (Rebecca)
>
> "It's almost as though I didn't exist. I couldn't believe that I was the person I was." (Andrew)
>
> "You lose yourself when things are going badly. I lost myself for seven months." (Marcus)
>
> "I wasn't me. The personality just gets wiped out, the person you think of as you." (Maureen) (Woods and Carlyle 2002: 176)

There is a clear correlation between my account and the descriptions offered by these teachers. I don't know if or how their described state manifested in their performance and relationships. I guess, in Berlak and Berlak's terms (2002), these are illustrative of dilemmas. The notion of professional identity is considered further in Chapter 16.

Whilst worrying statistics indicate that many staff leave the profession citing stress and burnout, I was thankfully afforded an opportunity, through my research, to examine the context within which I worked, to comprehend the invisible levers, and to interrogate my history for clues about my susceptibility to the demands placed upon me. Significantly, I came to appreciate that these demands were not always initiated by others, but by myself. Foucault's expansive definition of power is useful. Whilst in my arrogance there is clear evidence of my administering *sovereign* power over others, I also actively suppressed myself. Somehow, I had come to dominate myself through a *disciplinary* power, which "is exercised by people on themselves in the specific day-to-day practices of their lives" (Brookfield 2008: 121).

The process of building whole school responses to the disruption which occurred during this specific period was formulated through a master's degree. Soon after beginning the subsequent PhD, I finally acknowledged the gnawing yet undefined sense of dissatisfaction. This book articulates the process of reconceptualisation so that all, including me, might benefit – that I might look at situations similar to those described in this chapter and adjust my lens. After all, the realities of school life remain: would it be possible for me to begin to comprehend something of the composed figure etched into the optical illusion, or would the lines illuminating the distorted characteristics continue to shape my interpretation of classroom events? To continue teaching whilst researching meant s*he* always lingered there in the background. Thus, how might I define and distinguish between the ability to respond and the inclination to react? These were the challenges which I proposed to explore whilst I continued to deal with the daily demands inherent in teaching dynamic groups.

My reconceptualisation of the pupils emerged gradually. However, during and up to this period it is fair to say that I perceived the pupils as subordinate or, using Cannella's (1999) term, 'other' (for more on this see Chapter 5). What had led me to this subliminal conception of the children in my charge? It seemed inconsistent with the strong motivation I had to see my students do well and the immense enjoyment I took from classroom teaching.

Chapter 4

Conceptions of Good and Bad

Sean

The previous chapter portrays an adult subscribing to a rather harsh and indiscriminate functionalist disciplinary system. I have described how I dealt decisively with a significant minority of persistent offenders, whilst also operating in a manner which actively deterred the compliant majority. Of course, the account of my stint as lead teacher for behaviour does not represent the whole story. There would also have been lots of excellent, mutually respectful relationships within the fabric of the school. Indeed, many pupils who did not experience the detention or isolation facilities might not even recognise aspects of my account. For example, I suspect those pupils who predominantly frequented the top sets may have been insulated from the challenges which came to define much of my time there. Regardless, in this school and during this period, I have endeavoured to provide a genuine perspective of school life – going beneath the persona to provide a unique glimpse into the psyche of an authority figure. Whether it is broadly representative of the profession overall is something for each reader to decide; I merely offer a subliminal layer to normative discourse. However, the account remains incomplete if the pupils I write about are not afforded a voice. Thus, in both Parts III and IV I present my students' individual and collective views of their experience at school.

In this and subsequent chapters, I will proceed to address my concern, not about disciplining pupils (for sometimes that was the most appropriate thing to do), but more about how, in the enactment of my role, control had become my default position – it had come to define me. I had become a living contradiction. As I probed my sense of unease, I had begun to ask whether being overtly controlling might be part of the problem rather than the solution. Was I contributing to a climate of fear masquerading as respect? Did I induce compliance and conformity at the expense of cooperation? Did I contribute to producing docile pupils instead of enquiring learners? The status afforded me by the institution I represented determined that I was a teacher 'in control' of pupils, but I began to acknowledge that I was also a controlling teacher. For the first time, I came to view the traits which accompanied this stance to be unethical, and challenged the viewpoint which identified my methods as evidence of unquestioned strength.

The period at the end of the account I have presented coincided with the beginning of my PhD research. It represents a time when I was struggling to hear even my own voice. From early 2009, I was in a state of flux which lasted periodically for much of the research period. At times the dilemmas offered fascinating stimuli to objectively rationalise conflicting perspectives, as feelings became knowledge; at other times it felt like a deep fog descending – a crisis of faith as I struggled to fill the void left by a conviction not to resort back to dominance and shouting to establish quick wins. Where once there was steadfast (and self-righteous) certainty, now periods of confusion reigned. I describe aspects of these darker moments in Chapter 19 when, in the face of classroom conflict, doubt threatened to compromise the intentions I had set out in my research.

Although it is accurate to say that this sense of incongruity dogged my consciousness, for much of the time I was preoccupied with preparing for and actually teaching. Many of my daily classes over the three year research period passed without incident, yet I still took time to make reflection notes at the end of every school day. There I was able to notice that which usually passes as mundane – the aspects I might have taken for granted had I not given them due attention. It was from these insights that I was able to articulate the components which form the classroom climate.

I found it to be equally true, in my experience as a teacher and as a researcher, that the individuals and sub-groups who disturbed the equilibrium typically created a disproportionate amount of reflective notes, in addition to taking up a disproportionate amount of my time, energy, and thoughts. Perspective became a byword for holding on to and presenting the reality of classroom life, in contrast to sensationalised media accounts which portray a broad misconception of school life. Such accounts may sell newspapers, but they also seem to justify sub-standard behaviour management services, as well as providing validation for government policies.

Thus, an analysis of what I was coming to conceive of as a faulty perspective occupied my thoughts as I simultaneously reviewed the literature, grappled with different theories, and continued to experience the sharing of a classroom space with groups of pupils on a daily basis. My simplistic view of the school (or, more accurately, my role within it) was a place where I had a professional duty to be intolerant of bad behaviour, to sort out the 'bad' kids, and enforce the school rules. I would also add to this a conviction to safeguard learning, although in reality for much of my career (despite affirmations which suggest the opposite) I am not sure that I had a real grasp of what effective learning actually entailed. If pressed I would associate it with conditions which were orderly; other than that I would fall back on experience and tacit knowledge – a sort of knowing which was near impossible to articulate, let alone emulate. A fat lot of use then to the reams of trainees and newly qualified teachers (NQTs) who would visit my classroom to observe.

I placed under scrutiny the deeply ingrained assumptions and habits which had come to represent my professional identity. I had come to a default position in which I indiscriminately quashed disruption and enforced arbitrary rules on young perpetrators – because it was part of my job! Only now, I continued to do my duty with a knowing sense of dissatisfaction, whilst also entertaining questions about the origins of the implicit messages I had habitually absorbed and pretty much obeyed.

In this chapter I chart part of the process I took to make sense of contradictory views and conflicting ideologies as I sought to establish solid ground. The relatively stable platform which emerged would come to represent my conclusions. It is where I arrived at; and it is where I now stand, as I look back and survey the journey I have taken. The essence of this book is to chronicle many of the significant steps I took. The contradictions and conflicts I experienced represent the ruts, holes, and bogs that I negotiated as I stumbled around trying to gain a sure philosophical and psychological footing, and to (re)position myself as a classroom leader. Essentially, I tentatively moved away from an allegiance to a discourse of crime and punishment, where I subconsciously subscribed to thoughts dominated by offence and blame. Of course, I would never have used such terms in association with my classroom practice; nonetheless, it provided a vocabulary to reassess how I had come to operate.

Now, through the vehicle of research, previously uncontested reductionist notions of black and white, right and wrong, routinely caused me to interrogate my experience of reality as being akin to a hundred shades of grey; that classroom interactions are defined by multiple variables; that relationships are framed by context; that I, they, we are complex. I came to a gradual realisation that my ability to see clearly was being obscured by discreet messages which distorted my lens. My uncontested conception of 'good' and 'bad' students came under scrutiny most unexpectedly as I came to realise that the simplistic notion I held could be manipulated for political gain. I also came to recognise that the discourse framing civil disobedience and criminality were equally applicable to the world of education, and it was essential that I was no longer ignorant of them. Here I offer a number of pertinent exemplars to illustrate this view. In doing so, however, I want to dispute any presumption that I have abandoned all notion of boundaries to become some wishy-washy liberal; I most certainly have not. But I was now on a quest; looking for answers where once I did not even know I ought to be asking questions.

On one level, the very idea that pupil resistance might be justified as legitimate is not one I can subscribe to readily or easily, for the notion often undermines the adults who act as custodians of the system. More than that, educators are human beings who tend to be in the job for all the right reasons – that is, to help and support children. And yet as I sat through many an INSET, I inwardly screamed with boredom and irritation at the content and delivery. How ironic that the vast majority of INSETs I attended required the audience to just sit still and absorb the message, only for it to be forgotten within days, if not hours. I listened with empathy and sympathy to some of the so called educational experiences my own children had to endure, and could comprehend why they might revert to distracting ploys if only to break the tedium. I recall watching one teacher with a disruptive class who, of course, behaved impeccably due to my presence. At the end the teacher said it was the best lesson he had ever had with them, and could I stay for every lesson? Yet a part of me felt that the pupils deserved a medal for not messing about in light of the most tedious delivery of material! Where to start? On another occasion I had to respond to a stream of rebellious Year 10 boys being sent from the room as the teacher exclaimed to one pupil, "You will obey me!" I am not seeking to apportion blame, but I am highlighting the necessity for the SLT cavalry to ask a few questions before indiscriminately stamping their foot down. In Chapter 1 Sarah provided an alternative perspective which was quashed out of hand by the dismissive on-call teacher. Pupil removal and sanctions are often akin to a sticking plaster, because the same power plays are usually exhibited when they re-join the lesson.

Back in the classroom, the very idea that the adult might be an unwitting instigator of needless conflict, as I realised I could be, was intellectually stimulating. Discipline programmes such as Assertive Discipline say very little about the content of teaching programmes or differentiation. There is a lack of comment on the nature of educational experience and no discussion as to whether 'on-task' and 'learning' are two separate concepts. The role of the curriculum, the quality of teaching, and the social interactions taking place in the school are largely downplayed. Consequently, the institutional, political, and contextual dimensions of indiscipline are not deemed to be problematic. In the next chapter, Stephen builds on the thoughts he outlined at the beginning of this book to critique the nature and appropriateness of the curriculum. Although, cognitively, I would not have disputed that teaching methods, materials, the curriculum, and institutional or societal conditions were important, in practice I found it difficult to look beyond the conduct, and so attributed behaviour problems as belonging to the students. For me, it was simply a choice they were making. This was perhaps illustrated by my easy use of the terms 'good' and 'bad' pupils.

As stated earlier, the notion that both the child and the adult are mere pawns who, on occasion, dispute the restricted semblance of power afforded to them according to their roles and status, provides a different lens through which to contemplate perturbing exchanges between pupils and teachers. Such occurrences easily equate to the perception that the conflict itself is the problem. I came to regard such incidents as catalysts for a more profound problem (of which disruptive behaviour is a tangible symptom): a system defined by tensions and dominated by a moralistic discourse which plausibly dishes out the uncritical labels of 'right' and 'wrong'. Of particular interest to me was the way in which the discourse is used in association with schoolchildren. Usher and Edwards (2004: 90) observe that a "discourse authorises certain people to speak and correspondingly silences others, or at least makes their voices less authoritative. A discourse is therefore exclusionary." Intriguingly, the realisation came to me indirectly and from an unexpected source.

Fear and Blame

A series of incidents in 2011 gave me a unique opportunity to view unfolding media events through the theoretical lens I had spent countless hours reading and writing about. I recall vividly my disgust as images of riots in some UK cities beamed across my TV screen, which were sparked by the shooting dead of Mark Duggan by police officers.

I had just completed the third year of my study. With the action research phase largely complete, I was methodically conducting a literature review to gain a deep and broad appreciation of the field in order to position my work. I believed that I had moved on from the inclination to instantly punish pupils causing problems, yet, in the immediate aftermath of the disturbances of 2011, I found myself nodding as Education Minister Michael Gove stated, "We cannot say often enough that what we saw this summer was a straightforward conflict between right and wrong" (BBC 2011). I felt somewhat compromised as David Cameron (2011) announced:

> these riots were not about poverty … [We need to] confront the slow-motion moral collapse that has taken place in parts of our country … Schools without discipline …
>
> We need an education system which reinforces the message that if you do the wrong thing you'll be disciplined … [Citing exemplar schools] They foster pride through strict uniform and behaviour policies.

Previously Cameron had spoken of schools and discipline "where the kids [should] respect, and even *fear*, the teachers, not the other way around" (BBC 2007; emphasis added). His considered response reminded me of the concerns Walton raises in *Scared of the Kids* (2001).

Subsequently, the prime minister's decision to conflate respect with fear caught my attention. Ahmed (2004: 40) identifies fear as an "ill-defined and slippery concept". Distinguishing it from anxiety, he states "fear has an *object*" (ibid.: 64; original emphasis). Mindful of heightened tension and publicity, Cameron's words were no doubt chosen carefully. Brooks et al. (2013: 187) discuss how political leaders are able to "define what is or ought to be the public's chief object of fear", so that, according to Robin (2004: 16), it "dominates the political agenda, crowding out others". Which others? I suggest that his focus draws attention away from the significance of social mobility and educational inclusion (discussed later in this chapter), thus deflecting criticism of government policies in these areas.

Just prior to the riots, the coalition's white paper, *The Importance of Teaching* (DfE 2010) utilises Freedman et al. (2008) to state that the most common reason for undergraduates pursuing another profession, despite considering teaching, "is the *fear* of not being safe in our schools" (DfE 2010: 32; emphasis added). It is noted that Cameron contributed a foreword to the same document. The discourse insinuates that there is an apparent threat, inherent within the school population. Amidst the lawlessness and mayhem of the riots, it is children who are presented as the *object* of fear.

Only upon subsequent analysis of arrest data was it revealed that those who passed through the courts were predominantly adults and not children of school age (Home Office 2011). I had neglected to question the presumption of youth guilt because the evidence I had seen seemed so compelling – after all, many of the perpetrators wore hoodies! Illustrative of 'othering', which Hayden (2011: 4) describes as "a way of defining and securing one's own positive identity through the stigmatization of an 'other'", I reflect that I readily made an association between the culprits and Gavron's (2009: 4) definition of an "underclass perceived as feckless and undeserving". Here I can sense how my thinking might have been swayed, how I was susceptible to a discourse demanding that *we* take decisive action – an uncritical need to do *something*; to stand up for the virtuous.[1] In retrospect, it appears all too convenient (and indeed predictable) to identify the juvenile offenders as 'yobs', to misrepresent and magnify the extent of youth involvement, and to saddle schools with the task of curtailing them. Of course, the stated version of events evidently justified the stringent disciplinary systems, regardless of whether the proposed method insentiently tarred all children with the same brush.

My literature review served to further inform. Despite the media's propensity to sensationalise issues around behaviour, Hayden (2011) and Hayden and Martin (2011) stress that links between school behaviour and criminality are unfounded. Yet in this instance, there was a clear insinuation that schools were somehow culpable. Steer (2010: 8) provides perspective: "The misconduct of a few represents a small percentage of the seven million pupils in the

1 It is important to state that I am in support of all sentences passed down to those found guilty of crimes, irrespective of age.

school system."[2] Regaining a sense of equilibrium, I was able to look beyond the discourse to reason that the vast majority of those millions would never dream of committing such acts and probably shared my sense of disbelief at the scenes of criminality and destruction. As Steer (2009: 22–23) pre-empts, "It is important that the gap between the public perception of schools and the reality in schools is not allowed to grow." This is especially pertinent in light of shocking high profile incidents such as knife attacks on members of staff.

Historical critical incidents such as the murder of Philip Lawrence, a head teacher protecting one of his pupils at the school gates, and the Dunblane shootings a year later in 1996, continue to feed this discourse of 'badness' (Hayden 2011) and related fears around safety in schools.[3] Rigoni and Walford (1998) suggest that the Labour government's uncritical enthusiasm for Canter's Assertive Discipline (Canter 1988) in the white paper (DfEE 1997), published shortly after these events, was their response to a 'moral panic' (Cohen 1972) about declining standards of discipline in schools. In 2009, the East London borough of Waltham Forest became the first to install metal detectors in all of its secondary schools (Sugden 2009). In 2014, the fatal stabbing of Ann Maguire in a classroom in Leeds reignited debate about the extent to which screening should be adopted in the UK (Clark 2014).

Critical moments naturally come to characterise the debate about pupil behaviour and questions about the best approaches to tackle it. A definitive definition of the phenomenon remains elusive. In the literature I read of 'unacceptable behaviour', 'disruptive behaviour', 'bad behaviour', 'disobedience', 'misbehaviour', and 'challenging behaviour'. As Docking (1980: 42) observes: "labelling behaviour is bedevilled not only by technical problems of assessment but also by problems of value judgements".

As Hayden (2011) points out, pupil resistance to authority is not new. Contemporary headlines can be both extreme and worrying. During my stint as a local authority behaviour consultant, Professor Elliott (2004) claimed that Britain had the "worst pupils in the world". Ofsted (2013) states that disruption and inattention in schools had been accepted for far too long: estimating that around 700,000 pupils attended schools where behaviour needed to improve; a need for change was stipulated to avert a decline in

2 Now estimated to be in the region of 8.4 million pupils.

3 Illustrative of its impact, when I visit my old school, I have to wait to be collected and escorted by the ex-colleague I am visiting. Recently, one experienced staff member cancelled our meeting due to his inability to escort me from reception to his classroom, due to a last minute cover lesson. Despite having been signed in, given a visitor's badge, being in possession of a valid DBS (Disclosure and Barring Service) certificate, and having worked at the school for 12 years, I was not allowed to walk the 30 or so yards to the classroom unaccompanied. Despite my protests, which centred on common sense, the consistent response cited concerns about safety.

educational standards. Subsequently, Haydn (2014) argued that the true extent of poor pupil behaviour in schools, as depicted in 'official' reports, was seriously underestimated.

It is of no surprise that, in the wake of the riots, the coalition government championed their recently published white paper to justify a "sharper focus on discipline" (DfE 2010: 20). Who could argue? Regardless that the vast majority of those arrested and charged were no longer in the school system, the mantra was loud and clear: in the immediate aftermath it seemed patently justified. However, despite the emotive prejudgements, the fact remains that understanding young people's behaviour in schools is not straightforward (Hayden 2011). As the Steer report (2005: 7) comments, "issues around behaviour and discipline are complex and wide-ranging". Contrary to Cameron's dismissive claim to quash the notion that poverty was a contributory factor, young people appearing before the courts *did* indeed come "disproportionately from areas with high levels of deprivation" (Ministry of Justice 2011: 28), with offenders' eligibility for free school meals acting as an indicator. The apparent inequalities – termed an 'educational apartheid' by the Sutton Trust (2001) – are acknowledged as part of this book's contextual landscape, although they are not a detailed part of its analysis.

It also caught my attention that 66% of 10- to 17-year-old offenders also qualified as having special educational needs (SEN), compared to a 21% national average (Ministry of Justice 2011: 25). The report did not specify the nature of need. The fact that children with SEN consistently dominate exclusion statistics is well known. The latest available records show (at the time of writing) that "pupils with identified special educational needs accounted for just over half of all permanent exclusions and fixed period exclusions" (DfE 2016b: 5). Within the broad category of special needs are those children with behavioural, emotional, or social difficulties (BESD). Whilst BESD is an imprecise umbrella term (Cole and Visser 2005), aspects of the behavioural and emotional difficulties displayed by pupils with BESD typically include a lack of concentration, being hyperactive, presenting challenging behaviour, and being disruptive (DfES 2001).

My research, which is inclusive of SEN pupils' performance within secondary school mixed ability classrooms, appears particularly pertinent in light of analysis of SEN and exclusion statistics covering the period I was planning and conducting my study. These showed that BESD was more prevalent amongst boys than girls (DCSF 2009: 5). From age 12 onwards BESD became the special need for children associated with School Action Plus (DCSF 2009: 28, table 9).[4] The most common point for both boys and

4 School Action Plus (SA+) was used when School Action had not been able to help the pupil make adequate progress. At SA+ the school will seek external advice from the local education authority's support services, the local health authority, or social services. The process was replaced in 2014.

girls to be excluded was in Year 9 and 10 (equivalent to ages 13–15). Around 53% of all permanent exclusions were of pupils from this age group (DfE 2011b: tables 3 and 4a). Secondary schools' most common special need was moderate learning difficulty (DCSF 2009); Steer (2009: 43) affirmed its significance: "Much poor behaviour has its origins in the inability of the child to access learning". Youdell (2011) makes an interesting distinction between a failed student deemed an anti-school boy and his subsequent designation as BESD. Here the boy's recognition as 'cool-bad' was undercut by the label 'aberrant-mad' – he moved from won't do it to can't do it![5]

Together these determinants – deprivation and SEN are commonly used to define the 'significant minority' – make a definitive response to disruption somewhat delicate: politicians have to tread warily. Any teacher worth their salt knows that a minority can have a destructive and disproportionate impact on learning, on the rest of the group, and on the teacher's own sense of competence and well-being. So what is a teacher to do? What approach is best to enable us to move forward with clarity and conviction? It was the government's incongruous portrayal of (and approaches to) the significant minority which aroused my suspicion and cemented the scepticism I proceeded to develop.

The Significant Minority

Consistent with the contradictions and tensions inherent within the education policies advanced by the preceding Labour government (Harris and Ranson 2005; Burton et al. 2009), the coalition government initially disassociated SEN from the significant minority. The schools' white paper (DfE 2010) seems to carefully avoid any direct correlation between SEN pupils and the 'sharp focus' of the disciplinary measures it advocates. Reference to these children is minimal, aside from highlighting that a disproportionate number of them are victims of bullying.

In conjunction, despite detailed acknowledgement of some SEN pupils' inability to cope (and a brief, passing comment that they are more likely to be excluded than their peers), the green paper, *Support and Aspiration* (DfE 2011c), gives little or no mention of any phrase implying discipline in its 128 pages. Although it cites figures which show a 23% increase in the number of pupils with BESD between 2005 and 2010 (2011c: 20), undefined 'behaviour management' is the strongest correctional term used. Instead, in the foreword it purports: "*Every* child … identified as having a special educational need deserves our support" (2011c: 3; emphasis added). 'Support' is mentioned numerous times in the paper which exudes an ethos of care.[6]

5 For a critique of the terms 'bad', 'mad', and 'sad' see Wright (2009).
6 'Support' is mentioned 11 times in the foreword alone.

Consistent with David Cameron's deficient characterisation post the riots, there appears to have been a deliberate ploy to obscure the make-up of the significant minority – portrayals are conveniently incomplete, thus a definitive response eludes teachers who are charged with meeting needs and quelling wants. Whilst the 2011 green paper disassociated itself from discipline to project concern for the individual, the 2010 white paper emphasised the behaviour and championed "tougher discipline" (DfE 2010: 53). Accentuating the disparity between the publications, the percentages for physical assault are conveniently converted into a quantifiable headline figure by the forthright white paper to magnify the most contentious manifestation of disruptive behaviour in schools – 'violence'. The report states: "in 2007, almost 18,000 pupils were permanently excluded [11.6%] or suspended [4.7%] for attacking a member of staff" (DfE 2010: 32).

The source of the statistics (DfE 2009) does not define the nature of "physical force against an adult". The authors of the white paper also neglect to clarify the fact that the highest percentage of the fixed term incidents cited did not take place in state secondary schools. The statistics reveal a much higher proportion in primary and special schools (DfE 2009: table 10). "Attacking a member of staff" is such an uncompromising statement but it is unclear how it is defined – does it include a 6-year-old having a temper tantrum and hitting out when the teacher tries to intervene? In 2012 Ofsted published inspection criteria in which explicit reference to 'behaviour and *safety*' (emphasis added) was one of the four main categories deemed to be integral to a judgement.[7] Cornell and Mayer (2010) recognised order and safety as conceptually offering a more fertile ground than the emphasis on violence.

Certainly, my intention is not to trivialise or to make a judgement on those leaders who were tasked with making difficult decisions in the wake of such incidents. My concern here is more to do with the deliberate use of a discourse and statistics to construct a loaded narrative for the consumption of the general public and the teaching profession.

It is apparent that the significant minority are deliberately portrayed differently in accordance with the interests of distinct audiences. When the minority are depicted as notorious and associated with cited violence, as in the white paper (DfE 2010), they are met with (appropriate) stringent discipline measures. Conversely, when the minority are identified as SEN, as in the green paper (DfE 2011c), the coverage elicits fitting notions of concern and support. Yet an inconvenient paradox emerges. During the same period as the white paper's damning statistical reference (2007/2008) "pupils with SEN (both with and without statements) [were] over 8 times more likely to be permanently excluded than those pupils with no SEN" (DfE 2009: 3). Significantly, similar alarming data is stated in the green paper (DfE 2011c:

7 From September 2015, 'safety' was changed to the broader term, 'welfare'.

70–71) but the 'discipline as antidote' rhetoric is conspicuous by its absence. Instead, the acknowledgement of underlying causal factors, an emphasis on multi-agency assessment, and concern about a correlation with estimated costs on lifetime future earnings frame the paper's coverage of exclusions. All these considered aspects are non-existent in the corresponding white paper. It is reasonable to presume that pupils with SEN contributed significantly to the accentuated 18,000 incidents prompting exclusion. In light of this reality, how is this cohort to be defined? How are their actions to be interpreted – as 'naughty' or 'needy'? Clearly an awkward dilemma for policy makers stipulating directives for schools.

Thus, each representation of the individuals comprising the 'significant minority' is associated with apt provision which satisfies the sensitive requirements of the target audience. Each paper has a strong central theme which becomes a pale subsidiary in the opposing publication. The two papers under discussion strategically omit and cherry-pick information, effectively deflecting criticism from their proposed policies. The messages are enveloped in persuasive ideology which depicts them as common-sense givens. As Brookfield (2008: 41) notes: "On closer examination, however, we see that a degree of deliberation undergirds what appear as accidentally emergent belief systems." As with the previous Labour government, approaches which advocate a mixture of care and control for young people are identified as contradictory rather than complementary (Burton et al. 2009). Regularly absorbing these mixed messages is the teacher, although there was no hint of ambiguity in Education Minister Michael Gove's words[8] which contained a veiled threat: "Teachers have a responsibility to *make sure* pupils behave and succeed or they will find themselves 'in the firing line' " (Kershaw 2012; emphasis added).

Steer (2005) had already formalised this obligation, reminding teachers of the power enshrined in legislation through which they have statutory rights to discipline, to search and restrain pupils, and to hold pupils accountable beyond the school gates. This emphasis was maintained as the coalition government negated the legal requirement for schools to give parents 24 hour notice for detentions (DfE 2010). Schools' legislative powers also extended to head teachers being able to prosecute parents whose children truanted (Zhang 2004; Ross 2009). The dominance of a discourse which encourages punishment extends to administering fines, the threat of a criminal record, and even imprisonment for parents who choose to take their children out of school for a holiday during term time. This law does not apply to parents whose children are educated in the private sector. Riley (2007) argues that such legislation is consistent with attempts to hold parents accountable for their children's general antisocial behaviour through

8 Michael Gove had previously contributed to the forewords of both the 2010 white paper and the 2011 green paper.

criminalising previously non-criminal behaviour. Michael Gove was more specific, announcing proposals to impose stronger sanctions on parents whose children misbehave in class and who are not "showing respect for their teacher" (BBC 2014).

Rules

The primary mechanism for determining the validity of these controversial measures and more common misdemeanours is, of course, the observance and enforcement of school rules. Goodman (2006: 215) illuminates a perspective which was obscured to me as I uncritically enforced school policy: "From rules justified by order, it is a small step to rules justified for their own sake". She claims that if rules were self-justifying and the teacher's task is to exact compliance, then discipline becomes the procedure of punishing perceived disobedience: "Just as the distancing of discipline from learning opens space for moralizing rules, so, too, the distancing of sanctions from rules opens space for moralizing sanctions" (ibid.: 217). Rules then are conceptualised as a formative representation of deviant discourse. Often experienced as punitive – punishment as "moral affirmation" (Garland 1999: 24) rather than crime control – they represent the "rebalancing of moral scales" (Goodman 2006: 222), yet are employed by schools for non-moral offences.

The implied correlation by David Cameron (2011) between strict uniform and pupils' behavioural and academic performance serves to illustrate the points being made. Media headlines (typically at the beginning of the school year) frequently include accounts of students missing lessons due to being sent home for uniform 'offences'.[9] Hattie (2009: 33) describes this as "cosmetic or 'coat of paint' reforms" which involve the parents, lead to more rules, and appeal to common sense. In one case, the ensuing dispute even involved the police who were called as the parents of the 50 uniform offenders protested outside the school gates (Finnigan 2016).

Yet there is no doubt that rules matter. On an extreme level, you only have to look at the anarchy, chaos, and disorder which emerge when the rule of law breaks down in war-torn countries. On a more mundane level,

9 I have listened with interest to arguments justifying the enforcement of school uniforms. It is a topic which extends to other countries. Proponents claim it fosters a collective sense of identity, or, in Cameron's words, "pride" (as well as protecting those children who don't own fashionable clothing). I was intrigued to observe as I walked down my local high street early one morning that, in my town, uniforms not only identify the students who go to the local school, but they also advertise those children (or parents) who chose instead to attend a 'superior' school outside of the catchment area. There is a marked difference between the polo shirts and sweatshirts worn by one cohort and the ties and blazers of the others. Even more distinctive is the occasional striped blazer and straw hat which announces to all that this child is the beneficiary of a private education. A broad and fascinating debate!

motorists' adherence to traffic signs and signals ensure that all benefit. Rules also matter in an organisation such as school, and sometimes the best thing an adult can offer a wayward child are clear boundaries. I am not for one moment proposing a laissez-faire attitude to behaviour. Instead, I have come to ask if arbitrary rules imposed on students might actually provoke acts of resistance (which in turn embroil the authority figure employed to uphold pointless 'standards'), and whether the likes of Gove and Cameron – far removed from the frontline – have lured diligent professionals to become ensnarled in trivial conflicts.

In Part III I share my enquiry of classroom interactions and engage with the literature to see if there are more sophisticated explanations than a moralistic discourse which neglects to look beyond exhibiting behaviour or mitigating circumstances. In the meantime, I pass over to Stephen to provide some depth and breadth to the issues I have raised and to lay the foundations for the forthcoming discussion of methodology.

Chapter 5

A Consideration of Curriculum

Stephen

Sean's personal narrative, derived from professional experience and research, raises several controversial themes which deserve further scrutiny. This chapter provides a broader context for his coverage of an individual operating in a range of schools. The role of the curriculum and the social interactions taking place in school are largely downplayed in debate around behaviour. Consequently, the institutional, political, and contextual dimensions of indiscipline are not identified as being problematic; I will address this issue here. In taking steps to qualify the term 'system', I will also reflect on the incessant changes I have experienced over the past five decades.

I taught in secondary schools first and primary schools later. My first comprehensive was a dysfunctional affair: a grammar school and secondary modern which had been bolted together the September I began. It was bilateral rather than comprehensive, with grammar streams. My head of department had a nervous breakdown (I found him weeping in the toilets) and departed sick, leaving me as acting head of department six weeks into my probationer post. I had entered teaching without a PGCE, as one could then, as I had a mortgage to fund. Thus I learned pedagogy the hard way – without guidance or support. The year is remembered by the initials ROSLA (raising of the school leaving age): Year 11 pupils had expected to leave but were forced to return for one more year. They consisted of a quarter of my timetable. The school was on a split site, a two mile drive apart, with no time allowance for travel. My Wednesday afternoons required a change of campus between each of four lessons. One mature teacher I looked up to as a disciplinarian admitted to me one lunchtime that he could never sleep on Sunday nights because he was worrying about Monday morning. Whilst there is appropriate concern about pupils' well-being in schools, Sean's research shows the mental state of the teacher to be equally important. Currently, workload is identified as having a detrimental effect on teachers' sense of well-being. I taught religious education for one lesson a week to the whole school. I wrote reports each term for over 800 pupils. Teacher workload issues are far from new.

Next, I moved to another secondary school with a substantial A level offer in RE where I stayed for seven years. It seemed to me an unhappy school, which put me, as union representative, in some difficult circumstances.

There were confrontations but ironically I protected the head teacher by insisting on due process. Although the academic results were reasonable, I felt that the school underachieved overall. I doubt if pupils remember school fondly.

During the next decade I gained experience of early years and primary education. Primary school curriculum philosophy was then dominated by the experiential (and also experimental, in scientific terms) methods of John Dewey, which was characterised as learning by doing. Pedagogy was thus activity and action based, setting up and working through observation and experimentation. In this process, teachers facilitated learning and needed to be creative in curriculum planning. Lesson plans were not laid down. Although they wanted pupils to be proactive in their own learning, the effective teacher would have thought through the process to provide appropriate resources and stimuli.

Teacher training, which was then my central job, prepared students to be thoughtfully and creatively proactive and reflective. The university training process was guided by experienced teachers and head teachers. Central to the curriculum were the social and personal issues relating to equality of treatment and opportunity. The Inner London Education Authority staff were leaders in this, and nationally the Schools Council brought teachers together to develop curriculum projects. Both were targeted and closed by the Thatcher government leading up to the Education Reform Act 1988. 'Reform' is a weasel word. It is used to give the impression that it is improving something which has gone wrong, but it is in fact an ideological attempt to impose a new state of play.

The national curriculum after 1988 had a different vision. A broad and balanced curriculum was interpreted to mean covering all curriculum subjects by name, and stipulated content, even in infant schools. Panels were established to determine curriculum content. These suggested issues and processes, such as the geography curriculum highlighting values, but the final documents became reduced to raw subject content – so called 'facts'. The science curriculum moved from 18 process focused attainment targets to three, disguised descriptions of chemistry, physics, and biology. Some aspects were controversial and hard fought, such as the place of Empire in British history. The emphasis throughout was on teaching established knowledge rather than developing the critical skills to challenge given information.

Syllabuses are lists of topics declared to be significant facts. This is counter to the academic project in which current understandings are tested, refined, and where necessary jettisoned. Intellectual frameworks (paradigms) shift, as Thomas Kuhn (1970) famously declared. Just as Galileo replaced a very different view of the universe, so quantum physics is changing our understanding of the nature of matter. I hold that teaching should be a creative enterprise involved in analysis and change, and not a process of memorising and accepting ancient wisdom unchallenged. There are many ways of interesting children, including varying delivery to maintain engagement and curiosity, and using experiments, projects, and themes. From the 1970s, MACOS (Man: A Course of Study; today we would say Humans) enabled 11-year-olds to explore what it means to be human using history, literature, science, geography, and religion, all integrated into coherent sessions. An itemised national curriculum makes such integration impossible. A curriculum which is a list of unchallenged facts to be transferred from teacher to pupil does not lend itself to creativity. Cross-curricular links are difficult to make when syllabuses were not organised with these in mind. This is relevant to school behaviour because well-treated, keen, and motivated pupils have less incentive for rebellion and disruption.

The round of curriculum consultations demanded to know how topics such as multicultural education, personal and social education, environmental education, and economic and industrial understanding might fit into a subject curriculum. Their value was indisputable, but the curriculum was already bulging. They were inelegantly declared to be 'cross-curricular issues and themes' which all curriculum subjects should address. This curriculum, planned by committee, was rapidly becoming overloaded, and the 1990s became a decade of continual change as it was whittled down.

In 1999, a few Oxford colleagues and I explored how the subject curriculum could deliver cross-curricular learning about spiritual, moral, social, and cultural education about self, society, and values (Bigger and Brown 1999). Although some might disagree, I believe that the experience of pupils in finding school enjoyable and meaningful (or not) is at least as important, and arguably more so, than what marks they eventually get. In an era of incessant competition, a pupil's summative grades are conveniently used to judge the 'quality' of the schools', the teachers', and the pupils' performance against a narrow set of predetermined criteria. This is regardless of aptitude, interest, or social background. My colleagues and I emphasised that learning was about far more than encountering disparate facts and figures, but should develop the will for discovery and critical thinking about what things mean and what matters. Even when confined to a subject curriculum, we showed that it was possible to engage pupils on broad values.

What Is Education For?

Across the world, education is an expensive project. Schooling is declared to be a universal human right and an aspiration for the poorest of nations. Money is thrown year on year at schooling the next generation. But is this money being effectively spent? Or might schooling be an expensive failure?

Sean cited David Cameron's retreat to discipline and stricter uniform in the wake of civil disobedience of 2011, but such a focus presupposes that these measures legitimately safeguard the institution of school. Sean and I argue that an uncritical acceptance of these mechanisms and symbols protects an entrenched system, an establishment which serves the needs of those who hold power, and sustains the status quo. David Cameron neglected to ask deeper questions. Long ago, John Holt (1972, 1982 [1964]) emphasised how schools fail children and eventually threw his weight behind the de-schooling, home schooling, and un-schooling movements. We cannot take it for granted that schools *are* good for children. We hope they are, but we need to be vigilant.

The state is responsible for education. The bill for teachers' salaries is huge and the real estate heritage is extensive. The state develops its ideas about what it wants to get for its money through politicians and their advisers. This means a high level of ideology which has, since 1988, produced a centrally dictated curriculum and monitoring system. One answer to the question, "What is education for?" is that it produces educated employees for businesses. A company will assert that it requires literacy, numeracy, personal qualities, and skills – that is, it wants competent and trustworthy employees. This means a system which separates out the sheep from the goats, so assessment systems must rank pupils from best to worst. This is different from the more romantic agenda of wanting pupils to reach their full potential; employability rather emphasises the need for conformity and a basic skills minimum. The Education Reform Act 1988 demanded a broad and balanced curriculum, but some might argue that during the intervening years it has become anything but broad or balanced. The basics predominate; creativity, morality, and values are at the margins, if there at all. Earlier chapters have touched on the impact on teachers of this system; subsequent parts of this book will illuminate the responses of pupils. Sean writes specifically about the experience of individuals, whereas I critique the broad themes (and narrow definitions) which continue to define the experience of consecutive generations who enter and pass through the system.

The Politicisation of Learning

Stephen Ball (2003) speaks of performativity in schooling – that is, the obsession for measuring performance, especially the use of performance related targets and inspection. These come from a lack of trust in teachers and are risk averse to creativity. Performance monitoring conducted by uncreative bureaucrats threatens to damage teacher well-being. Compliance becomes a virtue and free thought a crime. Such innocent terms as 'learning', 'schooling', and 'education' are ambiguous. Their meanings may seem obvious when people use them, but dig a little deeper and clarity is somewhat cloudy.

Gert Biesta (2007, 2011, 2014) problematises these concepts in relation to adult education. I will draw out some points from his work in the belief that they can offer a critical commentary on schooling. Learning is something that young humans and animals do. It is natural. They play, imitate, experiment, and relate. Early babbling sounds become language in imitation of elders. This kind of learning can be absent in school where learning is not natural but artificial. In calling such learning *real* learning, natural learning is redefined as *development* and *change*. If we further examine school learning, we see it as closely linked to the power that schools and teachers exert. Teachers decide what should be learned and what it means. Knowledge is transferred from teacher to pupil. It is reproductive learning, regurgitated when required for tests and exams. The teacher is the expert and the pedagogy becomes a teacher monologue passively received. Some pupils will flourish, others will flounder; some individuals will exploit or even create opportunities to resist. Resistance leads to temporary suspension from classes and perhaps permanent exclusion from school. I am concerned with news that academies' 'freedoms' ensure that they have no legal responsibility for hard-to-teach pupils – for example, those with SEN or challenging behaviour. Sean showed in Chapter 4 that the identification of these cohorts is conveniently blurred in government literature.

School pupils are viewed as having little life experience but are dependent on older, wiser adults. Cannella (1999: 36) describes young human beings – labelled as "young child, adolescent, teenager, student, pupil, learner" – as "the ultimate 'Other'". They must have their decisions made for them by adults, whose knowledge has been "legitimized" and "whose ways of being in the world can be uncovered through the experimental and observational methods of science". She adds: "Parents and educators have accepted and contributed to the 'scientific childhood' without question or critique, without recognition that younger human beings may not always benefit from the pre-determinism imposed by others."

I critique the nature of knowledge in the next chapter. Dewey encouraged the use of existing experiences and the creation of new ones. Paulo Freire (2014; Freire and Macedo 2000) prioritises experiential discussion and political consciousness raising: education was not 'learning stuff' but 'learning life'. With children, the environment, social justice, animal welfare, and similar themes are all powerful stimuli to natural learning.

The school curriculum post 1988 has established other priorities. I perceive it to be a scarcely motivating overgrown list of topics chosen by committee which has, of necessity, narrowed over the last decade. What is taught is tested by one means or another, with high marks for accurate reproduction. The answers that gain marks are those intended by examiners, even if others are equally correct and more creative – unexpected answers are not on the assessment criteria. Thus, testing is second-guessing the examiner's intention and cannot be described as educational. Inconsistent and erratic marking have undermined the confidence in awards, as re-marks and appeals become endemic. In addition, shifting grade boundaries may render the summative grades awarded to pupils as arbitrary. In this insecure process, little has been learned. Much time for potential learning has been lost by preparing for the tests – playing the game. With reproductive learning, there is a belief that there is true knowledge which the teacher has to clarify. Everything in scientific research (and also other subjects) affirms the opposite of this, that hypotheses have to be tested, reformulated, or replaced.

Three decades ago the government announced National Education and Training Targets (NETTs) which set out the percentage of learners who should be attracted into education and training qualifications. To achieve this, a new range of qualifications were created, NVQs and GNVQs. This was far from a celebration of natural learning through motivated activity. Although for some pupils it equated to an escape from the classroom, for others it meant attending courses to sweat their way to work-relevant qualifications. Government funding depended on these targets being worked towards. This is not the only definition of learning possible, and it may not be linked to learning at all. Passing on enough short term knowledge to pass a qualification might not necessitate real learning. If schools focused on learning, and not qualifications, then different choices might be made and far different criteria applied. As it is, schools are measured by test and examination results. Not entering pupils for qualifications they might fail becomes a strategy to cheat the system, as does excluding pupils who might bring school averages down.

Let us be clear: head teachers who know how to cheat the system are those who make rapid perceived 'improvements' to a weak school. In the early 1990s, when working for Birmingham Compact to improve motivation and raise achievement across the broad school body, there were not significant increases in grades A–C results because these pupils were diligent anyway. The league tables that were introduced in 1992 only counted A–C grades. As a result, a number of schools dumped the Compact programme with *all* pupils so they could guide a few likely pupils who might with help be raised from a grade D to C, and so impact their league table position. Although this is an understandable political strategy, it was educationally inappropriate. This is the politics of learning: an artificial agenda imposed upon pupils for political purposes to meet national targets. We have institutionalised qualifications with a pecking order and an expectation that qualifications lead to careers. Careers rely on a good CV which is too often dominated by the A*–C currency, affirming engagement and mastery of the narrow curriculum on offer. It is hard now to disentangle ourselves from this agenda, so we are slaves to it, even though qualifications no longer guarantee future financial security.

Positive School Relationships: Critical Pedagogy

Critical pedagogy asks questions about authority, authoritarianism, hegemony (the holding of power), and democracy in schooling. There is a continuum between chaos, order, and repression which this book seeks to uncover. Sean and I believe that schools should be encouraged to develop order through self-discipline, discussion, community consensus, and freedom in learning, without tipping over into mob rule on the one hand or authoritarian repression on the other. The main strategy we are advocating is a change in how we view the teacher–pupil relationship, including the way we view authority. What one teacher can do in isolation is much more limited than what the whole teaching profession could do together, particularly if professional expectations were to change (as they did when corporal punishment was abolished in English state schools in 1986, though not worldwide).

Systematic change is hampered when repressive short cuts seem to work – that is, excluding the worst offenders and exerting fear of consequences on the others. 'Seems to work' is an apposite phrase, much peddled in the media. A few pupils can disrupt a whole class so removing that behaviour advantages the rest. But removed pupils still have to be educated, so exclusion leads to a group of disruptive pupils in a special unit. Where disruptive behaviour has not been dealt with extreme measures might be necessary. However, we point to alternative strategies to be used consistently throughout schooling that should improve behaviour earlier and so reduce disruption in secondary classrooms. Too often teachers are fire-fighting the effects of not transforming problem children in a more timely fashion.

The term 'critical pedagogy' implies criticality across broad areas; not just determining factual accuracy but also values, ethics, and social issues. The word 'critical' is overused for narrow general comment about knowledge claims: it can mean as little as having an opinion. We refer here to a more deep-rooted analysis of what passes for knowledge. At around the time when Hitler and the Nazis were seizing power, critical theory was developing in Frankfurt as a protest against social and political injustice. This was a mission reminiscent of the biblical prophets in support of the poor, the needy, the oppressed, and the stranger.[1] Such a social critique made the group targets of the Nazis, so the operation moved to the United States for the

1 Theodor W. Adorno's debt to Walter Benjamin, and indirectly Gershom Scholem, is explored in Jacobson (2003).

duration. The social critique they began has deeply influenced social studies ever since.

The message for the curriculum is that reflecting on social justice is a critical part of knowledge. 'Knowledge' is more than information: it requires understanding of the implications of the information – its accuracy, utility, and consequences. Pupils need to have thought about who has benefitted from the knowledge and who has been disadvantaged. Recently, a schoolgirl's question was reported on social media, "When are we going to study female scientists?" This is a reminder that much of the information around is produced by males about males. Wikipedia's early imbalance on the contributions of female scientists and researchers is currently being addressed.[2] The process of selecting what knowledge is worthwhile may be subtle or overt, which invites careful monitoring of the school curriculum. The critical process of analysing issues about knowledge claims needs to be explicit in school learning. Pupils are inundated with questionable information, especially from the Internet, which they need to evaluate carefully. This promises to produce independent-minded young adults, resistant to indoctrination and group pressure. Such free thinkers may not be welcomed by politicians and employers, much as they feared educating workers a century ago. This is not a problem but a reason to prioritise critical thinking. There are ethical issues which are part of life, and they should be part of schooling.

Critical pedagogy emphasises that authoritarianism produces resistance. School rules full of 'thou shalt not' cause pupils to want to break the rules. Regulations on dress, for example, produce the desire in some to get away with as much individualising as possible, thereby ridiculing the rules. Peter McLaren (1986) started his academic career with a study of pupil resistance to petty school rules in a Catholic school. This began his interest in critical pedagogy (McLaren 2002, 2009). Crowd control through austere rules is not education. Authoritarian demands tend to make crowd control more difficult when pupils object. Class control is much easier if pupils are interested and want to learn, and have good relationships with their teachers.[3] Barry Kanpol (1999), writing on teachers' lives in a period of crisis which has relevance today, finds control and authoritarianism to be anti-democratic.

---

2 See https://en.wikipedia.org/wiki/Wikipedia:WikiProject_Women_scientists.

3 See the contributions by McLaren and others on critical pedagogy in Darder et al. (2009).

Resistance to Authoritarianism

Authoritarian demands in some controlling religious upbringings, including my own, repressed personal rights to free thought; I showed more resistance than many. Religious authoritarianism and control does not guarantee long term loyalty. Wartime Nazi totalitarianism was met with resistance despite the risks. We have had a long educational tradition of authoritarianism, caricatured by Dickens' depiction of Wackford Squeers in *Nicholas Nickleby*. Schools have moved on, although caning was not uncommon during both Sean's and my own secondary schooling. Other authoritarianism strategies include sarcasm, belittling, name calling, shouting, and low expectations. Such things do not create helpful and positive classroom relationships, and there is likely to be a reaction – repression in some, but resistance in others. Resistance can be covert or overt, leading to low level disruption. (Sean explores this throughout his account.) Henry Giroux (2016) advocates resistance similar to civil rights activism, "to draw more people into subversive actions modelled after both historical struggles from the days of the underground rail-road and contemporary movements for economic, social and environmental justice". Giroux aspires to the global development of both politics and education rooted in social justice, with "education as a political and moral practice crucial to creating new forms of agency, mobilizing a desire for change and providing a language that underwrites the capacity to think, speak and act so as to challenge the sexist, racist, economic and political grammars of suffering produced by the new authoritarianism". Reflecting on US schools modelled on prisons, he argues instead for an education that transforms.

Critical pedagogy makes reference to the work of anthropologist Victor Turner (1969) who describes society as a self-adjusting process, with authoritarian structures creating resistance which can force structural change.[4] Turner points to carnival as one form of turning structures on their heads, a playful resistance to over-rigid authority and status. He calls the interface between structure and process 'liminal', an in-between state, fructile (his term) and rich in possibility, in which old assumptions are overturned. Turner advocates a positive community building process he called by the Latin term *communitas*. Translating this into schooling, it shows the wisdom of a school being first and foremost a community building exercise, developing personal and social skills within a democratically articulated community mission. This is the opposite of most school processes which are not democratic in any real sense. Learning to listen to the voices of the pupils is a major step away from such stifling practices.

4 For more on Turner see Ashley (1990), St John (2008) and Bigger (2009b).

Concerning resistance in school classrooms, Sean uses expressions such as 'undermining', 'testing', and 'challenging boundaries'. The educational literature offers terms such as 'counter-culture' and 'laddishness' (Willis 1977),[5] which might be attributed to the conduct witnessed during the London riots. Even though David Cameron was in error to insinuate that a substantial number exhibiting criminal behaviour during the disturbances were school pupils, he did make a valid point in identifying education as a primary vehicle to pre-empt apparent disregard for others, for property, and indeed for the self. However, his demand for even stricter discipline and uniform was little more than a convenient ideological sound bite. The mainly adult perpetrators were the product of at least 11 years in the education system, so their lack of moral and community awareness represents an opportunity missed.

Promoting Well-Being: Schooling and Mental Health

This is my take on the overall aim (or aims) of education: society needs well-balanced young people suited for whatever work evolves over the next five decades, the nature of which cannot be predicted now. Ideally, they will have respect for others and the ability to think matters through and decide on worthwhile courses of action; they will be contributors rather than consumers; in this information age, they will know how to find the information they need and assess its quality and trustworthiness; in a networked world, they will be able to contribute new knowledge; they will have interests which motivate them and enable them to operate in groups with similar interests. Some will have academic interests, others practical, both being considered important.

Successful learning clearly requires more than being confined to a desk completing worksheets. Jerome Bruner, a polymath focusing on schooling, psychology, and science education (whose death has been announced as I write) demanded holistic education enabling the whole child to develop. Bruner (1996) viewed pedagogy as a mix of demonstration/imitation, didactic information, thinking skills using discussion and collaboration, and the testing of what is taken to be knowledge. It is a mistake to allow these to be unbalanced. Active learning comes when pupils participate, work with their peers and adults, and are practically involved. Such learning can be inside the classroom or outside: outdoor education, including Forest Schools, can stimulate deeper learning and interest. This is the triumph of doing as opposed to listening and accepting. Doing involves working things out and thinking things through. The current model of schooling is cramming and

---

5 The female equivalent is considered in Chapter 12.

testing; in my opinion, a thoroughly depressing way for youngsters to pass their childhood. There were a few examples of 'anything goes' schools which came to public scrutiny in the 1970s, which unfortunately led to the false polarity that schools which did not adhere to cramming and testing were all like that. There is a middle way, a balance between freedom and discipline, between knowledge acquisition and creative experimentation. I suspect many head teachers and practitioners aspire to this but find themselves compromised as inspection, time pressures, and curriculum requirements dictate.

Pupils come to school with life experience, some of which is negative and challenging: poor self-esteem, depression, low body image, low confidence in worth and potential, and limited aspirations. Sean's story illustrates this well. School attendance ensures that there is an opportunity to acknowledge and address such issues. The implicit curriculum can do this through everyday expectations and the explicit curriculum through discussion, literature, and drama. In the broad and balanced curriculum proposed by the Education Reform Act 1988, creativity had an essential place, which has been gradually eroded as the curriculum has contracted. Emotional outlets through art and music can have implications for well-being. Leaving aside the need for creativity in adult life, leisure, and employment, creative ways of thinking enrich the world far more than conformism. What the world will need over the next 50 years cannot be predicted, and the more open and flexible (i.e. creative) young people are, the easier it will be for them to find a niche and make a significant contribution. World changing inventions and insights need to start with someone's flight of imagination. And that spark of imagination needs not to have been stifled.

The current campaign by prominent politicians and their advisers to associate creativity with ineffectiveness is advanced under the guise of evidence and standards. Amidst the debate which pitches progressives against traditionalists is the term 'core knowledge'. It is therefore appropriate to shine a light on the uncontested assumptions which underpin the latter's claims of apparent superiority and the association of facts with truth. The term is clearly applicable to any discussion on curriculum content, but it is extended here to consider how a researcher's theory of knowledge inevitably influences decisions around methodology. In the next part, Sean charts the tentative steps he took to forge a methodological pathway. There he was required to negotiate the intricacies of contestable terms such as knowledge and evidence. The following chapter prepares the ground for the reader.

Part II

Methodological Considerations

Chapter 6

Knowledge and Values

Stephen

The argument developed here is that there is more to education than the unthinking distribution of knowledge, whether through worksheets, books, or lecturing. Knowledge is not values free, and what is asserted as knowledge is not always true. It is constantly checked, revised, and restated. Scientific knowledge as stated today has changed vastly over the past few decades, and will do so again in the future. Testing the validity of knowledge is the academic enterprise.

Knowledge has ethical dimensions. Scientific advances have brought nuclear power and nuclear bombs. Nazi medical experiments regarded human life as expendable. Colonial land ownership claims provoke controversy, whether the context is Australia, the United States, Africa, Israel/ Palestine, or the Scotland of my ancestors (Wightman 2010). Colonisation has been sharply contested in the English curriculum. Selection of knowledge comes with a point of view – someone has decided that certain things are important and others are not. Such selections might disadvantage some people and advantage others – rich white men, for example. Deconstructing these assumptions should be an essential part of learning.

The pupils in school today are the citizens of the future. They will have much to consider when choosing their representatives and politicians. As untested online information increases they will need to be able to sift and evaluate information. Information will continue to be twisted to support political ideology: young people need to be able to recognise lies, half-truths, and fallacies in arguments. Therefore, the school curriculum needs to be less about information and more about issues of accuracy, interpretation, and the effect of information on society. In short, pupils need to model themselves on investigative journalists, digging for the truth. This requires from teachers a specific style of questioning: how do we know? What effect does it have? Does it do good or harm? Who benefits, and who is disadvantaged? The purpose of understanding underlying issues is a desire to correct wrongs and build a better society based on respect and fairness. This is not new. Jerome Bruner (1986, 1996) introduced the idea of scaffolding – that adults help learners through their conversations; that pedagogy should be holistic, combining arts with science; that the curriculum should be a spiral, introducing specialist knowledge to all ages, step by step, in gradual and approachable ways.

Application to Research in Education and Schooling

This vast field of educational research is covered in many journals with radically different methodologies. It has been compared to the positivism of medical research in terms of systematic review, but the reality is far more complex. Checking whether a medicine is effective is simply a matter of comparing a group who are taking it with a control group who aren't (but don't know they aren't), but even here the placebo effect may give false readings. Grounded theory was created in order to study what dying people think of their experiences (Glaser and Strauss 1967) using evidence of people's memories, attitudes, and responses, collected through interviews. This became an early example of qualitative research. Whilst some research, such as in psychology, reduces opinions to numbers (using a 1–7 scale, for example) for ease of collecting and processing large scale data, qualitative research resists this reduction and uses the words themselves as data. Despite a paradigm war, both methodologies can complement each other, one providing breadth and the other depth.

Positivist research in education makes a number of assumptions:

- That the truth is simple, observable, and measurable.
- That there is only one truth, one right way.
- That this can be proved by experiment.
- That such experiments produce evidence comparable to science.

The positivist therefore holds that truth is discoverable. There is no need for, or room for, interpretation. In education, this presumes effective pedagogical practice as waiting to be found. In practice, pedagogical effectiveness is hugely problematic. The phrase 'what works' – and if it works, it must be true – is commonly used. Of course this has to be flawed. Whether something works depends on aims and definition. If the aim of a school is to motivate learning, something works if it achieves that goal. A behaviour modification system which forces compliance does not meet this aim if it is demotivating. For it to be said to work implies that the aim of schooling is to force compliance. Indeed, some schools have been unapologetic in lauding compliance as an essential prerequisite to successful learning. Whole school Behaviour for Learning structures are used by some schools and praised by some politicians, although the strategies are based mainly on punishment (typically rephrased as 'consequences'). We can recognise these as 'naughty step' strategies from popular TV shows, establishing a set of imposed rules and punishing breakages of those rules. This is rooted in behaviourism (Watson 1924), alternatively labelled 'behavioural intervention' or 'behavioural engineering'. The classic situation is an out of control child (or children) needing to understand the boundaries between what is acceptable and what is not. I have no problems with establishing such boundaries where this has not been done before. Our questions in this book are about what happens next, so this is not the only strategy used over time. Is there a vision of learning, or is the object of pedagogy mere compliance with rules? And can disruptive attitudes be nipped in the bud at a younger age through more positive teaching and relationships?

Behavioural research explores the behaviour of both animals and humans. Observation has to go hand in hand with interpretation, and researchers need caution and humility in their hypotheses about what they observe. The history of behavioural analysis has included experimentation which was not particularly ethical. It has given us terms like 'conditioned reflex' (Pavlov), which was developed by Watson and Rayner (1920) as 'stimulus response' (including dubious experiments developing phobias in 9-month-old Little Albert). Pavlov was much hampered by Stalinist purges which resulted in the deaths of many of his co-workers, so his conclusions were politically manipulated. His biography (Todes 2014) speaks of naive thinking, conclusions beyond the evidence, and old fashioned theorising. Dissenting voices in Stalinist USSR tended to be shot, so hampering independence of thought.

Watson denied the existence of free will by reducing behaviour to stimulus and response. Unfortunately, complex behaviour remains complex. Different people respond differently to the same stimulus: Milgram's obedience experiment (1963) and Zimbardo's 1971 Stanford Prison Experiment showed that some people resist unethical orders and some capitulate. Skinner's (1953) theory of operant conditioning gave us the term 'reinforcement' for repeated stimuli which promote both positive and negative learning. Again, this is simplistic: conditioning can be resisted. On this insecure base has been built the various troubleshooting empires of behaviour modification, behavioural intervention, and behavioural engineering, using positive and negative reinforcements and punishments. Judging what works is nuanced, so school effectiveness requires complex judgements.

Positivism in research is problematic. You can turn an opinion into a number, but it is still an opinion. Even in science, deciding which results to publish and which to jettison is a matter of judgement. Implicit opinions, assumptions, and conjectures need to be articulated. Scientists try to replicate experiments to check results and conclusions. They look for weaknesses to develop understanding and theory further. Thomas Kuhn's ground-breaking work on scientific paradigms (1970) showed that once a theory becomes groupthink, it becomes hard to shift, so even flat earth theory was resisted to an extraordinary extent and the discovery of oxygen was not easily accepted. Theoretical models and suggestions are not so much facts as best guesses.

Darwin's theory of evolution was a way of making sense of known data; subsequent scientific testing has developed it and failed to disprove it. A creationist might deny it, not through science but via preconceived belief. My grandfather held the view that astronauts could not land on the moon because it was described in Genesis 1 as a 'light' and not a solid object. So too with pedagogy. There are preconceived ideas but no certain truth. There are dominant fashions of thought, sometimes called paradigms. However, a paradigm needs to shift when the evidence piles up against it. Like flat earth theory, the evidence piled up against it and eventually caused it to crumble.

Qualitative research tends not to make absolute claims about knowledge and its generalisability, but step by step builds up a body of reflection on issues otherwise difficult to research. Since the data comes from opinions (via interviews) and interpretations (via observations), the term 'interpretative' is used where appropriate. Note that the same opinions and interpretations are present in quantifiable research, but are hidden beneath the inflexible numbers.

Evidence and Evidence-Based Research in Education

Pronouncements on schooling frequently appeal to evidence and evidence-based practice. I have problems with this. Control groups and blind testing do not work well with education. I could teach a topic to group A and not to group B and test them. The result would be predictable and scarcely worth funding. Yet control groups are exactly what government wants. This debars classroom research, since control groups and blind testing are not ethical in normal teaching situations. You cannot mess pupils around or refuse to teach half the class.

Systematic review brings together different reports and papers on a topic, to see whether confident statements can be made about new knowledge. For education the results are less helpful. I have participated in a number of such reviews, and found them unsatisfactory. The parameters are set requiring studies with a particular methodology – that is, randomised control groups with double blind trials. Several hundred studies on a topic will be reduced to include only those with this chosen methodology. In my first systematic review the hundreds listed were slashed to 17. And what a motley selection they were: studies destined for the bin if one was reviewing literature for a PhD. The systematic side requires the reviewer to go through the article with a fixed set of questions, mostly relating to the narrow methodology. The general quality of the papers was poor, and it is certain that far better studies had been side-lined. Another review produced only two papers considered relevant, both by the same people and both poor. The organisers put pressure on me to be more positive.

There is a great deal of better research containing strong models for school improvement, but which falls outside this narrow government mindset. Political myopia has deep roots. I recall a former secretary of state for higher education telling educational researchers, "There are two kinds of research, good research and bad research. Good research agrees with government policy, bad research is flawed." The speaker did not seem to realise the ridiculousness of this statement, and different forms of this sentiment recur with tedious frequency in government pronouncements about education. Of course we need to beware of 'bad' research, where conclusions do not flow from the data, where causation is wrongfully claimed, where opinions masquerade as results. Questionnaires are particularly insecure. As a respondent, I may want to respond 'it depends' or 'none of the above'. I may try to second-guess what you want to hear. I may wish to present myself in a good light and respond dishonestly. In other words, if those numbers are insecure, then the conclusions based on them are insecure. You can get large numbers of informants, but large numbers of insecure quantifiers just add to the complexity. The end result may not be necessarily meaningless, but it is unlikely to be transparently meaningful. Questionnaires using free writing are obviously more difficult for researchers to process, but it is exactly what qualitative research is about. To sift through explanations and opinions requires an equally rigorous analysis. I have been interviewed, and quoted, and failed to understand the published quotation of my words. Reliability includes accurate transcription and checking. The mishearing of a few words can radically change the sense.

Many of the research terms we use in qualitative research come from questionnaire and experimental research, but function differently. Researchers need to make clear that their research is honest, rooted in reality, and relevant to the topic in hand and to the conclusions being drawn. Reliability and validity stem from these requirements. The issues will be different in quantifiable questionnaires and scientific/medical experiments. Another term used is 'replicability' – could a different researcher replicate the research and get the same results? This has a point in a chemistry lab, but qualitative research deals with unique occasions (groups of people in a particular place at particular points in time), so replication can only assess different people at a different place and time. The first researcher may have been trusted by the participants, the second not. Failure to replicate qualitative results does not invalidate the original results. Qualitative research accumulates research evidence until generalisations can be made.

Ofsted claim to provide 'evidence'. Inspectors observe work in a school and give their *opinions*; but it is an opinion, not evidence. Opinions are given number scores. A combination of these opinions leads to a final score for the school. Again, this is not evidence, it is a group opinion. These inspectors have been casually employed, often without adequate qualifications or training. They tick a prepared pro forma. We need to be cautious about the value of their group opinion. So, there are many Ofsted opinions, but there is no Ofsted 'evidence'. That their opinions coalesce is more a matter of group-think than scientific data.

In this chapter I have sought to alert the reader to the complex terrain that defines research methodology. Sean, an accomplished teacher, developed his understanding of methodology through his master's and PhD. Negotiating conflicting claims and forms of evidence, the following chapters convey his development of critical awareness, a healthy scepticism, and then a clear conviction as he forged his own unique methodological path.

Chapter 7

Quality As Measured

Sean

The early chapters of this book have stated that my research interest revolved around a better understanding of who I am (or more accurately, who I had become) and what I did when operating as a teacher and authority figure. The sense of incongruity between my espoused values and my enactment of my role is encompassed in the term 'living contradiction'. I have begun to acknowledge the impact of my childhood and that aspect is developed further in Part IV. I have also probed the idea that I had long been absorbing implicit messages from within the educational system – some deliberately (for they reinforced my perception of a strong teacher); others unthinkingly (for I was too busy to reflect on what lay behind them). It is the identification of unconscious influences, and their potential significance to my sense of identity and performance, which occupied my thoughts as I began to engage with research methodology.

This chapter charts an ongoing process of realisation and deliberation. I suspect it may be interpreted as naive by some; refreshingly honest by others – as is the case in the classroom, much will depend on the reader's prior knowledge. As I had little cause to contemplate the ins and outs of academia before my research, I was vaguely familiar with many of the terms, though I had limited understanding of definitions or contentions. My research required that I forge a methodological path, but as this was yet to be clarified, much of my early reading provided me with a better appreciation of the lie of the land.

As I delved into unfamiliar literature, I was unexpectedly offered another dimension to comprehend my operational state – I was afforded a glimpse behind the scenes. Whitehead and McNiff (2006) were the first to alert me to the connections between the customary world of the classroom and unfamiliar fields of academia. They allude to assumptions which underpin the prominence of positivist (and interpretive) methodologies within educational research, and thus schools:

> There seems to be a common understanding – better, misunderstanding – that 'theory' is a self-contained body of knowledge, usually scientific knowledge, which can explain and be applied to practice. This view of theory, which itself is a theory, and stems from the natural social sciences, has been around for so long that it has become

> entrenched in the public psyche, so it often goes unquestioned. (Whitehead and McNiff 2006: 29–30)

I learned that the hegemony I was identifying within school policy and practice could be traced to the hegemony which existed in the world of educational research. I eventually came to echo Whitehead and McNiff's (2006: 26) deep concerns about how teachers and other practitioners are "systematically bullied by dominant forms of research and theory, and are persuaded to think that they cannot think for themselves". The process of reconceptualising led me to conclude that, despite my so called authority and my apparent success, I was not much more than a pawn in the grand scheme of things – a puppet, a mere foot soldier. Extending the latter analogy, I began to question the legitimacy of the order to go 'over the top' to implement yet another initiative. I paused to query the qualifications, the competence, and the ulterior motives of the officers who remained far removed from the front line. The fact that the education minister, the schools' minister, and sundry lieutenants in influential think-tanks have never served as teachers, for me, substantiates the comparison.

Two common terms caught my attention – 'evidence' and 'knowledge'. I have since noticed that both are subject to much debate in my social media feeds where evidence has become conflated with 'what works'. Through my reading of research methods in education, I began to better appreciate how narrow definitions of these words equated to the barely visible strings which dictated my approach in the classroom.

I learned that the condition I was struggling to articulate was already being discussed in the literature. Stephen Ball's (2003) concept of performativity and his critique of accountability illuminates how the system's mechanisms of government, or control, subtly frame the modes of thought held by many diligent professionals. Entwined with a critique of systemic performance management processes, the teachers' sense of self is identified as a matter for concern in light of the requirement (or, in my case, incessant obligation) to uncritically uphold and implement procedures which sustain the system's control over its subjects. That I held myself to stringent account to ensure my performance aligned with external descriptors of 'outstanding', is of particular interest to me. Ball (2015) argues that the system encourages us to think about ourselves as teachers in *their* terms, to take on board the systems of recognition *they* offer to us (e.g. successful, average, unsuccessful), and subsequently to take responsibility for working on ourselves to improve. The expectation continues to have allure, for who can argue that it is not an appropriate and worthy ambition to make ourselves better at what we do?

I came to appreciate more deeply that 'evidence' is political – it is always constructed with social intent. Biesta (2007: 5) encourages us to ask for whom, and for what purpose? He argues that "the focus on 'what works' makes it difficult if not impossible to ask [these] questions".[1] As I will qualify below, the erroneous use of quantitative 'evidence' can be used not only to coerce teachers as individuals, but also to dictate to the profession as a whole.

In accordance with the system's embedded accountability processes, the quest for certainty and knowledge of 'what works', the desire to eliminate contradiction can lead practitioners, researchers, school leaders, politicians, and increasingly those who contribute to EduTwitter to convey claims for evidence through linear forms of expression such as statistics. Statistics deal in possibilities (rather than certainties), are open to interpretation, and can be devoid of context.[2] Such observations are inconvenient and, unsurprisingly, often glossed over with the help of a convincing narrative or headline. The aforementioned "equivalent to 38 days of teaching lost per year" (Ofsted 2014: 5) and Canter's (1988: 73) "5 hours per month more time teachers have to teach", serve as exemplars.

A Number

Ball recognised that we work in an era where there appears to be a reverence, a fixation, with the number. It is presented as a way of representing quality. I certainly subscribed to that notion, believing that the richness of learning could be reduced to a digit. As a consequence, people can be labelled, categorised, held to account, and subjected to predictions and forecasts. I argue that this fixation comes to infringe on one's sense of self, on relationships with pupils in the classroom, and on perceptions of colleagues in the staffroom.

The now obsolete practice of having Ofsted inspectors visit classrooms (sometimes arriving halfway through the lesson) in order to judge learning and assess progress serves to illustrate the uncritical assumptions so many of us came to accept. O'Leary (2013), in reference to graded lesson observations and the use of a four point scale for performance management purposes, writes of the deceptive allure of such an apparently robust mechanism. A single number is all it takes to seduce people into thinking that the process has some kind of scientific basis, that it has objective value akin to a calibrated instrument such as a set of weighing scales or a thermometer. The evidence that the procedure was both unreliable and invalid (Coe 2014), and the recognition that any such judgements are inevitably filtered through the subjective and biased interpretations of the observer, is by and by. I was as

1 It was reported that the education white paper *Educational Excellence Everywhere* (DfE 2016a) contained the term 'what works' 17 times and made reference to 'outcomes' 61 times.

2 I am interested to consider the distinction between *evidence* and *proof*. Evidence is contestable. I suggest that the difference is not always apparent to the layperson (the teacher) and can be profound when it is used to interpret the judgements of others. The concept of proof resides in the domain of mathematics, not the complex study of social science.

gullible as anyone. The uncontested validity given to numerical data was deeply ingrained within my mind, dominating my thoughts and constantly in my dialogue with colleagues. However, I came to the realisation that individuals like me had been made calculable and subject to the "power of the single number" (Rose 1999: 214). And I objected to the fact that *I* was constantly being measured, not just my performance – *me*. Measured and judged, shackled even, by objective metrics. My research afforded me the opportunity to progressively loosen those chains over a period of time, and my study of the methodology highlighted several key links forming that chain.

I was intrigued by the idea that adherence to a quantitative mechanism could somehow be integral to this sense of being trapped. How on earth did that come to be? Beyond summative assessments, this procedure wasn't part of the equation when I first embarked on my career as a teacher of children. In truth, it wasn't rocket science. The reality was that statistics representing effectiveness and performance had gradually come to infiltrate every aspect of my work environment. In my own classroom, 'learning' or 'progress' was erroneously quantified through graded observations; conclusions were drawn or reinforced through a dubious indicator coined the 'learning walk';[3] numbers were integral to the levelling of pupils' work; figures were apparent through inter-departmental comparisons, feeding into the published league tables on a national scale, and extending to international rankings through PISA. Schools are thus rendered as sites of normalisation and reality is presented in terms of quantifiable measures, which in light of standardisation "re-territorialize[s] difference as problematic" (Allen 2004: 420). And, of course, teachers and their departments are held accountable to the SLT, who answer to Ofsted, and so the school becomes vulnerable to forced academy conversion under the guise of standards but in the shadow of quasi-privatisation (NUT 2017).[4]

3 A school I have visited uses learning walks to check 'indicators' of 'good' and convert it into a percentage (alongside observations and staff self-appraisal) to provide evidence of teaching performance. Others use it as an opportunity to ask children what they have learned. I suggest that the practice simply captures something of the pupils' performance. If the observer returned to see how the initial indicators had become embedded, applied, or transferred to a different context, problem, or scenario, they might have some justification in stating that learning has taken place. Even then, without an awareness of the pupils' knowledge prior to the initial observation, they cannot attribute apparent evidence solely to the activities or to the teacher's input. Bjork (2012) is eloquent in deciphering the difference between performance and learning: performance is easily measured, learning can only be inferred.

4 The white paper *Educational Excellence Everywhere* (DfE 2016a) announced that every school would be forced to convert to academy status by 2022. This would not only infringe on democratic choice, but the proposal was also devoid of any substantial evidence to support the idea that schools (either primary or secondary) are likely to perform better as sponsored academies, rather than remaining under local authority control in the maintained sector. Amidst opposition from her own party, the then Education Minister Nicky Morgan was later forced to amend her proposal. The latest proposal to expand grammar schools is also inconveniently devoid of supporting evidence. I find the government's propensity to champion certain evidence, and selectively ignore others which challenge their policies, particularly galling.

Literature offered another dimension. Shirlow and Pain (2003) refer to different scales of fear permeating internationally, nationally, and locally; the fears may be about the UK performing relatively poorly on the global stage or fear of the 'naming and shaming' of 'failing' schools. Cascading down, 'performance' is understandably important to staff who fear the consequences of their pupils' 'failure' (Jackson 2010): the "force and brute logic of performance" (Ball 2013: loc. 1976) renders 'failure' in a performative system as letting down ourselves, our colleagues, and our institution. Radford (2008: 148) alludes to the influence of policy makers as integral to creating and sustaining the current state: "Educational standards identified almost entirely in terms of measurable attainment, have given rise to a whole new field of practical inquiry that provides multiple examples of how research can be contaminated by an ideological agenda." The mutually beneficial relationship between policy makers and educational researchers was described in Chapter 1.

Accountability

The quantitative measurement of performance has become widely accepted. Its seemingly irrefutable legitimisation has created a mechanism of regulation under the guise of accountability. The mechanism for systemic control is identified as performance management: a powerful and effective technique for managing complex systems which connects the will of government to the detailed complexities of classroom life through numerical measurement. Ball (2015) looks beyond simplistic, technical definitions of accountability to consider the impact it can have on those who are susceptible to absorbing its implicit messages. He draws attention to a more profound issue in which accountability measures create subjectivity – that is, they create subjects. This manifests through an impoverished view by which we come to see others and ourselves in terms of performance or productivity, rather than as competent human beings with an array of skills (many of which are not considered, let alone measured). Brookfield (1995: 18) extends the application to student evaluations. When subscribing to the 'perfect 10' syndrome, he describes a range of consequential teacher responses ranging from affirmative pride to feelings of incompetence and guilt. The process "primarily … serves individuals with a reductionist cast of mind who believe that the dynamics and contradictions of teaching can be reduced to a linear, quantifiable rating system". Holding propositional forms of logic, my prominent mode of thought revealed my propensity for polarised either/or thinking, habitually conceiving teachers and pupils as 'good' or 'bad' educators and learners. I was inclined to define people in accordance with categories, grades, and levels. I was under the assumption they provided me with an indication – even a confirmation – of an individual's competence (or incompetence).

We, as a school, were on a quest to move from 'good' to 'outstanding'. I was part of the system. My concern was that the system had become part of me. In essence, I was interested to ask why I, and others like me, had come to be so willing to adhere to this contrived notion of the 'professional' that we had lost something of ourselves along the way. Sacrificing lunchtimes, evenings, weekends, and holidays – family and leisure time – and working ever harder, equated to dominating myself through taking a perverse pride in perfectionist traits. The process of deconstructing this implicit influence on my psyche, and its expression through habitual behaviour, is the thread running through this book.

A Directed Profession

As I described in Chapter 1, by this stage of my career I had morphed from being a servant to an agent of the system. This transition is developed in Chapter 22. Not only did I uncritically integrate the latest government initiative into my practice, I was often at the forefront of disseminating it to others. By the time it got to my level, decisions had already been made by people I would never know, let alone meet. My role was simply to squeeze yet another requirement deemed important by external sources into the limited time I had available. Whitehead and McNiff (2006: 18) point out that premised social science standards of judgement, which continue to dominate to the exclusion of practitioner endorsement, ensure that "policy makers are assumed to make policy and arrange for its implementation by practitioners". This is perhaps indicative of a directed profession which is constantly told what 'good practice' is. It could be argued that the current grammar expectations, for example, which (at the time of writing) mean that 11-year-olds are required to use and apply a range of detailed grammatical terms, provide a perfect example of policy being shaped by the personal convictions of individual politicians.

The phrase 'evidence based' is used as shorthand for 'what works'; it represents the justification for imposing preferred methods of pedagogy on practitioners or verifying reductionist approaches. The emphasis is on techniques and making those techniques more efficient. Endorsed strategies are operationalised rather than questioned. Underpinned by positivist assumptions, which orientate towards hard facts, scientific research is predominantly experimental or quasi-experimental and designed to produce quantitative data as validation for theory. In the previous chapter, Stephen showed how the advancement of medicine has benefitted from such an approach.[5] Usher (1996: 13) explained how dominant scientific enquiries are based on propositional forms and have come to define and dominate the entire educational system. Propositional theories manifest through definitive statements which tend to categorise. They are grounded in a quest for certainty. They seek to reduce complex phenomena to an analysis of their components, which are presented as simple, absolute, and objective.

This esteemed objective knowledge can be broken down into separate components: 'know that' and 'know how'. Know that is associated with facts and figures and might be referred to as propositional knowledge or technical-rational knowledge. Knowledge is seen as a thing which is made more concrete. Know how, or procedural knowledge, is concerned with skills and competencies engrained within a constrained curriculum asserting self-contained bodies of knowledge. Both components lend themselves to tests and examinations, and are often used to define evidence, so informing policy and performance. This, of course, alludes to the idea that effectiveness and efficiency can be quantified and measured, enabling predictions and targets to be rational next steps. Ball (2015) associates this method of translating, of rendering education into the form of product – a commodity to be made susceptible to the market – as another function of performativity. An interesting elucidation of the uncritical processes which dominated so many of my waking hours.

However, it is also apparent that some studies and surveys – with the endorsement of politicians and kindred social media activists – take off and create those all-important media headlines which seep through to the social consciousness. As Biesta (2007: 8) identifies, having assumed that the ends of professional action are a given, "the only relevant (professional and research) questions to be asked are about the most effective and efficient ways of achieving those ends". As attention is increasingly focused on quantifiable outcomes, discourse around education has indeed been hijacked by numbers. There is an infatuation with refining the technicalities, rather than asking questions about the moral purpose of educating the young. My concern is that research is being subtly wrapped up in an ideological agenda. This agenda is cleverly concealed from keen and impressionable enthusiasts, who naturally want to find out what works and what is most effective.

By way of illustration, I recently read a persuasive and eloquent argument posted on an educational blog by a teacher who has a high profile on social media. The prominent practitioner is prolific in his writing (and often forthright in his views). Coming across as authoritative and incredibly

5 Greenhalgh (2015) provides an intriguing critique of evidence-based medicine (EBM). Points made in the 29 minute video are equally applicable to education and pertinent to the arguments being made in this chapter. Contributions from the floor explore the relationship between evidence and uncertainty, and the notion of 'boxed in thinking' (i.e. the uncritical acceptance of an evidence-based narrative).

self-assured, even on topics outside of his area of expertise, it is easy to conceive how tens of thousands of 'followers' might be influenced. This self-proclaimed bastion of 'standards' eloquently shapes perspectives, so definitions and subsequent 'solutions' appear to stem from sound acumen. There was enough in the piece for me to recognise something of my own experience and to find an affinity. Acceptance of his logic would have affirmed and entrenched the attitude and operational stance I have come to critique in my research – 'evidence', 'knowledge', and 'sanctions' are his mantra. Consequently, on a second reading, I adjusted my lens to ask, "Which questions have not been answered?" and perhaps more importantly, "Which questions have not been asked?" The limitations of his assertions began to emerge. Had social media been as prevalent and accessible a decade or two ago, I would no doubt have lapped up many of these persuasive arguments, no questions asked (just as I did when absorbing the claims accompanying unsubstantiated commercial packages such as Accelerated Learning and Assertive Discipline).

There is a danger that uncritical advocates of evidence-based practice may become *more* informed, rather than necessarily *better* informed. The latter requires decisions which are underpinned by consideration of what is educationally appropriate and desirable. It involves, in Ball's (2015) words, "Reflexive thinking about the relationship between practice and morality, practice and values, practice and principles," rather than an inclination to think of practice as performance. I argue that this comes from intelligent problem solving and a commitment to *living* educational values. I read Jack Whitehead's (2008) testimony with great interest, as he describes his personal struggles to have his voice heard and to have *his* explanations about *his* experience of *his* lessons acknowledged and verified through academia. He had burrowed through inhospitable academic territory, which he identified as the 'disciplines approach'; I was afforded an opportunity to follow a similar path. I will expand on this here and in subsequent chapters.

Site of Struggle

Whilst acknowledging the legitimacy of a collective resistance to policies, Ball (2015) prefers to use the term 'refusal' to conceive the individual as a site of struggle. The forms of refusal become not political or grand gestures, but rather a refusal around daily mundane practices which constantly elicit one to subscribe to the demands of performance. In accordance with my own experience, he describes a struggle with the self, or rather a struggle over which kind of self you want to be. My research sought to deconstruct the persona I had come to adopt in role. For me, refusal was defined as an objection to being rendered 'competent' or 'incompetent' in accordance to the regime of numbers.

Away from social media platforms, I suspect that much research is rejected or ignored as irrelevant to the real world of teaching. Many staff just get on with their job and are oblivious, as I once was, to the controversy which brings research into the public arena for debate. Even then I suspect that selective research findings continue to feed into the collective educational psyche. I pause to consider two examples of educational buzzwords to illustrate: 'mindset' and 'effect sizes'. Periodically, such initiatives add flavour to the prescribed curriculum diet. Both contributed to my own teaching and then, as I describe below, acted as stimuli to clarify my position.

Carol Dweck's comprehensive evidence base in *Self-Theories* (2000) (or, more accurately, as popularised in *Mindset* (2006)) has generated an industry which has led others to jump on the bandwagon and convert her principles into posters, YouTube videos, and training events. Dweck has since expressed concern that her research findings are being misrepresented. This illustrates the challenge of ensuring that (even the most reputable) educational research leads to the enhancement of classroom practice.

As an intellectual exercise, I was interested to reread the original text (Dweck 2000) to consider its potential contribution to this chapter – a chapter concerned with the teacher's mentality when quality is incessantly measured. Naturally, educators apply the principles to pupils – the aim to cultivate a 'growth mindset' and to vanquish the 'fixed mindset'. However, there seems to be an assumption that the teacher is immune to fixed mindset thinking because, after all, they are the adult in the room! I noted that the implicit messages associated with a fixed mindset are sustained by conditions in which people feel that not only their performance but also their very self-worth is being judged. Dweck's consideration of the implications of her theory for mental health appear particularly pertinent when read against the backdrop of targets, observations, pupil 'progress', disruptive classes, and so on:

> Ideas about the self can create a meaning system that leads people to adopt goals and interpret events, sometimes in ways which make them vulnerable … our work suggests that an entity-theory framework [fixed mindset] can lead people to overgeneralise from one experience, to categorise themselves in unflattering ways, to set self-worth contingencies, to exaggerate their failures relative to successes, to lose faith in their ability to perform – even simple actions … if people have a very strong belief that they *should* be able to do everything, and their self-worth is tied into it all, then problems are likely to arise. (Dweck 2000: 144–145; original emphasis)

I would suggest that even this short extract makes a thought-provoking contribution to the current debate on teacher stress, well-being, and retention.

Interestingly, I reflect that this state would not have been apparent in my own classroom performance or communication. However, aspects do resonate with the private thoughts and underlying fears which I confronted in my study. I was, in the main, an encouraging and affirming teacher who espoused all of the qualities associated with a growth mindset – a belief in developing potential through effort and strategy. I could justifiably point to evidence that I employed this approach to enhance my own performance and effectiveness as an educator. I now realise that the underlying, debilitating traits associated with a fixed mindset tended to come to the fore when judgement, challenge (to my status/competence), or perceived threat became part of the equation. Prior to my research, such notions were habitually and subconsciously suppressed as I gradually became more rigid, working harder in order to cope. As a matter of course I was bullish in my response, but it is with some discomfort that I acknowledge that, on occasions, insecurities manifested through defensive and emotional reactions.

In a section entitled 'Final Thoughts on Controversial Issues', Dweck poses herself a question: "If an entity theory is maladaptive, why do so many people hold it?" I am compelled to state the obvious: every teacher, by and large, adheres to the system they have come to serve – like me, they are successful products who have proved themselves competent at every stage through the mechanism of testing. It is worth remembering that Dweck's research is concerned with beliefs about the self which have formed over a lifetime. My interest is in how they might come to hold sway when we are required to operate as adults in a functionalist institution. The answer she provides to her own question includes the notion that: "an entity theory may give people a sense of security in a complex world … a sense that they can predict things … that their social world is highly predictable" (Dweck 2000: 151). The descriptors resonate with the propositional logic which permeates this chapter. At the core is a mode of thought which champions binary divides, such as good/bad, successful/unsuccessful, outstanding/in need of improvement, and assumes that quality can be abbreviated to a quantified measurement.

Another buzzword has seeped into the vocabulary and psyche of the teaching profession. It substantiates claims for the validity of numbers and holds that figures can illuminate the effectiveness of teacher performance. John Hattie's influential work suggests that the connection between science and the classroom can be achieved through adherence to the comprehensible quantitative medium known as effect sizes.[6] Marketed well, I suspect its sales have benefitted from uncritical acceptance from a busy profession attracted by a tagline which promises to reveal 'what works'. The approach

6 For example, 0.40 is above average for educational research, 0.50 is equivalent to one grade leap at GCSE, and 1.0 equates to a two grade leap.

champions the idea of a 'knowledge-driven profession', in which judgements are based on other people's research.

Ill-equipped to critique, and not inclined to look beyond the headline or blurb, I was quick to accept the claims at face value. Looking back, there is no doubt in my mind that the accessibility of meta-analyses have made a valuable and interesting contribution to debate around teaching and learning. However, in accordance with Biesta's (2007: 17) review of Dewey's work, I have come to conclude that evidence-based practice "does not provide us with rules for action but only with hypotheses for intelligent problem-solving". However insightful it is, it should always be remembered that meta-analysis presents what *has* worked, it does not stipulate what *will* work. As Dylan Wiliam (2009: 15) reminds us: "Almost everything works somewhere, and nothing works everywhere." Biesta (2007: 5) advises caution around claims derived from broad quantitative conclusions, stressing: "evidence-based education seems to limit severely the opportunities for educational practitioners to make such judgments in a way that is sensitive to and relevant for their own contextualized settings".

However appealing to those who desire a prescriptive list of what constitutes excellence, effect sizes are not totally reliable measures, and the limitations of evidence in the form of generalised findings are apparent to those who will acknowledge them. As Hattie himself says in *Visible Learning*: "It is not a book about classroom life, and does not speak of the nuances and details of what happens within classrooms. Instead it synthesizes research based on what happens within classrooms; as it is more concerned with the effects than the interactions" (Hattie 2009: loc. 1). And yet, as I sought to comprehend the dynamics within the groups I taught, it was the interactions which intrigued me most. I did not want my research to be confined to observing them; I wanted to research *us* as we shared the same space. To chart a way forward, I would be required to clarify my position, lest I be misunderstood.

Positioning

In earlier chapters I have made it clear that, despite my qualms around draconian approaches to discipline, as an authority figure I *do* advocate boundaries. Here I need to clearly state that, even though some politicians exploit the term, I am much in favour of an evidence *informed* profession which is able to explore the potential insights from research to improve pedagogy and stimulate new practice. Yet, at the core of my narrative are caveats. These come in the form of a concern about psychological default positions adopted by the practitioner which colour interpretations and direct their action as a matter of course. Regarding school relationships, an authoritarian stance was the one I habitually reverted to; in relation to performance, propositional logic dominated. One decreed that I asserted my power over subordinates, the other that I categorised and labelled pupils and colleagues alike. A disproportionate amount of energy (which I came to recognise as perfectionism) was spent on trying to make techniques ever more efficient and effective so that my performance, my very 'self', might be verified by a number.

By contrast, I am also interested in the subtleties found in definitions, such as the distinction between compliance and cooperation when critiquing the concept of order; between pupils being busy and learning. I am also attentive to nuances. I am reluctant to dismiss the useful contribution of either authoritarian strategies or propositional logic to circumstances and domains which are appropriate. *My* domain is the classroom, situated in a school, which forms part of an established network integral to society itself. As a teacher I had obligations. I had to find a balance between my role as an employee of the school and my quest to question, even disturb, the status quo. There was to some degree a requirement to be pragmatic, recognising that education meets utilitarian ends in developing human capital for a competitive 'knowledge economy'. I aligned with Elliott (2006) who advocates a blend (in Aristotelian terms) of *techne,* 'know how', and *phronesis,* 'practical wisdom' (Dottori 2009: 184). I acknowledge the value of evidence and knowledge, but more so I insist that they are used to enrich rather than suppress. That is my position.

My Contextual Settings

Regarding my own opportunity to produce evidence – to make a contribution to knowledge – I realised I wanted to explore a different way to that which I had critiqued. I had contemplated the prominent methodologies directing and leading the profession. I had identified key propositional forms of theory, knowledge, and logic priming the profession to accept, rather than dispute, claims for knowledge. I was now determined to wrestle with the perceived hegemony I was encountering at every turn. I concluded that I wanted to champion the idea that classroom practitioners are more than capable of becoming a profession that can *create* knowledge. As I have argued, too often we are constrained (and misled) by dominant and biased forms of research presented through numbers. Our engagement should, and can, extend beyond going to conferences which tell us about other people's findings – as interesting and valuable as that can be. Whitehead's articulation of living educational theory (LET) was immensely attractive from the outset, encouraging me – a practising teacher – to believe that I could make a unique contribution to knowledge, that my theories about life in *my* classroom might be deemed worthy enough to be subjected to a validation process. Whitehead and McNiff's *Action Research: Living Theory* (2006) provides a coherent and comprehensible overview of the academic world and helpfully defines its specialised terminology – words such as ontology (a theory of being), epistemology (a theory of knowledge), and methodology (the underlying set of principles and rules which frame the enquiry). A consideration of the social purposes of one's research is integral to LET. I used the terms 'transform' and 'emancipate' to identify my intention. It was as if I was standing on top of a mountain with a clear view of the route I had followed so far (measured at every section) and an opportunity to chart a better onward course because of my new vantage point.

Whitehead and McNiff invite the reader to decide what kind of research they wish to do and what kind of theory they wish to generate. I wasn't too sure, in all honesty, as I had never before considered such a question. I knew, however, that my work would be predominantly qualitative, and I also knew that it would be action research. Because I was interested in understanding how power permeates education, it would be critical action research. So, whilst I was sure of the direction I wanted to take, I was hesitant about taking the first steps. My previous reading of dense methodological texts had led me down countless cul-de-sacs due to my limited understanding of the terrain. In order to proceed, I engaged myself with ideas of theory, knowledge, and logic. I worked to comprehend the methodological roots – the theory of how we do things. I had a compass, but I found that I had to construct my own map.

I needed to find an alternative methodology to those I had come to question and reject. Mills (1959: 123) argued that "Every man [is] his own methodologist." In attempting to articulate my study's methodology, I took up Clough and Nutbrown's (2012) invitation to discover a 'methodology for myself' within my research, to establish my own blueprint as a researcher. Accordingly, I employed Dadds and Hart's (2001: 166) concept of 'inventive methodology', which recognises that, for some practitioner-researchers, creating their own unique way through their research may be as important as their self-chosen research focus. Drawing on Datta's (1994) metaphor that neither the quantitative hook set for the big fish, nor the qualitative net scaled for the little fish, adequately captures life in most seas, Phelps and Hase (2002) suggest that we need to become scuba divers. I made a commitment to get into the water and swim, even when the sea was turbulent, unpredictable, and threatening to sweep me away.

Thus, I engaged with three specific approaches to inform my action research. The first was 'living educational theory' to articulate my own tacit knowledge; the second was 'complexity theory' to explore the intricacies of groups; and the third was 'critical theory' for critiquing macro–micro power relations. Stephen provided the grounding for critical perspectives in Chapter 5. I conceive the triad as intertwining circles on a Venn diagram, with my unique contribution positioned in the central intersection. Unpacked in the following chapters, each offered an alternative to the prominence of the positivist and interpretive paradigms within educational research.

If this chapter has raised concerns about the notion of quality as measured, in the next chapter I want to advance the term 'quality as experienced' (Stake and Schwandt 2006). Quality is a contested term for which the practitioner-researcher must make a case. Rather than seek validity through quantitative measurements, I made judgements about the quality of practice in terms of what I found valuable about my own practice (Whitehead and McNiff 2006). The phrase implied that the discernment of quality could be located in the form of practically embodied knowledge. Elliott (2007: 230) suggests that embodied knowledge, which is "at once both cognitive and emotional", is acquired in the course of "direct experience of practical situations. The process of awareness manifests in the language and actions of participants" to fulfil the conditions for *quality* in narratives of personal experience.

I would like to encourage colleagues that research need not be confined to random controlled tests, producing abstract and generalised outcomes. Alternative approaches offer teachers a legitimate platform to address their immediate concerns about life in *their* classrooms. I want to endorse a knowledge-creating profession which is capable of making informed refinements to practice, either as individuals or as part of a collaborative venture with colleagues – that is, for teachers to be masters of research rather than enslaved by it.

Chapter 8

Quality As Experienced

Sean

Whilst the stimulus for my research was founded on a concern that I habitually compromised my values in the name of professionalism, it also provided me with an opportunity to reflect upon and comprehend what I actually did well.

Throughout my career I had a steady stream of visitors coming to observe my practice. Accompanied by an SLT member, esteemed guests and prospective parents would regularly pass by because I was a sure bet to have an ordered classroom where all pupils could be seen to be on-task. Likewise, the school's trainee manager and a host of mentors would point their trainee teachers and NQTs in my direction for them to see 'how it should be done'. Typically, the latter would observe, take notes, and on occasion stay behind to ask me questions about what I did and how I did it. The first question was easy: I would rattle off objectives, strategies, and techniques in accordance with the technical-rational knowledge encompassed by the terms 'know that' and 'know how'. In effect, I simply reduced complex phenomena into simple parts and framed them with terminology such as 'starter' or 'plenary'. The facts, content, and skills created a common ground for my pedagogical intentions which satisfied the majority of enquiries. What I was ill-equipped to do, even after all those years at the chalk-face, was to articulate how I did it – the vast storehouse of hidden tacit knowledge which provided the invisible thread and somehow tied all those reductionist approaches into a coherent whole. The essence of the lesson remained intangible. There was no magic formula. In reality, what worked with one group might not work with another. A definitive explanation of how I did what I did remained elusive.

It had occurred to me that my influence actually went beyond what I did to who I am. The appealing idea of being able to capture the 'secret' of my apparent success, so others might replicate it, was my presumptuous intention when I first submitted my doctoral proposal to Stephen. My preliminary research question centred on the debate around whether 'excellent' teachers are made or born. My efficient arrangement of technical tasks and the obvious control I exhibited, in accordance with my reputation and status, were clear for all to see. However, it soon became evident that so much of the philosophy I had developed or acquired was devoid of any critique (apart from the official criteria affirming and spurring on my performance). I just did what I did.

Later in my research, I would come to realise that much of my success was dominated and driven by my perfectionist traits. My excessive mentally rehearsed lessons were then delivered and personality affirmed by those making judgements. I gave no hint of the psychological cost of meeting external standards or striving to meet incessant internal expectations. However, my 'no nonsense' attitude and overly serious outlook subtly began to manifest in my lesson delivery, especially when I was tired, and it became apparent to me that these habitual mannerisms needed to be addressed.

Thus, the opportunity to identify the fundamental values and principles which governed my intentions, informed my practice, and shaped my relationships became essential if I was ever going to be able to disseminate useful aspects of my practice and findings to others. The idea of becoming more patient and less dominating was all very well, but I still needed to fulfil my role as an educator. I wanted to be able to describe and explain what I did when I was operating at my best, as a person and as a teacher – that is, when I was most effective. At the core was a necessity to better understand how I functioned, but I also needed to comprehend the class dynamics in order to create an environment where learning might have a chance to occur. This was somewhat of a challenge, as the contextual variables and personnel were far from constant and always unique to each group and occasion.

I adopted a participative approach. As a practitioner-researcher my ontological position was naturally that of an insider, offering descriptions and explanations of classroom relationships and their influences upon the climate and learning. There, I sought to create knowledge or explanations whilst interacting with others, testing and critiquing what was already known and seeking to explore ways to transform it into something better. I was researching the unique phenomenon which passed as *us*, and specifically my contribution and educational influence.

Subjective Knowledge

Whitehead and McNiff's (2006) living educational theory provided a vehicle to assess and articulate my professional judgement. LET advances the claims of validity for subjective, tacit, and personal knowledge. This form of knowledge is framed as "I know this" when considered with a direct object (as in "I know this song"). Subjective claims to knowledge, such as "I have a toothache" or "I know what I'm doing" are legitimate claims, but they do not lend themselves to the type of empirical evidence that is so prominent in the educational world, where quality is dominated by that which can be measured rather than quality which is experienced. Nonetheless, a lack of empirical and testable evidence would not invalidate the experience of having a toothache. Subjective knowledge is not always rational; intuition derived from a deep sense of knowing can't be quantified, yet it was nonetheless real and present as I chalked up years of practice within the classroom.

I wanted this intangible aspect of my experience to be recognised as valid. LET affirmed this, explaining that subjective knowledge as expressed without a direct object – "I know" uttered in response to the prompt "You need to hurry up" – is integral to lived experience. I loved Polanyi's (1958) affirmation that people have a vast repertoire of experiential knowledge which they draw on for making any one of the split second decisions that are a feature of everyday practice. He emphasised an implicit dimension to personal knowledge, pointing out we know more than we can say; sometimes we just can't quite articulate decisions which derive from a base in which we can justifiably say "I just know".

Schön (2010: 5–6) recognises experiential knowledge as being integral to professional knowledge. He qualifies his thoughts through writing about "our feel for the stuff with which we are dealing" and highlighting times and occasions when we are at a loss to adequately produce descriptions of what we implicitly know to be right. The essence of the spontaneous, intuitive performance which makes up our everyday practice is, he claims, wrapped up in our tacit patterns of action. We may say that our knowing is in our actions, where we make "innumerable judgements of quality for which we cannot state adequate criteria, and … display skills for which [we] cannot state the rules and procedures". He adds that "Common sense [is] knowing-in-action … 'thinking on our feet,' 'keeping your wits about you'", suggesting that we can think about doing whilst doing.

Biesta (2007: 13) informs us that "knowing is about grasping and understanding the relation between our actions and their consequences, knowing can help us to gain better control [mastery] over our actions – better at least, that is, than in the case of blind trial and error". It is this process which enables us to acquire habits or dispositions to act. Intelligent use of my imagination would enable me to contemplate possible lines of enquiry which would inform my professional action and facilitate an acquisition of knowledge. This could be done through reflection, but it was often enacted on the spot. Elliott (2007: 230) suggests that quality could be discerned through "direct experience of practical situations", whilst reminding us that quality "is always multifaceted, contested and never fully representable".

LET, then, is grounded in the personal knowledge of 'know this' and (to) 'know', because practitioners systematically relate their work to their values and draw on those values as standards of judgement. My ontological values were identified as 'respect' (mutual), 'fairness' (in my dealings), 'responsibility' (for my reactions), and 'trust', as I sought to provide opportunities for the pupils to become more autonomous and self-disciplined. It is the 'living I' which was "placed at the centre of educational enquiries, not as an abstract personal pronoun but as a real-life human being" (McNiff et al. 2003: 72). My ontological and epistemological stance (i.e. I viewed myself as part of the group rather than as a fly on the wall; *we* create knowledge as we interact) meant that my "methodological values lent discipline and systemization to my enquiries" (Whitehead and McNiff 2006: 25). I would endeavour to detect these values in my practice and to notice when they were conspicuous by their absence. I would then discuss this with critical friends as part of the validation process – this was termed social validation. For Schön (1983), the process of reflection-in-action is central to the 'art' by which practitioners sometimes deal well with situations of uncertainty, instability, uniqueness, and value conflict. And because qualitative research is often defined by uncertainty, fluidity, and emergent ideas, so too, argues Lincoln (1995), must the validity criteria be flexible. Significantly for me, as I critiqued the notion of effectiveness, McNiff et al. (2003: loc. 135) reminded me that "To be action research, there must be *praxis* rather than practice. Praxis is informed, committed action that gives rise to knowledge rather than just successful action."

In the role of researcher, it was essential that I made authoritative claims to knowledge. This was to be achieved by demonstrating how I improved my personal practice in the classroom, and my discernment of the process. I needed to articulate what it was that I had come intuitively to do. In addition, as my study was a collaborative venture, I needed to show how I improved the wider educational situation – for pupils and colleagues who were affected by my work (McNiff et al. 2003).

Living Logics

In order to achieve these aims, I embraced the concept of living logics to transform my practice and to make sense of my experiences. By now, I was aware that propositional logic esteems the security of structure. As Biesta (2014: 3) observes: "We live in impatient times … the call to make education strong, secure, predictable, and risk-free is an expression of this impatience." Fromm (1941) claims that the greatest fear is the fear of freedom, whilst Rayner (2005) suggests that it is the fear of uncertainty (quoted in Whitehead and McNiff 2006: 37). I could detect these ideas in the literature as well as in my lived experience of schools. In an era of accountability, it operated as an undercurrent beneath much of the practice and procedures I participated in and observed. I came to realise and admit that fear, however well it was masked through dominance, assertiveness, or bravado, was ingrained deep within my psyche. This is considered in Part IV.

If propositional modes of thinking championed an emphasis on truth and the elimination of contradiction, dialogical forms of logic placed a value on rightness, on asking questions, dialogue, and modification. It is grounded in contradiction – an acceptance that there are multiple ways of thinking, holding one and the many together at the same time. I liked that: it suggested to me that I could begin to discern this feeling that I was pushing and pulling at the same time, acting in ways which were contrary to what I believed and valued. However, it was the description of living logics which enthused and energised me to investigate beyond the superficial answers which were so readily available upon a cursory search on the Internet.

Whitehead and McNiff (2006) caution that living logics, or modes of thought, are risky; exciting, but risky. Their work encouraged me to make a commitment to risk as I operated on the brink, not knowing what the next step would be, accepting that embracing the present would help to create an unknown future. I loved this perspective, as part of my research revealed that much of my waking day was spent under the burden of 'living' in the future, whilst my quiet moments were consumed with reliving the past (encounters, conflicts, decisions, etc.). An exemplar is offered in Chapter 19. Through this lens I could see potential in everything, and became open to the idea of working with colleagues in a later research cycle (see Chapter 25). The opportunity for collaboration was liberating for someone who had become increasingly insular since swapping the PE department for an RE classroom. When the last pupil entered the room and I closed the door behind him/her, the domain had become my kingdom – I was overly possessive about my space and entrenched in my thinking.

Living logics are inclusional of both propositional and dialectical forms of thinking, and open to the possibility of synthesising. It was important that I didn't throw the baby out with the bathwater; there would still be a requirement to teach the content, occasions when I would need to direct learning, and instances when I would have to deal with disruption. The techniques I continued to employ simply derived from a more considered perspective, which was underpinned by core values to which I had made a commitment.

I was further enticed by a description of living logics as, "The shift in perception … focussed on the development of a relationally dynamic awareness of space and boundaries with other people … the boundaries are co-created and flow with space" (Whitehead and McNiff 2006: 40). Drawing on Bassey (1995), Whitehead (1998: 3) extends the ambiguous nature of the concept and its dependence upon specific situational contexts: "A *boundary* can be defined in space and time, for example as a particular classroom … or, in a particular period; or it may be defined as a particular person, or group of people, at a particular time and in a particular space."

Whitehead (1998: 3) advises that "By researching one's own professional practice as a 'singularity' within a particular social and professional context [such as the classroom], [I] can contribute to a new paradigm of educational research." Bassey (1995: 111) offers a definition of singularity as: "a set of anecdotes about particular events occurring within a stated boundary, which are subjected to systematic and critical search for some truth. This truth, while pertaining to the inside of the boundary, may stimulate thinking about similar situations elsewhere." It is my hope that readers of this book will recognise something of their individual state and circumstances in my experiences.

In the next chapter, I broaden my definition of 'boundary' with my conception of the classroom as an 'open system'. I acknowledge that the contextual interactions I observe, experience, and record are informed by elements external to the immediate environment under scrutiny. Aspects such as pupils' prior knowledge, relationships with peers, the curriculum, the school culture, and so on all feed into the classroom to remind me that, in reality, boundaries are permeable.

That accepted, I could now imagine the possibilities for my study, and could conceive its potential to help colleagues who recognised the struggles, the successes, and the scenarios I was encountering. I had established LET as a methodology which would enable me to articulate my specific contribution to classroom life, but I needed to show context. I shared the space – the boundaries – with groups of children who, as I will show in Part III, have the capacity to morph into different collective entities on an hourly basis. Dilemmas resided in situations as well as in individuals. I needed to cater for this reality, if the decisions I made to enhance teaching and learning were to be understood in context.

Chapter 9

Complexity

Sean

As we have seen, my work began by entertaining the notion of dilemmas, contradictions, and tension. I acknowledged paradox and interrogated instances of hypocrisy in my practice. I recognised control as a problematic term and traced its influence to systematic and institutional sources (which can emerge through ideology, discourse, and selective evidence). In Chapter 7, I described how I had identified propositional logic as being a key component in the perspective I held, categorising school practice as right or wrong, and even its participants as good or bad. My adoption of living logics invited me to tolerate risk and uncertainty. The test bed would be during lessons in the company of others. I needed to construct, and then commit to, the methodology I had identified as being integral to me living out my stated values.

Interactions

If LET shone a discerning light on my specific contribution to the group, complexity theory provided the rich terminology to illuminate the dynamic relations which manifested within the classroom. It offered an excellent contextual perspective: "a complexity ontology provides a way of thinking about institutions, cultures, groups and individuals *as systems of interactions* which are, in some ways, always unique" (Haggis 2008: 160; emphasis added). Thus, "conventional units of analysis in educational research (e.g. individuals, classes, schools, communities) should merge, so that the unit of analysis becomes a web or ecosystem" (Cohen et al. 2007: 33); that is, a web of interrelated learning which has, suggests Morrison (2008: 23), the potential to break "the simple linearity of positivism and behaviourism". It provided the nexus between macro and micro research, as I acknowledged that what I did was likely to be influenced by "local, regional, national and global policies and the power relations that sustain existing social formations" (Whitehead 2006).

This broad scope enabled me to position my study, as I sought to comprehend the group dynamics and consider how I might best influence the 16 groups which were part of my research. Ball (2013: loc. 1) encouraged me to believe that my intention might be feasible: "even in our woeful ignorance of why humans behave the way they do, it is possible to make some predictions about how they behave collectively. That is to say, we can make predictions about society even in the face of individual free will." Human-Vogel (2008: 99) observes that "Interactions have an emergent property that can perhaps be described as the atmosphere or culture of the particular classroom." With regard to the contribution of the class leader, she asserts that within these complex systems it is teachers who shape the learning environment, whilst recognising that some have a stronger impact than others.

This was the type of research and challenge which stimulated me over a six year period. Conceiving of the class as a complex system encouraged me to discern patterns of behaviour within the group and provided me with the terminology to describe it. I also grappled with critical incidents which had the potential to skew my perspective and sabotage my commitment to operate in accordance with my stated values.

Conceptual Fudge

Enticingly, Ball (2003: 5) identifies complexity as "a science of collective behaviour", whilst the Carnegie Corporation (1996) calls for value-laden dynamics such as 'school coherence' and 'classroom ambiance' to become subject to enquiry. However, although the tenets of complexity theory appeared attractive, I found it to be initially abstract and rather difficult to grasp – as Haggis (2008: 64) puts it, it is "conceptual fudge". By way of affirmation, Tosey (2002: 6) points out: "Many practitioners remark that complexity theory is conceptually interesting, but seems difficult to apply in practice." Clearly it had potential for my study; however, accounts of the theory were always tantalisingly incomplete. I had to search through countless abstract references to piece together a coherent picture which would provide me with a framework to proceed. Although this process might be interpreted as negative, for me the focus remained on the potential the theory offered to reconceptualise common phenomena. Comprehension of a number of key definitions, and its contrasting position in relation to positivist methodology, confirmed the possibilities that complexity theory offered as a discerning light to shine on educational endeavours.

Complexity theory, an umbrella term, offers a conceptual framework for analysing the behaviour of systems that consist of a large number of interacting components. It claims that order can emerge from apparent disorder – where certain phenomena appear to be chaotic or random, they are actually part of a larger coherent process – and that control is illusory.[1] These ideas, or more specifically their application to the classroom, grated with the propositional logic which had defined my career thus far, yet it chimed with perspectives integral to living logics. Complexity theory is associated with, although distinguished from, chaos theory (a pure mathematical concept).

1 The efficiency of a flock of birds serves to illustrate.

Computer simulations and the study of natural phenomena provide models and exemplars which offer an alternative representation of the universe to that which is deemed deterministic and ordered. The dominant positivist paradigm informs laboratory experiments and seeks to establish a simple cause and effect linearity. This logic and associated principles continue to underpin much classroom research, which strives to separate and measure variables through quantifiable means.

Complexity theory suggests that attributing a single cause to an outcome in the classroom is problematic: to reduce phenomena to a restricted number of variables, and then to focus only on certain factors, is to miss the necessary dynamic interaction of several parts. For example, a pupil's performance in maths may indeed be influenced by the method being used, but it may also be prejudiced by the student's relationship with the teacher, which peers s/he is sat near, whether setting is an issue, whether the lessons tend to be in the morning or afternoon, and so on. Baranger (2001) emphasises the point through a helpful metaphor: "If you study only a head, or only a trunk, or only a leg, you will never understand walking." Measurement, however acute, may tell us little of value about a phenomenon. As Cohen et al. (2007: 11) state:

> [The positivist] approach is less successful in its application to human behaviour where the immense complexity of human nature and the elusive and intangible quality of social phenomena contrast strikingly with the order and regularity of the natural world. This point is no more apparent than in the contexts of classroom and school where the problems of teaching, learning and human interaction present the positivistic researcher with a mammoth challenge.

Complex Adaptive Systems

The literature describes various attempts to conceptualise classroom life through complexity principles, arguing that many non-biological systems (e.g. classroom groupings) share most of the typical properties of complex biological systems. However, there is a special category of complex system which was created especially to accommodate living beings (Baranger 2001): the concept of the complex adaptive system emerged in the 1980s at the Santa Fe Institute in New Mexico (Alhadeff-Jones 2008). I found it refreshing to review classroom interactions through this lens. 'Complex' refers to the interconnectedness, 'adaptive' indicates that the pupils impact on the environment (and in turn the (local) environment affects them), whilst the 'system' is defined as a web of relationships. This enabled me to analyse the dynamic interplay as pupils adjusted their conduct when moving from lesson to lesson. The findings from this focus are presented in Part III. There it becomes apparent, indeed essential, that the teacher needs to be able to pre-empt and adjust to emergent conditions.

Horn (2008: 135) suggests that every teacher needs to understand and realise "that she is working within a sensitive learning ecology whose directions can be altered by small changes in the boundary conditions and interaction patterns of the classroom". For example, the butterfly effect, a phrase coined by meteorologist Edward Lorenz in 1972, alerts us to the sensitivity of initial conditions in having a disproportionate effect on unfolding events (Gleick 1987; Baranger 2001).[2] This principle made perfect sense to me. I was well aware how a seemingly insignificant altercation with one child could, in an instant, alter the whole atmosphere in the class. Or, as highlighted in Chapter 19, how the introduction of a single new pupil (often due to a 'managed move'), could have a disproportionate and detrimental impact upon the entire group.

In complexity theory, there is an acceptance that it is beyond our ability to study a system in its entirety; instead there is a recognition of the importance of local relationships. As illustrated in Figure 9.1, the buzzwords are 'self-organisation' and 'emergence' because the theory seeks to understand how order and stability arise from the interactions of many components, according to a few simple rules (Mason 2008: 1).[3] Whilst I will engage with these simple principles in later chapters, I offer a word of caution. Models and theories which reduce complexity to a handful of rules are not pure 'representations of reality'; instead, they should be viewed as provisional: tools designed to help us renegotiate our world.

My application of this tool provided me with a fresh lens to analyse class dynamics, low level disruptions, and teaching and learning interactions – to articulate the tacit knowledge I had acquired over the years. In response to the notion that control is illusory, I focused my energies on how I might influence (learners) and manage (situations and environments). The acceptance that ultimately I can't control others was liberating, and the corresponding idea that I could only control myself made sense, although in my experience it was sometimes easier said than done.

Whilst the concepts of complexity theory, such as control and self-organisation, are the everyday stuff of educational discourse, the elusiveness inherent in the theory was well documented in the literature. It does not represent a neat prescriptive solution, and there is no unified view of the nature of complexity theory. Complex systems exhibit emergent behaviour as agents or individuals interact. Although patterns might be apparent there

2 The flapping of a butterfly's wings in Brazil can cause a tornado in Texas.
3 Nature provides an ant colony as a perfect example of self-organisation.

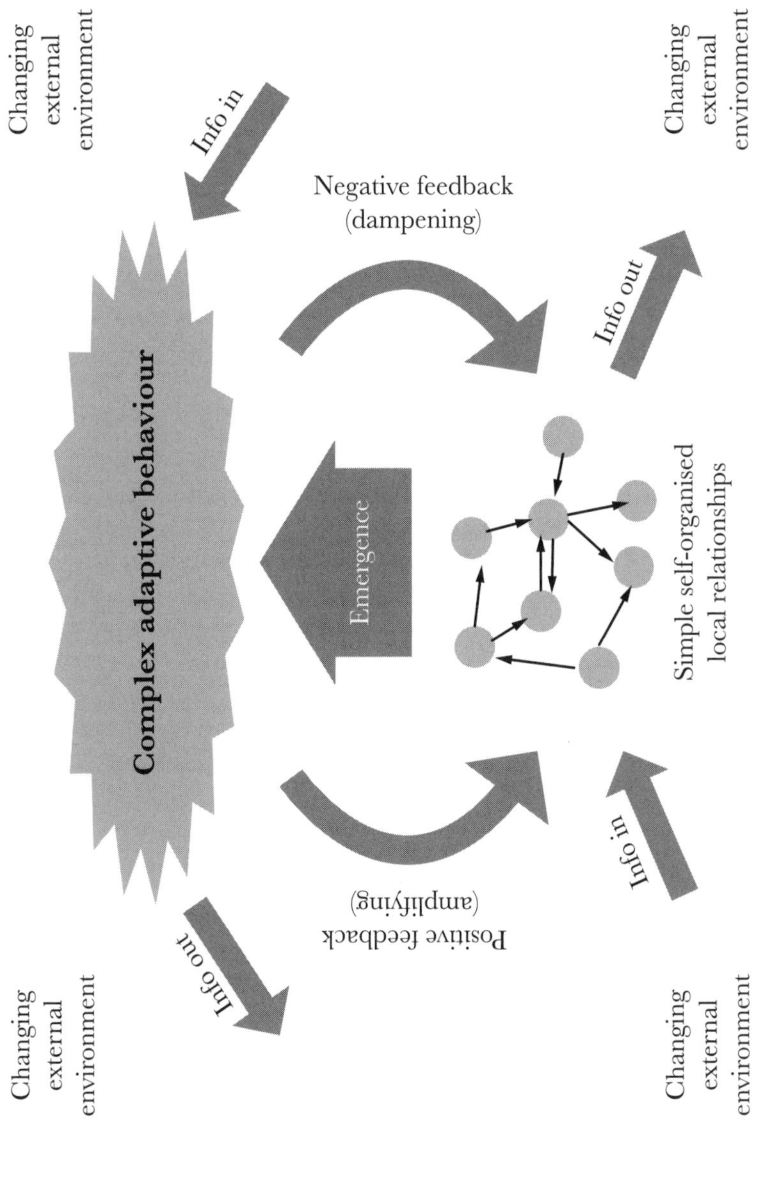

Figure 9.1. Complex adaptive behaviour

Source: D. Calvin Andrus, Wikimedia/Creative Commons Attribution-Share Alike 3.0 Unported

is always scope for unpredictability.[4] I could easily see an application for my impending study of class dynamics. I now had terminology to recognise, anticipate, and name it.

'Is' Not 'Ought'

In an era where diktat is the method most convenient to policy makers, Kuhn (2008: 178) warns that there is a danger of drifting into the erroneous misapplication of a paradigm's essence because, "Complexity metaphors are descriptive but are often taken as prescriptive … complexity's 'is' is moved into an 'ought', an injunction to change 'how things are' (that is, to make them self-organising, dynamic and emergent)." This descriptor chimed with my evolving perspective which viewed classrooms as essentially adaptive environments. Thus, whilst my work acknowledged these concerns, it embraced Kuhn's invitation to consider which aspects of complexity I found useful and to identify how these ideas related to other discourses and beliefs with which I engaged. This allowed me to proceed with confidence, despite lacking expertise in the area – it gave me the permission to learn and to be creative in my application.

However, it is important for me not to present complexity theory as the antidote to the dominance of positivism in the sphere of education. Like other methodological approaches, it has its limitations. The tenets are unlikely to be embraced by school leaders who are immersed in an education system in which they are accountable, according to Morrison (2008: 21), for the: "Regulated prescriptions of governments for the aims, content, pedagogy and assessment of learning and education … and constant surveillance of an individual's performance against predicted targets." He adds that the theory's comments "on autocatalysis and self-organization fit poorly to systems of schooling whose hidden curricula comprise obedience, compliance, passivity and conformity, unequal power, delay, denial, rules, rituals and routines" (2008: 28).

Morrison reminds us that "Complexity theory under-theorises power … regarding it as the momentum of the moment; it gives no guarantees; it is a theory without responsibility or accountability [hence] the charge of relativism is one complexity theory cannot shake off" (2008: 26, 28). Applying complexity theory to educational research involves researchers in a complicated process of marrying complexity habits of thought with a range of aims. It means "recognising that complexity theory, per se, does not have an ethical intent. *It is the researcher who is committed to human betterment*" (Kuhn 2008: 179; emphasis added).

4 Again, flocking suffices as an example from nature. Flocking can be described by the behaviour of individual birds, yet it is perhaps more accurate to say flocking is the behaviour that *emerges* from the behaviour of individual birds as they adapt to feedback.

Complexity theory, in offering only organisational principles, encourages researchers to engage in critical and reflective discourse about the nature of education and conceptual frameworks (Kuhn 2008: 177). I did this by selecting living educational theory and critical theory as integral to my methodology. However, in relation to the latter, I acknowledge Cohen et al.'s (2007: 30) critique that the emancipatory claims of action research "might be over-optimistic in a world where power is often through statute … the reality of political power seldom extends to teachers [so it] has little effect on the real locus of power". Going further, I am mindful of Mayes' (2010) findings which suggest that applied critical theories are often too simplistic, assuming that power can be straightforwardly transferred from the powerful to the powerless. Cohen et al.'s conclusion is that those approaches which remain theoretical fail to take into account the importance of micro-level actions and will not succeed in changing the power relations between teachers and pupils.

However, this did not distract from my individual contribution as I realigned my stated values and took responsibility for my influence; my work negotiated the creative tension that exists between the requirements of group structure and individual freedom (Chaltain 2009). I included pedagogical strategies which encouraged the pupils to be active learners: as I provided opportunities for greater independence, I encouraged them to be resilient and to set their own moral boundaries in response to the trust I afforded them. This defined my conception of improvement: it can tolerate episodes of apparent disorder, alongside the need for stability and boundaries; it places an emphasis on cooperation whilst recognising occasions when compliance is a requirement.

As the author of this research, I stood at the hub of the dynamic flow within my classroom, formulating a living theory which sought to find an authentic correlation between deeply held values and my conduct as an adult in a position of authority. I took full responsibility for contributing to the well-being of the children with whom I related. I recognised 'values' as a contested terrain which needed to be negotiated, and accepted that there are few overarching universal values (Berlin 1969). In problematising the question of values, I came to understand them as dependent upon social practices rather than as abstract principles (Raz 2003). I advanced their significance as key in determining the application of 'appropriate' authority to emergent behaviour in my classes. My core values provided a format and a structure for responding to individual incidents and contemplating their impact on my decisions, conduct, and relationships.

Clocks or Clouds?

Thus, I came to reconceptualise my classroom, recognising the difference between the terms 'complicated' and 'complex' (Alhadeff-Jones 2008). As Doll (2008: 187) articulates:

> In simple terms, one important for education, closed systems transfer and transmit, open systems transform … Closed systems function toward a pre-set goal, such as in the workings of a thermostat [or, as Haggis (2008) suggests, a mechanical engine or a clock]; open systems, in differentiation, function just to keep the right amount of imbalance, so that the system might maintain a creative dynamism.

Whilst the analogy emphasises how different parts are brought together to form a complicated whole – designed to function in a closed, predictable, and predetermined fashion – another is offered as representative of an open system – indeterminate and unpredictable – a *cloud*. Radford (2008: 144) explains that:

> The difference between 'clockish' and 'cloudish' perspectives is that of their usefulness in terms of explanations for the ways in which the universe seems to work … If we accept that the characteristics attended to by complexity theory are those that we experience in the world, then we may come to the conclusion that the reductive, analytical approach may be limited and misleading, as well as impracticable. Clouds do not lend themselves to this kind of analysis.

If these explanations appear vague and abstract, Radford proceeds to make a succinct point which captured my attention: "The question for educational researchers [and teachers] is whether schools are more like clocks or clouds" (2008: 144).

There is no doubting the reality that a functionalist system dominates one's experience of education in the UK – whether as a teacher or a pupil. With all of the competing interests, there is a sense that the system is intricate and complicated, having many different parts, but each part can be explained and is required to operate in a clockwork order in the name of efficiency. Quantitative data infused with market values encourages competition, demands accountability, and invites prediction – there is a quest for 'what works' in accordance to predetermined criteria. As a result, researchers seek to find out which parts are most useful, thereby enabling practitioners to be ever more efficient and effective in their delivery. I have experienced the resultant tension. I detected the strain between apparently conflicting parts of the system, and became agitated by the constraints.

Consistent with my positioning in Chapter 7, my answer to the clocks or clouds question (as illustrated by the composed/superior optical illusion from Chapter 1) is both. Schools do function like clocks, but their inhabitants, despite conditioning, remain essentially autonomous and interdependent. I consider the 'clockish' state to be contrived and entangled in tradition and ideology: schools generally exist in accordance with a depiction of how things *ought* to be – they emphasise the reactive character's features, drawn with defined, prominent lines in accordance with propositional logic. And yet the presence of a second profile, however faint, reminds us that we are coexisting human beings whose potential and respective worth cannot be defined by a number.

However well-organised schools and classes are, there is always scope for unpredictability. For some teachers, I would suggest that this is what makes their job interesting, even exciting. But, on some occasions, the unpredictability comes in the form of disruptive behaviour from individual pupils. The volatility can disturb the teacher's sense of order and well-being; the instability can impinge on the harmonious state of the group. In the following chapters, I will attempt to shine a light on this tension by critiquing the phenomenon of frequent low level disruptions – events which can leave the teacher feeling decidedly under the weather. I sought to understand the different degrees of resistance which manifest as pupils test, resist, and challenge boundaries.

Part III

Degrees of Resistance: Low Level Disruptions

Chapter 10

Variance

Sean

Ofsted's *Below the Radar* (2014) contains a couple of sentences which are largely lost amidst the headline findings. Beyond the emphasis on whole school organisational responses to quell low level disruption, it hints at complexity. It mentions (but does not elaborate on) the fact that children are well versed at adapting their behaviour according to context and circumstance:

> This *variation is at the heart of the problem* and is confirmed by inspection evidence, which shows that variation in behaviour not only exists between schools but can also be found across different classes within a school … behaviour in different classes commonly varied from good to inadequate and, on occasions, was outstanding …
>
> The same students were observed behaving impeccably in other lessons with different teachers. Students echoed these observations by indicating that their behaviour varied according to the teacher. (Ofsted 2014: 10, 23; emphasis added)

My own experiences underlined the validity of this observation. In 2003, whilst working for the local authority as a behaviour and attendance consultant, I visited the most deprived school in the county. The newly appointed head teacher gave me an interesting task: "Shadow the most disruptive Year 8 and Year 9 pupils and tell me something of their experience."

The first morning set the tone for the next two days. Equipped with a timetable, I located my Year 8 companions. Period 1 seemed to confirm all I had heard about this school. The arrogance and disdain on display convinced me that some of these kids ought not to be in mainstream schooling: the children neglected to even test or resist; instead they openly challenged the adult seeking to teach them, before dismissing her. A significant minority ignored the teacher throughout the lesson, bar engaging in exchanges which undermined her authority for the benefit of their classmates. The majority were indifferent. The poor woman might as well have been invisible. I felt embarrassed for her as I sat in a corner at the back of the room and simply recorded all that I saw and heard. Clearly, having a visitor from the local authority was no deterrent – I sensed my presence actually provided an audience for this exhibition of the 'Wild West'. And then the bell went to signal the end of a long hour and a change of lesson.

Keeping my distance, I continued to observe as I made my way from the mobile classrooms and through the bustling crowds towards the main block. Waiting for the group was a small woman with a big smile. She greeted them and a conversion occurred before my eyes. The same children transformed into the most polite and diligent bunch of inquisitive learners you could hope to meet. Seemingly oblivious to the hypocrisy, several even acknowledged me for the first time that day to ask if I would like to see their work! And so the pattern was set. Periods 3, 4, and 5 continued to illustrate the students' roller-coaster performance.

The same spectrum was repeated the following day as I shadowed a notorious group of Year 9 pupils, and watched them adapt their entire personae, seemingly at will, on an hourly basis. At one point a 'leader' chatted to me between lessons. Somehow it emerged that we shared an interest in boxing and I was elevated to top man as the lad endorsed me to his mates. This experience reaffirmed for me, or more accurately reminded me (for I too was a pupil once), that behaviour changes according to context and has a tendency to magnify in the presence of certain peers and adults. I recall that this malleable response to authority was acutely apparent during my time as a PE teacher. On the two occasions I have in mind, the pupils, the adult, and the site were near identical – just one variable differed. Firstly, when refereeing an inter-house football match I noted that there was a tendency for my Year 9 boys to dispute, even challenge, some of my decisions. It was then fascinating to observe the very same cohort accept every ruling I made when refereeing a rugby game. It seemed that each code shaped the expectations and manifested in both the individual and collective conduct.

It was ridiculous not to realise this, I know, but when taking a lesson I neglected to consciously look too far beyond the behaviour that the pupils exhibited with me. Of course I was aware of the discrepancy between my experience of them and their conduct elsewhere – because I took the detentions and read the detention reports – but the sheer velocity of adaption took me aback. In my own school, every time I had visited another lesson the pupils' conduct naturally changed as a result of my presence, status, and our relationships. I am reminded of the comment that the Queen must think the entire world smells of fresh paint!

This dilemma intrigued me. Subsequently, one of my stated objectives was 'to better understand contextual factors which influence whether my pupils are more or less likely to disrupt learning'. To gain depth and provide perspective for my own data, I surveyed theory and literature. I sought to challenge the fallacy of a prominent moralistic discourse which, for convenience, labels pupils as 'good' or 'bad' in accordance with their behaviour. Araújo (2005: 264) legitimised my intended line of enquiry:

> Official and teachers' understandings of indiscipline opened a space for the polarization of perceptions of pupils' behaviour, as being either disruptive or disrupted. However, indiscipline in real classrooms is more fluid than official and teachers' discourses allow. Disruptive pupils are not always disruptive, as those who tend to behave well are not necessarily disrupted or behave well on all occasions. In a given classroom situation it may only be possible to position a couple of pupils at each extreme end of a behaviour spectrum, but most pupils would fall in the middle. Pupils do not merely slip into disruptive or disrupted bodies; rather, discipline is negotiated daily in classrooms through interactions with both teachers and peers.

Positionality

Araújo's description encompassed Foucault's (1980) notion of power. The French philosopher had identified discipline as an exercise of power operating within the minutiae of practices inside schools. This discourse of power as mobile and contingent includes the possibility of resistance (Youdell 2011) through low level disruptions. Thompson's (2010) exploration of the hegemonic good student challenges polarised descriptors of pupils, arguing that the notion of the 'good' student is antithetical to the lived experience of students, as they too negotiate their positionality within complex power games in secondary schools. As with the 'naughty' child, the 'ideal' pupil (Hempel-Jorgensen 2009) is immersed within competing and contradictory discourses and micro-practices of power. I continue to find the playing out of these undercurrents fascinating. Resisting the temptation to blame or to instantly quash, my research provided a platform for me to decipher this complexity.

The power/resist dynamic is accurately articulated through this emotive quote from the Department for Education's memorandum on behaviour and discipline in schools:

> Bad behaviour spreads like a cancer; it is very difficult to contain it. One very badly behaved student impacts on a second one, who is quite badly behaved. It spreads, so that even the very good students become somewhat unsettled. That creates a situation where you have low-level behaviour. People often dismiss that, and say, "It's just low-level behaviour, that's okay". You'd be amazed, however, at how disruptive low-level behaviour is. (DfE 2011d: 11)

This description will resonate with most teachers. It conveys a pervading sense of disorder, of escalation. The literature is awash with terms which qualify low level disruption, such as incessant chatter, answering back, inattention, and other forms of nuisance that irritate staff and interrupt learning. Testimonies from teachers in primary and secondary schools are used by Ofsted (2014) to illustrate low level disruptive behaviour, and include talking to each other (not about the work), texting, calling out answers instead of raising a hand, swinging on chairs, tapping pens, turning round, quietly humming, rolling eyes at the teacher, or other impolite gestures. One could interpret these examples as simply a lack of good manners or a general lack of respect. I have some sympathy with that view. However, in the cold light of day, the list of misdemeanours doesn't read as overly offensive. It strikes me that my inherent reaction to punish appears quite irrational. I confess that I had levelled the same (silent) judgement of irrationality at colleagues, as I observed and intervened in altercations between teachers and pupils. Here, sporting my high visibility waistcoat to affirm my on-call status, I was rationality personified as I calmed the situation and sought a logical solution for all involved. There was an emotional distance so I was sufficiently removed from the circumstances to fulfil my task effectively. How bizarre then that this professional response could so easily regress to a personal reaction when *I* was the teacher being undermined or challenged, and a random colleague (regardless of their hierarchal position) arrived in their luminous outfit to calmly resolve the situation *I* was in danger of escalating.

As a researcher, I was intrigued to decipher what exactly was going on in these common and reoccurring incidents. I suspected it had something to do with power, authority, interpretation, perspective, roles, context, needs … I couldn't quite grasp it. But what I did know was that the observable behaviour was only the tip of the iceberg. It was uncomfortable to admit it, but for me it may have had something to do with fear, because disturbing dreams (not quite nightmares) were testimony to the mild panic which occasionally descended when I found myself feeling powerless in front of an unruly class. The fact that I never had the displeasure of feeling truly helpless and vulnerable was apparently irrelevant to my subconscious, as I tossed and turned in the small hours. I drew periodically on snippets of literature, theories, and analysis of my own data in an attempt to gain a clear and coherent understanding of these situations – each one qualifies as generic, yet is also paradoxically unique.

Back in the classroom, a retreat to sanctions or consequences offered predictable answers to narrow and insular questions about what needed to be done. My challenge was to look beyond the behaviour and the quick fix, to momentarily put aside the urge for harsher discipline. As we have seen, I had already charted that course: I knew what worked. In accordance with Ofsted's (2014) recommendations, I was well aware of the strengths that came with a stringent organisational approach, but I also became acutely aware of its limitations. I was now concerned with the obscured psychological and operational effects on those charged with administering a rudimentary behaviour policy. Equally concerning was my realisation that in my quest to become consistent I had inadvertently become progressively inflexible.

I wanted to ask other questions which risked being passed over because they lent themselves to complex lines of enquiry, rather than convenient and simplistic answers. I wanted to delve into the nuances to see if it was possible to identify variables which might affect the likeliness of misconduct and the degrees of resistance. Perhaps even more important for my research, I sought to comprehend emergent perspectives which might help me to reinterpret misconduct. All easier said than done, especially when disruption is taken as a personal slight and provokes an overwhelming urge to indiscriminately reclaim control, regardless of the potential harm to individuals or relationships. I wanted to understand the interactions better and I wanted to find out why, despite my convictions, children's seemingly insignificant acts too often sabotaged my best intentions. Critical awareness, such as those illustrated in earlier chapters, was only one side of the coin. My self-awareness did not arrive as a formula; it emerged over a period of time.

In the meantime, the drip, drip of obstructive pupil behaviour, and my reaction to it, would act as a constant barometer. The group dynamic described in the Department for Education memorandum (DfE 2011d) provided the test bed for my research: it represented a bridge between the macro and the micro. Through each of these possibilities, I wanted to consider how I might, in Bill Rogers' (2006) terms, "crack the hard class".

Chapter 11

Weather Forecast

Sean

To gain a fresh perspective I utilised insights from a number of theories. (If in doubt, Jack Whitehead's helpful advice is to simply exchange the word 'theory' for 'explanation'.) I used identity theory, originally formulated by Stryker (1968, 1980, 1987; Stryker and Serpe 1982), to explore the mediatory space between social structure (Burke 2004) and the individual (Stets and Burke 2000). Hogg et al. (1995) explain it as the self being constructed through multiple identities that reside in circumscribed practices (e.g. norms, roles). This view invites a consideration of individuals' role related behaviours within the institutional structure. According to Stryker, role identities are defined as distinct components of self – that is, self-conceptions that people apply to themselves as a consequence of the structural role positions they occupy (Burke 2004).

As I was interested in studying the pupils *in situ*, rather than in isolation, I extended my reading to social identity theory. I sought to look beyond pupils' identities as individual learners to see how they negotiated the institutional roles they occupied – that is, to understand how they form and adjust their identities according to organisational structures and situational cues.

The emphasis on the social self, through studying inter-group relations and group processes, resonated with the principles of complexity theory which would provide the structure for my investigation. Referring back to Baranger's thought (2001), "If you study only a head, or only a trunk, or only a leg, you will never understand walking," I read this as being descriptive of my experience of watching pupils abandon apparent gains made through one-to-one behaviour intervention when they were reintegrated back into the classroom dynamic. I was particularly interested to comprehend the make-up of 'problem' groups which seemed to consistently walk with a metaphorical limp! I would turn my attention to the subtle patterns of interactions in an attempt to recognise and articulate, even to anticipate and steer.

'Can' Not 'Do'

Firstly, I wanted to interrogate the validity of the broadly accepted and seemingly innocuous terms which categorise young people's behaviour. In previous chapters I have drawn attention to the moralistic terms 'good' and 'bad'; here I ponder the all too convenient use of 'majority' and 'minority'. I have already asserted that politicians, the media, inspectors, and certain researchers have a propensity to misrepresent young people's behaviour. Therefore, it may seem strange that I would question a statement from the Steer report (2005: 5) which appears to defend the conduct of students. The report, in line with Ofsted (2005) findings, claims: "the great majority of pupils work hard and behave well". Note, not just the majority (conceivably 51%), but the *great* majority. I believe that the quotation has some substance, and yet the terminology invites further scrutiny for it is illustrative of sweeping, uncontested generalisations and subsequently simplistic solutions. The statement insinuates that the vast majority 'do' work hard and behave well – period. It omits any consideration of the issue at the core of this chapter: variance. I produced evidence which showed that it would be more accurate to say that the vast majority of pupils 'can' work hard and behave well, but they do not necessarily do so all of the time. This may initially appear to be an irrelevant detail, but I suggest that this understanding can help to frame the disciplinary approach that we, as teachers, employ because it contextualises our perspectives and filters our experiences.

In addition to using the term 'majority' to associate individuals with working hard and behaving well, the reader is also invited to presume the opposite and associate poor conduct with a 'minority' who do *not* work hard or behave well. Although my study affirmed my own experience of schools (in particular, when running detentions and the isolation unit that there is indeed a hard core – a significant minority), I firmly believe that *all* pupils can display these positive qualities, and on occasion do.

Attributing desirable and undesirable behaviour to broad categories of unidentified pupils lends itself to a moralising view of children. Such language conjures up polarised conceptions of young people as good/bad and conformist/deviant, and conveniently contributes to a discourse of crime and punishment. Yilmaz (2009) associates the historical view that individuals are hereditarily bad with consequential strictness, which is traditionally associated with schools. This puritanical view of children's behaviour leads to notions of socialising, taming, civilising, and disciplining through punishment. This chimed with my own early default position, irrespective of the perspectives I espoused and the impression I gave at events like parents' evenings and open evenings. The phrase 'zero tolerance' had come to legitimise my intolerance of disruption. However, Downes and Rock (2011: 144) argue that our reaction to deviant behaviour can alter when we realise that it is "a variable, not a constant". Waterhouse (2004: 74) concurs, stating: "the labelling tradition has been particularly sensitive to recognizing that the origins of deviance are to be found not in the characteristics and dispositions of 'deviants', but in the interpersonal processes occurring in situated incidents". These interactions represented my site of interest, with the incessant political interference providing the broader context.

The research process afforded me an opportunity to review, and become more sensitive to, the quandaries facing students in the classroom – to pause and look beneath the observable, obstructive behaviour which so often equated to instant retort or reprimand. I had long been instinctively dismissive of the very idea that pupils' ploys might in any way be deemed a valid response to their school experience (often expressed in an inappropriate way). I effortlessly assigned individuals to categories based on my limited experience of them; when teaching, I effectively defined them as either behaving or not behaving, and tended to treat them in accordance with these circumscribed beliefs.

Conduct Offers Up Clues

I began to consider the purposes behind a pupil's behaviour – could it be a crude indicator that a child was feeling psychologically vulnerable? However, I was keen not to restrict this variable to those children with SEN. I was interested in any pupil who found it difficult to cope with academic tasks and the prospect of being seen to fail; those who struggled with working memory functions such as retaining and processing information; those who had to constantly deal with the challenges of fitting in and negotiating interpersonal relationships with peers. That consequential behaviours, defined as low level disruptions, might be defensive mechanisms seemed too complicated, too inconvenient, and threatened to compromise the instant 'solution' offered by 'telling off' and sanctions.

There is yet another layer to this complexity, which is often bypassed when commentators resort uncritically to espousing the need to take control. I tread carefully, but I feel compelled to draw attention to pupils' experience of being regulated and curtailed as a matter of course. It is not the whole story, but it is part of the equation. I am thinking specifically of times when they are forced to absorb boring, irrelevant content. I have to be frank and admit that I have empathised with the plight of some classes as I sat at the back, also enduring a lesson which was quite some way from being educational, interesting, or engaging. I understand the temptation to break the tedium, if only momentarily, by chatting or turning around (two of the descriptors used to define low level disruption). At the risk of sounding patronising, it is highly likely that on these occasions colleagues were simply doing what they had learned to do or had time to do. (I also need to stress that I am not suggesting that I have captivated and inspired every class I've ever taught – far from it.) I can also draw on parallel experiences as a trainee in lectures, and even as an established teacher when I have been obliged to sit through INSETs, and been bored stupid. Obviously, I was far too responsible to have been outwardly disruptive, but I have been irritated and resentful that my finite time was being wasted. So I empathise, even sympathise, with the children and adults who partake in this uncomfortable dance. And I am not surprised that blame becomes the currency, as participants point fingers at each other whilst the organisational and ideological levers which frame and constrain the interaction continue to go unexamined.

The purpose of making these points is to advance a more considered approach, which at least pauses to question the legitimacy of resorting indiscriminately to simplistic and unsophisticated behaviourist strategies which derive from this predisposition to blame. If only it was as neat and tidy as dividing into conformist/deviant or reward/punishment. The literature shows that behaviourist experiments carried out in labs are atypical and that, despite providing useful principles for discussions around discipline, their application has limitations in light of the array of intricate needs within the dynamic classroom. Approaches such as Assertive Discipline, for example, tend to restrict their coverage to the need for limits to substantiate their polarised philosophy and methodology – and, of course, to promote their multi-million pound franchises. Schools are a bit more complex than that.

Therefore, addressing the headline concerns around low level disturbances, I wanted to challenge the false impression that pupils are either exclusively disruptive or disrupted, to flesh out the undeveloped Ofsted (2014: 10) assertion that variance is "at the heart of the problem". If this was so, it would require me to focus my energy on becoming progressively aware, increasingly skilful, to pre-empt and respond to unique contextual interactions. I wanted to drill down and investigate the conditions which prompted those individuals in the archetypal 'majority' to join in with disruption, and to identify the variables and nuances which determined whether pupils who are typically associated with the 'minority' choose to behave well. If I could reframe the problem, then schools might question the validity of resorting to traditional solutions and arbitrary sanctions by default – because 'they work'. The Ofsted (2014) report states that students vary their behaviour according to the teacher. Clearly, then, the adult is a key variable. Their qualities and the impression they make on the audience require scrutiny. I present my pupils' collective evaluation in Chapters 13 and 14.

Possibility of Localised Showers

In accordance to complexity theory principles, I held that schools were essentially responsive to emergent properties inherent in natural phenomena – metaphorically, like the formation of clouds. I also subscribed to Ginott's (1972: 10) assertion that it is the teacher's personal approach that creates the climate and it is their daily mood that makes the weather. Thus, I conceived the idea of employing the metaphor of weather to denote classroom behaviour:

Since I typically had the pupils' company for only one hour per week, I sought to extend my knowledge of them. I needed to be able to compare the actions I witnessed in my class with their general performance – that is, my pupils' susceptibility to disrupt.[1] I asked them about their conduct in other lessons and stipulated that they were not to name teachers or subjects. Each student (*n.* 334) independently provided a self-evaluation of the percentage of time they considered themselves to be motivated to do well. To be helpful, respectful, and cause no disruptions to learning would be termed Blue Skies or Sunshine. The times when they were not very disruptive but tended to be unmotivated was to be labelled White Cloud. These two categories together constitute the idea of 'order' in a classroom. This phrase was not subjected to critique in the Ofsted (2014) report; consequently, I address this to make the distinction between cooperation and compliance.

Now to the notion of disorder – the aspect which tends to get most attention. I proposed a third category which was termed Grey Cloud. It represented those times when pupils tended to join in with disruptive behaviour, if others were doing it and they thought they could get away with it. A brief explanation was provided: "This is usually in the form of low level disruptions like calling out, talking over the teacher, etc." The final category asked students to think of times when they showed a determined effort not to learn, to disrupt the lesson, and to make things difficult for their teacher. Here we have the notion of Rain Cloud. Together Grey Clouds and Rain Clouds constitute Dark Cloud behaviour. Pupils were asked to allocate their

1 A limitation of my research was that I did not distinguish between mixed ability and setting to explore whether this was a significant factor.

100% across the descriptors and were informed that 0% was a valid response.

In addition, a proportion of the original cohort of respondents (*n.* 241) were asked firstly to estimate the amount of disruption they witnessed in their classes around the school, and then to consider to what degree they joined in with the disruption. Analysis of their responses to these three interrelated questions provided broad strokes for comprehending behaviour in the school. The correlated data sought to delve beneath the successive Ofsted judgements of 'good' for behaviour which were awarded to the school during this research period.

It is important to point out that my data, whilst inviting quantitative answers to kindle qualitative responses, was not intended to be statistically significant. I did, however, find it fascinating to consider how the different segments of data could conceivably be misconstrued to substantiate hypothetical media headlines. For example, I found that for a majority of time (55%) pupils witnessed disruption in their lessons (in fact, my research produced evidence to suggest that *every child* experienced some disorder in their lessons (*n.* 241)). At first sight this appears to be damning. However, whilst we learn that only 45% of the week was devoid of disturbances, significantly, during the disruptive 55%, the pupils in those classes displayed self-discipline for 80% of the time by not joining in. This affirms that the decision of whether to engage in low level disruptive behaviour is highly selective for most pupils. Later in this part I will discuss which factors informed and influenced pupils' decisions.

Going a little deeper into this reported self-disciplined response (which indicates that for the majority of time most pupils did not actively obstruct learning even when they witnessed others disrupting), we might assume that, if able, those who were amenable were attentive to the task at hand and learning. However, the data revealed that around a third of the time pupils were not engaged but coped by being passively compliant. This pliable condition applied periodically to the vast majority of the 334 students surveyed, as only five claimed they were motivated to do well in *all* of their lessons by recording 100% for Blue Skies. Later, in Chapter 13, students describe the types of teachers who encourage these states.

An Assumption of Quality

This, of course, has implications for learning and provokes a number of philosophical and pedagogical questions in light of Steer's (2005: 2; emphasis added) assertion that "the *quality* of learning, teaching and behaviour in schools are inseparable issues". Subsequently, I pondered the distinction between disciplinarian and educator, and I was reminded that being effective at getting the class to work well is not the same thing as being an effective teacher. The Ofsted (2014) report, for example, makes an uncritical association between learning and teaching to substantiate its headline claim: "pupils are potentially losing up to an hour of *learning* each day ... This is the equivalent of 38 days of *teaching* lost each year" (Ofsted 2014: 4–5; emphasis added). Yet the act of teaching does not necessarily equate to learning, and the report does not even raise the issue of quality – it is presumed. Sarah's diary extract (in Chapter 1) serves to illustrate this. Learning is not necessarily a linear transaction that is transmitted from adult to pupil in the allotted hour just because the location is a classroom. I think it would be more accurate to have said, "losing up to an hour of *potential* learning", for the concept of learning needs to be distinguished from performance; learning can only be inferred, and I suggest that the *potential* is largely dependent on the adult and the *quality* of the interaction.

As I contemplated the notion of quality, I was mindful of how often my own children were taught by non-specialists, cover, supply, or trainee teachers who were learning their trade. I pondered whether the complex and contested notion of learning is sometimes reduced to students being quietly occupied. Here, I plead guilty as I recall the limited capacity I had to contribute to learning in cover lessons or when my timetable required me to 'teach' other subjects. Restricted by time and more pressing priorities, I tended to operate just a chapter in advance of the students. Inevitably, I was stumped if they asked questions which were not in my notes, or if they veered from the prescribed chapter or the lesson plan I had inherited. I can assure you that it was not quality teaching and learning in comparison to that experienced by other children who happened to be paired with the head of department or faculty. Likewise, as a head of department, I can recall how many times I had to dumb down lessons and provide a skeleton version to colleagues from other departments who had been assigned to me for the year. And also how often it was senior leaders who got called into a last minute meeting, so palming off the delivery of the lesson to a cover or supply teacher. If Ofsted wish to raise the issue of precious time lost in lessons, I reflect on how much potential learning is compromised by the increasing necessity of using non-specialist teachers to fill in. And I have not even begun to consider the implications of schools employing adults who are not qualified to teach.

It is these contextual realities that provide the backdrop for my pupils' evaluations of their conduct in light of the adult allotted to them. I wonder if, in the mind of some teachers (specialist or non-specialist), an ordered classroom – regardless of pupils' levels of cognitive engagement – is seen as a positive indicator of learning, as evidence for assessors, or even as the antidote to disruption. I suggest that keeping children busy, as I habitually did when forced to teach outside of my comfort zone, can represent containment – and an educational moment missed. I began to compare teaching as an act to teaching as a set of intentions (with a subsequent need to tolerate and be confident with uncertainty). I reflected that it was easier to do so when I was secure in my own subject knowledge. I confronted these questions as I researched my own practice, monitoring and reflecting on the impact of taking calculated risks – whether it might lead to more fruitful learning or simply provide opportunities for pupils to coast or play up.

In reporting that 55% of time spent in school could be categorised as disruptive, it is worth affirming that most pupils believed themselves to be responsible for making only a minimal contribution to disruption. However, substantiating the assertion that the disrupted are capable of disrupting, only 23 from the 334 maintained that they did not join in with disruption at all. Data analysis showed that those responsible for the majority of the 55% of time when learning opportunities were impeded could be traced to a few prominent classmates who were habitually disruptive, rather than selectively disruptive. The self-reporting 'significant minority' were responsible for initiating disruption (contributing to the 2–3% Rain Clouds), which encouraged others to join in when they deemed it safe to do so (13% Grey Clouds).

Paradoxically, despite identifying a significant minority who frequently and wilfully disrupted learning, only 13 of the pupils claimed they were completely devoid of cooperative behaviour in their lessons (by recording 0% for Blue Skies). As only one pupil was devoid of both Blue Skies and White Cloud compliant behaviour, the remaining 321 students – the great majority – can work hard and behave well *in certain circumstances*.

I wanted to understand the nuances which determined whether a child was likely to choose to be disruptive. I started with the notion of deterrence as a variable to bring about constraint – after all, according to responses from the second set of questions, collectively pupils resisted the temptation to join in 80% of the time when disruption was apparent. Were they predisposed or persuaded? Acknowledging the contribution of internal influences such as family, upbringing, and the child's own moral code to affect self-discipline, I reasoned that this amenable state might come from two key contextual sources: the specific teacher and the possibility of undesirable consequences. Later, I would probe even further by dissecting the comparative influence of variables such as curriculum subject, peers, and friends. However, initially I began plotting my evolving findings on the simplest of diagrams which symbolised the core ideas of complexity theory (Figure 11.1).

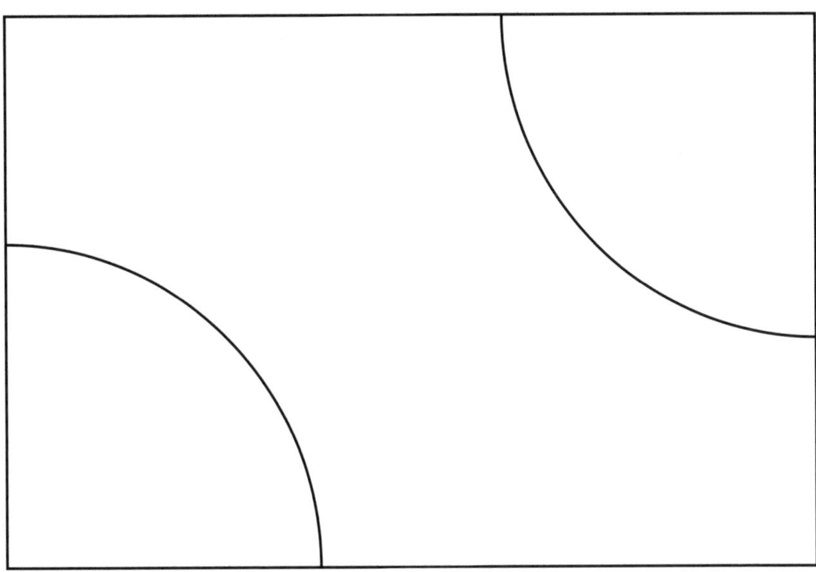

Figure 11.1. Complexity sectors

Chapter 12

Testing and Challenging Boundaries

Sean

The next step was to customise the template for the classroom (Figure 12.1).

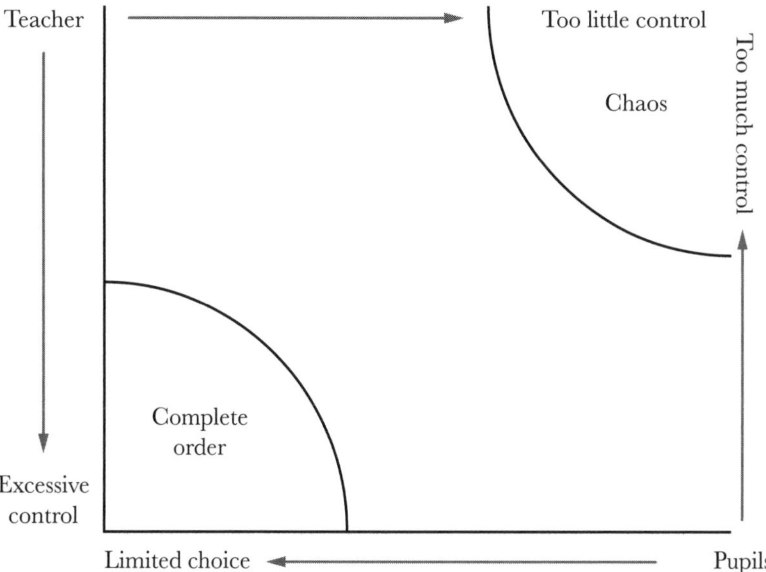

Figure 12.1. The polarised classroom

I used the term 'dynamic boundaries' to present two polarised segments. To the left we have complete order, to the right the idea of chaos (or disorder). The order of the left might be indicative of a very strict teacher, of the adult's status, or maybe an activity where the pupils are particularly attentive. I will argue that this requirement is sometimes necessary, but it can become suppressive if resorted to excessively. The curved boundary on the right indicates when pupils have 'crossed the line'. In conventional classrooms, one would expect to see a strong reprimand, sanction, consequence, or detention in response to unacceptable behaviour. Staff who blur this line through inconsistency or ineffective authority might be deemed by school leadership to be 'struggling' teachers, on the basis that unproductive disorder impinges on opportunities for learning. Later, I would ask my pupils to share their insights and perspectives of staff they intuitively identified as 'strong' and 'weak'. It would emerge that weak became synonymous with their conceptions of supply/sub/cover teachers – that is, adults whose authority is often not recognised or acknowledged by pupils. This definition is further qualified in due course.

To reiterate, both of these polarised sectors suggest a degree of clarity – that is, conduct which has happened and is unacceptable (to the right) and, conversely, individuals' self-discipline, influenced by interpreting cues which are likely to deter such events from happening in the first place (to the left). Here, the combination of the threat of sanctions and an appropriate authority figure signify order and induce self-constraint from the majority of pupils for the majority of the time. This response is regardless of their level of interest in the prescribed curriculum matter. Subsequent enquiry revealed this combination, aligned with the capacity to stay calm whilst giving a clear choice and following through on consequences, brought 'new' teacher to 'senior' teacher status in the eyes of both Year 7 and Year 9 cohorts (*n.* 51). Whilst I advocate that trust is integral to relationships and authority, the reality is that it takes time to cultivate. Therefore, my findings support the literature which suggests that credibility and competence are the key attributes that pupils recognise as currency in a teacher, and which are assessed instantly. However (as I explain in Chapter 13), these tend to bring about order defined by compliance, rather than cooperation. Cooperation cultivates pupils' goodwill; it is an ideal which can be worked towards through investment in relationships. Compliance is a necessary foundation in accordance to the reality that the classroom can be a harsh world.

Through my research, I was interested to explore both segments of the diagram and, more significantly, the terrain in between where pupils might resist, test, or even challenge authority to determine where the boundary lies with that specific teacher, in that specific lesson. The middle zone is deemed fertile ground for low level disruptive behaviour to occur and potentially escalate towards chaos. I wanted to start by shining a light on those pupils who, it emerged, habitually scouted this terrain on behalf of their peers.

Rain Cloud Behaviour[1]

Due to the wilful and deliberate ploys which often determine Rain Cloud behaviour, there are occasions when the teacher will be confronted with disruptive behaviour, irrespective of lesson content or preventative measures. These incidents appear to manifest, regardless of whether or not the behaviour is likely to lead to a detention. The child can be defiant, stubborn,

1 Pupils whose self-evaluation indicated high habitual RC behaviour may be indicative of descriptors in the literature alluding to backgrounds of deprivation and SEN. My study did not seek to substantiate or disprove this association.

obstinate, and determined. At other times, emotions may dictate proceedings. Of the percentage initiating disruption for 2–3% of the time, a number of scores skew the total. Of the 68 pupils who recognised Rain Cloud traits in their own conduct, 36 students (identifying with this category to some degree) recorded single figures, suggesting an issue with an individual teacher. The remainder (the real core instigating disruption) typically spent between 10% and 20% of their time seeking to obstruct learning. Some individuals recorded higher rates. This suggests that their behaviour was highly sensitive to contextual variables which affected whether they conformed to classroom expectations or, conversely, manipulated the class dynamic.

I was keen to examine school detention data to glean insights from teachers' perspectives on students who were deemed to have 'crossed the line' (September 2008–July 2011). It was easy to get sucked into the tide of negativity and tales of conflict as I surveyed the detention data. Descriptive facts recording the pupil's conduct were often fused with hints of exasperation from the adults who were required to address the rudeness, the obstinacy, and the disturbances to learning. However, the pupils' accounts reminded me that even those displaying wilful disruptive behaviour up to 2.48% of the time might be amenable for 97.52% of the week, if conditions dictated. They might desist, comply, or even engage. Perspective and proportion were therefore integral to my attempts to redefine reality in the midst of classroom contestations, which Bill Rogers' white space/black dot (mentioned in Chapter 3) serves to illustrate.

Nevertheless, I do not wish to minimalise or trivialise the impact such incidents have on the learning, and also, more significantly, on the sense of well-being of the teacher and sense of security for class members. As we saw in Chapter 9, the 'butterfly effect' denotes the disproportionate impact that a seemingly insignificant variable can have on the whole system. I know from tough experience that the presence of even one unruly individual pupil can have a profound impact on my performance, on the group, and subsequently on learning (we will explore some examples in Chapters 18 and 19).

Crossing the Line

It might be presumed that the antics encapsulated within the Rain Cloud descriptor would evoke the school's consequences system. Data supporting my assumption that apparent deliberately disruptive acts logically led to official reprimand is presented through documents detailing the reasons for sanctions. Each incident warranting a detention was recorded by the teacher involved. An analysis of the descriptive content from 4,059 incidents clearly shows that male pronouns comprehensively outweighed female pronouns over the three year period (Table 12.1).

Table 12.1. Gender terms within detention data (*n.* 4,059 incidents)

Term	Number of references in detention data
He	1,123
His	556
She	415
Him	353
Her	336

This suggests that boys were more likely to exhibit wilful Rain Cloud behaviour, which was liable to result in detention, whilst much of girls' involvement in Dark Cloud behaviour was confined to joining in with Grey Cloud conduct. Further analysis showed this was consistently the case in data attained from pupils in Years 8, 9, and 10 rather than Year 7. The comparative lack of consequences suggests that either females typically ceased obstructive behaviour before C3 was administered (for more on the consequences system see Chapter 3), or their attention seeking traits did not necessarily equate to detentions in specific lessons, or that girls were more attuned to calculating behaviour according to circumstance and the individual teacher(s) – and therefore were more likely to get away with it.

The literature offered me some perspectives on the notion of 'laddishness'. Myhill (2002) uses the terms 'bad boys' and 'good girls' to illustrate the moralistic discourse in play. Myhill and Jones (2006) highlight a reinforcement of social stereotyping of female compliance and conformity vs. male challenge and individuality. Pupils reported teachers' expectations of boys and girls as being different, with more being expected of girls both in terms of achievement and behaviour. They noted that girls received less negative attention from teachers, whilst boys were reprimanded and monitored more. Francis (1999) draws on notions of masculinity to differentiate between boys' and girls' behaviour, whilst Hirst and Cooper (2008: 439) suggest there was an acceptance that "boys will be boys". Conversely, Jackson (2006: 350) critiques the term 'ladette', which was defined by one of her research participants as "typical male but a female" to draw some parity between the genders. Charlton's (2007) review of 'good girls' and 'bad girls', and Myhill's (2002) study, further challenge the current tendency to construct underachievement in terms of gender. My dealings with disruptive female students was a feature of my action research (see Chapters 18 and 19).

Staff Language Conveying Disruptive Incidents

Aside from scrutinising gender terms, the detention data was broken down further to extract the most frequent phrases. Prominent terms were then identified. These are categorised for convenience under the labels A–G:

A:

Refused (mentioned 506 times)

Refusal (171)

Refusing (111)

Defiant (123)

B:

Rude (380)

C:

Disruptive (376)

Disruption (269)

Disrupting (143)

D:

Continued (358)

Continually (141)

Stop (147)

Failure (117)

E:

Asked (538)

Told (252)

Warned (211)

Warnings (193)

Instructions (185)

F:

Sent (205)

G:

Silly (209)

Shouting (141)

Messing (137)

Throwing (117)

Across (115)

The list advances a number of themes worthy of mention and further discussion. Possibly representative of a pattern, the initial terms (A) may indicate a power struggle which is interpreted by the teacher as personal (B). The incident is interfering with the learning process (C) and there is a sense of escalation (D) where teacher language is ineffectual in deterring the child (E). There is an indication of attempted respite as the term 'sent' is almost exclusively used in reference to being 'sent out' (F). Unsurprisingly, there is no mention of SEN, setting, or home circumstance as the offence is detailed. The focused and emotive expression apparent in the records may indicate teachers' acceptance of a discourse of 'badness', which contributes to teachers' efficacy beliefs, attribution theories, and the subsequent levels of emotion and stress I noted in my literature review. The final set of descriptors gives a sense of the behaviour in which the individual pupil feels very much part of the collective, and perhaps feels anonymous, as their antics merge and feelings of responsibility wane (G).

Undeterred

The relative size of the terms 'male' and 'female' in Figure 12.2 are proportionate to the number of incidents recorded in the school's detention data. Allison (2013: 14) makes a distinction between "incidental boundary-crossing and deliberate boundary-flouting". Illustrative of the latter, the self-confessed tendency of some pupils to deliberately provoke staff is encapsulated by the Rain Cloud percentage (2.48%); the volume of detention data suggests that the threat of sanctions may not be enough to deter the wilful child.

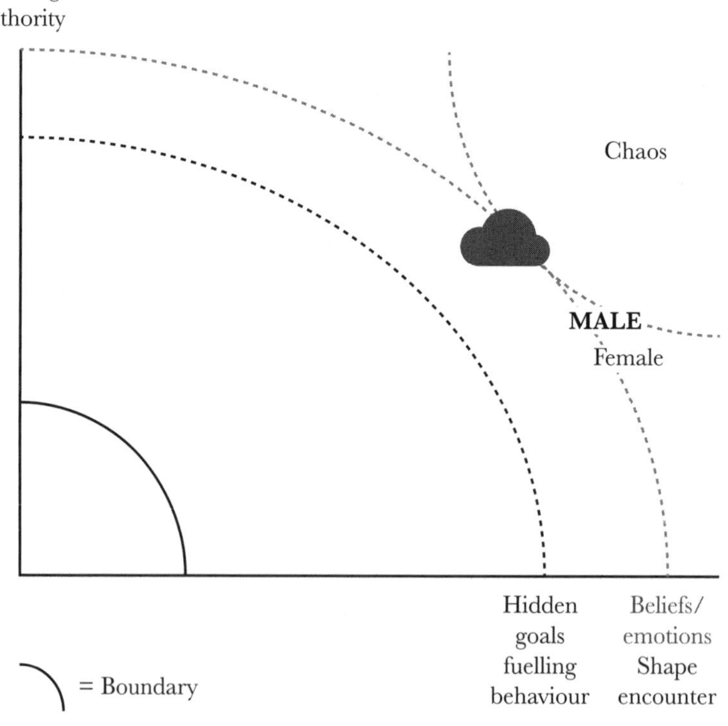

Figure 12.2. Undeterred by institutional boundaries: gender Rain Clouds

The episodes exemplify the notions of 'laddishness' and 'counter-culture' (Willis 1977). This supposition is illustrated through the plight of one of my trainee teachers. I will refer to him as 'Mr John'. During Mr John's three month placement, the 23 pupils forming his Year 8 class represented the only group with whom he experienced behaviour problems. Overall his teaching practice was successful; however, this specific class (containing a strong cohort of boys whose behaviour was recognised as an issue throughout the school) seized the opportunity to test boundaries when I eventually withdrew my presence and allowed my colleague to take full control. Months after he left, I was able to ask the pupils to reflect on their comparative experiences and to report back anonymously to aid my research.

One male pupil identified himself as the instigator of the class climate, declaring: "Eighteen people provided an audience for me to perform to and everyone was looking to disrupt. Often I was at the centre and led others astray but if they never egged me on I would stop." The stage on which this specific pupil performed was, I believe, constructed in accordance with two factors identified by two female students, one stating that, "The teacher was mainly to *blame* as he couldn't control the class", and the other suggesting, "People mess around because he is less like a *proper* teacher" (emphasis added). In their eyes he lacked credibility. Teacher credibility is defined as the degree to which the students perceive the teacher to be believable. The concept of authority, as recognised by pupils, is presented in Chapter 13 and further defined in Chapter 21.

Interestingly, Mr John's disciplinary approach was not dissimilar to the one I was trying to cultivate myself. He was a respectful and caring individual who wanted the best for his pupils. Attempting to decipher the degeneration of the class's performance, I turned to Zimbardo's (1970) process model of deindividuation to better understand the notion of peer amplification. I was aware of the identity and influence of the main instigator – we will call him 'Billy'. Billy seemed to have been given permission by fellow pupils to experience a sense of power. Although occupying a subordinate hierarchical position, Foucault (1980: 98) reminds us that the individual is both an object of power and an instrument through which power is exercised: "Power must be analysed as something which circulates, or rather as something which only functions in the form of a chain … individuals are the vehicles of power, not its points of application."

Langer et al. (1978) use the term 'mindlessness' to denote when individuals act before thinking. I surmised that key individuals recognised the conditions of relative anonymity due to Mr John not knowing all of their names. This led to a sense of reduced responsibility ('everyone') within the group and a perceived lack of deterrents (through consequences or respect), leading to heightened arousal and boisterousness. Zimbardo does not define group size, although studies often denote crowds (Mann 1981) and mobs (Mullen

1986) when there is evidence of a lower than normal threshold of restrained behaviour (Zimbardo 1970). I observe this in action whenever I attend a football match and watch the fans become a collective entity, which permits individuals to hurl verbal abuse at game officials, players, and opposing fans (which would be deemed unacceptable in other circumstances). We might also review the UK riots through this lens.

Back in the classroom, consistent with Juvonen and Cadigan (2002), attention was focused outwards, so that individuals may have overlooked discrepancies between their personal moral and social standards and their wider behaviour as they became absorbed in a sense of group unity (Forsyth 1983). As we have seen, two female pupils argued a sense of legitimacy by blaming the teacher, whilst there is also a sense that Billy was dictating proceedings and his behaviours were influencing others to join him. Le Bon's 1895 classic study, *The Crowd*, described this process as contagion. Hollander (1981) found that high status individuals, like Billy, are usually protected from sanctions despite shows of non-conformity. Their idiosyncrasy credits, previously earned within the group, prevail unless the deviancy is extreme and peers distance themselves from association. However, 'messing about' and 'just having a laugh' were terms frequently used in discussion with me. Huuki et al. (2010) identify humour as a resource and a strategy for boys to gain status amongst their peers. Meeus and Mahieu (2009) note that students' humour is used as a form of boundary seeking and boundary crossing behaviour, whilst also having the potential to make a positive contribution to the relationship with a teacher. This is descriptive of my own childhood behaviour (see Chapter 21).

On this occasion, as the class cited low level disruptions and general noisiness as descriptors, it seemed that Billy was able to stay within these peer accepted boundaries. My impromptu reappearance in the middle of this – using the pupils' term 'performance' – was akin to witnessing the breaking of a spell which had gripped the group. In this instance, it was clear that neither the authority of the adult, nor the possibility or threat of sanctions, acted as a deterrent for many of the pupils – and one in particular, who seemed to have become intoxicated with the experience of contesting power.

Theorising Through a Complexity Lens

I was interested to apply the complexity model (see Figure 9.1) to see if it could supply a coherent explanation for the class dynamics I had experienced and observed. I wondered if the descriptive process would provide structure to the collective accounts I was gathering, and whether the terminology might help to further comprehend and articulate Mr John's uncomfortable encounter.

In accordance with the model and the data, it became apparent that upon arrival pupils will naturally self-organise, in keeping with local rules and relationships, and absorb contextual cues before conveying their assessment to others in order to influence the group's emergent behaviour. In my study, this was done consciously by key individuals who deliberately engaged in chatter and deferred the start of work. I was curious to consider whether the exchange between members of the group might also operate on a subconscious level – whether pupils could instantly discern or sense the ambiance within the room. Complexity theory suggests that the system is sensitive to feedback: "*Emergence* is an interplay between both negative and positive feedback; it is not the absence of tension, but a *dynamic balancing of opposites*" (Newell 2008: 9; emphasis added). The system adapts, moving between states we might describe as near equilibrium and far from equilibrium – order and chaos, predictable and unpredictable. This dynamic encompasses the terms 'fold' and 'stretch'.[2]

My immediate and ongoing task would be to cultivate, or negotiate, a balance to ensure that the classroom climate was conducive to learning by attempting to read the mood or flow of the group. In keeping with my evaluation, I would either amplify or dampen the system accordingly and intermittently stimulate, settle, or redirect. If I was to enable my pupils to become more autonomous and self-disciplined, I would need to continuously monitor to attain equilibrium between their learning needs and their social needs. I was keen that one did not become detrimental to the other. Working in silence, as a matter of course, might impinge on relational opportunities, whilst unproductive chit-chat would most definitely impact negatively on achievement.

The notion of the 'strange attractor' (Remer 1998) became part of my vocabulary. The concept is defined as "the foci in [complex] systems around which patterns evolve and are maintained" (Remer 1998: 1), yet, importantly, these are infused with unpredictable details. I liked this idea because it married with living logics descriptors which spoke of taking risks and operating in the present. For example, a classroom buzzing with productivity might be descriptive of the attractor *excitement*. However, primed about its unpredictable nature, a diligent teacher is forever mindful that it might escalate into *over-excitement*, with the possibility of descending into chaos. Typically, this might come through an activity which stokes up enthusiasm but fails to establish boundaries to direct the group's energy. Alternatively, it could come through disruptive pupils amplifying their peer group's emergent energy to create a 'run-away system' which 'crashes' (Rea 1997), as the

2 In nature, this ebb and flow can be illustrated by the delicate ecological balance between prey and predator. Unhindered positive feedback loops (resulting in rapid population growth) are curtailed by the negative feedback administered by the predator. The equilibrium in this system would crash if hunting exceeded growth (Rea 1997).

teacher finally loses his temper and brings the commotion to a grinding halt.[3]

How might this scenario be prevented? Going back a stage, the attractor of low level disruption is likely to escalate if the teacher fails to intervene early by dampening. This was apparent with Mr John. Billy, the ring-leader, and his audience fed continuously into the positive feedback loop, thereby making the system unstable as noise levels rose and an array of seemingly trivial off-task behaviours manifested. As a result, the teacher found himself fire-fighting as the energy shifted around the room. He was made to feel disempowered – as though the group were beyond his control, immune to his influence, and dismissive of his authority. My reappearance in the doorway ensured the system crashed abruptly and silence quickly descended on the room. On reflection, Mr John either hadn't dampened the group's energy as they entered the room or he had neglected to quash key individuals' initial ploys to deviate from the learning. Whether this might have been achieved by employing appropriate disciplinary procedures, or perhaps more subtle means (such as a brief copying task to focus attention), is largely dependent on contextual variables and relationships. The identification of said variables, cues, and relationships continued to emerge from the analysis of the data.

The Significance of Timings

As I sought to construct a picture of the complex dynamics which can lead to disturbances, another factor appeared to be significant: the timing of the lesson. Of the recorded incidents, 3,122 noted the time the sanction was issued: there was a clear trend to disruptive incidents which built as the day progressed. According to the data, period 5 (2.15–3.15 p.m.) was nearly two-thirds more likely to witness disruptive behaviour than period 1 (8.55–9.55 a.m.).

3 Again, in the natural world the unconstrained population growth of some animals is an example of this. 'Crash' refers to exponential growth patterns exceeding the capacity of the environment (Rea 1997). Financial markets are another example of a system which maintains equilibrium through feedback loops. In 2008, moving far from equilibrium, it also provides an exemplar of a crash as a result of the banking crisis.

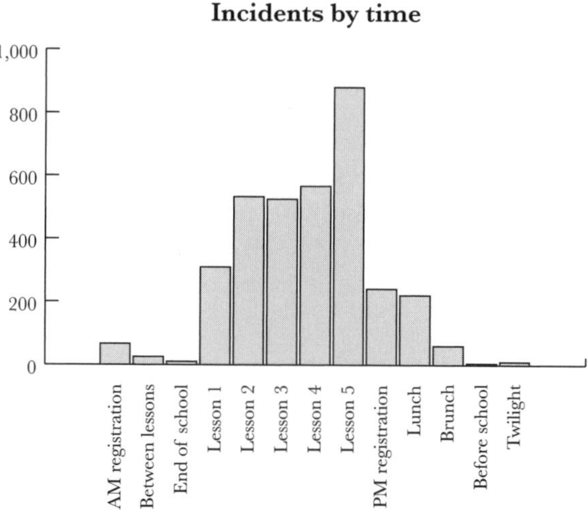

Figure 12.3. Incidents by time (September 2008–July 2011)

The trend was also substantiated by a small sample of Year 7 and Year 9 pupils. It became apparent that the periods were not dependent on specific subjects, lessons, or teachers. My own perplexity in light of this experience is documented in my diary blog:

> I take Y9 history group Tuesday period 1 and again on Thursday period 5 – what a difference! Tuesday it takes all my energy to get them going, whilst Thursday they arrive 'buzzing' with social baggage and very much offended, even insulted, by the prospect of having to divert to the learning agenda.

The statistics indicate that the arousal level of the groups increased throughout the day. I diligently read an excellent resource, Forsyth's *Group Dynamics* (1983), which cites a number of seminal texts which I will briefly make reference to within this chapter. Studies of the arousal/aggression hypothesis are usually applied to conflicts within groups (Berkowitz 1974) and are attributed to frustrations in response to environmental constraints (Dollard et al. 1939). However, I did not consider the external factors in the afternoon to be significantly different from circumstances earlier in the day. Alternative explanations for conduct (which is generally more pliable in the mornings), beyond the scope of this current study, may be found in the exploration of the effects of sleep deprivation (Durmer and Dinges 2005) due to children's extensive use of electronic gadgets (Hastings et al. 2009). Conversely, more excitable behaviour seen in later lessons might be attributed to additives and sugar intake (Steer 2005; Feingold Association 2007) during breaktimes and lunchtimes.

An interesting comparison can be made of the performance of pupils in the isolation unit. Deprived of their usual food and drink intake and the company of a peer group, I observed that the performance of occupants was constant throughout the day. As a result of these observations, we, as a school, sought to dampen this emergent energy by changing the assembly tutor time from morning to afternoon and extending the morning break to shorten lunchtime. The data also has implications for organising rotas to support colleagues through an analysis of hot spots: days, times, and locations. For us, these considerations informed our on-call provision.

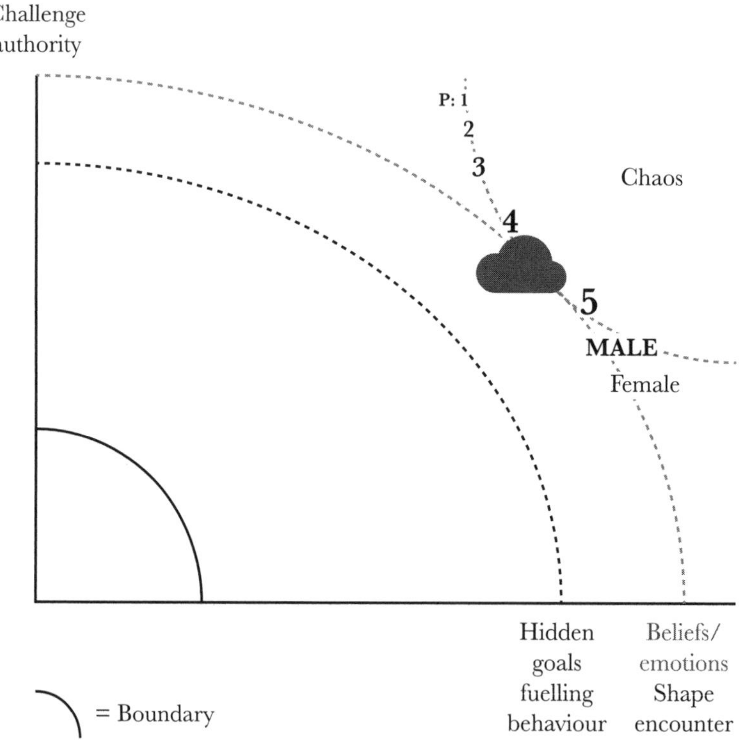

Figure 12.4. Undeterred by institutional boundaries: plus times of disturbances

The right hand side of Figure 12.4 was becoming ever more populated, so I now turned my attention to better understand the segment on the left.

Chapter 13

Recognising Boundaries

Sean

Irrespective of the time of the day, I wanted to further explore pupils' inclinations not to join in with or instigate disruption. I sought to discover the conditions they claimed were necessary to deter them from disrupting learning. I posed the following question:

> You arrive at a classroom for the first time and survey the scene. What signs/cues would inform you that 'good' behaviour is a wise option for you to take with this teacher? (*n.* 225)

The question draws out qualifying accounts to offer explanations as to why disruption is not seen and to identify influences which deter students from joining in when they witness others disrupting the lesson. Although I did not specify, two respondents interpreted the question as an invitation to describe teachers who elicit Blue Skies cooperative responses which deter temptations to disrupt:

> 8F: [The teachers are] quiet, calm, in control. They trust you.
>
> 10F: The teachers I really like are the ones you can have a laugh with but they have such a big amount of respect from the students that the students listen and always do what they say. It is such a good balance as you feel like trusting them and you feel quite matey with them, but I get great marks because they are fab teachers and you want to impress them. When you feel as if you're on the same wavelength as them, the lessons are really productive and you want to learn more.

I would explore the essence of these responses further when I examined the pupils' assessment of their behaviour in my own lessons. For now it is sufficient to plot this constructive behaviour category onto the evolving model (Figure 13.1).

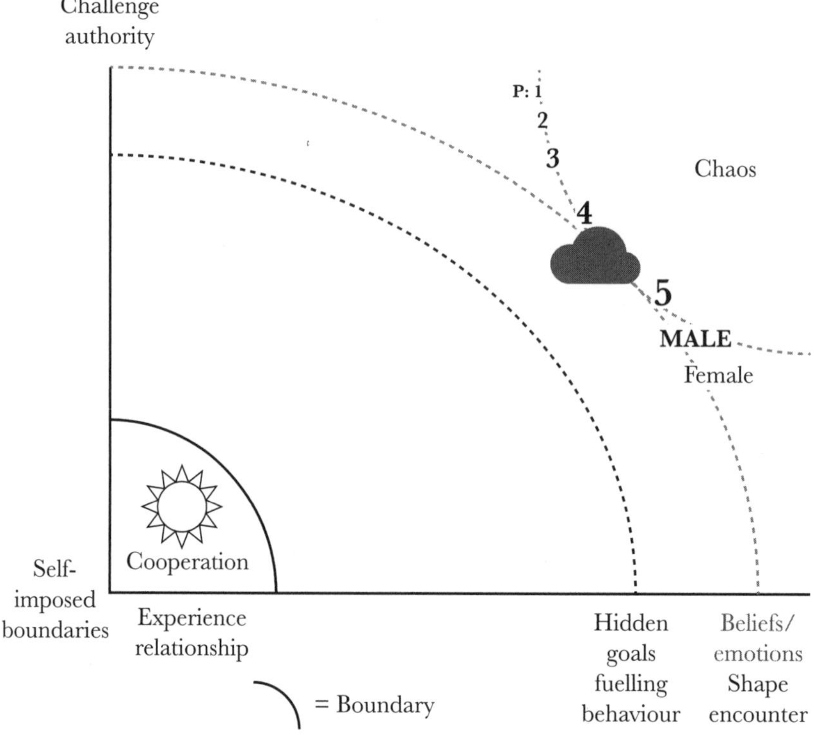

Figure 13.1. Student recognition = self-imposed boundaries: plus cooperation

The responses reminded me of a little lad I worked with some years ago. 'Joe' was in Year 8, had a troubled background, and was getting detentions galore. An analysis of the data showed that hardly any sanctions had come from male teachers; the vast majority occurred when he was being taught by female staff. However, further analysis revealed that two female teachers on his timetable had not given him a single detention. I was curious. "Joe," I said, "I notice that you seem to keep out of trouble when Ms X and Ms Y teach you – how's that?" His answer was simple: "They like me." And they genuinely did. I spoke to both colleagues, and it was clear that they could see through the antics and the reputation to see a vulnerable little boy. They acknowledged him when he arrived at lessons and expected him – indeed, trusted him – to do well. He felt as though he was someone, so he didn't have to get himself noticed. Instead of taking his habitual place to the right in Figure 13.1, for at least a couple of hours a week he projected a radiance. Brookfield (2006) suggests such teachers exude two qualities in the eyes of their pupils: credibility and authenticity. The former denotes a perception that the teacher has something important to offer from which the student will benefit, whilst the latter incorporates notions of trust and honesty.

In contrast to the two comments above, the bulk of the pupils interpreted the question in terms of their relationships with 'stricter' teachers, with whom notions of deference seemed to merge elements of respect and fear. My coverage will draw on Foucault's portrayal of discipline as a mechanism of power which regulates the behaviour of individuals in the social body. This is done, in part, by regulating or normalising the organisation of space, time (timetables), and the institution's representative curtailing of children's activity and behaviour through the use of symbols, drills, posture, and movement (see O'Farrell 2005). In my own lessons, I would come to re-evaluate lining up outside the classroom and taking the register. Foucault emphasises that power is not discipline, rather discipline is simply one way in which power can be exercised. Such practices aim to produce 'docile bodies' and 'obedient souls' (Foucault 1979). My work depicts this passive expression as White Cloud and is illustrated in Figure 13.2. I populated the bottom of my evolving model with variables, offering a progressive list of deterrents which might influence pupils.

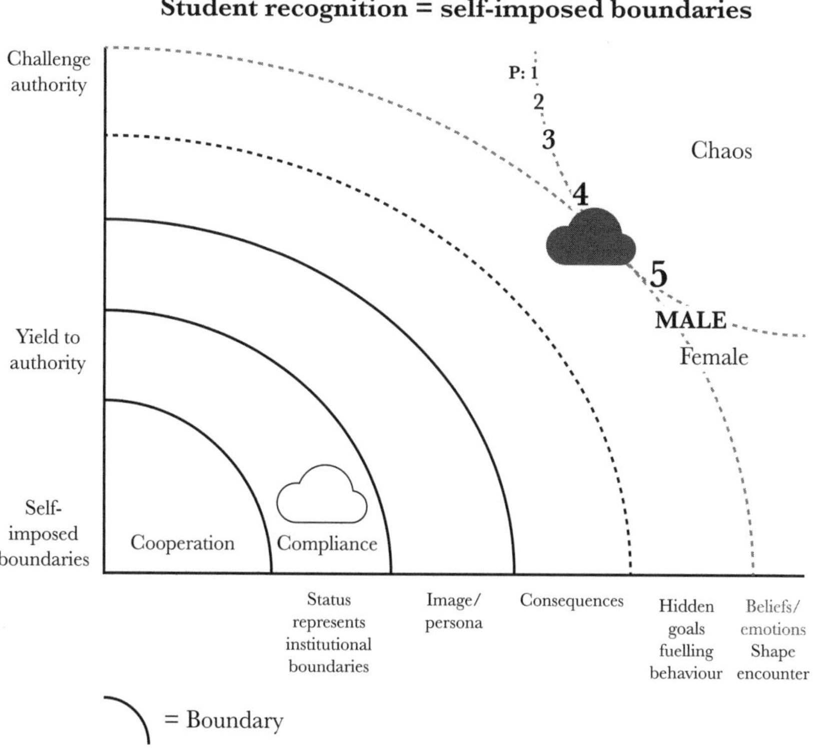

Figure 13.2. Student recognition = self-imposed boundaries: plus compliance

I was interested to explore the importance of relationships and experience, and how they fed into notions of status, image, and persona to induce self-imposed boundaries. Principally, I was curious to probe the determinants which contribute to an individual yielding to authority. My model makes a specific association with the concept of status as being representative of institutional boundaries. I recalled a salutary lesson some years before which reminded me that recognition of authority is interpretive and subjective. Whilst visiting a school in my capacity as a behaviour and attendance consultant, I was wandering between lessons and was approached by a middle-aged female teacher who assumed that I was one of the 'mature' trainee teachers who had recently started their placement. "Are you alright, dear? Do you need any help?" she asked, head tilted to one side. On finding out I was with the local authority she transformed before my very eyes, becoming almost subservient. One can only imagine her response had I been an Ofsted inspector! Regardless, something internal had registered in that teacher, and I was curious to apply this principle of recognition to my students.

I had established that pupils were well versed in adapting their conduct in accordance to situational cues. For the majority, these determined whether – or, more accurately, to what degree – they were likely to engage in the learning process or contribute to disruption. Conversely, there were times when individuals chose to tolerate the task and keep a low profile. What induced this passive White Cloud state? What indicators and variables influenced their decision to cooperate or obstruct? I wanted to hear it from the horse's mouth. Selecting both verbal and non-verbal cues, I attempted to accurately capture the essence of the 220 contributions I received. I took time and care to ensure my presentation would not mislead or misrepresent the original meaning of the comments. My account is consistent in conveying the general themes provided by my pupils.

I identified reoccurring terms using NVivo data analysis software, and then selected extracts to further qualify the themes emerging from the pupils' collective comments. This form of presentation is a variant of Youdell's (2011) assertion that a storytelling approach has a place in social science. Drawing on Delgado (1989, 1995) and Gillborn (2008), a range of experiences which have been extracted from numerous resources are represented as a single narrative. Those responding were able to draw on their personal experience, which suggests familiarity with the scenario in which the cues induced 'good' behaviour. Only five pupils out of the 225 chose not to respond. Consequently, I feel justified in presenting my students' collective definitions of the 'Means Business' teacher and the 'Scary' teacher.

The 'Means Business' Teacher

> You can tell if a teacher means business or if they are a pushover. Everyone is quiet and in their seats when you walk into the classroom. The teacher looks at you as you come in. Things seem organised, everyone is sat in their normal seats in accordance with the seating plan, and they settle everyone down quickly with a kind of 'teacher radar' as they get order. They greet the class and seem aware of what everyone is doing as they address the whole class. Everyone has got everything ready and everyone is listening to them. Rules have been stated from the beginning and everything is picked up on. We had heard the rumours, and other students told us of their reputation for strictness even before we attended a single lesson. There is work on the board and other people are working, which suggests they have already been told to be quiet. It is creepily silent. You can tell what is going on by the other students in the room; they give a lot away. All the people that usually mess around are quiet and even the troublemakers, the ones who are usually bad, are good and getting on with their work. The teacher looks confident in what they are doing; they have control. The tables are in rows and it feels like there is less chance of getting away with anything. The teacher knows how to keep calm, so the class is calm and everyone is interacting with the tasks. This teacher has a strong mind, a strong personality, and is persistent.

It is noted that the organisation of the space, through the arrangement of furniture, can play a part in creating classroom ecology (Sommer 1967). 'Sociopetal' table groupings can promote interaction, whilst 'sociofugal' layouts, such as rows, discourage collaboration. The organisation of tables was another facet I would come to reassess in my own lessons.

The terms 'everyone' and 'all' are considered key in light of established social-psychological studies. We observed this earlier with Mr John's class. The descriptors affirm Sherif's (1936, 1966) conclusions that group norms can act as a frame of reference for individual members who internalise and adapt accordingly. Asch (1952, 1955, 1957) shows that the larger the unanimous majority, the greater the conformity. Moscovici (1985) asserts that perception of majority consensus has a direct influence and is likely to induce conformity. This contrasts with the latent, indirect influence of a minority – as in the case of this fictional authority figure, the Means Business teacher – which induces a longer lasting effect, termed 'conversion'. Whilst accepting that an external authority or class leader can establish a standard, Sherif (1976) notes that most group norms develop through reciprocal influence. Usher and Edwards (2004: 92) point out that "when discipline is effective, power operates through persons rather than upon them". The narrative might, at first glance, appear to be describing an oppressive climate; alternatively, it may represent a solid foundation from which strong boundaries are established and respectful relationships are allowed to develop. As depicted by the following comment, "it is when disciplinary regulation breaks down that coercion comes to the fore" (ibid.: 92).

The 'Scary' Teacher

> There's the physical appearance, but the body language of the teacher gives a lot away too. Sometimes they are already annoyed (e.g. scowling, tapping foot, arms crossed). It's not just the way they look at you, they give you *the* look – the look of authority. They just look at you and stare; a stern stare. This teacher can be harsh, even evil; someone or something has made them angry. That teacher look – it's scary, especially when they then shout. Some male teachers look so big, so intimidating. The look on their face and the way they sit and talk, it makes you feel small and scared; they don't smile or say hello. They say, "Don't mess about or I will come down on you like a ton of bricks." The pupils know not to mess about; you know s/he has a short fuse. They say, "Silence", and they don't let you speak or anything, not even fidget. They might be in a mood. Using that voice – it is a loud, demanding, bad voice which shows you up in front of your mates. The teacher is stubborn, strong-willed, and strict – never afraid to overuse the 'C' system in order to punish.

Interestingly, detentions are only mentioned twice; the force of the Scary teacher's presence or persona alone appears to be synonymous with the concept of boundaries. I was reminded of Sarah's account as I read similar descriptions from over 200 of her peers.

Commentary

The collective agreement in the pupils' answers reflects the conformity described by the White Cloud percentage (32%). This concurred with my experiential knowledge which suggested that coercive tactics exemplifying power often lead to submissive responses and compliance. This is contrasted with an identification based on relationship and subsequent internalisation, where pupils adopt behaviours which are congruent with their value systems (Kelman 1958). These two sketches are reminiscent of how I might have been described by some pupils prior to this study. Interestingly, of the 220 responses only two pupils mentioned a teacher's formal status (e.g. head of department, head of house, head teacher). Status, it seems, is not always confined to organisational position or rank, but is largely dependent on individual and collective observations and interpretation.

Whilst I have used the terms 'comply' and 'conform' to convey inhibiting instances of order, I was interested to consider the tendency of pupils to follow the directives of individuals who they had identified as being representative of authority. Milgram (1974) shows that the inclination of subjects to submit to commands goes even further. He describes an agentic state in which participants' own personal goals become subordinate to the obedience of another. The models I present suggest that an individual teacher's facade or character is an effective deterrent for those inclined to test authority.

Whilst authoritarians might argue that the educational ends justify the disciplinary means, I hold two objections. Aside from the psychological effect on the individual teacher (as shown in Chapter 3), my concern extends to a consideration of the suppression of those children predisposed to follow and accept the commands of the prominent adults entrusted with their education. I have become uncomfortable with the idea that when a teacher says "Jump", the advocated response should be "How high?" I want more than that for my own children. In Chapter 21, I will argue that the child's subtle internalisation of adult role models can have a profound and lasting effect on emergent behaviour. I will show that an authoritative approach (as distinctive from authoritarian) can provide appropriate boundaries, enabling the pupils to negotiate relationships and decipher the subtleties of power and trust. I consider such goals as definitive of educational achievement, and need not be sacrificed in the sole pursuit of educational attainment.

In deciphering the difference between cooperation and compliance, I highlight the dichotomy between the two comments shown at the beginning of this chapter and the plethora of subsequent responses. Upon reflection, I am drawn to make a theoretical distinction. The two observations appear to derive from the pupils' 'personal identity' (Hitlin 2003). This notion invites discussion of value commitments and is associated with moral identity (Stets and Carter 2011). I argue that acquiring trust encourages the pupil to express authenticity through responsibility and self-consistency.

By contrast, I draw attention to the nuance between students' role identity and their social identity to convey a distancing between individuals occupying different positions within school (Burke and Stets 2009). Despite Burke's (2004) definition of roles (e.g. pupils and teachers) as broad categories that people within a culture learn to apply to themselves and others, my data suggested that this is informed and adjusted by observation, perception, and experience. Often pupils' verification of authority is attained by what the teacher does and says, not merely by who s/he is (Stets and Burke 2000). In accordance with the two depictions above (Means Business and Scary teacher), Brookfield (2006: 57) suggests that in a classroom where credibility is present but authenticity is somewhat absent, students usually feel their time is well spent and that they benefit, even though the distance is experienced as "cold, unwelcoming, intimidating, or even threatening ... makes it hard for learners to ask for assistance, raise questions, seek clarification, and so on".

Although teachers are employed by the school and naturally assume an elevated place within the hierarchy, my research confirms that pupils' acceptance of their authority is nonetheless highly variable. For example, a concurrent line of enquiry suggests that pupils' dislike of their teacher was significant in determining classroom relationships. Predictably, disruption follows on as a common consequence. In fact, this variable of 'not liking' was identified as the main determinant which could lead to pupils undermining even senior leaders. Interestingly, I found that the factor also impacted on esteemed orderly classrooms, as pupils withdrew their goodwill by limiting their participation and doing the bare minimum of work required. This state of affairs contributed to my understanding of the distinction between compliance and cooperation. My data shows that individual pupils are adept at modifying their relative roles in accordance to context. In Chapter 19, I apply Berne's (1964) fascinating terminology, 'victim' and 'persecutor', to exemplify the fluidity in which classroom participants can adapt to different situations.

Whilst the responses analysed in this chapter allude to notions of order and control, the person often attributed with popularising the phrase 'low level disruption', Lord Elton (1989: 65), offers a pragmatic perspective for those addressing behaviour in schools:

> Reducing bad behaviour is a realistic aim. Eliminating it completely is not. Historical and international comparisons help to illustrate this obvious but important point. Children have a need to discover where the boundaries of acceptable behaviour lie. It is natural for them to test these boundaries to confirm their location and, in some cases, for the excitement of a challenge. The proper answer to such testing is to confirm the existence of the boundaries, and to do so firmly, unequivocally and at once.

My pupils seemed acutely aware that some staff appeared to be less able to do this effectively.

Chapter 14

Indistinct Boundaries

Sean

My pupils' collective voice informed me that they yielded to authority for up to 32% of the timetable. I have categorised this state as White Cloud behaviour and used descriptive terms such as compliance, conformity, and even obedience, although Sarah's account (in Chapter 1) exuded an undercurrent of frustration and hinted at resentment. Stets and Tsushima's (2001) research into negative emotions, derived from role based identities, recognised suppressed anger as prevalent. Whilst they reported identities characterised as low status to be more intense and having longer lasting anger, my data suggests that pupils' timetables afforded them periodic opportunities to contest power with selected authority figures. Foucault (1980: 95) argues that such resistance is intrinsic to power: "where there is power there is resistance".

My work suggests that, whilst this is more common for a minority of pupils, the vast majority are capable of participating to various degrees, should the 'right' circumstances present themselves. This chapter builds on the previous one and shows that students' perception and degree of acceptance of an individual teacher's authority, informed by observation and experience, is integral to such situations. As long ago as 1957, Strodtbeck et al. recognised that those adults perceived by pupils as low status are less likely to induce conformity to school rules. Using the students' terms, my work has personified these under the umbrella of supply/sub/cover teacher.

Here, we will consider the classroom climate where boundaries are less transparent. In relation to pupils' identities, I am interested to explore the 'disturbances' (Burke 2004) to individuals' 'identity standard' (Stets and Carter 2011). This phrase is defined as meanings which constitute the self (Burke 2004). Reid and Deaux (1996: 1090) point out that an awareness of one's personal traits can be heightened through social definition – "personal attributes can be used to describe how one is similar to others in a social category or to highlight one's unique characteristics". Meanings are our responses to perceptions. Perceptions are associated with roles, positions, and groups that exist within a social structure. These are often shared within the local settings of a social structure – namely, the classroom – and, of course, according to complexity theory, these relationships operate in accordance to local rules.

In lessons where pupils' self-control is less apparent, due primarily to a lack of cooperation or absence of coercion, an interesting shift in dynamics is reported. The individual pupil's identity is liable to relate to the ambiance emanating from the group, and the teacher may be perceived as a collective target. It is perhaps this phenomenon which practitioners are referring to when they describe disruptive behaviour in schools. Whenever I have started work at a new school, I have encountered power contests where pupils have sought to challenge and test my authority. This can be a complex and perturbing experience for the teacher, causing them to feel compelled to assert themselves using simplistic, draconian behaviour management approaches. However, my interest here is in the apparent deficiency in the teacher's personal and professional qualities which are discerned by individual pupils and affirmed by a proportion of the class. This is damaging to the authoritative stance I am advocating because when pupils unite to disregard a teacher's authority, the sense of security the class require is absent.

My understanding of my pupils' collective perception is conceptualised through self-categorisation theory (Turner 1985, 1991; Turner et al. 1987), which represents a theoretical development within social identity theory. The propensity to label sharpens inter-group boundaries to illuminate awareness of an in-group and an out-group. The classification gives meaning to experiences in which one is (or feels) included/excluded. The notion of the in-group/out-group is considered further in Chapter 15. Hogg et al. (1995) argue that categorisation essentially 'depersonalises' individuals, such as those labelled as cover or supply teachers, but it is devoid of the negative overtones of 'dehumanisation'. Rather than representing a loss of identity, the emphasis is on contextual change in the level of identity from individual to group member. The validity of this theory is borne out in my own research which showed that when asked, "Would you 'mess about' if it was just you and your teacher in the classroom?" not one child out of the 51 surveyed answered yes. I am particularly interested in considering the apparent subordination of individuals' personal values during this process. The focus builds on Juvonen and Cadigan's (2002) findings and exemplifies the 'them and us' dichotomy which depicts the ineffectual authority figure as representative of an out-group.

My recognition, both as a child and as an adult in education, is that the extreme positions (denoted by order and chaos) are largely determined by the direct relationship between the pupil and the person occupying the role of teacher. As stated earlier, I am fascinated by the dynamic boundaries which define the complex space between the polarised positions. I anticipated that pupils' unmotivated passivity and tendency to participate in low level disruptions would be located in this middle zone. Here, the dynamics of interaction between peers often compete with interest in the subject matter and the authority of the adult. This can present a tension between pupils' social agenda and learning engagement. This potentially chaotic dynamism can perplex a 'struggling' teacher. As we saw with Mr John, if left unaddressed the cumulative effect disturbs the classroom climate, which can leave the teacher feeling frustrated and disempowered.

When pupils exhibited the type of behaviour recorded in the detention data, it suggested that either the threat of sanctions did not deter them or there was a feeling (or calculation) that the sanction would not be administered. However, it is assumed that not all disruptive behaviour resulted in a detention. The school system during the period of my research allowed two warnings for less serious behaviour. These were assessed as C1 (recorded in 235 incidents) and C2 (recorded in 691). I was curious to know whether the students used these warnings as a buffer or as a gauge to measure, test, or resist boundaries.

The next question further probed the idea that some teachers were not perceived by pupils to be as 'important' as other staff:

> What experiences or signs have helped inform you that it is 'safe' to resist a teacher's requests and instructions so you choose to 'mess about' instead?

The Means Business teacher and the Scary teacher showed that behaviour could be deterred by encounters which were principally defined by power (in accordance with hierarchal roles), yet devoid of established positive relationships. I was interested to note that the former's mere presence and mannerisms ensured that they did not have to resort to constantly giving sanctions, although the Scary teacher was inclined to administer them arbitrarily.

As with the previous question, I collated the pupils' responses into a single description, whilst preserving the essence of their individual replies (*n.* 225; 16 non-replies).

The Ineffective Teacher

> The first signals are that they're not ready when you enter the room so you know it will be hard for them to get order later. Pupils are already messing about as the teacher fumbles about, disorganised, and seems without confidence; that is like a licence to misbehave, especially if the normal teacher isn't there. You think, "Yes, sub!" because they don't follow things up. They just give you instructions and then read or go on the computer, so it feels like it's not really a proper lesson. If the teacher hasn't been clear in telling us to do something, everyone does their own thing. They're clueless about what is actually happening; we students have a 'teacher radar' – it judges what the

teacher is like, it's automatic, we can't prevent it. It's just like with some you know you can get away with it and with others you can't.

These signs confirm what people have already told us. We soon learn what a teacher is like. As we get used to them we can see they are weak as they don't give you consequences. They rarely shell out consequences, especially inexperienced teachers who are not fully aware of the sanction system. They continue to give warnings but don't give out any actual punishment; they take no action. They don't have a backbone, don't put others in their place, and fail to make an example of them. They let you off very easily. They don't stick to uniform rules; instead continuously telling us how few detentions they've given out – it generally means they don't want to. They simply repeat a C1 so the students get loads of warnings, but these are just empty threats.

The teacher just stands there doing nothing with their arms folded waiting for the students to be quiet – they rarely are! Even after the teacher has addressed the class, nobody pays attention and people carry on talking. If they don't know what they're doing, people walk all over them. You can tell by their facial expressions, body language, and tone of voice that they are nervous. The teacher is just a pushover; people are screaming and the teacher is just talking louder to try and talk over them; and even if they shout at you, they have a high voice – it's just funny.

The teacher then gets off-task and concentrates on controlling one unruly student, but everyone's messing around. You can sit with your friends if they don't know the seating plan, so everyone is sat in a different place; people stand up and we can get away with it. If others who normally don't mess around do with this teacher, and everyone else is doing it, I join in to fit in; I will follow my friends because you want to be cool and don't want to look like a wuss. If my mate gets bored, he starts being naughty so I copy him. When everyone's messing around and when you know what the teacher is like, you know how far you can go without getting told off. If you see one person getting away with it then you can too, and soon everyone is. Because we're in a big group, it overawes the teacher; with everyone doing it, you wouldn't get caught. The teacher can't keep control and they don't do anything to stop the chaos, they just let you do what you want.

It is suggested in this chapter that the modes of behaviour categorised by the weather might typically manifest in response to whether the pupil recognises the teacher as being a creditable representative of institutional boundaries. For some pupils, adverse learning conditions might evoke active disruptive behaviour such as attention seeking (Grey Cloud), whilst on other occasions a covert obstructive response might be passive (White Cloud) – the pupil sits there, unnoticed, and does next to nothing. We know that each of these different stances has the potential to be adopted by each individual pupil depending on context, variables, and circumstances.

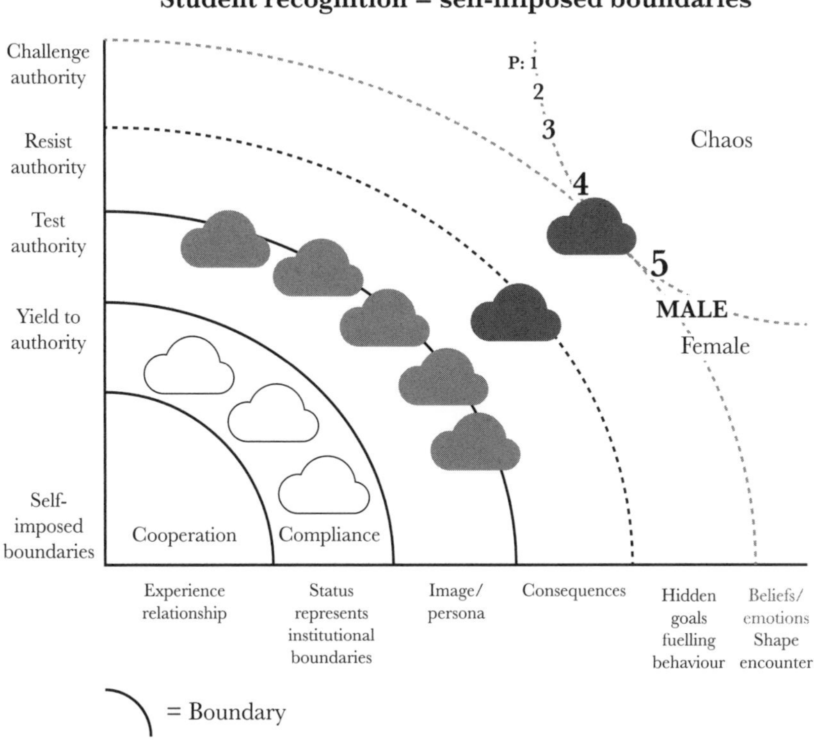

Figure 14.1. Student recognition = self-imposed boundaries: scenario

For example, Figure 14.1 represents an unknown cover teacher who was not attentive or assertive upon meeting the class, who may have experienced continual low level disruption as many pupils gauged the climate and by-passed the initial restrictive boundaries to converge on the fourth line from the right, awaiting cues to stop or carry on. The data suggests that some students will take the lead in this situation, risking sanctions whilst winning the approval of their peers. Billy was a prime example of this. The often ambiguous testing and resisting of authority takes place in this 'zone of complexity' where the boundaries are open to interpretation. These expressions of low level disruption will usually precede challenging behaviour, which by contrast indicates clearer boundaries to all through the sanction system. The pupils' psychological games to draw the teacher into contestation in this zone are explored in Chapter 19.

Chapter 15

In-Group/Out-Group

Sean

Examining the pupils' collective account through the lens of self-categorisation, it is clear that many of the pupils subscribed to a common social identity which depicted them as the 'in-group'. By definition, the authority figure – representative of a structured organisation which attributes power, status, and prestige (Hogg and Abrams 1988) – is depicted as the 'out-group'. Pupils' reference to 'everyone' affirms a sense of solidarity. In accordance with Verkuyten (2002), there is clear evidence of pupils claiming their actions to be partially legitimate due to the qualities or performance of the adult. The data suggests that the blame for the group's emergent behaviour lies with the teacher, and specifically their failure to adhere to the pupils' established expectations of authority and control. This again affirms Mr John's experience. That the pupils' accounts are consistent with authoritarian descriptions of discipline suggests that they have absorbed a degree of conditioning throughout their experience of schooling concerning apposite institutional roles and associated power structures. I will attest that aspects of my own indoctrination re-manifested as I began teacher training and began to construct an identity to befit my new-found elevated status.

In accordance with the literature which denotes pupil behaviour as 'anti-structure', individual pupils have to position themselves with their peers in the disruptive classroom. Forsyth's (1983: 149) analysis of different conformity models concludes that "social impact depends on the size of one's own sub-group in relation to the size of the group as a whole". Burke (2004) points out that verifying the self as a group member involves being like the others and receiving recognition, approval, and acceptance from those others. For Stets and Carter (2011), identity standards can be viewed as goals that are obtained by manipulating meanings, so that alignment with the peer group's social agenda (the others are messing about, I want to be seen to be cool, I need to join in) can diminish the importance of the prescribed learning agenda. This may be the source of the incongruity individuals experience between the values inherent in their personal identity and apparent in-group norms. I was curious to delve deeper into the contextual factors which might influence the likelihood of pupils to employ tactics that divert from the prescribed learning task to affirm perceived in-group status.

The significance of some of these sub-themes began to emerge from the data; in particular, pupils' perception of, and response to, those adults whose arrival as an impromptu authority figure (in the form of a supply or cover teacher) disrupted some members of the group. The recurring strand depicted an adult in the role of supply/sub/cover teacher as a comparative non-entity (in comparison to a 'strong' teacher). Whilst I was intent on providing an illustration of in-group/out-group categorisation through the exploits of a particular group and a trainee teacher, I never anticipated that the coverage would be applicable to myself at this stage of my career and within this school. And yet there it was: the phenomenon wasn't the sole preserve of new and unfamiliar teachers. Apparently, my status could be rendered next to useless when certain variables aligned – in-group/out-group, space, roles, resentment.

Territory

The validity of this unpredicted avenue of enquiry became apparent to me when I was required to cover a Year 10 tutor group. I realised that an understated factor (which is not explicitly mentioned in the data but is a constant ingredient when analysing the contextual factors impinging on any supply teacher) is the concept of territory. There has been substantial research in this area, commonly associated with gangs and the animal kingdom (Forsyth 1983), but I saw its relevance in terms of the complexity I was studying. The resistance I experienced to my authority was profound: pupils who would not dream of challenging directives in my own classroom openly and deliberately ignored my requests and seemed to resent even my presence in their tutor base. As my diary notes record, my sense of equilibrium and established assumptions about my status were further disturbed:

> Tuesday: No work left. Social group usually do no work but are allowed to sit around and chat – or so I found out. I was going through the process of cajoling when the HOH [head of house] pops in and directs 'silent reading and sign diaries'. Easier said than done, I thought! Even more interesting was that the class seemed to recognise the HOH's presence the moment she entered the room. Pupils quickly sat up straight and looked attentive. I was perplexed that they would recognise my colleague's authority over my own.

The brief exchange I had witnessed was between pupils with the temporary role of tutees and a teacher they recognised as an appropriate authority due to her position as head of their house. I was particularly perturbed as my colleague was both junior and less established. I suspect that had she walked into a different form base, associated with another house, her presence would have been negligible. As I tried to make sense of this unsettling incident, I reflected that it was also significant that the class contained two influential girls who I had previously encountered and with whom I had developed a strained relationship. If a child doesn't like you all sorts of subtle (and not so subtle) obstacles can impede civility, let alone learning. I recall one Year 8 girl who simply refused to leave the room when I did an 'on call'. I had to resort to calling on a colleague – with whom she smugly complied.

Regarding the variable of territory, I experienced a similar phenomenon when registering certain tutor groups, usually in established upper school bases. The dynamic was also apparent when I was required to cover a 'challenging' Year 8 tutor group once a week for two terms. My research had afforded me the opportunity to explore possible solutions, but none seemed to work. The eventual switch from their established base in the maths block to my teaching room instantly resulted in the pupils reverting to the amenable conduct I had witnessed during their lessons with me (the influence of social dynamics on peer conduct is considered in Chapter 23). On one occasion, I made the risky (or stupid) research decision to allow a Year 10 group to choose where they sat and with whom. I experienced pockets of hostile territory within the room – adolescent power bases, strong in their unity and collectively obstinate towards me and the prospect of learning. As I was wearing my research hat, I was able to revert back to a strategic seating plan and informed the group that they had (re)taught me an important lesson.

Accepting that the arrival of a supply or cover teacher has the capacity to disturb the established routines of classes, and mindful of the influence of territory, I was drawn to further enquire about the impact of changing just one significant variable: a trainee teacher would be introduced part way through the year. This focus ensured that standards would remain constant as the trainee became integrated into customary procedures.

Disregard

Rather than the direct comparison (which is apparent when a supply or cover teacher arrives, perhaps unexpectedly, to take charge instead of the usual teacher), this situation enabled the trainee theoretically to build up relationships with the pupils, whilst the host teacher continued to maintain the established norm. Ideally, the trainee would integrate within the recognised patterns of behavioural exchange between children and adult. We saw with Mr John that the perception that he was not a 'proper' teacher prompted the class to engage collectively with obstructive behaviour. I was interested to learn about pupils' responses if a trainee teacher decided that her strategy was to be strict. The Year 8 class I surveyed seemed to enjoy the subject when with their regular teachers and in an environment where the norm was for them to behave. After the trainee (Ms Smith) had left, I asked retrospective questions to draw out reasons for the reported difference in the class's conduct once the host teacher had withdrawn himself as the primary adult focus for the class.

I shared the teaching of the class with an experienced colleague and the teaching practice took place in his classroom. During interviews with the pupils a number of interesting themes emerged. It was immediately clear that Ms Smith's relationship and strategies were in stark contrast to my colleague's. Merei's (1958) research shows that those who try to change a group immediately face rejection, whereas those who work within a group, and gradually introduce innovations, are more successful in influencing the group. It seems that on this occasion, all these years on, the principle still held true. All 20 pupils interviewed affirmed Ms Smith's apparently ineffective strategies and the escalation of off-task behaviour, or resistance, once they had tested and worked out the boundaries.

The ensuing dialogue affirmed the pupils' perception of authority to be implicit, whilst assumptions which qualified their choices (based, in part, on external contributory factors such as status and appearance) emerged as unexamined and therefore invited scrutiny. Rather than just cite key phrases from the transcript, the flow of conversation here better captures the degree of consensus which was apparent in the interviews. The conclusions the students eventually arrived at affirmed the literature and supported the validity of my research. They had recognised that the qualities which conveyed authority in their eyes were essentially intangible, yet alluded to the significance of credibility and trust which were derived from their interpretation of experience.

> "She like just put her hand up in the air as her signal for us to be quiet … it could be like five minutes," said one pupil.
>
> Another recalled the experience and expanded: "At the start she never used the 'C' system. She just like put her hand up and gave us like warnings … And then she would say, 'I'll give you a C1,' but she never did. But like in the last two weeks she started giving out C1s and that and keeping us back after class."
>
> "Did that have an effect on you?" I asked.
>
> "Yeah, we started behaving a bit better."
>
> "You started listening to her?" I probed.
>
> "Yeah, [but] sometimes she was sending people out for five minutes and then getting them back in, and then sending another person out for no reason, and it was like just not fair telling them all off."

"It seems to me you feel there was a bit of unfairness in what was happening."

A moment of unity as all four agreed, "Yeah."

One of the pupils qualified further: "I think more people were getting annoyed with her because sometimes after lessons she would keep us in for five or ten minutes for no reason."

"The whole class?" I asked, knowing the probable answer.

"Yeah," they all affirmed in unison.

The pupil continued: "And people were getting more and more annoyed with her and that's why they were naughty in the lesson."

Her classmate started to explain the collective rationale for the acts of defiance: "I think when she did keep us back, and this is like school kid behaviour, but it was like we're not going to work for her if she's going to waste our time. We're going to try to waste hers."

Further dialogue led to the students considering their reaction to the prospect of suddenly being aware of my presence in the doorway whilst they were in the midst of their rebellion. The interview led to me challenging many of their underlying assumptions, as I highlighted the contradictions between what they said I represented and their actual experience of me.

"I would probably have shut up and nudged the person next to me and we would have all like seen you and …"

"Even if I hadn't said anything?" I interrupted.

"Even if you hadn't said anything, even if you were just standing there."

"We would have stopped and listened to Miss," chipped in her classmate.

"And would you have?" I enquired looking at a third child.

"Yeah," she nodded.

"So what happens in your head, and the heads of your classmates, which directs them to suddenly be quiet?" I asked with genuine interest.

"We would have got a telling off or something because we were being really naughty," volunteered one. I was fascinated by the freedom in which these 13-year-olds used juvenile terminology to convey their behaviour.

"But Ms Smith could have told you off," I stated, mildly challenging the erroneous line of the argument, whilst seeking not to belittle her contribution.

"Yeah," she said slowly, absorbing the point.

"And also consider I have never told you off in our two years together, have I?" I reminded.

"No," all agreed.

I half-feigned confusion, "So where did you get the idea that *I* would give you a telling off?"

"Well, we have you every week and we are used to you ..." started one.

"So it's to do with you knowing me well?" I interjected.

"Yeah," all affirmed.

"Because we know you can control us, if you know what I mean," offered one. I came alive. She had inadvertently offered up one of the project's key terms.

"What do you mean by 'can control you'?"

"Like ..." she paused.

"Because I can't actually control you, can I?"

"Yeah, but ... I'm not sure, I think that I just behave."

I tried to help her out, "Because I guess I could do C1s, C2s and all that."

"Yeah," she hesitantly nodded.

"But, then again, so could Ms Smith." I had her snookered.

"Yeah."

"And I don't give you C1s and C2s. So what is it about me, my presence in the doorway, which makes you think 'I had better shut up'?"

Her contemplative friend broke her silence to offer her thoughts: "Maybe because we kind of respect you more – we've been with you for two years."

In retrospect, I wondered if disapproval might be key here. At the time I took another tack: "What about if it was the head teacher ... you've not been with him for two years?"

"We definitely would stop straight away, I think."

The ensuing discussion covered predictable ground citing status, expectations, and relationships before progressing to consider the significance of physical appearance.

> "Is it anything to do with the way someone looks? If you didn't know me, would the way I look standing at the door make any difference?" I asked.
>
> "Yeah, because you've got like this … you stand, like, really hard, if you know what I mean," offered one, with an amusing pose and expression to emphasise her point.
>
> "Yeah," agreed her friends.
>
> I sensed an opportunity to probe once again. "What if I was a smallish woman, would that make a difference?"
>
> "I think it would, I don't know. I think we prefer male teachers," said one prompting affirming nods from her peers.
>
> "Are there some teachers in the school who don't resemble anything of me but you would still behave for if you saw them standing in the doorway?" I asked, knowing full well the answer, as I pictured prominent female staff within the school.
>
> "Ms D," offered one. "Yeah, Ms H," chimed another.
>
> "So, it's not necessarily to do with how someone looks then?" I clarified.
>
> "No," reflected one, "not really."
>
> "It's the way they stand and talk," another said quickly, searching for the right answer.
>
> "Yeah," came the support.
>
> "The way they present themselves?" I pondered out loud.
>
> They all assertively declared, "Yeah," to suggest that we were on to something.

Chapter 16

Professional Identity

Sean

I did not get to know Ms Smith very well and so my investigation was done in retrospect and omitted her perspective. However, Mr John contributed enthusiastically to my research, even after he had left to take up his final placement. My ongoing dialogue with him affirmed my observation of a competent human being morphed (with that one solitary Year 8 class) into a persona completely at odds with his natural personality.

Split-self

This resonated with Woods and Carlyle's (2002) descriptors of teachers' incongruence around the notion of identity when placed under stress. Reddy (1997, 2001) uses the term 'emotives' to refer to emotional gestures and utterances, citing their capacity to alter the states of the speakers. Zembylas (2003) argues that, repeated over years, these could have profound effects on a teacher's identity and relationships, resulting in a feeling of burnout. Wright (2009) describes teachers creating a 'split-self' through which they adopt a different persona and which distances them from the emotional response that troubled children transfer. These, I argue, are integral to the dilemmas Berlak and Berlak (2002) refer to in the opening lines of this book. Sutton et al. (2009) report a dearth in good research evidence on the appropriate balance of positive and negative emotions for teachers in various contexts or on the most effective strategies to use to manage emotions. I hope to make a contribution to this knowledge, showing that this is a process rather than an event. The distinction between an authentic individual and the portrayal of an institutional position came to be highlighted independently from a convincing source – higher level teaching assistants (HLTAs).

During my research, HLTAs were well placed to be unobtrusive observers of classroom interactions. A group interview involving four colleagues drew out a distinct difference between a teacher who is successful with the children and one who remains distant. Qualifying the former, one stated that successful teachers "are confident about showing the students themselves as a person, they have personality; they might say things about their own lives and interests".[1] I wondered whether they were insinuating that others played a role. "Yes," was the reply. "They haven't the confidence to say, 'First of all, I am a human being, and I have chosen to teach because I like teaching.'"

Curious to learn about their observations of adults 'playing a teacher', the HLTAs came to a consensus which highlighted (stiff) body language, (higher) voice, lack of eye contact, and being generally more tense. A distinction was also made between them talking *at* students – "We need to get through the lesson, so we will do this, we will do that and bang, bang, bang, work, work, work" (this also included demands such as, "You will do this …" and, "We are going to …") – and talking *to* students. These perennial observers concluded that those teachers who experienced more difficulties with pupils "concentrated on content rather than the kids". Indicative of prominent educational discourse, Lodge's (2001) study of language used by teachers who profess an interest in learning found that the word 'learning' was used only 2% of the time in comparison to 98% for the term 'work'. Wolfe and Alexander (2008) argue that patterns of interaction are deeply habituated in teachers' consciousness and are tied to culture and history (Alexander 2001).

Self-laceration

Rodgers and Raider-Roth (2006), contemplating the perceived split or tension that NQTs experience between themselves as an individual and as a teacher, write of an inevitable tentativeness. Ever mindful of expectations purporting what a teacher *should* be (Goodson and Cole 1994), and fearful that their personal selves are not acceptable or appropriate, Rodgers and Raider-Roth identify an undermining of trust in the self, and thus their pupils' trust in them. The remoteness of an artificially constructed notion of who he ought to be made 'presence' difficult for the likes of Mr John (and I suspect Ms Smith), bringing about a disconnection with the group. Brookfield (1995) uses the term 'self-laceration' to describe the tendency of teachers who take their work seriously to blame themselves if their pupils are not learning; they feel, at some level, as though they are the cause of the hostility, resentment, or indifference they encounter. When students resist the pedagogical encounters that have been formulated to address their needs, such teachers can allow themselves to become consumed with guilt for what they believe to be their pedagogic incompetence. Likewise, they

1 Brookfield (2006: 57–58) observes that a teacher who is strong on authenticity, but weak on credibility, is perceived as a 'soft touch' – nice enough as an ally or confidant, but nothing much of value is learned. He argues that in optimal learning environments two characteristics – identified as credibility and authenticity – "are kept in a state of congenial tension". Unless a teacher gives a sense that s/he knows what s/he is doing, that s/he is competent and convincing and has been around the block a few times, then his/her authenticity counts for little.

immediately blame themselves when, for example, levels of learner achievement are deemed to be below national benchmarks.

I detected a vulnerability in Mr John, as the pupils seemed to reject him when they made a direct (and unfavourable) comparison to me, their 'proper' teacher. Beijaard (1995) describes how the more personal and professional selves are integrated into teacher identity, the more this is likely to be affected by positive or negative pupil attitudes and behaviour. My strategic role (documented in Chapter 3) meant that I had become progressively disturbed by conduct which I perceived to be obstructive. It is the apparent incongruity between these two facets of self which was encapsulated for me by Whitehead's (1989) phrase 'living contradiction'. Back in 1975, Argyris and Schön wrote of the discrepancy between our espoused theories (those we would like to identify with and convey to others) and our theories in action (those we habitually use). In accordance with my study, they advocate an examination of the assumptions engrained within a person's governing variables. Specifically, my identity, in my role as leader before and after the action research, was subjected to examination through my study (Lührmann and Eberl 2007).

Such self-definitions determine the nature of micro behaviours which the teacher habitually performs (Hay McBer 2000). This focus constituted my professional identity. I am mindful that some researchers, such as Nias (1996) and Bucholtz and Hall (2005), claim that teachers have a relatively stable identity rooted in a core set of values, beliefs, and practices. I came to subscribe to Cooper and Olson's (1996) analysis that professional identity is multifaceted – that historical, sociological, psychological, and cultural factors may all influence one's sense of self as a teacher. In addition, Reynolds (1996) advances the importance of the contextual, affirmed by Olsen (2008: 139) who suggests that identity is "an ever-changing construct … that becomes inter-twined inside the flow of activity as a teacher simultaneously reacts to and negotiates given contexts and human relationships at given moments".

Sub-identities

Mishler (1999: 8) writes of many sub-identities that may conflict or align with each other, which is expressed as a chorus of voices and "not just as the tenor or soprano soloist". Drawing on Gee and Crawford's (1998) view that social setting determines relationships between different identities, Beijaard et al. (2004) conclude that the better the relationships between identities, the better the chorus of voices sounds. I found this metaphor to be consistent with my notion of authenticity. Highlighting potential discrepancy, referring specifically to 'professional identity', Ball (1972) "usefully separates situated from substantive identity. He views the situated identity of a person as a malleable presentation of self that differs according to specific definitions of situations (e.g. within schools) and the more stable, core presentation of self that is fundamental to how a person thinks about himself or herself" (Day et al. 2006: 603).

And so I proceeded to apply these insights to my action phase, to explore whether non-authoritarian teacher approaches can steer pupils to contribute towards a well-ordered class dynamic, whether I could exhibit an authoritative presence which was governed by my living values, and whether I could be 'confident in uncertainty'.

I was mindful that the broad 'weather' categories presented in this part to convey instances of contestation, compliance, and low level resistance were inherent in every child I taught. The coming together of individuals to temporarily form unique and dynamic groupings contained the potential for each of these behavioural attributes to manifest, at any point, during any lesson. My task was to anticipate, recognise, and respond to these inevitable moments, so they did not escalate to draw in peers or disintegrate into conflict with me. I also aimed to notice and appreciate the positive (Bill Rogers' white space), establishing a norm in which the pupils themselves recognised disruption as being inappropriate.

I will show in Part IV that the requirements for compliance, and the need to revert to sanctions, can be effectively limited to specific and appropriate occasions, thus encouraging self-discipline to become the norm as pupils recognise the boundaries which enable learning. I will also consider how teachers might operate to achieve this: to have presence by being present, by encouraging a state or space where neither overbearing force nor chaos governs proceedings. I will argue that pupil energy need not descend into disruption or evoke the teacher's inclination to suppress, but instead might be harnessed to produce an emergent, cooperative classroom climate which enhances both learning and relationships. The concept of liminality is used to describe this state in-between authoritarian hierarchy ('structure') and social freedom/well-being ('*communitas*'), recognising the negotiation as a continuing process of readjustment (Turner 1969).

I envisaged operating in the zone of complexity (Stacey et al. 2000), without reverting to a draconian system or a domineering personality. Instead, I hoped to interpret apparent disorder as a creative opportunity for greater democracy and pedagogical choice. Turner (1990: 11–12) described this as "a fructile chaos, a fertile nothingness, a storehouse of possibilities". Research has shown that increasing the opportunities for choice making can be effective in reducing occurrences of problem behaviour (Shrogren et al. 2004). As a practitioner-researcher, I was ever wary of the possibility that pupils' interpretation of apparent disorder might provoke conduct in which relative freedom descended into disarray. The nature of my concern was articulated by pupils as part of their experience of school. Their perspectives provided an understanding as to what extent their behaviour was dependent on contextual factors when they sensed conditions which conveyed ambiguity. As such, I placed an initial emphasis on establishing boundaries within a transparent structure, where I was attuned to the need to either amplify or dampen the group's emerging energy. From this foundation, I hoped that the collective wisdom offered by my pupils and my application of theoretical insights would enable me to increasingly trust my students as we moved away from a constrained experience of pedagogy to partake in productive risk taking, and, in Bruner's (2014) terms, entertain "the world of possibilities, [which is] where intelligence lies".

Part IV
Power With

Chapter 17

Classroom Climate

Sean

It strikes me that when people consider pupil behaviour using propositional logic they invariably arrive at a polarised view – it's either/or. One side may justify being strict by pointing to the ineffectiveness of leniency; the opposing side may have a philosophical aversion to dictating to students and look to create an environment where children are free to express themselves. In viewing the classroom as a complex adaptive system, it is apparent that the teacher needs to be flexible in order to operate effectively – to be able to adjust and amend their approach in accordance with changing circumstances. And it is the teacher who sets the barometer that pre-empts many of the seemingly insignificant incidents which discerning pupils interpret as behaviour cues. As we have seen, trust is the ideal, but trust takes time and investment; so the starting point should convey a sense of credibility and competence that the adult is representative of institutional boundaries. Some pupils will accept it, others will need a bit more convincing and to observe what the teacher does and says – whether they follow through on things or whether their threats and warnings prove empty. With the latter, escalation will invariably follow. The balance is found in strategies and approaches which qualify the terms I presented in Chapter 12: amplify and dampen.

Someone asked me recently what I would do if a pupil was misbehaving. The honest and most accurate answer I could provide was, "It depends – context, relationships, and circumstances are everything." If she had asked me the same question a few years ago, my psychological default settings would have launched me into a bullish crusade to sort it out – consequences and sanctions, sanctions, sanctions – no questions asked! I wonder if she interpreted my response as weak and a cop-out. I can assure you it was not; it takes great strength to be an appropriate adult when the pupils around you are intent on kicking up a storm.

Figure 17.1 illustrates that, as with the weather, unilateral control of pupils' behaviour is illusory (Mason 2008). However, as a teacher occupying the position of responsible adult, I was required to uphold school rules which were stipulated in policy. Within these broadly accepted boundaries, I aimed to administer varying degrees of control in accordance with the emergent circumstances. For example, I reasoned that the pupils' self-control, apparent during cooperative Blue Skies behaviour (bottom left), ensures that the adult is able to yield control (C), whilst the manifestation of wilful Rain

Cloud traits (bottom right) warrants a strong directive response in accordance with school disciplinary procedures. In such situations the notions of democracy (inclusion) and trust (openness) are temporarily withdrawn.

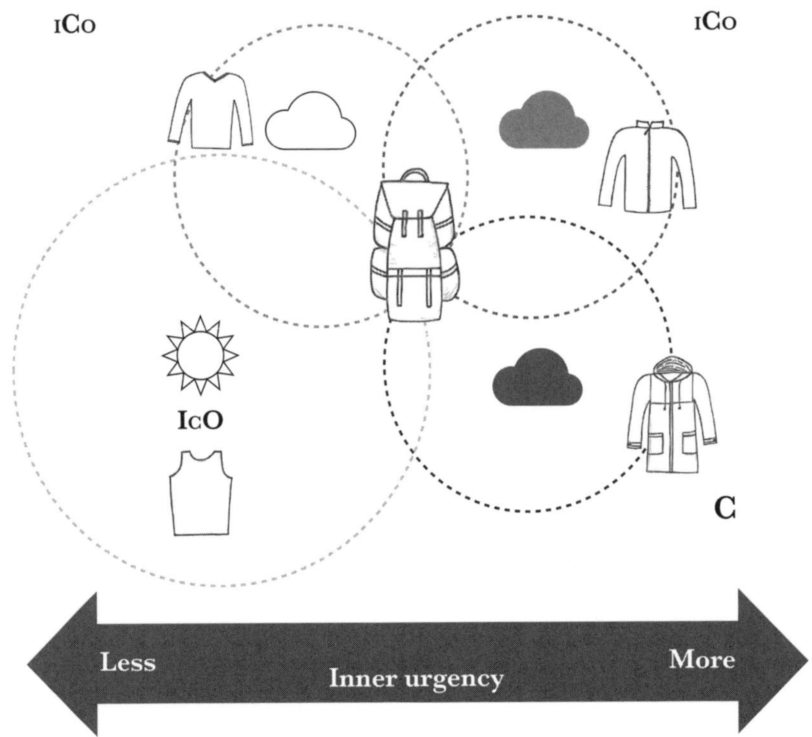

Figure 17.1. Dynamic control – differing degrees of inclusion, control, and openness (ICO)[1]

The degrees of control (indicated by the size of the C) are symbolised by the different clothing the teacher 'wears' or operationally adopts in response to the conditions. The clothing itself is representative of a disciplinary approach which complements the climate – for example, a Vest is worn in response to sunny conditions, in contrast to the Waterproofs which are donned in the event of rain. In essence, the figure advocates appropriate control and recognises its application as dynamic. Hart's (2010) research on effective behaviour management concludes that there is no one specific technique or approach that can be identified as superior; rather, a number of elements contribute (Little and Akin-Little 2003). Marzano et al.'s (2003)

1 The terms inclusion, control, and openness come from FIRO theory. It forms part of the four model link-up which is presented in Figure 17.2 (openness is also referred to as affection). I expand on my application of inclusion and openness later in this chapter. A distinct model of FIRO is provided in Appendix A.

meta-analysis of which classroom management techniques work best affirms a blend of different aspects. This is further endorsed by the Department for Education (2012: vi) in their review of pupil behaviour in schools in England, who acknowledge that "Using a combination of strategies is also a theme of the literature."

In Part IV I will present a detailed analysis of the four respective garments below: Vest, Fleece, Light Jumper, and Waterproofs (which, I argue, exude a sense of fairness and competence, if suitably worn). Although a definitive formula remains elusive, the approach addresses the concerns inherent in descriptors of strict and lax teachers that the pupils attributed to Means Business/Scary, and Ineffective teachers in Chapters 13 and 14. In consideration of authority, Bigger (2015: 10) articulates the inappropriateness of polarised stances in an educational setting, suggesting that an educational establishment operates within a continuum: "if too authoritarian it is repressive, forcing compliance rather than enabling independence; [alternatively], if there are no boundaries and rules, a pecking order will quickly establish who holds real authority, by dominance and aggression rather than through wisdom".

I would suggest that such instances of inappropriate disciplinary approach might be helpfully demonstrated through reference to the Vest, Light Jumper, Fleece, and Waterproofs. One teacher I know dominated the loveliest of Year 7 classes as a matter of course, regardless of the fact that the vast majority were timid and compliant. This is demonstrative of wearing Waterproofs in warm weather. At the other end of the spectrum, I can think of teachers who wanted to be the children's friend: they referred to them as 'guys', habitually tried to cajole the class, and almost pleaded for the cooperation of individuals who had sensed an opportunity to test and challenge boundaries (often on behalf of peers who awaited the outcome). Here we might envisage a teacher who is seemingly oblivious to the weather forecast, continuing to wear a Vest as the dark clouds gather. To simplify, we might say that one used too much control, whilst the other did not use enough; one tended to be hot and bothered, whilst the other was inevitably exposed.

At the beginning of their course, each pupil would be carrying their own provisional imago[2] based on their prior experience of the group and their previous contact and/or perception of the teacher. The significance of prior knowledge of a teacher's standards or approach was illustrated in Chapter 13, indicating that teachers' reputations were discussed and passed on by peers. Data consistently showed that the pupils' sensibility to classroom climate was most acute at the beginning of interactions. I therefore sought to ensure that my boundaries were apparent upon first contact with the groups, and were subsequently reinforced through routines each time we met. Rather than constrain the pupils, I hoped this clarity might provide a sense of security from which to develop positive relationships and to tolerate uncertainty in learning. Gerlach and Bird (2006) refer to findings in neuroscience which affirm the importance of relationships to determine whether children are able to access adequately the cognitive or 'thinking' brain.

In recognition of the needs of a developing group, and mindful of its individual members, Temple's (1992a) four model link-up (Figure 17.2) provides two models with an emphasis on the individual and two with a group focus. Considered together, they show how different developmental phases require different aspects of leadership as the group process unfolds (Temple 2005). I selected data to illustrate my engagement with each stage, and focused on some of the obstacles which impeded us from moving seamlessly through one stage to the next.

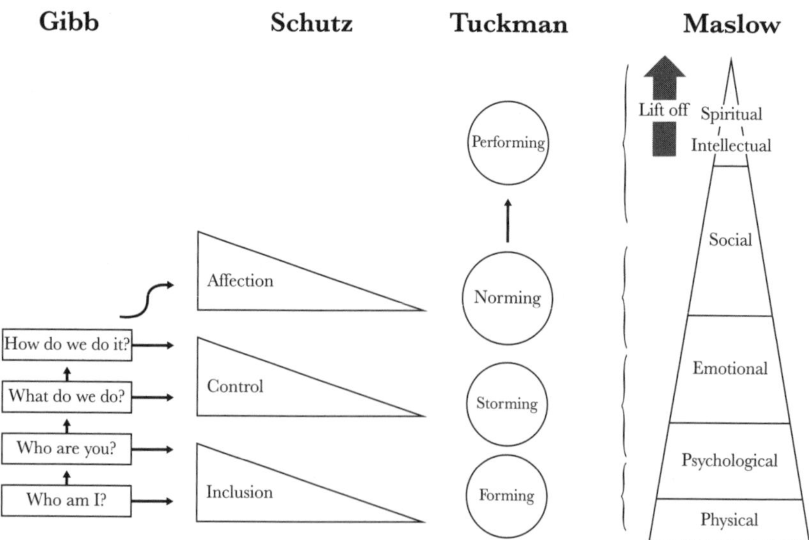

Figure 17.2. Group formation: four model link-up

2 An imago is defined as an unconscious, idealised mental image of someone, especially a parent or authority figure, which influences a person's behaviour.

The sections at the base of Figure 17.2 represent the early stage of group formation. Temple (1992b) uses the model to articulate the unconscious concerns of pupils when they meet for the first time:

- Group questions about who the group members are (Gibb 1978).
- Initial focus on whether to join in or not: "Can I belong here?" (Schutz 1979).
- The first stage of foundation forming, relating to the adjustment of the provisional imago (Tuckman 1965).
- Primitive concerns about survival, both physical and psychological (Maslow 1950).

Every time I have watched the opening episode of a series such as *Big Brother* or *I'm a Celebrity … Get Me Out of Here!* I watch this process unfold with unerring accuracy. All the while, we (the viewers and producers) know that beneath the facade of initial politeness, a storm is brewing as contestants manoeuvre, contest power, and push boundaries. In accordance with these insights, I was keen that significant pupils took their cue to behave well from me, in order to influence susceptible peers. My investment was done in these early stages. My negotiation and use of control were key to my performance. As demonstrated in Chapter 13, too much control and I would continue to elicit mere compliance, too little and I would expose myself to pockets of testing, resistance, and challenge (Chapter 14).

Initial Forming Phase

The deliberate aim of my initial meeting with groups was to convey a sense of safety and care within a structure framed by transparent boundaries. This involved a genuine welcome and an invitation to come into the room, without the formalities of lining up outside. This was in recognition of the fact that sub-groups converging outside classrooms were more likely to engage in boisterous behaviour, which then had to be diffused upon entering the classroom. Previously, my practice had been to demand a straight line before they entered the room, in silence. My attention would have been on stamping down individuals I perceived as seeking to disturb my class. The decision to funnel pupils into the room as they arrived meant that I was able to shape the classroom climate and influence potentially troublesome individuals as they joined us.

Positioning myself to monitor the evolving group, I made a commitment not to get distracted by administrative tasks which would prevent me from paying attention to individuals as they entered. This allowed me to make enquiries of their day and well-being. My hope was that the pupils, despite their reservations about the relevance of my subject to their ambitions and interests, would feel accepted and increasingly experience a sense of belonging and confidence; I gave them permission to talk to their friends but also made them responsible for getting themselves ready for learning. I used the notion of a relationship bank account to frame classroom exchanges. This was informed by Schutz's FIRO theory categories of inclusion, control, and openness (included in Temple's four model link-up and explored later in this chapter; the theory is also expanded in Appendix A). 'Deposits' (as depicted by the piggybank in Figure 17.3) are made when participants feel significant, competent, and valued, and are extracted when they are feeling ignored, humiliated, or rejected. Alongside competence, I view trust as being integral to significant deposits.

A task on the board often acted as a backdrop for those arriving early. I am mindful of Morgan et al.'s (2010: 191; original emphasis) claim that "it is the *absence* of positive experiences which undermined commitment and efficacy rather than the *occurrence* of negative events". Noddings (2003) viewed presence as a fundamental feature of care, which she argued is an essential stance in teaching. Referring to the concept of connection found in personal relationships, and resonating with my practice at the beginning of lessons, she offered a pragmatic application: "I do not need to establish a lasting, time-consuming personal relationship with every student … What I must do is to be totally and non-selectively present to the student – to each student – as he addresses me. The time interval may be brief but the encounter is total" (Noddings 2003: 180).

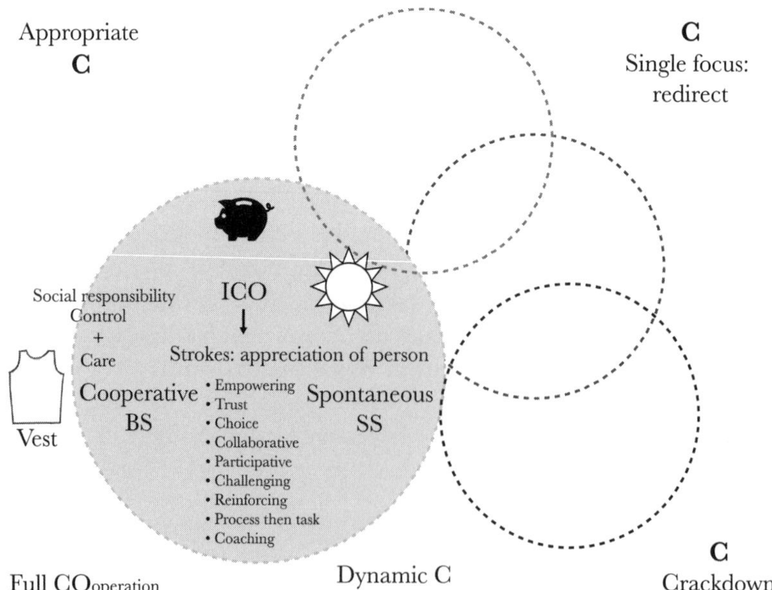

Figure 17.3. Disciplinary approach: Vest

Reinforcing Cues During the Re-forming Process

In the first lesson, I tended to insist on an initial seating plan which sat the students as boy/girl. This was the most convenient categorisation to separate likely social alliances until I got to know the group better. I then informed the pupils that I was open to possibly amending and trialling different combinations as the term progressed. As previously mentioned, my research had explored the possibility of allowing peers in a Year 10 class to choose their seating arrangements. As in my experience of covering a Year 10 tutor group, I witnessed both overt and covert resistance to learning through the establishment of several cliques. Reverting back to a formal seating plan instantly dissipated the pockets of opposition.

The idealistic aim is to be able to wear a Vest as the group initially forms, and subsequently at the beginning of each lesson. Whilst some pupils allowed this, due to their cooperative nature, my experience affirmed that this stance would inevitably leave the teacher feeling exposed if clouds formed overhead. Field data on the students' propensity to interpret signals and read cues revealed that some perceived an open, caring welcome as a sign of weakness.

Although I can advocate giving – in transactional analysis terms – genuine 'strokes' or units of recognition (Barrow et al. 2002) through appreciating the individual for who they are (rather than what they do), I found that a more formal structure was required if I was to create (and sustain) learning conditions which were full of context and purpose. This was to ensure that opportunities for pupils to be more independent and interdependent did not descend into chaos (as characterised by social distractions and power struggles).

The optimum state at the start of lessons was characterised by a sense of order. For some classes this was insisted on in order to quell their energy or detract from their social agenda, for others the sense of collective goodwill created a feeling of harmony. Behaviours contributing to this affable state require further explanation. In Figure 17.3, I make a subtle distinction between Blue Skies (BS) and Sunshine (SS). For the sake of simplicity, I chose to use the generic term Blue Skies in questionnaires and graphs to encompass this constructive category. However, Temple's (2004) Functional Fluency model (which became integral to my research) enabled me to articulate distinctive attributes which only a minority of children have demonstrated to me throughout my career. Sunshine stems from the spontaneous mode (see Appendix B). My experience of these children had thus far been indefinable. They exhibited a spark which I found energising, as though schooling could not stifle their natural exuberance. Blue Skies is associated with cooperative pupil conduct, as it is a mode of behaviour which develops from the socialising of the child. It suggests that, as the expectations inherent within the role of pupil begin to become established, the well-adjusted child is able to exercise positive traits which enable him/her to communicate and function effectively with others. However, Chapter 14 shows that even pupils who habitually display these positive characteristics are susceptible to peer pressure – if the teacher is ambiguous or fails to convince significant pupils that they are representative of the school's boundaries.

Hence, the most appropriate attire to adorn whilst the group formed, and at the beginning of each subsequent lesson, was a Light Jumper. This approach caters for the reality that some children will arrive harbouring negative thoughts which may lead to passivity, whilst others arrive with strong social agendas which can undermine the crucial establishment stage. This category represents the formal stance that I used to settle the group at the beginning of lessons (and the year), and a position I reverted to intermittently as I was called to (re-)establish a sense of calm and order. The Light Jumper approach incorporates more control than the Vest, as it habitually includes directives as part of the communication with the group. We also recognise and appreciate what they do well. In accordance with Dweck's (2000) research, this is done by emphasising both effort and strategy, rather than the idea that a child is 'good' or 'clever'. Elements encapsulated in the notion of the Light Jumper are presented in Figure 17.4.

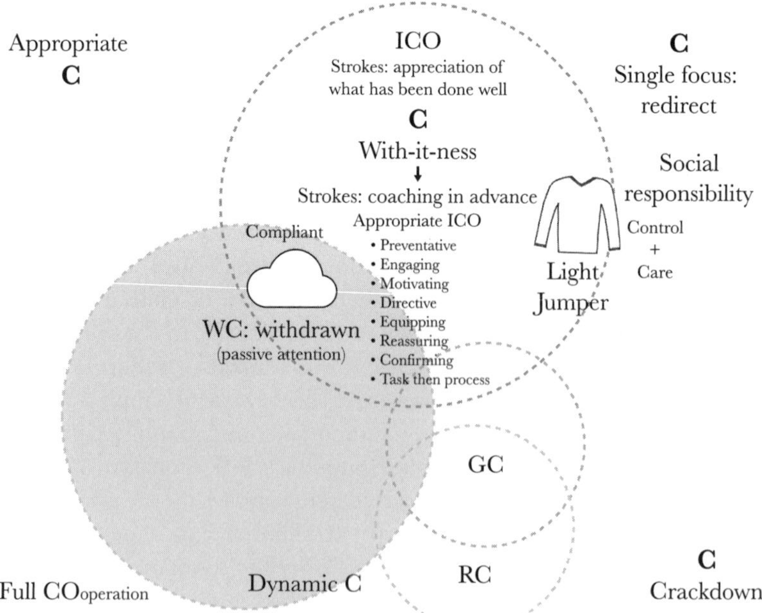

Figure 17.4. Disciplinary approach: Light Jumper

To build a picture of classroom climate, I will describe the established procedures I constructed and present pupils' initial impressions upon entering the classroom. In response to the question, "How would you describe your experience at the beginning of lessons in my classroom?" (*n*. 334) prominent key terms (mentioned a total of 229 times) confirmed a sense of organised calmness which is quiet and relaxed, enabling pupils to settle and chat as they got themselves ready. One Year 8 girl summed up: "We usually just get into class, get our stuff out and give out the books and just have a two minutes' break and then start the lesson."

The terms used in the extract below capture the balance between structure and freedom via expectations communicated through routines. This encompasses the essence of 'coaching in advance'. Routines were explained, discussed, agreed, recorded, and practised in the first lesson before any subject content was introduced. The entry and settling period conveyed the norms of behaviour expected, along with the security of knowing what was coming next. I deliberately wandered amongst the group, having positioned myself initially near the open door. My persona was noted by a group of pupils ranging from Year 7 to Year 10, who wrote:

> Mr Warren always welcomes people even if he is under pressure/stress.
>
> He waits till everyone comes into the classroom.
>
> He always seems happy to see us.
>
> I feel … looked after because he takes into account your problems and feelings.
>
> As soon as we walk in he says hello with a smile.
>
> We are welcomed because he always smiles.

Mindful of the notion of 'face', I was able to smile, greet, remind, and reinforce agreed routines as individuals passed me to join classmates who had already started the process of getting out and handing out equipment; others were having a drink and chatting whilst getting themselves acclimatised. Bags placed under the table and coats on the back of chairs were also signs that distinguished this environment from many others in the school. Rud (1995: 123) draws upon Nouwen (1975) to advance the notion of 'hospitality'. Primarily, it refers to "The creation of a free space where the stranger can enter and become a friend instead of an enemy … where students and teachers can enter into a fearless communication with each other."

Contributing to the different phases of the lesson was the use of music. Selected classical tracks played in the background rather than dominating the room. The volume was selected to moderate noise levels: if the music could not be heard it suggested that some of the children were a little too excitable and needed a subtle reminder to calm down. Music was mentioned by many pupils in their responses to the questionnaire. Terms such as 'calm', 'soothing', 'peaceful', 'nice', and 'background' were prominent descriptors. Conversely, if the atmosphere was flat, pop music was used to inject an upbeat feel and to accompany selected tasks.

My movement to the front of the classroom would occur after I had announced, "Starting in 30 seconds." A 10 second warning usually accompanied the cessation of music as I moved to the centre of the room. It was a directive rather than a request and signalled that their attention was required: "And stop … pens down … (looking around) … looking this way … (surveying the room and making eye contact) … and listen (pause) … Thank you – good morning." A shortened version was used to interrupt activities, when I paraphrased Rogers' (2002): "Eyes and ears this way, thanks" (whilst describing any distractions I observed, e.g. "one or two still fidgeting with equipment"), then repeating the direction, "Pens down, eyes and ears this way … thanks."

If the room was full of energy and enthusiasm I tended not to compete with it, but instead interrupted by breaking into loud rhythmic banging on the lockers (bang bang-a-bang-bang) to elicit a concluding response to the beat from the pupils (bang bang). This was often repeated in quick succession until the vast majority were diverted from their former focus to join in. Their collective response left a split second of silence, which I would fill with an affirmation or a directive such as, "Pens down …" At times, I might apologise for interrupting and inform the class of how long I would need their attention. An alternative signal the pupils came to recognise was a high pitched bell which announced the end of the settling down period and the beginning of my instructions. Allowing a selected pupil to act as bell ringer also brought attention and acted to minimise the number of times I had to insist on attentiveness.

The expectations conveyed through these routines were supported by an immaculate classroom, which was left that way by the preceding class. Tables were aligned, litter was put in the bin, and light and temperature were carefully monitored in response to the (actual) weather outside of the room. This stipulation was influenced by Kelling and Coles' (1996) broken windows theory, which suggests that signs of neglect can escalate unsociable behaviour.

Whilst pupils from other classes waited to enter adjoining rooms, typically pushing and jostling outside in the inadequate available space whilst the teacher insisted on straight lines and silence, my groups had already settled and were primed for an opening task. This would either aim to capture their interest or reinforce previous learning in readiness for the opening activity. In accordance with Fiedler's (1978) leadership model, I would keep communication to a minimum and deliberately place an emphasis on the learning task to focus the pupils' attention and energy. As I got to know the groups better and cultivated relationships, I could judge when I could afford to be a little more informal.

'With-it-ness'

Central to the persona I deliberately adopted when wearing a Light Jumper was the concept of 'with-it-ness' (Kounin 1970). This was to influence pupils' interpretation of my standing as an authority figure. It complemented the intention to be 'present' – that is, "bringing one's whole self to full attention so as to perceive what is happening in the moment" (Rodgers and Raider-Roth 2006: 267). Providing a pragmatic strategy to my philosophical stance and methodological commitment, with-it-ness is defined as a teacher communicating with the pupils by her/his actual behaviour that s/he knows what the pupils are doing – the proverbial 'eyes in the back of the head'.

I believe it is necessary to transmit the degree to which I am with-it. Kounin (1970) suggests this is best demonstrated through desist events. Desist events are examples of incidents where I do something that communicates to the children whether I know (or don't know) what is happening – for example, a pupil would be doing something, I would intervene, and my action would cause the pupil to stop. I might position myself so I have a peripheral view of the lad who has wandered over to the bin to sharpen a pencil whilst I am busy speaking with another child. Legitimate as it may be, I note that he has had adequate time to complete his task and seems to be smiling. "Johnny (pause, eye contact) … sharp enough for you?" He knows that I know, and so do his audience. Hargreaves et al. (1975) consider whether the teacher is able to pick the correct target, whether they do it on time, and whether they might make some kind of mistake which communicates that they don't know what is happening.

The idea of a lighthouse constantly surveying the surrounding area is another helpful metaphor for this attribute. As one Year 9 pupil identified: "They have eye contact with you … and address the whole class aware of what everyone is doing." Thus, the term with-it-ness describes the capacity to be aware of a wide variety of things that are going on simultaneously in a classroom. This is a constant challenge for any teacher, and it can be a particular strain for a new teacher until this skill is acquired. Teachers perceived to be with-it are able to anticipate and see where help is needed, as well as where and when they might get drawn into a psychological game (see Chapter 19). They are able to nip trouble in the bud: they are skilful at scanning the class whilst helping individuals, and they physically position themselves so they can use their peripheral vision; they are alert; they pre-empt disturbances and they act fast; they sense the way a class is responding; they read the climate; and they act to maintain a positive atmosphere. As two students observed:

> At the beginning of the year he made it clear he doesn't tolerate misbehaving and I saw that he wasn't wrong when he dealt with a few silly boys.
>
> I figured Sir out by someone who took it too far and he sorted it.

It would be apparent to any observer that there was a degree of calmness and order in my groups. However, I was interested to gain the pupils' perspectives. I asked two further questions to obtain a comprehensive view – the first subjective and the second objective:

> Can you help me understand what it is I do, or the way I am, that influences your behaviour in my classroom? (*n*. 246)
>
> Why do you think most classmates choose to behave rather than disrupt my lessons? (*n*. 240)

I wondered whether their collective responses would identify the value underlying my performance at the beginning of each and every lesson: respect.

Many of the students seemed to recognise and respond to the reciprocal relationship which is defined by mutual 'respect' (50 mentions). Also significant for me are two other aspects. The first is the identification of 'fun' (151) and 'funny' (77). Although I used a repertoire of jokes, silly walks, wigs, and masks, it has become apparent to me that this description is of me at my best as a human being. It is when I am most at ease with myself and my surroundings and my conduct is not governed by me playing a role. Much of my subject content was of a serious nature (ethical and moral issues) which required me to display a sense of proportion and appropriateness. I was aware that, on occasion, a quip has backfired and embarrassed a child (which I was quick to apologise for), and at other times I have unwittingly offended through comments which have pricked sensitive ears. A minority have also communicated through the research process that they did not find my jokes funny! The data showed that a couple of individuals had interpreted my attempts at humour as sarcasm. Again, whilst not seeking to minimise their views, I have accepted that I can't please everyone, but my best intentions and sincere apologies aid my attempts to be authentic.

The second interesting term to emerge from my analysis of the pupils' responses to my questions is a reference to 'breaks'. For the majority of my career I have believed it to be unreasonable to expect children to concentrate for a full hour, lesson after lesson. In 1998, I accepted Smith's (1996) maxim regarding attention spans: as a rule of thumb, I used chronological age plus/minus two minutes (Smith 2002). Break(s) are mentioned 79 times as a contributory factor to the class climate. The comments showed that the pupils recognised that the purpose of breaks was to change pace, prevent boredom, bring renewed focus, and to simply refresh. Pupils were told in advance when the next planned break was scheduled, or sometimes I gave a selected pupil the responsibility of gauging when the class needed a break. On occasion I detected that they were not ready to settle or focus so enquired of them whether they needed a 30 second break to get the chatter out of their system. My rationale is succinctly put by a Year 7 girl: "Mr Warren understands our needs, like breaks."

The strategy also allowed me to get ready for the next phase of the lesson – for example, getting technology set up. Plus, it enabled me to follow up on earlier lateness or have a quiet word with individuals who needed a reminder or the offer of a choice to ensure they did themselves justice. Often, it was simply a chance to ask individuals how they were feeling and to make contact. Experience has taught me that many colleagues will not contemplate the idea of breaks as they are not confident that the pupils will resettle. However, I have found that, aside from establishing routines for re-engagement, the ingredients of trust and reasonable negotiation tend to derive from respectful relationships.

Seeking to attain further insight, I asked four Year 7 classes:

> What signs/clues informed you that it would be in your best interest to behave rather than mess about and disrupt my lessons? (*n.* 95)

This question is reminiscent of the earlier question I posed to classes about their perceptions of a 'strong' teacher (see Chapter 13). However, this version is personalised and enquires about *my* performance. In response there is a (complete) absence of any references to the traits apparent in Scary teacher and Ineffective teacher, although there was an echo of the Means Business teacher underpinning my considered approach.

Collective Responsibility

I was particularly interested in examining the reasoning which followed the connective 'because …' One theme stood out as significant: it was apparent that many pupils had an acute awareness of the 'freedom' they felt privileged to have been given. In addition, several pupils cited a practical instrument as a tangible cue to amending behaviour. The tool, colour coded in accordance with traffic lights, is usually assembled in a binder to form an A4 sized flip chart, with one number on each page (Figure 17.5). It monitors whole class collaboration and acts to stimulate peer pressure on those individuals who would otherwise stay disconnected during group tasks.

Figure 17.5. Group monitoring tool

As the pupils explain further:

> I knew how to behave because of the countdown and the numbers on the different coloured paper.
>
> The behaviour/number thing is good because [if] you lose points and get to 0 you'd do bookwork.
>
> The whole class will suffer, [so] you know not to mess about but have fun and learn.

Interestingly, I can recall only a couple of occasions during the research process when a group actually lost all seven points. Often, just picking up the tool and wavering whether to turn over the page was enough to deter off-task behaviour. I also observed a particular student who had deliberately squandered the points appear genuinely taken aback when his peers communicated their disapproval. Over time I considered it more ethically sound to deal with a persistent perpetrator separately at an opportune time so as not to punish the whole class. I was also interested to note that one comment equated bookwork with punishment – an interesting connotation, as this was never my intention. On reflection, what I did was to take away their choices which inevitably left them with a task that was directed by me. It so happens that this tended to take the form of bookwork. In essence, the activity ensured each pupil focused on their own space and task, and so effectively dampened the collective energy that was causing me concern.

Classroom Climate Questionnaire

To affirm the emphasis I placed on this foundational aspect of group formation, I posed two further questions:

> How do you feel about coming into my classroom?
>
> What advice would you give to a new student who has just joined the school and is accompanying you to my class for the first time? (*n.* 354)

I wanted to encourage the pupils to build on their emotive responses by articulating an objective perspective. An interesting array of terms emerged from the data. Positive descriptors such as 'good', 'happy', 'calm', 'excited', 'relaxed', 'fine', 'comfortable', and 'confident' were prominent. The word 'fun' appeared 202 times. I was mindful that this term was absent in descriptions of other teachers for whom they did behave (see Chapter 13). I felt validated in making the distinction between 'messing about' and Rea's (1997) portrayal of 'serious fun' as integral to learning performance (see Chapter 24).

As my initial focus was on building a positive learning environment, I was keen to explore the context in which 'atmosphere' was phrased. The mention of 'nice', 'good', 'peaceful', 'friendly', and 'calm' gave me encouragement. However, Schutz's (1979) FIRO theory, which is integral to Temple's four model link-up, prompted a further enquiry of my groups' inter-relational state.

Secure, Significant, and Valued

The FIRO model uses the acronym ICO: I considers to what extent the pupil wants to be and feels *included*, C refers to levels of *control*, and O relates to degrees of *openness* (or affection) and is more personal than inclusion. (See Figure 17.1 where I consider different disciplinary approaches in response to 'weather conditions'.) The inter-relational theory challenged my assumption that I should make an indiscriminate effort to include everyone in whole class activities. I came to realise that whilst some pupils with high extrovert preferences might desire continued involvement in order to feel significant, others (perhaps those who were more introverted) naturally preferred to observe developments and/or work independently. Rather than compel pupils to speak, I began to respect the level of contribution individuals wished to make by creating more choice in how they engaged with others during the learning tasks. (This is explained further in Chapter 24.)

Whilst I did not subject pupils to the intricacies of the theory, or expose them to the complications of submitting scores, I did enquire whether the climate I was trying to cultivate equated to them feeling significant, valued, and/or liked (see Appendix A). These aspects were investigated through administering questionnaires to four Year 7 classes in July 2011 (*n.* 106). Expanding the scope of my original questionnaire, they were asked:

Do you feel safe?

Do you feel as though you belong and are welcomed?

Do you feel as though you are treated well and valued in my class?

Data analysis revealed 287 references to 'yes', which were then qualified. Further enquiry produced zero returns for the word 'no' as part of any of the responses to the three questions from the participants.

The data presented so far suggests that I was largely effective in establishing a solid foundation for my classes, so enabling pupils to contribute positively to the class dynamic rather than being coerced. General affirmation for this view is illustrated through comments such as:

> [I behaved] because I liked you.
>
> You just take care of us and stuff.
>
> You don't shout or be mean so I don't have any reason to be naughty or nasty.

On the whole, I can claim that paying attention to how the groups formed at the beginning of the term, and periodically in subsequent meetings, ensured that the majority of my classes passed effortlessly through Tuckman's (1965) forming and storming stages and settled or normalised (norming). Forsyth (1983) characterises this latter developmental stage as class members sharing a feeling of group unity and exhibiting a sense of cohesiveness. However, this is not to suggest that all pupils experienced my lessons positively. Some comments alerted me to aspects which were not initially apparent to me when teaching. There was evidence that some children who felt uncomfortable to varying degrees tried to cope so they did not upset the class equilibrium. Consequently, their sense of unease also escaped my attention. For example, some participants made the clear distinction between the subject and the teacher. One Year 10 pupil stated: "I do not enjoy RE but I do like Mr Warren as a teacher," whilst his peer said: "Its fine, but I prefer Mr Warren rather than RE. He has made it a good subject but normally I don't like RE. I used to dread it last year." The theme is reinforced by a Year 7 boy who reported: "I don't really like RE but it has grown on me."

Furthermore, despite my efforts to create a positive, secure, and foundational base for my classes through the establishment of routines (alongside a commitment to notice and appreciate pupils, especially those who were usually quiet), one Year 7 child wrote (emphasis added): "I feel OK … *But I don't think Mr Warren really knows me.*" Another answer reminded me of the vulnerability some children feel as they move from one cohort to join another: "I feel scared … sometimes. Yes, [I feel welcomed and valued] by the teacher, but not by pupils."

These insights reinforced for me the fact that on an hourly basis pupils are required to navigate their place amongst their peers, and so the adult needs to be ever vigilant. In addition, although the questions generated a broad range of affirmative responses, drawing comments such as, "You are a calm person which sets an example to others," the data also produced negative judgemental remarks such as I was boring and strict. In qualifying the phrase 'OK', older pupils in particular openly revealed their indifference. Dismissive of my attempts to improve his experience of my subject, this is perhaps best captured by the response: "Fine, like any other lesson, just plain simple school."

Contrary to the majority of replies, my research reminds me that typical classes are likely to contain some individuals who, despite the teacher's best efforts, are reluctant to be won over. Standing out as exemplars, three Year 9 boys from the same class wrote: "I do not look forward to Sir's lessons and I dislike the method of teaching," "Getting ready to be bored," and "Bored and thinking 'Oh no'," whilst a Year 10 girl offered a different interpretation of 'fun' saying: "Don't really look forward to it, find the lesson boring and not too keen on stupid jokes every lesson."

From an initial surge of being uncomfortable with such comments, I eventually came to a place of acceptance. This represented a small release from a rigid and controlling mindset – there was a growing sense of realism to my perspective. These individuals may well have equated their experience of the subject with negative feelings towards me. As I was unaware of such opinions during the lessons, and it was unrepresentative of the groups' collective appraisal, I suspect a facade of politeness or passive defensiveness may well have existed if the respondents sat with peers who they did not relate to or who did not share their view. This is the essence of White Cloud behaviour, which is likely to be seen as unproblematic if it masquerades under the veneer of order. Breidenstein (2007) links boredom with being detached. The three Year 9 boys were of particular interest to me and are scrutinised further in Chapter 24. My research notes also detailed sustained periods of active opposition from other individuals. These invited intense scrutiny during the research period and are viewed through the lens of transactional analysis.

Chapter 18

Dark Clouds

Sean

Whilst I can argue a consistent progression from the 'forming' stage to the 'norming' stage for the majority of classes, obstacles impeding my work became apparent. Tuckman's (1965) model of group processes suggests that as individuals come together there may be a calm before the storm. This is especially so if group members are not overly familiar with each other or if an unfamiliar authority figure takes the helm. My pupils independently and collectively participated in a process where significant individuals would subtly test the boundaries on behalf of their peers, whilst others were explicit in stepping over the boundaries and challenging the authority of the adult. The chapters that comprise Part III produced data which was stimulating to put together. However, this chapter adds another dimension, for I now speak as the teacher from a position where my research was to become personal and uncomfortable.

The significant Dark Cloud behaviour I encountered blew in from two specific groups. The ongoing incidents meant that these classes witnessed a prolonging of the storming stage. My ability to deal with these conflicts is at the heart of this aspect of the study. The repeated challenges to my authority provoked in me an overwhelming inclination to revert back to domineering, quick-fix strategies. The subsequent reflexive process by which I sought to overcome these deep-seated traits is documented in the next chapter. The ensuing focus might be summarised as a study of pupil provocation eliciting an external professional response, whilst at the same time stoking engrained defensive reactions which I fought to contain. This aspect of my performance uses two values to act as standards of judgement: firstly, 'fairness' is advanced to assess my authoritative response to students, and, secondly, the notion of 'responsibility' guides the decisions I made – especially during critical moments of contestation.

Hidden Goals

The broad obstructive category I refer to as Dark Clouds is defined by Grey Cloud and Rain Cloud behaviour. The considered response to Grey Clouds is to pull on a Fleece (see Figure 18.1) in order to maintain an internal and external equilibrium when experiencing a changeable climate. By donning this garment, I aimed to redirect pupils back to task in a non-confrontational manner.

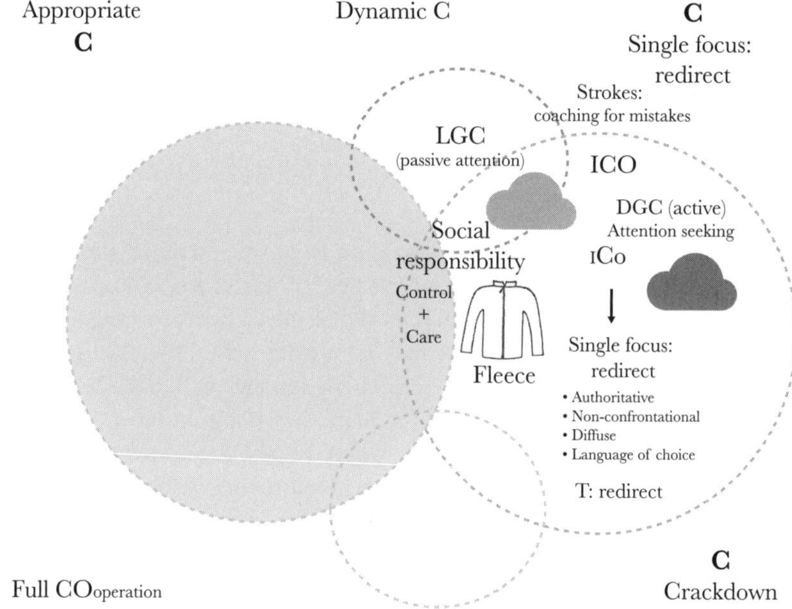

Figure 18.1. Disciplinary approach: Fleece

Note: LGC: Light Grey Cloud; DGC: Dark Grey Cloud

For the majority, the use of the techniques espoused by Rogers (2002, e.g. "Eyes and ears this way") were enough to desist and return them to their learning. In accordance with the descriptors presented in Chapter 14, Grey Cloud behaviour is equated with attention seeking and is usually dependent on approval from peers. Often it is active but sometimes it is passive (e.g. feigning incompetence to get the attention of the teacher). This represents the distinction between *Dark* and *Light* Grey Clouds. As such, I found that if the class norm was task orientated and sufficient scaffolding was in place, then such incidents were fleeting. Comments from students ranging from Year 7 to Year 10 indicate their awareness of boundaries (emphasis added):

> If I get a bit out of *line* [you] talk to me and then I am OK.
>
> We know you don't stand for nonsense, and we know when to draw the *line* because without shouting you present warnings.
>
> You are caring and funny but you put people who cross the *line* in their place; I think you just set the rules so we know where we stand. Also you respect us and we can have a laugh with you but we also know when not to cross the *line*.

However, during the research phase I encountered some pupils who deliberately pushed boundaries, rejected the group norm, and chose to 'cross the line'. Teacher–pupil encounters at the borders have the capacity to escalate, drawing in observers and impinging on productive behaviour and learning opportunities. On the occasion depicted in Figure 18.2, a new lad joined my Year 8 class. I had taught the group since their first day at the school and I had developed a strong bond with them. The new boy tried to impress his peers by turning off the power switch, which sabotaged the lesson. As the interactive whiteboard and computer died, he was met with a most unexpected response as he sat there looking smug and innocent. Instead of gaining their approval the entire class shunned him. It wasn't nasty, it was just completely apparent that their loyalty to me was uppermost. Speaking to the boy quietly outside the classroom, positioning myself in the doorway to simultaneously occupy part of the classroom and the corridor, I simply told him how it was: that the class and I had history. He nodded and said, "I realise that now. I've made a mistake – sorry." In the coming weeks and months, the young man simply merged in with the group expectation. If only it was always resolved like that ...

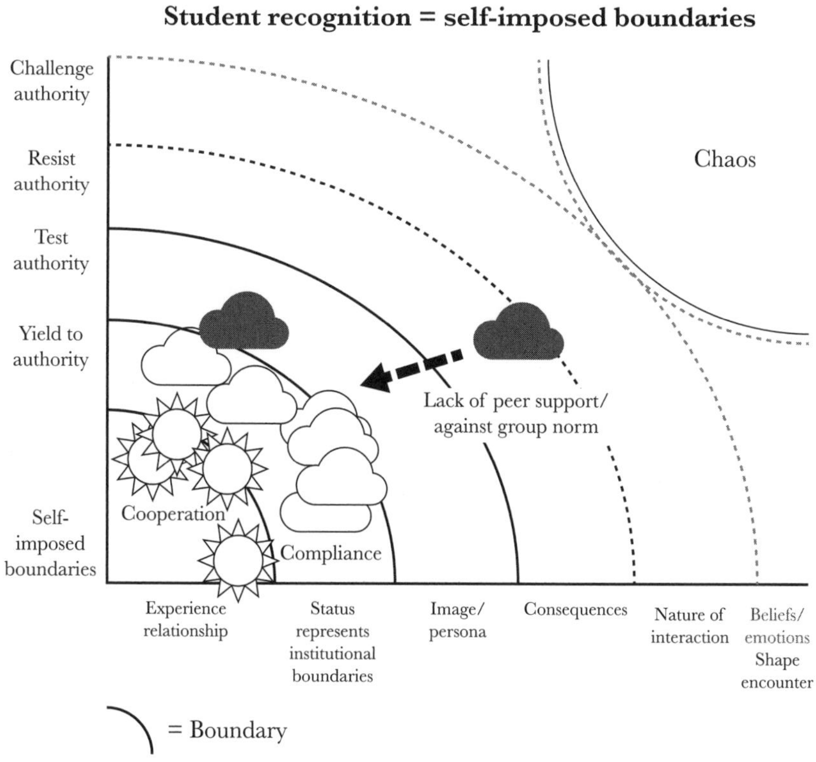

Figure 18.2. Student recognition = group norm

Dreikurs et al. (2004) helped me to distinguish between Grey Clouds and the hidden goals I attributed to Rain Cloud conduct. With Rain Cloud, wilful behaviour is fuelled by 'misguided power'. There is evidence of this strand in the detention data shown in Chapter 12. The conflicts can be predetermined and may be accompanied by heightened emotions such as anger. I realised that I would have to distinguish between behaviours deriving from the will and fearful and emotional responses which stem from the lower brain (Siegel 2014). Goleman (1996) draws on neurological data to advance the notion of emotional hijacking as an explanation for seemingly irrational reactions. Sunderland (2006) advocates the need for adults to get close to children experiencing distress tantrums. Acting as a container, they demonstrate that the emotional state is survivable and assist the child to develop self-soothing techniques and self-regulation. However, the idea that some incidents might be contrived was interesting; this would require the teacher to demonstrate heightened awareness alongside a dignified disciplinary approach. But it is not always easy to distinguish between genuine distress and manufactured emotion – Sunderland's term 'little Nero tantrums' captures the distinction. It requires a very different response from the adult, lest they become embroiled in power play. Berne (1964: 23) refers to these destructive patterns of communication between pupil and teacher as 'games'. These are defined as "an ongoing series of complementary ulterior transactions progressing to a well-defined, predictable outcome".

To illustrate these complex and uncomfortable exchanges, I initially select two data sources to present the critical moments of my research. Firstly, in this chapter, an obstinate Year 8 girl who became increasingly non-responsive to redirection strategies, and secondly, in the next chapter, my dealings with the deliberate ploys of a Year 10 female sub-group. Later on, in Chapter 23, I briefly relay my dealings with an established class which I inherited halfway through the year who had the potential to collectively challenge boundaries. I present my descriptive accounts of these episodes and provide the context for my reflexive grappling and attempts to stay consistent with the values I had identified as standards of judgement. The incidents suggest that a deeper level of antagonism was motivating the children's conduct. In situations like these, when reason becomes subordinate, a Fleece quickly becomes inadequate.

Demonstrative of my old way of behaving, I refer briefly to my former reaction to similar provocation, recorded near the start of my research on 19 January 2009. It is significant because it represents the last time I shouted at a pupil.

Y10: MB tried his luck very early on … gave him a truth tablet, showed him the reality of taking on an adult in a power struggle. Slammed my fist on his desk and shouted for the world to hear that he was giving it the 'biggen' but couldn't fight for toffee and was no more than a three foot gangster. This took the wind out of his sails and got the attention of the watching class.

Solitary Rain Cloud

The first analysis involves a female in Year 8. My research diary shows that I recorded nearly 10,000 words to document our ongoing dispute over the course of a school year. I will offer selective entries to illustrate the nature of the conflict, as well as my operational responses and my attempts to use redirection techniques.[1] Although the weather categories refer to specific behaviours rather than as a label for a person, I take poetic licence to intermittently refer to the focus child as RC, identifying her with the Rain Cloud traits she habitually displayed.

---

8 September 2009 (beginning of second research year)

Lesson 1:

Had not taught any of these students in Year 7. I was dressed in a Fleece as I aimed to disperse any clouds that might have gathered outside the room at the cessation of break.

An established (whole school) Rain Cloud (by reputation) quickly emerged from the crowd to challenge my instruction regards split gender table groups. Full of attitude and spouting the familiar "Whatever", this charming young lady's 'weather' was quickly countered by my adoption of Waterproofs. An immediate response which established that I was not interested in her opinion (I was not seeking her agreement, nor was I looking to persuade) was followed by deliberate silence and selected eye contact as I scanned the class settling to create very clear boundaries, which they accepted. The power was established in the silence and inner confidence that exuded from it. I did not feel threatened by this challenge although it did put me on my guard. The shift from Fleece to Waterproofs had been subtle and effective. Clear *directives* (rather than requests) reinforced my authority and centred on symbolic detail as I *described the obvious: "Still waiting for a couple … bag under table … thanks* (language of appreciation and expression of expectancy) … *pens down … eyes and ears to the front. Thank you – good morning.*"

A strategic request for RC to close the door (as she was closest to it). Matter of fact enquiry of RC's name (with class watching in their silence) led to a mature, adult recognition from me that we had got off

---

1 The italics in this section indicate use of Bill Rogers' (2006) language of redirection.

on the wrong foot – "Let's start again from the beginning and give it another try." Fluent switch back to Fleece and then Light Jumper as the climate was established and any threatening clouds had quickly dispersed.

Lesson 2:

It was fair to say last week's RC was quiet today. A behaviour report and specific targets helped. I had it confirmed that her constant frown is her natural demeanour, as is her uncultured aggressive replies to any civil request. I shall have to be on guard not to take things personally, yet will seek to amend her communication if it might be perceived as disrespectful.

Lesson 6:

She 'rained' today for the first time in four weeks. This time an enquiry at noticing she had her book closed and head on table. Keeping away from 'why' I *described the obvious* and asked, *"What should you be doing?"* I was met with a dismissive "Not bothered". Great, that's two of us then! Language of *choice*, *strategic retreat*, *take-up time,* and *return to redirect* prompted some sort of appropriate response. Was able to lean on the behaviour report which has become her second skin. Her noises are apparent to all as she left my classroom at the end to punch another child outside. Part of a family fuelled rivalry apparently! And there is me trying to teach the intricacies of research and mind-mapping!

Lesson 8:

First lesson after half-term. RC fully involved throughout.

This caused my research supervisor to comment on the research blog: "It is time to rename Rain Cloud, perhaps. I see traces of a silver lining."

I replied: "Quite right. 'Silver Lining' was polite and quiet. Form tutor informs me she tends to push boundaries around the school and we are doing well if she at least lets a teacher get on with teaching. We certainly have that now. He says she is terrified of contributing in case she is seen to look 'thick'. I recognise this trait in many of them."

Lesson 9:

It has been a good three weeks since I delivered the last fragmented part of the unit. All enthusiasm seemed to have waned and the lesson started with a strong whiff of apathy.

This atmosphere was then challenged as a 'new' girl (NG) introduced herself.

"Where do you want me to sit?" she asked.

Again I have been stitched up as a decision is made somewhere to add a child to an existing group. I only have enough room for 30 chairs and table spaces; NG makes 31!

Whilst in the process of trying to figure out if anyone was absent so I could shoehorn her into their seat, trying to find my keys to get her an exercise book, it emerges that NG was with us in Year 7, moved to another school, and now she is back!

These additional unscheduled tasks prevent me from starting the lesson and now I am becoming aware that resident Rain Cloud is keen to impress NG. Great! The delicate balance of an established group is about to be disrupted for the third time this year. It seems every time we take on another pupil they are the sort that take – take time and energy.

I placed NG on the edge of a full table with her back to RC. There was nowhere else.

RC's little comments were becoming apparent and then drew a measured response from me. I then addressed NG who had turned herself into a position to converse with RC sitting at the back. I spelt it out clearly, "You are not to turn around to talk to RC. RC is not to distract you. No one is going to join this class and stop me from teaching and others from learning – no one!"

Body position suitably amended we carried on.

The group, whilst compliant, were established in their apathy by now. The [comparative] Friday group also exhibited silence whilst absorbing poignant lyrics from songs, but did so with a sense of absorption and engagement. Only the subtlety of noticing, or at least sensing, might have spotted the difference at a glance, however a chasm in attitude existed.

One final piece of interruption from RC whilst I was in the middle of giving whole class instruction, "My pen's not working", brought my words to an abrupt halt.

"So, who cares?" I was aware I was slipping into a tone and dialogue I recognised from an age gone by. She mouthed something back wrapped in attitude and the hook was attached, causing me to react to the *secondary behaviour* rather than responding to the *primary issue* of pen/interruption. Acutely aware of her history of bullying peers, and having recently become aware of her success at 'playing' teachers since Year 3 (my wife taught her), I interpreted her tactics as trying to intimidate me. I made it very clear that she was barely a teenage girl and I most definitely *was* standing against her without any fear. I could hear myself say it and felt the weakness of my condition.

I knew I had failed. RC refused to do any work and just sat there with her book closed – defeated though defiant. There were no more interruptions and no more trying to impress NG. I could have sanctioned and removed her for not doing the work but knew I'd had a part to play in the situation, even though I had been set up. I just resigned to leave her to it, resisting inclinations to enforce my normal procedure of maintaining standards at all times.

I made my mind up over the weekend to pull RC out of her class and make some sort of apology along the lines of "I regret … if I could have done it differently then …" I would also look to restate the behaviour that started the issue (calling out, attention seeking, seeking to undermine, etc.) and confirm it remains inappropriate. Rogers (1994: 50) refers to this focus as "repair and rebuild".

Felt quite apprehensive about doing so due to uncertainty of her emotional response and the possibility of stirring up the lesson for the teacher I would have to pull her from. In the end the class were not where they were timetabled to be and so the opportunity passed. Limited time to catch her before lesson tomorrow morning.

Lesson 10:

The opportunity presented itself as RC arrived late.

I stood in the doorway and was able to steer her to stay outside. She was not best pleased, full of defensive anger it seems, but my tone quickly sought to disperse this before it had a chance to build.

I said my bit about if I had the chance again … would do it differently … fresh start …

There was not much of an acknowledgement but I hoped the intervention, in accordance with the responsibility I have as the adult, would go some way to enabling a safer [emotional] environment for the child.

Unfortunately, all I had anticipated began to manifest as the lesson unfolded.

An opportunity to work in colour groups saw NG make for RC. Should I stop it? I wondered but decided against my instinct in the spirit of a 'fresh start'. As the activities proceeded it became apparent the two were up for a social (RC now had an ally). Quick reinforcement of task (covered by doing the same for other pupils in the vicinity) fell on deaf ears.

Raising awareness of a reasonable consequence then followed as I made clear, "If you want to work together then I need to see …"

Deaf ears. RC, feet now up on chair doing next to nothing whilst NG is able to crack on whilst under pressure from her friend to be idle.

"*Name* (RC) (*pause, eye contact*) you are not attempting the task (*describing the obvious*). Do you need help?"

No response, no acknowledgement.

I explain anyway.

She starts to use her pen to tear holes in her exercise book. I am aware but do not jump in. It is more important for me to continue teaching the whole class who are responding in various degrees to the group tasks provided. Within five seconds of addressing the class RC begins whistling to interrupt.

The short instruction finished, I was able to turn to RC and remind her (if she needed reminding) not to whistle when I am teaching. Backchat led to her being asked to leave the room.

"Why?" came the whine.

"So, I can speak to you; leave the room."

The grunt and defiant posture rose (*secondary behaviours*) but got no response from me.

I quickly moved NG back to her original seat and then followed the school policy of speaking to a student who has had time out. Clearly, with her will firmly set against me, experience told me it would be folly to try to convince the child through reasoning. Instead, whilst positioned in the doorway to maintain contact with the class, I gave a clear description of observable behaviours and reminded her of the context of a fresh start (which was about to be withdrawn).

Within minutes of re-admittance, a constant tapping of her pen accompanied my whole class reinforcement and the battle line was well and truly drawn.

RC's decision to leave the classroom before the rest of the class cemented a lip service detention that I was supposed to administer.

This final episode demonstrated a clear breakdown in communication. Essentially professional throughout, I found myself up against wilful, defiant, and rebellious behaviour. Wearing Waterproofs (see Figure 18.3) involved a conscious decision not to be drawn into a power struggle. This meant resisting the temptation to focus on getting the child's agreement. In such instances, Dyer (2005) argues that the best thing we can do for a child is not to compromise, barter, or plead, but to show that a boundary means no – that the child is responsible for his/her own conduct once reasonable means of negotiation have been exhausted and reached designated limits. My deliberate distancing from the contained rage she emanated prevented me from getting drawn into a power struggle on this occasion: I had taken my sails out of the wind.

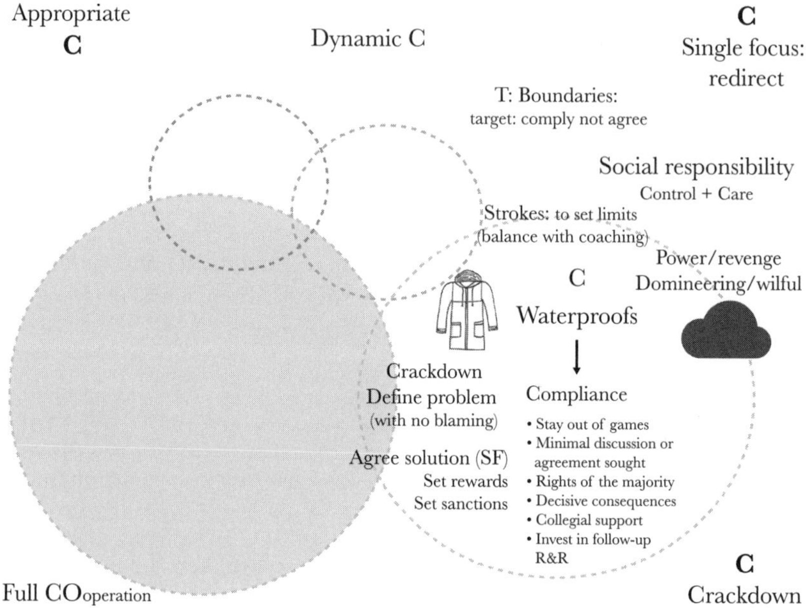

Figure 18.3. Disciplinary approach: Waterproofs

Note: SF: Solution Focus

The process of negotiation, summarised in subsequent field notes, detailed my extensive efforts to make things right, to put money back in the relational bank account and rebalance the scales. Arranging a reconciliation meeting to 'repair and rebuild', apologising for my initial 'mistake' of embarrassing her in front of her peers, correcting her view that I 'hated' her, 'agreeing' targets, and organising temporary alternative provision with colleagues were met with a range of creative reasons to be late/absent and sustained strategies to deliberately disrupt the lesson. I became aware at one stage in a lesson that I felt uncomfortable. Bizarrely, I found myself being over-accommodating. I was fearful of correcting her, so negating the inroads of a fresh start. I saw small glimpses that my reasonableness was being perceived as weakness as she pushed and tested boundaries (e.g. shouting out answers, pulling and pushing the boy next to her).

Further enquiries revealed that extensive work with external agencies filled a file which seemed remarkably devoid of sanctions. Two colleagues who had carried out their duties according to reason and policy had found themselves confronted by her aggressive mother when in the process of teaching another class. I did not encounter this. I attribute this to RC's older brother being an advocate of mine within their home (a fact I later learned). After experiencing a verbal attack from RC when intervening on behalf of a child who was being subjected to her abuse during a lunchtime, I insisted to the deputy head that measures would have to be taken to reassert my authority. I deemed this essential if I was to be able to fulfil future obligations to address such incidents on behalf of the school. This failed to happen, despite my best efforts, and so I felt compromised. Early in the new academic year, I was again in an area where RC was swearing loudly. For the first and only time in my career I looked the other way and carried on walking.

Chapter 19

Stormy Weather

Sean

Concurrently with my battles with RC, my conviction to find a 'better' way was being sorely tested by a Year 10 sub-group. Again, I refer directly to my field notes which capture the inner struggles dominating my reflexive thoughts during this period. After initially calm and constructive lessons, everything changed.

---

29 September 2009:

This was a struggle from the off. Period 5, just after tutor time, we had another 'madam' join the group. This one from a neighbouring school was looking for a "new start … to overcome her previous difficulties", or so the email said last week.

Immediately her persona pitched itself against me, looking to see if I was a soft touch or not. The group's established Rain Cloud (smiling girl (SG)) arrived: oh great, they seemed to have already found each other!

The fire-fighting that followed would have been fascinating, if I hadn't been caught in the middle of it. All the power appears to be with the girls in this year group. The males are largely unobtrusive or immature 'boys'. The three main lads of the year group were each expelled in the Year 8/9 period.

The amount of overconfident opposition to the tasks and my instruction was staggering. Peacocks strutting to let the new girl (NG2) know they too had credence in this town! They were willing to take a hit from me; in fact, it seemed a definite strategy to confront me, so raising their kudos. Even a girl (N) who had *never* been anything other than delightful began to get in on the act.

They would have witnessed a calm, assertive, insistent adult who met each and every challenge by redirecting, issuing sanctions to register boundaries, and putting them straight. Inside I was spitting mad, every ounce of me at work to prevent myself from losing it and scaring the living daylights out of them. It left me in a state of flux as I was already exhausted from a desperately busy day leading into this final lesson.

The entire episode exemplified the fact that small changes (presence of new 'madam') can have disproportionate effects. Though dressed appropriately, my perspective and state (symbolic 'fog') prevented me from experiencing the inner calmness I would hope for. After all, they are no threat whatsoever, other than a challenge to my professional obligation to enable learning. However, my inner state begs to differ, as it was reminiscent of an occasional nightmare I have where the class are out of control and won't listen to me.

I stuck with it and built upon the calmness I presented. Strategic placing of new girl, low level 'folding' task in the form of a controversial case study grabbed their attention – and the storm had passed. Brief 'showers' occurred but were quickly and assertively met. No pleading or second and third chances from me!

6 October 2009:

Wasn't able to teach the Year 10s this afternoon as a last minute notice informed us of house competition games. It ended up that I sat with the 'non-doers' in a classroom anyway. Fascinatingly, one of the group's (and school's) Rain Clouds, a young lady who, like her brother before her, dallies between helpless and obstinate in my lessons, was one of those in my charge. It so happens she was scheduled to be with me that very period if the house issue had not presented itself.

What an amazing difference. Gone was the growl; in its place a smile and easy demeanour. Chatting away with me and peers you would never have recognised the rude, obnoxious young lady I had previously encountered with my education hat on. It seems such a shame to spoil a good relationship by insisting she does the work next week when we resume our formal roles!

13 October 2009:

I decided to take a risk today and operate primarily with my research hat on. I was intrigued to observe how the lesson might manifest if I resisted the (easy) C1 sanction option (unless obviously appropriate) or resisted the temptation to assert my authority through shouting. My self-boundaries were focused on using the techniques I espouse during behaviour management training, in which I advocate a calm demeanour as one diffuses and redirects low level distractions.

NG2 arrived with N and immediately got herself noticed. SG (the 'smiling girl' from last week's blog) arrived later, non-uniform and a big commotion about the smell of BO in the room. And so the scene was set!

N was constrained by the house report she was on but was desperate to be part of the mini grouping. None of the other students seemed remotely interested in joining them as the clique probed for a platform to perform.

The strategy of undermining and distraction took on a variety of forms periodically throughout the lesson. An assertive C1 may well have laid down a marker but probably would have been an over-reaction to any single incident and likely to have started a verbal, high profile protest from the individual (and her allies).

It was interesting at one stage to observe SG deliberately put on her gloves during the lesson (thus inviting the teacher to ask her to take them off) and then NG2 putting her scarf on shortly after (thus forcing the teacher to ask her to take it off). Lots of eye contact between the two left N somewhat excluded as she yielded to a reminder that she was on report.

SG played her usual card of 'learned helplessness' – "Can't do it, won't do it ..." – despite me taking time to individually explain what I had already explained to the whole class, providing examples and encouragement. Her declarations of impotence moved beyond apathy in response to a resource that could hardly have been made easier. NG2 appeared to be coping well with the resource, but found an opportunity to get the teacher's attention with the one aspect she couldn't get straight away, thus mirroring SG's strategy.

To illustrate the extent of the problem I was facing habitually, I conducted a discreet tally chart (see Figure 19.1) to capture the interactions of the lesson. Of 18 disturbances recorded within the hour, 16 (89%) emanated from the sub-group.

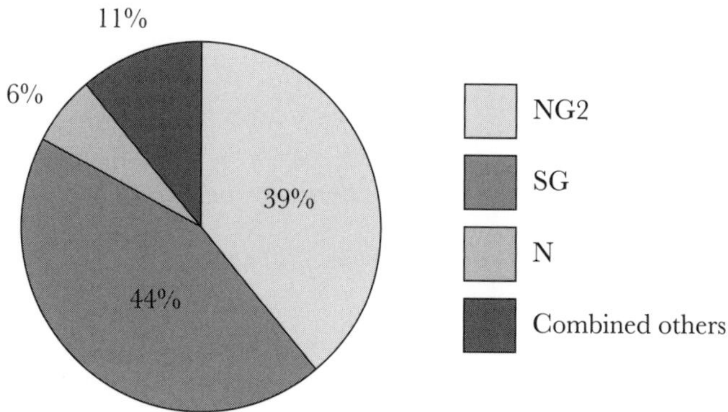

Figure 19.1. Low level distractions (Year 10, period 5, Tuesday 13 October 2009)

As a researcher, I found the task wearing. The exercise reminded me of the frustration a teacher may feel when they are emotionally involved in such an experience, rather than operating as a participant researcher. Whilst it was an interesting exercise to practise constraint, my role was not, of course, constrained to that of an 'objective' observer. Afterwards, it seemed to me that somehow the girls had got one over on me. The prospect of going through it all again for the rest of the year drained me of energy, and I feared it would lead to me reverting to defensive mechanisms. Indeed, the lesson represented in Figure 19.1 prompted me to ponder the implications of such a situation as I lay awake from 1 a.m. to 5 a.m. Despite the Christmas break, extracts from my research diary show that there was no sign of the challenging behaviour abating upon commencement of lessons in January.

In the extract that follows, I have presented the interaction as I initially recorded it in my field notes, rather than as individual extracts, because I feel single phrases would disrupt the dynamic and detract from the sense of escalation. Again, efforts to redirect by adorning a Fleece are recorded in italics.

---

12 January 2010:

First lesson back after the holidays and snow.

Was in a decent frame of mind but felt a pervading heaviness as this lesson drew nearer. Recognised it as ridiculous but it was there nonetheless.

Group came in and began getting themselves organised. Routines working well. I noted NG2's arrival (it occurred to me that I was particularly aware of her entry as I was conscious of the inner relief I had experienced previously when realising that any of the three were absent).

N arrived with a frown and a strut and immediately made her way to NG2. I observed from afar.

SG arrived late. *Resisting the temptation to ask why*, I said quietly, "I'll see you at the end to find out your reason for being late."

"I'm not late," she stated. *I didn't allow myself to get drawn in to the accompanying attitude (secondary behaviour).*

The lesson got underway and the majority were ready to be engaged. Surveying the room for positives to comment on I noticed that only three students had left their bags on the table.

Matter of fact, "N (*pause/eye contact*), sort your bag."

It was simply pushed across to the other part of the table. "N, bag." A tut greeted a heavy-handed removal of the offending item.

"SG bag, thanks."

"NG2, bag off the table."

All had made a start except three!

"N, you have not started." (*describing the obvious*)

"I haven't got a pen."

"Here you go."

No thanks forthcoming.

Playing along for a moment, "SG, you have got your book closed."

"I haven't got a pen."

"There you go."

"NG2, do you need any help?"

Ignored but then a pronounced effort and sigh masqueraded as a response.

"SG, you are looking at your phone under the desk. Put it away or on my desk. C1." (*choice/take up time and standard sanction consequence*)

N piped up, "I can't do this."

I patiently reminded her of the printed directions and example available to her.

SG whined, "Why can't I move seats?" No response from me.

The rest of the class continued to ignore the tactics.

SG closed her book.

"SG, are you refusing to attempt the task?"

"Not doing it."

"Fine, C2, *time out*. Out you go."

N turned around to offer her laughing, mocking contribution to the situation. I mimicked her to suppress an overwhelming desire to put her in her place.

This stirred NG2 up. "You always do that. You are to blame for winding us up. You do my head in."

"Yeah," joined in N.

"Really," I said. (My head was screaming shut your XXX mouth!)

Analysis of Games

In accordance with Schön's (1983) insight into contemplative processes, as a practitioner I did pause to reflect on his concept of 'knowing-in-practice'. Unerringly accurate, he wrote of the possibility that, in the relative tranquillity of a post-mortem, teachers may think back on a lesson and the situations they have lived through as they explore the understandings they have brought to their handling of the case. 'Post-mortem' – how apt, that's exactly how it felt. Berne (1964) conceptualises unhealthy communication as descending into psychological games, whilst Karpman (1968) presents the exchange through a drama triangle (Figure 19.2). The negative expression is shown in a smaller font, with the top two terms (accuser and rescuer) representative of negative parental expressions of control and care. (These are explained further in Appendix B.)

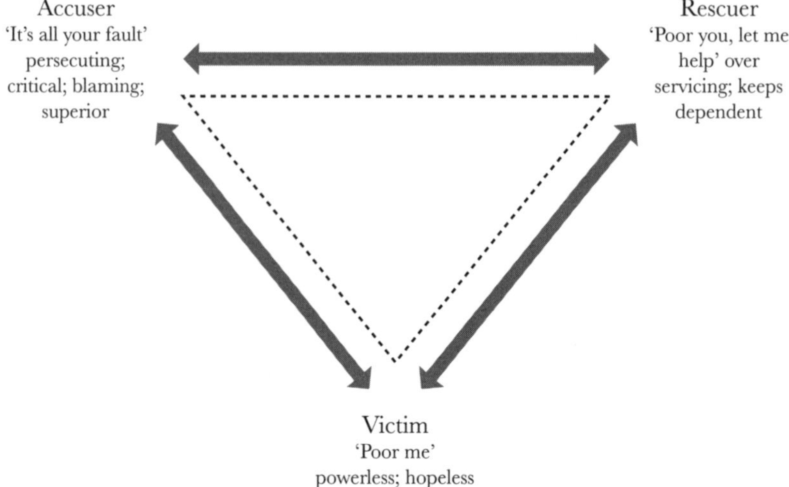

Figure 19.2. Drama triangle

The use of these terms in situations such as the one outlined above can be represented as a formula: con + gimmick = response–switch–cross-up–pay-off (C + G = R–S–CU–PO), which aims to draw the teacher out of Adult.[1] To illustrate this process in action, I analysed the diary extract retrospectively.

1 Transactional analysis refers to ego states – the parts which make up our unique personality. Parent consists of all we have absorbed from 'big people', and Child consists of behaviours, thinking, and feelings which can be replayed from childhood experiences. Whereas these are subjective, Adult is an objective, direct response to what is happening in the here and now. The terms Parent, Adult, and Child are written with capital letters so as to distinguish from mothers/fathers/caregivers, grown-ups, and children.

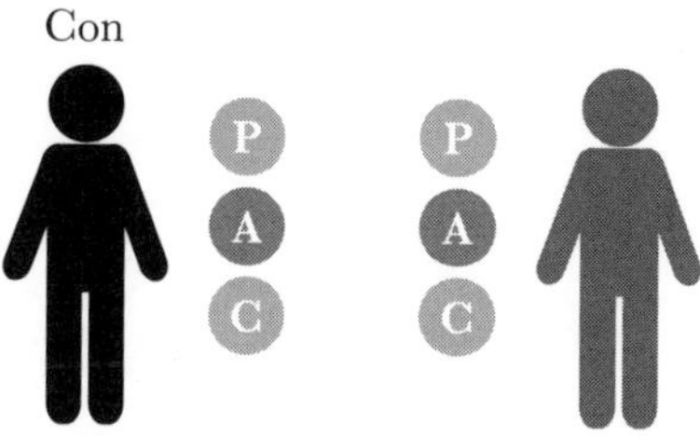

Figure 19.3. Con[2]

The game begins with a 'con' (or invitation) in the form of a split transaction from the pupil – there is an ulterior motive behind the actions witnessed (Figure 19.3). The statement, "I haven't got a pen," was part of a plan to stoke a reaction. Although the information might initially appear to be reasonable, it derived from the resistant Child – the body language and tone alerted me to a ploy.

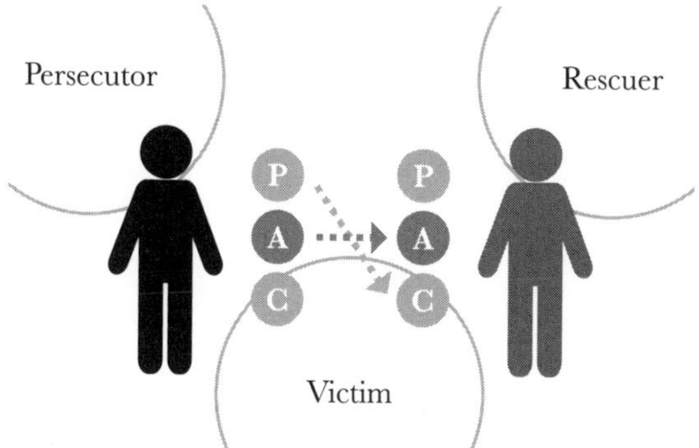

Figure 19.4. Games

Players can enter the game in any role. On this occasion the three collaborated to adopt the position of obstinate 'persecutors' (on the top left in Figure 19.4), seeking to draw me in by provoking me to correct them. This would have enabled them to 'switch' to another position and perpetuate the exchange.

2 The three screenshots (Figures 19.3, .4 and .5) are from Theramin Trees (2010).

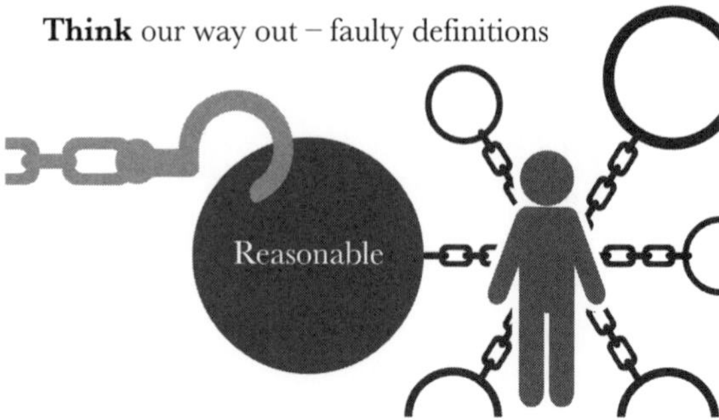

Figure 19.5. Gimmicks

The game can only proceed if I get hooked in – that is, if my 'gimmicks' compel me to react (Figure 19.5). Gimmicks refer to a psychological need which the initiator(s) of the game can exploit; they act as a target for the perpetrator(s). These needs are expressed through absolute terms: "I must ..." or "I must be seen to be ... reasonable." In my case, my long established hooks come in the form of control: "I must be strong" (or, more accurately, "I must not be seen to be weak") and "I must be perfect" (or, more accurately, "I cannot be seen to be less than outstanding"). The games which engage participants are usually repetitive, largely outside of Adult awareness (Stewart and Jones 1987), and originate in childhood. (The origins of my core gimmicks are considered in Chapter 21.)

On this occasion, I was not drawn into the game so I was afforded the opportunity to reflect on the tactics they had used. The girls, looking for a response (or, more accurately, a reaction), sought to outmanoeuvre the operational stance I had taken. Subsequent ruses indicate a switch to 'victim', inviting me to either administer blame from a 'persecutor' position or to 'rescue' by pandering to their needs and over-servicing – placating so as to not stir them up and allowing me to get on with the lesson (Karpman 1968). As I resisted getting entwined in the game by responding through an Adult professional Fleece, SG switched back to passive persecutor, moving from victim: "Can't do it as I haven't got a pen" to "Not doing it".

My momentary slip when mimicking her revealed an ulterior transaction which was constant beneath my professional mask, signifying my slipping out of Adult. This prompted the girls to instantly change tactics, switching to blame me for the issue and portraying themselves as victims of a persecutor. Had I got further drawn in to justify myself, the game would likely have progressed to a 'cross-up' and 'pay-off'. Hence, if I had been unaware of the game, Karpman (1968) suggests I would have experienced a moment of disorientation or unease when I came to realise I had somehow 'been had'. The pay-off refers to the instigators, having enhanced their script and life position, feeling smug and superior whilst the teacher feels deskilled and foolish. My past experience verified the validity of this formula.

Reflexive Turmoil

On this occasion, although consciously I had read the situation well, later my subconscious proceeded to champion the validity of my gimmicks and objected at some level to my constraint. This resulted in me retrospectively experiencing the cross-up. I used my research diary to capture the essence of my turbulent thoughts upon waking:

> I awoke in the early hours and found myself caught up in a familiar struggle. The incessant replay of the previous day's events encourage me to repeat the confrontations, but each time I visualise a self-righteous retort which feels intensely justified. Thoughts which accompany the images tolerate accusations: "Surely it's a weakness, not a strength, to abandon shouting. I bet getting angry would have put SG/NG2 in their place. They wouldn't have messed with the man I once was." In my slumber I felt impotent. I felt my self-control made me look feeble in the eyes of those who continue to disturb me. Conversely, I could sense the Rain Clouds' stand as they revelled in the stronghold of their defiance, their indifference, which derived from their collective will, furnished by periodic displays of contrived emotion. I am fully aware I cannot win if I follow them onto that chosen battleground. I want consequences. In my tiredness I am convinced I want to cheat and win back territory by imposing my will.
>
> How can I rebalance?
>
> "They can't control me unless I let them." Yes, I have said that phrase to countless colleagues over the years. I deliberately relax my muscles, now aware of how physically tense I am. I am stirred to the very core of my being. Whilst the school lies empty I lay reliving the past, whilst framing the future, trying to understand that which strips the present of all peace in the dead of the night.

The value which I identified as a standard of judgement in these critical moments is that of responsibility – that I would be responsible for my actions. In the midst of critical moments, and during fretful sleep, these isolated episodes, disproportionate though they are, continued to skew my perspective. Through acquired skills and a commitment to the study's values, my exterior concealed the inner turmoil I experienced in the second year of research. Dewey (1938: 18) counsels, "only when the past ceases to trouble and anticipations of the future are not perturbing is a being wholly united with his environment and therefore fully alive". I was about to understand how the notion of presence might contribute to my desire to be authentic and more trusting, whilst continuing to necessitate the requirement for me to be an effective authority figure.

Whilst this was a valid exploration for me to pursue as part of the research process, a sobering perspective emerged after the doctorate was done and dusted. Taking my little boy for a haircut, his usual haunt was closed. Looking around for an alternative, I wandered into one hairdresser's and there was a familiar face awaiting me. Smiling girl (SG), the character integral to the clique documented in this chapter, offered me a cup of tea. She was by now about 18 or 19. We chatted and laughed about the old days and I reminded her of the issues she had caused me. Her response was priceless: "I know, Sir, I was a right cow." The exchange served to remind me that it wasn't personal. We had just walked along a path for a little time together until we separated and went on our merry way. At the time, however, when we shared time together in school, I was still embroiled in trying to gain a perspective which would enable me to cope rather than defend; to respond rather than react on occasions when my buttons were being pressed.

Interestingly, I spoke to Sarah again recently, who went on to do well in her examinations. Reminded of her diary entries (in Chapter 1), what were her retrospective thoughts? She is now not so angry. She seemed acutely aware of the inconsistency between rhetoric and practice, but she has learned to tolerate – if not ignore – the contradictions, as her energy is now focused on those individual adults with whom she has built a connection.

Chapter 20

React or Respond: Examining the Patterns

Sean

My methodology, underpinned by living logics, encouraged a perspective which accepted risk and accommodated the idea of transformative qualities which were emerging from my research. This mode of thought could be as threatening as it was intoxicating; I had to learn to tolerate the unique demands of operating in the present – being "on the brink" (Whitehead and McNiff 2006: 40).

Later that year, a sense of congruity began to emerge through engagement with Temple's Functional Fluency model (2004). Temple (2005) advocates that personal development should underpin the professional effectiveness of educators. For the first time, I was able to shine a light on the possible origins of the cons I initiated and the gimmicks which hooked me into power games in the classroom. The model also enabled me to comprehend more fully the distinction between compliance and cooperation, to affirm the ethical balance between control and care, and to recognise the defensive approaches that can undermine the effectiveness of control and care.

The data deriving from my Temple Index of Functional Fluency (TIFF) profile had to be patiently sifted to reveal the underlying beliefs which manifested in my habitual behaviour.[1] Providing prompts and stimuli, the profile represented a unique snapshot of obscured patterns and balances, revealing how I functioned and used energy in the various roles of my life. The exploration proved to be both illuminating and uncomfortable: an examination of how negative aspects of my ongoing behaviour as an authority figure, which had their roots in my past, came through in the analysis of modes and patterns within my profile. This was a result of a two hour consultation with Dr Susannah Temple, and subsequently through reflexive thought about the make-up and origins of my ego state structure and what made it. The model provided another theoretical framework to facilitate my methodological conviction to live in the present, as I engaged with risk and tolerated uncertainty – to function effectively in the here and now.

1 TIFF is a PhD validated tool which I believe has great potential to assist all adults who work in schools. An online questionnaire is analysed by a TIFF provider who gleans insights from the data over a two hour consultation. Further details can be found at: http://functionalfluency.co.uk/tiff-provision/.

React

Essentially, and of great significance to me, I was afforded an opportunity to decipher the conceptual differences between responding and reacting as they became apparent within my profile. The four negative behaviour modes, illustrated in Figure 20.1, indicate "old [out of date] teachings and old learnings" (Temple 2008: 7) – they are contaminated, causing a person to react, or even to re-enact, when unresolved issues relating to archaic events trigger reactions in the present moment (Paul and Epanchin 1991).

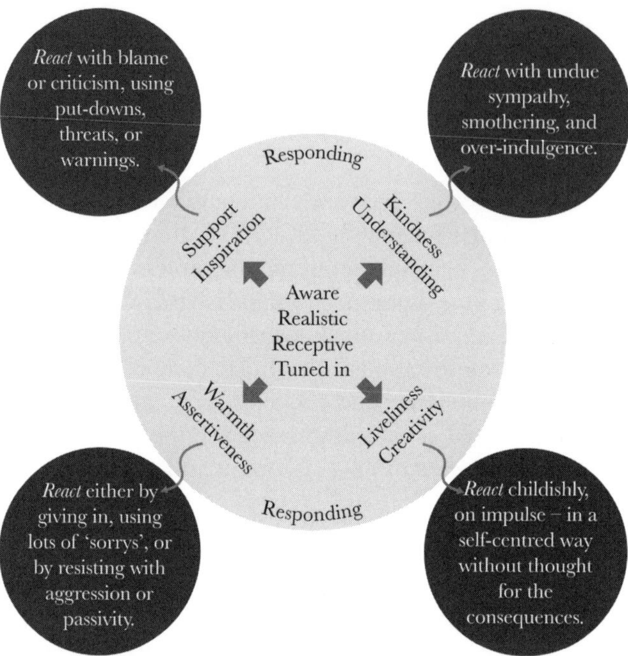

Figure 20.1. Responding or reacting

I now concentrated on exploring the significance of past experiences and relationships, in the form of disproportionate defensive reactions which habitually gripped me in the present day. I believe that these aspects of my past worked to sabotage my intention to live in the present. The literature describes the experience as regression. I became acutely aware of its validity as this abstract concept became concrete. On an occasion during the first year of my research, I interpreted continued provocation from a defiant boy as an attempt to bully me. This triggered an irrational re-enactment in which I 'flipped' and actively stood up to this perceived aggressor. The episode was very unsettling – it occurred in an instant and was gone again. In Chapter 22, I describe how this wasn't the first time that this type of disturbing scenario has occurred. I suspected that the roots of the trigger had remained dormant for many years. TIFF provided a non-threatening platform to coax the origins to the surface.

It should be noted that giving primary attention to negative modes is contrary to the TIFF methodology, which emphasises recognising, building on, and celebrating the positive. However, the arrangement of the data in this book, which begins by highlighting my dealings with the affable majority of pupils, is consistent with this philosophy. Through these more constructive episodes, I have demonstrated an increased ability to utilise both the structure and nurture modes to frame my authoritative stance as I sought to use positive expressions of control and care (see Appendix B).

However, my TIFF profile revealed that an inclination to control (or, more accurately, to subdue pupils) was still apparent during this phase of the research, and so necessitated reflexive thought (see Figure 20.2).[2]

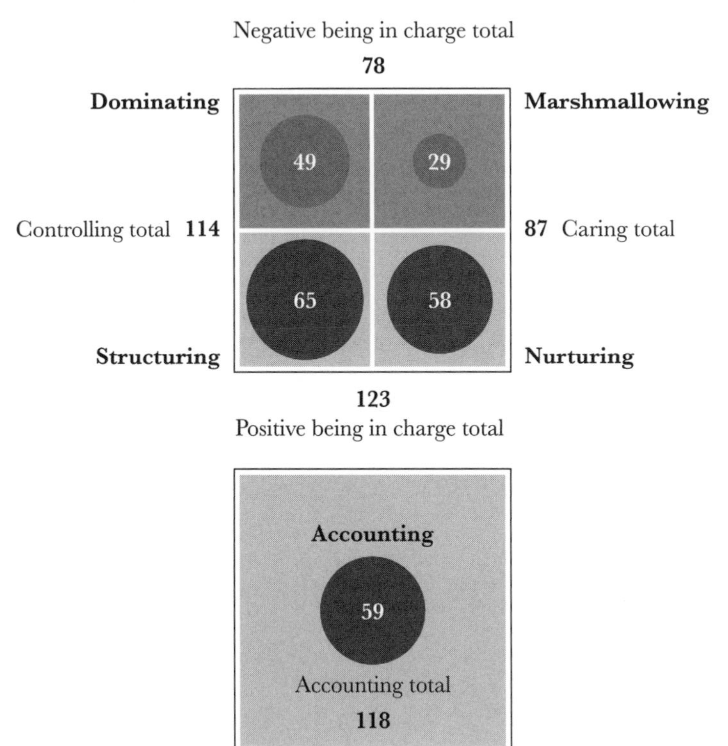

Figure 20.2. Functional Fluency profile: being in charge

2 Mode scores only have relative meaning as they are viewed in relation to each other (i.e. are they lower or higher?). The numbers representing different modes of behaviour are examined to explore quantitative patterns and balances (as illustrated in Figure 20.2). The relationships between scores are considered to draw out any potential significance or insight for the client. TIFF also provides ratios. The profile is unique to an individual person and is not an indicator of 'type'. The focus is on the behaviour, not the person. In accounting, 57–59 is considered 'evenish', 55–61 is simply termed 'a bit more uneven'.

Interestingly, Temple has since pointed out in conversation that the word 'control' comes from an old French verb 'controller' and refers to regulate. It is a value free term when expressed through words such as 'guiding' and 'directing' (Temple 2008, 2009). Control is thus an umbrella term which I had come to interpret first as 'good', and then questioned that assumption as I became more aware of its negative connotations and impact on my well-being and classroom relations.

Dominating

The top layer of the model presents terms which indicate a value judgement – that is, they are deemed positive or negative. The Functional Fluency model's two expressions of control – structuring and dominating (shown on the left of Figure 20.2 and explained in Appendix B) – are distinguished and defined by asking whether people benefit or suffer when the modes are in use. The content of Chapter 3 is clearly illustrative of the negative behavioural mode termed 'dominating'. This mode of behaviour derives from a life script position which suggests, according to Functional Fluency sub-descriptors, that I believe "I know better" (and this perceived opposition elicited in me blame, accusations, put-downs, and fault-finding). These represented my default. These prominent traits, which still threatened to manifest themselves when I was dealing with disruptive pupils, are encapsulated in the phrase, "I'm OK – you're not OK" (Harris 1995). It also describes the psychological foundations inherent when a teacher dresses inappropriately for the weather conditions due to an inclination to dominate the children, even if (as in my case) inadvertent effects are obscured from the enforcer due to a self-justifying belief that their choice of 'clothing' is for the sake of standards.

Upon interrogation of my scores, I realised that my persona had come to imitate the perception I held of my dad as I grew up, although they don't represent the man I came to know as I got older. As I became a teacher, the trait of being 'strict' as a technique nearly always involved a mode of behaviour defined by Temple (2009) as dominating. This was not a surprise to me. More unexpected was the enquiry which probed how much energy I used to dominate myself. This opened up discussion with Temple about my perfectionist traits. Reflecting on excessive mental rehearsal, which drained me and deprived me of peace, opened up an avenue which was hidden from me. Much of my internal energy, or 'accounting', was spent reliving the past or projecting into the future. An impromptu piece of research, in which I engaged with Zimbardo and Boyd's (2008) work, enabled me to appreciate more fully the grip a faulty time perspective had on shaping my thoughts and thus my experience of being. My internal construction of reality drew on extensive energy reserves as I donned the mask of professionalism. I suspected this was draining me of the capacity to be 'present'.

November 2009:

I was interested to see if I could begin to analyse the thoughts and emotions that fuel my inherent discomfort and which cause me to either compromise my values (experience being a 'living contradiction') or remind me to put on my professional mask.

I invested in a digital 'tally counter' and explored the idea of clicking every time I recognised a negative thought connected to work, no matter how fleeting.

Today was the launch; I attached it to my wrist. An interesting day because I had little or no responsibility as I was supporting an external team who were leading Year 10s on a 'challenge day'. I therefore anticipated a minimal number of clicks as I was removed from direct authoritarian teacher/student/formal curriculum.

From waking until the end of school (3.15 p.m.) I recognised 41 occasions when a thought/discomforting moment either danced across my consciousness or I caught it as I began the process of entertaining it. Of the 41, 22 were registered even before I came into contact with a single student!

The majority were directed in my head towards staff colleagues. In particular, those whose decisions are having an effect on me or what was considered *mine* at work. The form tutor who uses my classroom, the head of house who made a decision to put her in there, another head of house who nominated my room as one of the core classrooms for today's event, and him again because I would lose two free periods today whilst supporting this Year 10 challenge day. All of these 'incidents' manifested in hypothetical dialogue in my mind, each time resulting in self-righteous indignation. As none of the incidents had actually taken place they were based on speculative future occurrences.

The thoughts were reoccurring for much of pre-work and started almost immediately upon waking. Each time I recognised and clicked,

> and then let it depart. The more they reappeared, the quicker I was able to recognise them and reject them. I was also aware of the tenseness that accompanied those thoughts which had momentarily slipped under the radar and settled before I recognised them. Upon letting them go, I was able to physically feel the difference in my muscles and expression (I caught myself frowning) as deep breaths dissolved its effect.

I was open to the idea that the TIFF profile's quantitative data might act as a prompt – a key to unlock the chain of critical thoughts which impeded my commitment to operate in accordance with my values. The intention of the ensuing reflexivity was to reveal injunctions or 'drivers' (Widdowson 2010), such as the urge to control, which continued to affect my ongoing performance.

Clues gradually emerged from exploring my autobiography, and a thread slowly became apparent. It seemed sensible to start at the beginning, so seemingly irrelevant details and events were accepted rather than dismissed, allowing insights to come to the surface. In line with Walls et al.'s (2001) findings, my recollections revealed an extreme paucity in recalling academic memories from schooldays. Banks (2001) advances photo-elicitation as a basis for provoking vague recollections; thus, armed with a camera I revisited many of my old haunts to capture something of my murky memories to make them more tangible.

Chapter 21

Core Gimmicks

Sean

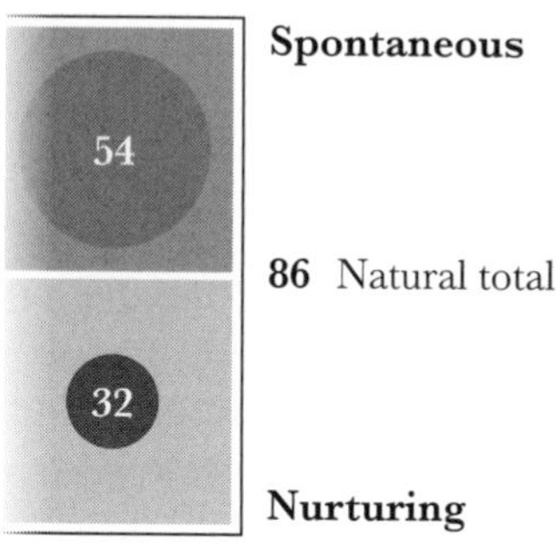

Figure 21.1. Functional Fluency profile: upbringing – natural self

The TIFF profile (Figure 21.1) stimulated a great deal of reflection, which was recorded in diary notes. In response to the scores attributed to my 'natural self' (questions which focus on my openness to spontaneity, as well as my propensity to behave immaturely), I allowed myself to revisit my earliest memories. I wanted to identify early experiences and messages which I might have absorbed when young, to see if I could account for habitual traits apparent in the way I behaved in subsequent decades. I started at the beginning.

> I initially find it difficult to formulate memories, let alone words to explore the notion of my formative natural self.[1] I suspect that being the first born I was the apple of my parents' eye for a while. I then consider the reality that another four siblings arrived year after year so there were five of us by the time I was age 5. I imagine time and attention became rationed in that pokey little two bedroom council flat.

---

1 See Appendix B for definitions of spontaneous and immature modes. Together they constitute positive and negative expressions of the 'natural self' or 'free child'.

However, long suppressed memories soon came flooding back as I continued to type. The following extract is written in the context of my dad leaving our family when I was 5 years old.

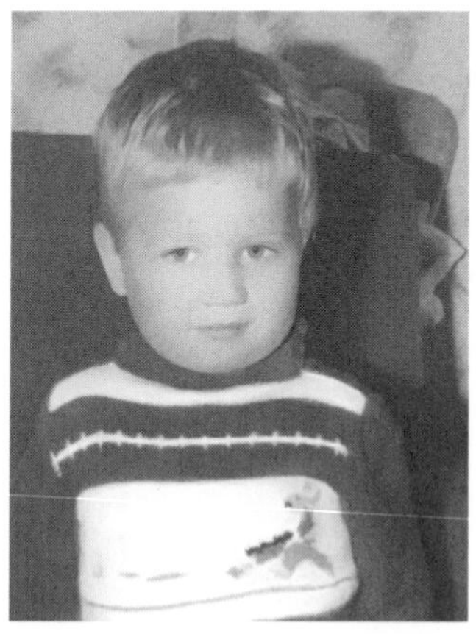

The family was dependent on the state, frequently going without food for days until we could draw family allowance on the Monday. This instantly dwindled as the previous week's debt was paid back so ensuring another hungry weekend awaited. A recollection of being hungry, dirty, and scared dominates my memories. We had no central heating in our council estate block; the bath took up most of the space the kitchen offered. Shivering in lukewarm water, created by mixing the cold tap and a couple of boiling kettles, comes back to me now. Living in a constant state of dread also resurfaces. I have since come to shrug my shoulders at the retelling of my lot, but I am more cautious here to consider the impact on that little boy who did not have the luxury of knowing it would all turn out OK. In adulthood, I have so easily dismissed the fact that our young family believed passionately that our flat was haunted; so much so that the five children slept in the same bedroom as our mum. We were so convinced that none of us would venture out into the darkness to go to the toilet, instead using a potty kept in the room. This subconscious state manifested most pertinently in my bed wetting up to around age 13. I would suggest that this child and his siblings would have social services on full alert in today's climate. However, they did not interfere in my lot back in the early to mid-1970s.

Our plight ensured we were destined to become victims, prey to the bigger boys from other families. It was in these situations that I felt most vulnerable and incompetent, for I was the eldest. Within the confines of our walls, as years passed, I am aware I often took advantage of my elder status to dominate my three younger brothers, my sister, as well as my mother. However, the little 'general' became inhibited as his dominance diminished at the very mention of his father's name, who was a well-known 'hard man' around the East End. I am saddened to think of the injunctions that young boy internalised: "Don't be a child for you are now the man of the house." And the inference from his dad's exploits: "To be a man means being tough; to be the son of George Warren screams out, 'Don't be weak'."

Transactional analysis suggests observation of authority figures are significant [Temple 2008]. The disparity in scores between 'control' and 'care' [114 and 87 – see Figure 20.2] might be attributed to beliefs assimilated by my formative self. I strived to imitate my dad as head of the family and did so through selective domination. As I reflect on my relationship with my younger siblings, I am reminded that a correlation between 'immature' and 'dominating' modes provides the key ingredients of a bully. I wonder if these early experiences have shaped the default template which primed my operational approach as I took on positions of authority. Conversely, I rejected and became hardened to my mum's right to govern me as she flitted between ineffectively trying to control and allowing me too much freedom – or in TIFF terms she 'marshmallowed' me [see Appendix B].

The Socialised Self, School, and Teachers

Nuthall attributes much of our perception of education as adults to the rituals we learn as pupils, when we are members of a captive audience. The common experiences that the vast majority of us pass through are "sustained by a stable web of beliefs and assumptions that are part of the [wider] culture" (Nuthall 2002: 6). My reflections enabled me to draw into consciousness long forgotten memories.

Although I had younger brothers I suspect my first real experience of having to cultivate a socialised self [see Figure 21.2] happened when I went to school. In truth, I cannot remember much about the first pages of my script in primary school. I can vaguely recall a couple of teachers' names (from current Year 4 and Year 5) to accompany Mr Bond in Year 6. He was the first man to teach me in my school career and had a lasting impact on me. I am not exactly sure why. It could be that he filled some of the unconscious void of a fatherless boy; it could be that we did lots of PE which was my area of interest.

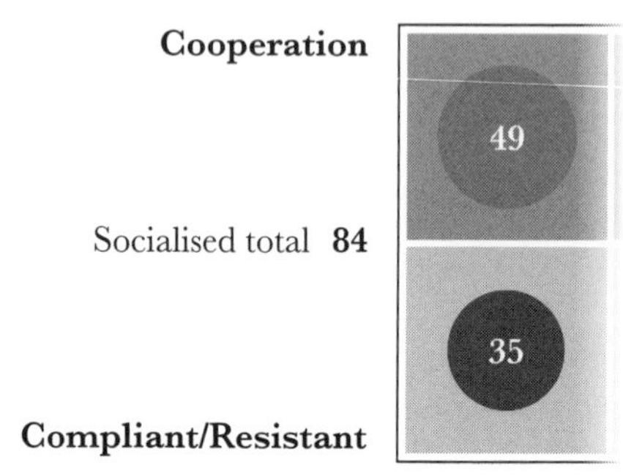

Figure 21.2. Functional Fluency profile: upbringing – socialised self

I learned that a classroom could be dominated by the very presence of a teacher. That a man's reputation could dictate self-imposed boundaries before you even came to be in his classroom. Weird how it seems somehow endearing that he used chalk as a cigarette and would sling it at any kid silly enough to misbehave. Can you imagine that nowadays!

Other embryonic lessons from Year 5 came from sitting up straight and silently to get the colour table star during story time at the end of the day. This could last for about half an hour, but peer collaboration meant complete compliance in order to have that little sticky star shaped reward next to blue table's name on the chart. Not for a moment did I conceive of it as a form of coercion.

I learned lining up straight from the dinner ladies. Not to push and to walk – not run – would enable you to be let in for dinner first (and be allowed to go for seconds). Although I didn't run, I do recall developing a rapid walking action as we raced, plate in hand, around the tables in the hall to get to the front of the queue – the motion akin to a speed walker.

I remember the echoes of identity forming in primary school. The wariness of having older kids in the school and then the liberating superiority of being the eldest pupils and representing the school in sports teams. This theme, this familiar cycle, would repeat itself again in secondary school, and strangely enough in teacher training, as well as through promotions during my teaching career. The cycle ensured I became, or at least felt, superior for a short period of time.

I don't recall misbehaving at primary school. It was a place where I felt as though I belonged. Education was not overly important: we did it because that was what we did. It was just part of the deal in a place where I could meet my mates, eat a decent meal, and play football every spare minute.

Clearly apparent in this extract is the development of the socialised child as I progressed through the key stages then termed infants and juniors. My earliest experiences remain a blur; how strange when you consider I would have lived through every one of those days. I wonder what messages I absorbed. Interestingly, I learned to make the distinction between being cooperative with my classmates and compliant towards the teacher in order to earn rewards. I was aware that hierarchal status mattered as big kids occupied the part of the playground where the best goalposts were situated. I was wary of some of the older children. As I grew up and started secondary school, I easily converted from inferior at school to superior at home. I dare say that I was grappling with the notion of identity.

How stimulating it is to apply this deep layer of insight to the data I obtained from the pupils as part of my study: each pupil is truly a unique individual in their own right. My primary school was a safety net, and I was painfully ill-prepared to go to 'big school'. I was about to become a number again – an obscure name on multiple lists. On reflection it represented a period of immense vulnerability as I experienced the transition from primary school to secondary school. My mum facilitated my truancy, which eventually resulted in a transfer to another school at the end of Year 7. This is the first time I have stopped to reflect on the challenges facing that innocent little boy and to contemplate his evolving identity and the implicit messages he absorbed.

Exposure

With some of the older boys I could not begin to try some of the antics or employ the attitude my mum and select teachers witnessed. The lads' standing and reputation left me feeling insignificant and powerless. These feelings became acute through a very uncomfortable experience one day when walking home from school. Now in the fourth year [Year 10], I had to travel through a notorious estate and was confronted by residents who also happened to be in the year group above me. They were bigger, stronger, and more self-assured than me. I was aware that one of them was a boxer. Without him actually hitting me, I was left feeling totally humiliated by their mocking attitude, and my confused state left me near paralysed as they continuously blocked my path.

Such a feeling of incompetence was not new to me. An absent dad meant that my siblings and I were subjected to the dominance of the 'Irish family' throughout our primary school years. These boys were older and bigger than us, and we became their prey. My shouting mum did not deter them as we resorted to running whenever we saw them and entering and exiting our house by climbing in and out the back window. The same pattern repeated itself on our new estate which we moved to in 1978, which also coincided with my move from one secondary school to another. Again, relative security was withdrawn as a new, older family moved in and turned from being my mates to being my intimidators. The fact that I was the eldest of my clan highlighted my impotence even more. That I can name every single boy and recount in great detail incidents from all three sets of oppressors is testament to the deep impact these incidents had upon my formative psyche.

Temple (1999: 171) suggests that troublesome incidents such as these can become fixated if unintegrated into Adult and are "therefore available for transferential cathexis in moments of stress … [and teachers are] liable in the professional situation to be triggered out of Adult into replaying material from Parent or Child".

According to Gudmundsdottir (1997), narratives and biographies can be used to gain an insight into teaching, unlike those attainable via other approaches. My analysis of memories of my schooldays also provided additional and unexpected insights to comprehend the pupil behaviour presented in Part III; my conduct was just the tip of the iceberg.

> School for me was 95% social (and it gave me free dinners). My self-image was shaped by the icon of the age – John Travolta (as Danny Zuko in *Grease*) – and I took on his mannerisms and adjusted my uniform. It is quite understandable, looking back, that such an unstable foundation was bound to be inconsistent in its expression. I had no discernible ambition or aspiration connected to school subjects, I felt popular amongst pupils in the year group due to my contribution to the football team, and I was very secure in the immediate sub-groups I was integral to. I even felt 'superior' to younger kids in the school, but inwardly terrified of some bigger kids who would sap my confidence in a second. It was little wonder that I wore a 'mask' as I negotiated my way through the daily interactions.
>
> I saw, for the first time, that my teachers provided a relatively safe stage on which I was able to assert, challenge, and resist periodically. True, some could (and did) give me the cane, but that was a decent trade-off and actually deemed a symbol of status. It was almost a preferable choice to the deadening requirement to copy out line after line of a corrective sentence in detention, starting with the words, 'I must not …'
>
> My teachers, whose very presence protected me from the 'imagined' threat of the older boys, inexplicably also provided a target which enabled me to feel powerful and significant again. Some did so by becoming a scapegoat for my non-compliance and rebellious show of defiance. I could get away with it, just as I did with my mum. Others restored my sense of security as they provided boundaries which signalled order and safety. The latter acted as a proxy of sorts, filling the void left by an absent father figure. They enabled me to adopt the appropriate role of a child.

Parental Figures

My process for recalling significant teachers was aided by sketching images which represented my memories of them (Figure 21.3). I found the exercise absorbing.

Figure 21.3. Teachers

The tall guy at the back with a beard is Mr Searle. A wonderful, caring man who showed me glimpses of how important values and principles are. When I say he 'showed me glimpses', I am referring to my ability to recognise and appreciate them. He was and is a passionate man, set against the inequalities and injustices of this world. It is he that I think of most as I undertake this research. I spoke to him recently on the phone. Wonderful! His recollection of me was of a very angry young man. I was surprised, as I assumed I had shielded that side of myself from him. It prompts me to remember that my social conditions were always the context behind every single experience of school I document here – from primary through to secondary.

The chap at the front right is Mr Moran, another I kept in touch with and came to know as a man. I helped him build three houses. He was the one who inspired and assisted me in going back to education and becoming a teacher, having originally left school with next to no qualifications to drift into work on building sites. Very cool, a reputation for being 'hard'. His very presence did the trick. As head of year he had status to back him up, but he didn't have to rely on that. Only a short bloke, but he came across as very self-assured, which shaped our perception of him. I remember being very receptive of his approval. Observe me with these two and I would be labelled a compliant, even cooperative and likeable young man. Indeed, I could be and was able to adopt this mask at a moment's notice, so wearing it at the appropriate hour was no problem.

With a strange logic I reasoned that Mr Root and Mr Pegram (second left and middle) 'can't control me' and so I ran riot, whilst the very strict Mr Leitch (left) provoked fierce, subversive resistance as he had 'no right to try and control me'. Further still, the kind and caring Mr Searle and the head of year, Mr Moran, did not require any form of control as I yielded without fuss to their right to educate me. My interest settles for a moment on these two significant authority figures in my early adolescent years – Mr Searle (Chris) and Mr Moran (Trevor). The fact that I maintained contact nearly three decades on poses the question as to what the bond was. Was it apparent then? Was it an interest they took in me? Was it a principle in them? I doubt if they kept in touch with many of the thousands of students they must have taught throughout their careers. If I had to get it down to one factor it is this: my overriding memory is a feeling that Chris cared for me and Trevor liked me. Can it be as simple as that?

In retrospect, what a relief it must have been to be able to revert to my appropriate role as vulnerable child when a strong, non-threatening adult was involved. I turned to the literature on gender; in particular, Biddulph's (2003) emphasis on the significance of men in the lives of 'under-fathered' boys. Although the exercise enabled me to consider the variable effect of prominent adults on my formative years, I sensed that even the most important of teachers were merely subsidiary figures in comparison to the place reserved for my absent father in my young life. And so I passed out of the system – with one decent grade to my name. Aside from the incidents when I was intimidated, I had a great time – I look back on my schooling with much fondness. True, I would have presented a sad score on the school's value-added data – a failure who fell well short of his potential. But that would be from a narrow perspective which neglects to take into account the enormous growth from a little boy to a young man. I had somewhere to go every day, I was fed, and I could have a laugh with my mates. I am sorry that so many decent, well-meaning adults paid a price during my more selfish episodes.

There were still no signs of the drive and incessant insistence on work which would later emerge; just a range of role models for me to absorb in my perception of what it meant to be a good teacher. Yet it is only through this process that I have consciously realised the essence of who they *were* to supplement what they *did*. If I subconsciously took anything from my embryonic image of a teacher, I am sad to say that it was an imitation which was only surface deep – I had little to sustain me beyond the persona I adopted and the performance I had mastered.

I will expand briefly on the issue of imitation. My children often 'played' teachers: my youngest daughter, then aged 7, wanted to be a teacher. The common trait she displayed was authoritarian mixed with a caring, sharing, and encouraging tone. She used phrases such as, "Line up straight", "Face this way", and "Quiet please – thank you". Unaware of my presence, she used one of my mini whiteboards and proceeded to take away 'golden time' for those misbehaving by writing their names on the board (her little brother and some dollies were subject to the sanction).

In an attempt to substantiate my assertion that the traits of a teacher are already ingrained a long time before applicants undertake formal training, I conducted an impromptu piece of research. I invited a Year 11 tutor group to submit the phrases they would use if they were to role play a scene in which they had to adopt the position of a teacher. I didn't specify the circumstances they would have to enact, however, a phrase was provided as an example: "Quiet". The class were encouraged to call out as I jotted down their responses:

> Don't talk back … Don't answer back … Calm down … Sit down … Do as you are told … Oh, for God's sake … Excuse me! … Turn around and face the front … Stop singing … Silence, I want silence … I can't hear myself think … Bloody hell … Hands up … Pens and pencils down … Don't call out … You are stopping other people from working … You will be staying behind for break … Other people are trying to work … You're late … Oh naughty words [a specific phrase one of their teachers used to prevent herself from swearing!].

Yes, the momentum dictated the exchange, but I considered it a worthy pursuit to elicit the expressions, mannerisms, and even tones that these students drew on to inform their hypothetical character. Now in my forties, I had to delve much deeper into my subconscious script to expose the origins of my habits and perceptions.

Exposed Again

Overlapping my time in upper secondary and the world of work was a definitive experience in my adolescence. I joined a boxing club at age 15. When I say 'joined', my dad took me because he wanted me to learn how to fight. After having had only limited contact through earlier years, this at least represented a chance to bond. I had actually expressed interest in joining a weight-lifting gym but that fell on deaf ears. It is only on reflection that I realise the gentle encouragement, affirmation, and caring I received from the adults at the club provided a foundation in which self-respect and identity grew.

There were few rules, just a code which guided all we were becoming.

The club was open seven days a week and my joining coincided with the end of my turbulent testing period at school. This is indicated in one of my school reports from 1980:

Inner London Education Authority

Langdon Park School

DATE July 1981 FORM 4O.

SUBJECT REPORT

NAME Sean Warren

SUBJECT History

REMARKS:

Over the year, Sean is possibly the most improved pupil in either of my two 4th Year groups. This means, admittedly, that he made a poor start to the course, making very little effort at all with his written work. However, I am very pleased indeed that Sean has really begun to take himself + the course seriously.

Obviously, there is still a very great deal that will need to be done next year. Sean has had problems with the material for his project, but now these are beginning to be sorted out, he has made much more progress.

Sean will have to concentrate on the written course work next year. He is an intelligent student who has displayed a very clear grasp of many of the topics, but he must make sure that this potential is fulfilled + that he begins to do himself justice on paper. With the right approach, he could do very well.

Sean is now pleasant + co-operative in lessons.

HPC 2389

A. Tarrant SUBJECT TEACHER

At the club I did well. Although I lost my first fight, I put up a great show in front of my dad, and I recall his pride as he paraded my battle scars to his mates in the pub afterwards.

Interest grew as my dad sold tickets with glee to family members and his drinking companions. My first home bout as a 15-year-old novice catapulted me to mini celebrity status as around 40 of the crowd filed in specifically to cheer on George Warren's boy.

I won five out of my next six fights, losing only to a majority decision. Even then my reputation was enhanced as it was revealed that I had broken my thumb in the first round. It is clear now, and what I suspected then, that the expectations were too much for that young boy to carry. By the time I was 17 all I wanted to do was to hide. I pulled out of a home show, but was convinced by my dad that I would be letting everyone down. I reluctantly agreed to fight. The brief flirtation with the prestige of being a winner was replaced by intense insecurity and doubt. Climbing into a ring and being centre of attention in front of so many people I knew provoked an acute sense of vulnerability.

The ring can be a very lonely place. I got soundly beaten, although it is fair to say that I was beaten before the bell even rang. I wasn't to know that my opponent would go on to become a professional champion. Regardless, the event left me embarrassed, humiliated, and very angry. I buried these feelings; this is the first time I have confronted and expressed what happened back in 1983. I had been publically exposed. I recognise the feeling too well, and it resounds through my narrative.

I detect now the beginning of a new hardness in the reconstruction of my persona as I present myself to people who are oblivious to my catalogue of shame about being a victim – a victim to my circumstances and fodder for older, bigger lads. On this specific occasion, I think it was more the imagined shame I felt on behalf of my dad as he watched on with his pals. Something changed that night in my perception of how others perceived me. As I stood there, occupying space in the local boozer, my dad, his mates, and members of my extended family continued to socialise – business as usual. However, I no longer experienced the pride I used to feel as I was inevitably referred to and introduced as 'Sean the boxer'. It qualified who I was; it was part of my identity. I don't recall anyone mentioning the defeat. I just sensed an avoidance of the subject. Embarrassed and angry in equal measure, I sought to deny the experience in the ring and bury it because no one ever offered me an alternative. I resolved never to be a victim again. Sensitive souls at the club held me up by creating opportunities for me to work with the younger boys and sought to restore me by appointing me as junior club captain for three consecutive years. The club's guardians are dead now and the club is no more.

Chapter 22

Transitions

Sean

Product

In 1981, I emerged as an unsuccessful product of the education system. Armed with just one decent CSE qualification and little ambition or direction, I was confronted with the challenges of (un)employment. As with the transition between primary and secondary school, I was painfully ill-equipped and I was to learn some harsh lessons about the uncompromising world of work.

Having examined my formative experiences, the TIFF model enabled me to explore how some of the implicit messages I had received might have moulded my habitual traits. I was interested to review my journey as an evolving adult, or more specifically as an authority figure, to see if I could unearth any clues about my current performance. Brookfield (1995: 50) claims that "Our autobiographies as learners in childhood, adolescence, and young adulthood frame our approach to teaching at the start of our careers, and they frequently exert influence that lasts a lifetime." Reoccurring issues around control and resistance soon emerged within the narrative.

> Leaving school with poor examination grades left me with limited options – that was the harsh reality. Infrequent and unreliable stints on building sites, market stalls, factory assembly lines, and door-to-door sales brought in little money and even less aspiration. I experienced a hard lesson that the patience exhibited by my teachers did not extend to the real world. Labouring on a cold building site, days before Christmas, I was put on a task inside. The project was close to completion and the finishing touches had been applied. I committed the crime of walking on the carpet whilst wearing my boots. The visiting site manager, with his hard hat and status-enhancing jacket took exception to this act and scolded me in front of the managers escorting him. As my bosses looked on in clear discomfort, I reacted habitually and told the self-important one where to go. His response was swift: "Sacked – get off my site." My retort about not caring fell on deaf, uninterested ears. The feeling of being justified lasted for much of the rest of the day. The reality of being without a wage again slowly dawned on me as the days turned into weeks. I was increasingly reliant on the state and succumbed to a cycle of getting up late,

watching daytime television, and lying awake until the early hours unable to sleep.

The decision to return to education came at age 18. I embarked upon the task of attaining the qualifications I would need in order to become a teacher.

Here the mantra of the system became all empowering because grades represented a passport. I became the oldest student when returning to school to attain the GCSEs I required. Unquestioningly, I learned to play the game, attending sixth form and night school whilst still working in my dad's pub. However, I struggled to do well as I was devoid of the skills required, as recall without the capacity to analyse and evaluate placed a limit on my capacity to gain good A level grades. Lots of effort without much strategy enabled me to limp over the line to take my place on a teacher training course at the age of 22. Upon arrival, I had already acquired a range of relevant skills which would see me succeed with children whilst trying to figure out the academic requirements.

The four year teacher training course subtly informed and reinforced my understanding of teacher–pupil relationships. The teaching practices simply lent themselves to moulding, or at least accommodating, the style of the teacher I was developing into. Implicit expectations which were embedded in my psyche (a requirement for children to line up straight, stand in silence, etc.) were reinforced and became expected if one was to gain the approval of those with the power to pass/fail (i.e. the host teacher and lecturer/supervisor).

Holiday work in play centres, football coaching, and summer camps in the United States allowed me to practise mannerisms which had first produced 'success' when I worked in the primary play centre back in London. I found I could discipline way before I knew the first thing about teaching. Each successful experience reaffirmed my mindset and approach because 'no one messed about in my lessons'. No one questioned my approach or showed me a different way, so I assumed that whatever I was doing, I was 'doing it right'. In 1988, I was deemed ready to go out and represent the establishment of which I was now a successful product. Again, I passed through the four year course, reassured that I was a valid teacher when I received my BEd (Hons) in physical education and history. I grabbed the diverse opportunities ahead of me. I was not burdened by responsibility, and the trait for perfectionism had yet to embrace me.

Servant

A range of experiences upon graduation allowed me to really settle my approach. Continuing roles coaching football in the United States, lecturing trainee teachers in Papua New Guinea (PNG), and working with children in Romania honed my skills and cemented my conception of who I was as a teacher.

A confusing episode occurred whilst working in PNG, which I have rarely considered, let alone discussed. I had taken the opportunity, with a colleague, to partake in a prospective alliance between Marjon, the teacher training organisation from which I had just graduated, and the National Sports Institute in PNG.

I had quickly developed a great affinity with the locals but found the 'superior' attitude of the deputy director and his wife progressively irritating. They were both Australian. Referring to me as a student on a secondment, rather than the 26-year-old qualified teacher I perceived myself to be, drew a line in the sand for our relationship. His overtly controlling tendencies stoked something deep inside me and resistance quickly turned to challenge. This came to a head one morning in the communal office. Standing over me whilst I sat at my desk, his attempt to physically dominate me in front of my colleagues led to me rising, man to man, to challenge him to "Make me" – to fight. He quickly backed down and left the room. Internal politics dictated that the deputy director was supported by his manager, and I was subsequently suspended from duties for the final month of the three month assignment.

Far from experiencing shame or regret, I was lauded by the locals for standing my ground. Numerous tales of his underhand bullying tactics with others emerged to enable me to justify my stance. That I was now powerful enough, and confident enough, to stand up against attempts to bully me is a significant thought. The trait – to stand up to perceived adolescent bullies – was one that would help to define the type of teacher I became. This deep unconscious conviction was yet to be realised, as a confident persona and an array of experiential skills now supplemented my curriculum vitae.

These were put to the test during a period of six months of continuous and varied supply teaching, in which I relied heavily upon the mannerisms which had paved the way for my success so far. Any consideration of the inappropriateness of getting instant results by being overly assertive and intimidating, even bullying, was obscured because I did not define my approach as such, and neither did those senior colleagues who were impressed by my ability to 'control' kids in an instant. As far as I was concerned, I was just being strong. It is important to remind myself that I was not a monster. Within this framework, which I tended to assert on arrival and then refer to as and when needed, was a range of rich and fun relationships with hundreds of children.

The issue is that I had no conception of another way of 'controlling' classes. Of course the relationships with the pupils contributed, but this was not at the forefront of my thinking. Compliance was everything and the relationships emerged from that structure. As I got better, my reputation began to do much of the work for me and a presence was established in the minds of the children whom I had encountered previously. I was now ready for my first full-time job. When it arrived, it stoked up dormant traits as I reverted back to my turbulent years as an early adolescent.

My teaching post in Kent lasted less than two years. I remember being asked at interview what would be my response if I arrived at the gym and the pupils were already in there misbehaving. I simply said, "It wouldn't happen." The head teacher pushed for an alternative answer, but my steadfast, overwhelming conviction was that it simply wouldn't happen. I got the job; as it turns out I did well at pretty much every interview I attended, even though I wasn't particularly skilful in how best to conduct myself or provide eloquent answers.

The same formula of being very assertive, thus paving the way for solid relationships, endured, and I hold immensely fond memories of the children and the amount of energy I had then. The issue came with the head of department, who was totally controlling with everyone and everything within her realm. This included providing the department with different colour polo shirts and insisting we all wear a certain colour on each day. I was now 27, fully qualified, and feeling really quite established after what had amounted to several years working in various guises with children, so this deeply irritated me. I was totally rebellious and openly sabotaged and undermined her. This was a regretful episode from which I only found a way out by moving schools.

The other thing to note here was that an additional response to my situation was to chuck myself into my work. An Ofsted inspector had described me as a 'rough diamond' and I now undertook the task of being very good. This meant many hours preparing resources. If I bought a resource book, I was not content until I had photocopied it, cut it up, and laminated it onto my index cards. I had taken the first steps and was on the road to becoming a perfectionist.

Joining a new school in January 1995 led me to employ my overly assertive approach again. New classes pushed boundaries but quickly found that I was more than a match for them. Most yielded straight away, and reputation and presence enabled me to again develop strong relationships with the vast majority of students.

My bullish street approach led to one Year 11 'yob' complaining to the deputy head because I had met his attempt to challenge me by telling him he was a 'fat tosser'! I record this to show how blinkered I was in my assertion that my job was to control kids and not to tolerate any form of challenge.

This trend repeated itself as I moved from PE to RE and stayed in a school in Colchester for four years. I was very much a PE teacher in the classroom in the first two years, as I studied part time to gain a diploma in my new subject. A range of conflicts occurred with the established disruptive pupils of this 'tough' school. My tactics were ugly on occasion (lifting up desks and throwing them) in response to a particularly challenging student attempting to perform for his mates at my expense. However, the methods worked, my reputation spread like wildfire, and before long I could merely walk into a room and elicit silence with my very presence.

As with the conflict I encountered in PNG, my habitual tendency to 'righteously' stand up against what I perceived as wrong became complicated – I was in danger of setting myself up to accusation. Again, fully justified in my own mind, I found myself intervening in a grappling fight between two Year 10 pupils outside my room. Amongst the multitude of students in the confined space between four adjacent classrooms, the lads had hold of each other and ignored my roaring warning to stop. Everyone else did, but they carried on. I walked over, assertively got in between them and separated them, a fist clutching each of their shirts. The conflict stopped immediately. However, the act was not perceived well by one of the boys' fathers, who put in an official complaint that I was too aggressive and had ripped the buttons off his son's shirt. The involvement of the regional union representative led to even more entrenched justification on my behalf. Although I was comprehensively cleared of any wrongdoing, I was still to acknowledge that the drive which prompted such a reaction was not strength but a potential weakness in my character.

Likewise, when my head of department – who was widely acknowledged as unprofessional and devious – tried undermining me, I met his antics with barely contained anger. The situation became even more entwined as official accusations of his incompetency as a manager led to me being offered the leadership of the department whilst he reverted to classroom teacher. My deepening disgust in response to his laziness and covering lies led to another outburst. Whilst I considered this a man-to-man stand-up and fully justified, he perceived it, or at least took the opportunity to report it, as an act of bullying. Again, enquiries exonerated me, but I became increasingly insular in my work in the department.

Unfortunately, my excessive preparation of resources developed into making me a fully fledged workaholic. Here, teaching the subject well overtook my tendency to value relationships with the pupils. There was still a mix but the balance had changed.

Another significant event occurred during these years in the 1990s, in that a guest speaker by the name of Bill Rogers attended my school, and for the first time all of my methods were held up to scrutiny and found wanting. I had seen that there was a different, better way. Unfortunately, in the subsequent years I found that simply knowing about an alternative disciplinary approach wasn't nearly enough to alter my conduct.

Agent

After two years as head of department I took up the post at the school I described in Chapter 3. By now I had responsibility for the performance of others and I worked hard to ensure colleagues carried out their duties – I had become an agent of the system, an upholder of standards. By this stage of my career I was married, I had become a parent, and I was an accomplished teacher. As years and promotions passed I had also become an experienced leader. On paper I was all grown up. However, even in the midst of my research, I found myself resorting to a resistant mode in the face of authority – a mode developed in my formative years.

During my research, I recall trying to negotiate an awkward, liminal phase in which idealistic values were out of sync with reality. I was frustrated. My extensive reading had enabled me to reconceptualise my daily experiences in school and alerted me to the hypocrisy within the education system. It had raised the possibility that staff had been hoodwinked into uncritically enforcing rules and procedures. I, of course, had unwittingly turned out to be a prime example. Whilst my research provided avenues to progressively address my own conduct, I had yet to figure out a coherent way to express my emerging objections to the manners and methods of others.

On this particular occasion I did so by being mildly rebellious. The school leadership team had imposed a requirement that all staff should wear fluorescent waistcoats when on duty. Ironically, it was exactly the type of policy I would have supported, or even initiated, whilst occupying my strategic roles for the county and the school. However, now I was back on the receiving end. As I had not been consulted and was a professional in my forties, I objected to others telling me what to wear. I steadfastly refused to wear it – a psychological folding of arms. Instead, by way of protest, I carried it screwed up in my hand as a token gesture.

It wasn't long before the acting deputy head approached me as I, for the hundredth time, stood in my allotted area overlooking the artificial grass. I saw her from afar out of the corner of my eye. I knew what was coming next. She immediately informed me that I needed to wear the garment and asked why I didn't have it on. I responded by enquiring of its purpose. "So the Year 7s can see you if one of them has an accident," she replied. I scoffed, "I have been out here on duty without fail for years, twice a week, rain or shine (and hardly ever late). Not only have I yet to have a Year 7 fail to find me, but many other staff, who *are* wearing their fluorescent waistcoats, arrive on duty ten minutes late. They are standing in warm doorways as we speak, with their cups of coffee in hand, keeping as far away from the pupils as possible." Rant over. She was stumped.

I was, on reflection, rude and mulish. My act of subversion was more self-righteous and superior than principled, for it derived from an obstinate trait established long ago. If I had a valid point to make, it was lost. It was only much later that I learned the incident must have been conveyed on the grapevine. On leaving the school, my colleagues presented me with the offensive garment, which they had personalised, and with great amusement made me wear it:

The coverage in this section represents reflections which emerged from an exploration of my TIFF profile. Reflecting on the period documented in Chapter 3, I can now recognise an aversion to any insinuation that a pupil (or senior colleague) is trying to bully or impose their will on me. With pupils it provoked a dominating reaction, with leadership it caused me to revert to resistant mode, stoking a rebellious reaction.

Authoritative Presence

Figure 20.2 revealed that there was an imbalance in the way I used control and care when in charge of others. Further, I was able to distinguish between positive means of controlling (structuring) and more negative ways of being in control (dominating). I have used this section to examine some of the experiences and beliefs which may have led me to react rather than respond.

The positive modes of behaviours (identified in Appendix B as spontaneous/cooperative/structuring/nurturing) are dependent on my accounting as an Adult. In accounting mode (Figure 22.1), I use my internal energy to assess current reality to enable me to function effectively in the here and now – to be 'with it'. The capacity to live in the present, rather than reliving past events or envisaging the future, was a significant challenge for me, especially when I frequently lay awake troubled in the middle of the night.

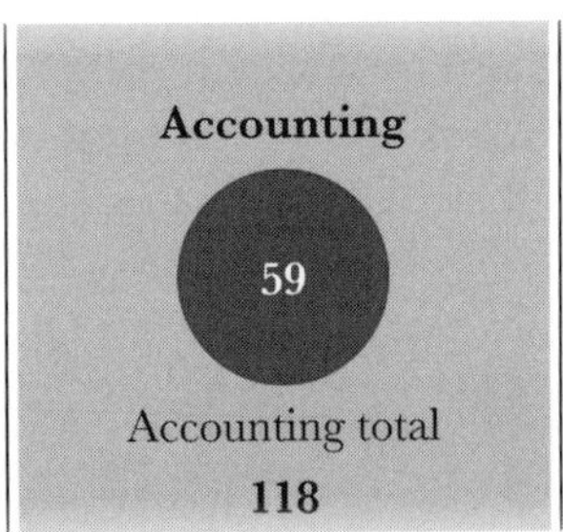

Figure 22.1. Functional Fluency profile: accounting

Accounting represents the rucksack in which the teacher's range of garments are packed: it ensures I can select appropriate clothing in response to emergent pupil behaviour, and it denotes the 'essence of presence'. The effect of giving my full attention to my pupils by accounting in the present was profound. By applying the TIFF model, I began to appreciate my young students, to notice and approve, to observe and redirect, and to begin to decipher invitations to play games, even in the midst of disruption.

Rodgers and Raider-Roth's (2006: 265) description of presence in teaching resonates with me: "a state of alert awareness, receptivity, and connectedness to the mental, emotional, and physical workings of both the individual and the group in the context of their learning environments, and the ability to respond with a considered and compassionate best next step." Rodgers and Raider-Roth (2006: 273) draw on Hargreaves (1994: 72) who saw "the importance of rooting self-knowledge in 'conceptions of the good and the welfare of others'", for presence has a moral imperative. Evidence to suggest I was getting closer to a balance was becoming apparent within the research data.

Respect is a value which acts as a thread throughout the research period. It is mentioned 105 times in questionnaire responses. I have amalgamated some of the students' comments below which correspond with the study's core aim.

> We know that it's a balance – if we treat the teacher with respect, we get fun and enjoyment back.
>
> You are firm but fair and never raise your voice because you treat everyone like young adults and with respect.
>
> You respect us and believe we can do things.
>
> You give the same amount of respect to anyone in the classroom.
>
> You give us freedom, but not too much that we can take advantage of it, because you explain to us what you expect in the lesson.
>
> You kind of look disappointed which makes us feel obliged to behave.
>
> If you are annoyed you don't shout but explain your disappointment which has more effect.
>
> You'd make me feel bad if I was naughty because I know I'd let you down … Because you show respect towards everyone so no one wants to throw it back in your face.
>
> You treat us with respect and this makes us want to do the same back.
>
> You're not too strict so people aren't afraid to answer any questions you ask.
>
> You don't take everything too seriously but you are serious when you should be.

Palmer (1997: 20) argues that in a "culture of objectification and technique we often confuse authority with power, but the two are not the same. Power works from the outside in, but authority works from the inside out." Warnock (1989) asserts that whilst teachers are given authority in the *de jure* sense, through hierarchal position or status, *de facto* authority – or application – must ultimately depend on the person who exercises it.

Whilst Warnock (1989: 74) was concerned with the individual teacher's personal ability, competence, knowledge, or status, she also hints at something deeper, something intangible: "He is the author. He must possess his own 'auctoritas', or the delegation of authority to him will simply not work: it will be empty."[1] Palmer (1997: 20) concurs, contributing to my notion of authenticity:

> External tools of power have occasional utility in teaching, but they are no substitute for authority, the authority that comes from the teacher's inner life. The clue is in the word itself, which has 'author' at its core. Authority is granted to people who are perceived as 'authoring' their own words, their own actions, their own lives, rather than playing a scripted role at great remove from their own hearts. When teachers depend on the coercive powers of law or technique, they have no authority at all.

I thought back to the default position I had come to occupy, the persona my research colleagues reverted to when under pressure, and my pupils' collective testimony that they are able to discern the substance of the adult in front of them. I realised that a delicate balance needs to be negotiated in order for the classroom to function effectively, efficiently, and ethically. I had sought to apply this sense of equilibrium to my own state of mind, and continued to explore how I might extend the notion to influence the class dynamic.

1 *Auctoritas* is Latin for 'authority'.

Chapter 23

Social Dynamics

Sean

Through the reflexive process, I was gradually becoming more aware of my own internal triggers, and I was increasingly able to decode the hidden goals behind pupil behaviour. The directed intention (derived from my engagement with TIFF) was to expand on positive modes of behaviour and to progressively transform the negative.

Temple's (1992a) four model link-up enabled me to guide group formations. Thus, a unique opportunity arose to add another dimension to my study of classroom climate when I inherited a Year 9 class after the February half-term (2011). Three aspects made this group potentially difficult: firstly, they were timetabled for RE on a Friday afternoon; secondly, they had formed the previous September and had become well established with another teacher; and thirdly, the cohort had been put together by the PE department and contained most of the Year 9 rugby boys' team. They would prove to be the perfect challenge to try out all I had been practising and to maximise insights from my data on peer social patterns and preferences.

An administrative error meant that I was unaware of the precise class list prior to meeting the group. The first entry into my research diary captured my response:

> When I saw this motley crew converge outside my room I began to quickly mentally dress for rainy weather. Many of the 'who's-who' of the year group came along the path, most of them were boys with strong social connections. I recognised many of them but had not taught about half of them. My first attempt to get their attention outside the room was either ignored or not heard. I suspected the latter and so I waited for a break in the verbal traffic and held a confident silence until eye contact and non-verbal direction gave me a platform to speak with quiet authority in relaying instruction and direction. I noted the school's latest recruit from another school (whose reputation was quickly growing here) roll up at the back of the group. Great!
>
> The class came in and settled quickly, organising themselves as boy/girl in accordance with my direction. I waited for my moment, sitting confidently on a raised piece of furniture. They listened and followed simple instructions. I relayed that my first impression of them was a positive one. Looking around the room, I redefined their tendency to

exhibit unhelpful behaviour in other classes as being 'spirited', rather than bad behaviour. "I like spirit," I told them, "but I am aware that some misrepresent themselves and are not always sure of boundaries and when to stop." They seemed to like that affirmation.

As with all the new classes this week, I explained that I thought it unfair if they had to guess the teacher's expectations. I had on the board a list of expectations wrapped up in 'routines'. If they agreed with the routine and felt they could adhere to the requirements, they were asked to write the routine on the inside cover of their book. I explained the routine whilst recording progressed and I invited any questions or objections. I was able to stroll into their territory as they were writing. One routine on the list involved my intention to offer them breaks following periods of about 13–15 minutes of concentration. A quick drink, chat, or wander would be possible, on condition of returning ready for the next episode. They liked the idea of that and we demonstrated it within the next few minutes. Will have to be on my mettle for next time as I don't want to fall into the trap of coming to the lesson underdressed and getting caught out, exposed by unexpected changes in the weather.

I later reflected:

I was interested to observe my inner reaction upon recognising the group's characters as they converged. Just prior to meeting them a deep unconscious negative and defensive 'thing' gripped me. It was gone before I could respond with any inner pep talk to challenge it. Maybe that is what fear or insecurity is when it reaches beyond the experienced professional I present at my place of work.

Self-organisation

The definitive insight this class provided came through a concentrated analysis on an aspect of research I had been tentatively trialling with other groups. Sociometry, originating from Moreno (1934), provided visual representations of the established social friendships within the class. Some of these might have stemmed from primary school or sports teams, whilst others could be fleeting or come in the form of cliques. The literature outlined the pros and cons of employing the approach, which informed the ethical procedures I took care to implement. With appropriate sensitivity, I sought to qualify complexity theory's emphasis on the importance of local relationships and self-organisation to emergent behaviour (Figure 23.1; see also Figure 9.1).

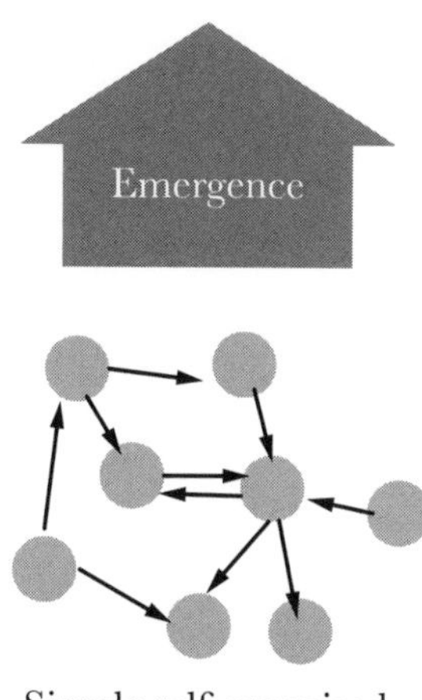

Figure 23.1. Complex adaptive behaviour

The sociogram data immediately challenged my preconceptions about which pupils were the 'leaders' within the class. In their second lesson with me, I presented the pupils with four questions:

1. Who would you prefer to sit near?
2. Who would you prefer to work with?
3. Who would you prefer to share a room with on a trip abroad?
4. Who would you prefer not to sit near?

The students could indicate from zero to five peers for each question. It was clarified that the last question was optional and the answers would remain confidential. It was assumed that if pupils did select classmates from the 'negative' question, the choice would be significant for them. I present data from the first question to illustrate insights gained (Figure 23.2). The data assigns pupils to five groups: 'popular' students who are well liked by many peers and seldom disliked (high social preference); 'rejected' students who are frequently disliked and not well liked (low social preference); 'controversial' students who are both liked and disliked (high social impact); 'neglected' students who receive very few liked or disliked nominations (low social impact); and 'average' students who receive an average number of liked and disliked nominations (see Košir and Pečjak 2005: 128).

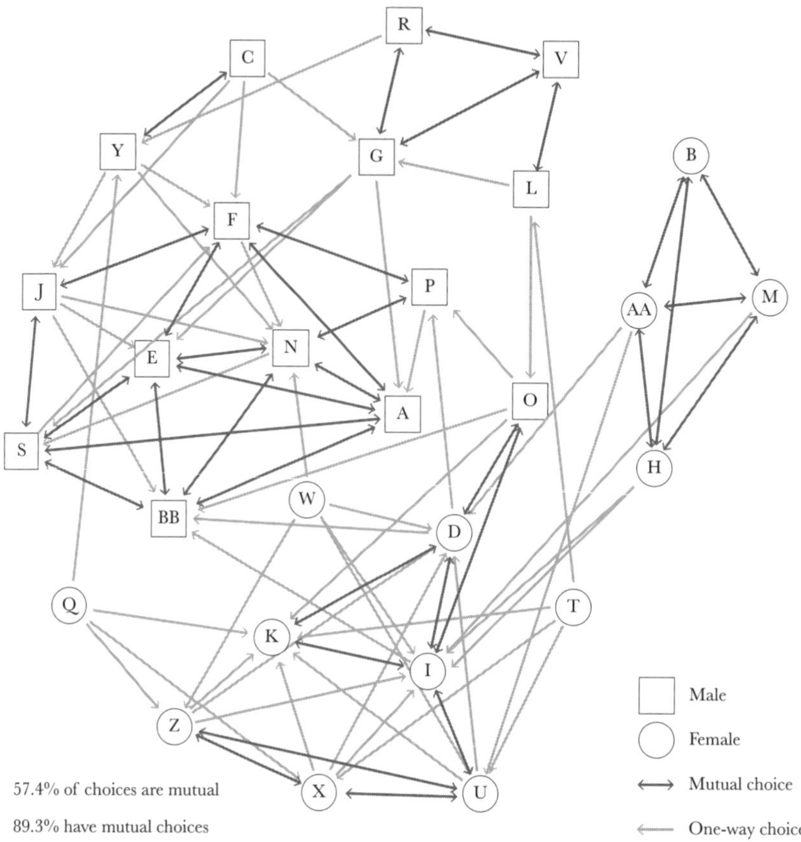

Figure 23.2. Positive question: Who would you prefer to sit near?

I realised that I was already spending a disproportionate amount of time subtly trying to appease those individuals that I thought influenced the climate (L, O, and R). I came to appreciate that the 'stars of attraction' (those who were apparently the most popular within this specific group) were actually relatively quiet, unassuming children. And I was also now aware of the peers who were significant to them ('stars of influence'). Francis et al. (2010) observe that it is possible for some pupils to achieve the balance between sociability and achievement, so avoiding being marginalised with the label of 'boffin' or 'geek'. Often exhibiting behaviours which were not excessively disruptive, they displayed good-humoured cheek and attitude rather than overt resistance or confrontation. Those pupils who chose each other offered me a clue about the strength of the alliance.

Clear patterns began to emerge which suggested that if I won over a few individuals I could indirectly influence the majority of the group. This informed my decisions to amplify or dampen the system. Those who were most popular represented an obvious choice, although consideration of the controversial pupils (those causing the highest social impact) was key to ensure cohesion within the group (A, S, and Z). DeRosier and Thomas (2003) identify this cohort as most likely to be bullies and relationally aggressive. I began to ensure that when I sought class opinion, I discreetly noted their responses. I carefully canvassed their opinion and included them amongst the pupils invited to lead or direct the lesson flow.

Nuthall (2002) notes that the personal and social world of pupils functions in the midst of classrooms, irrespective of curriculum content or the teacher's learning agenda. He identified social status as a key contributor to determining how peers glean subject content from each other as part of the learning process. By definition, some have limited alliances or are even excluded. I needed to understand these subtle gates and barriers. The negative nominations enabled me to be aware of possible areas of contention and amend seating arrangements. They allowed me to spot previously obscured cues, such as a lack of contribution to group discussions. The insights also afforded me an opportunity to periodically place pupils together for specific tasks, to combine their strengths and begin to address and amend the aversion to each other they shared. A delicate business.

Isolates

The data also revealed (or confirmed) the group's isolates. Labels such as 'isolate' and 'star' need qualification and should not be taken at face value. For example, Ashley (1992) describes witnessing the pupil with the lowest sociometric score intermingling with many other children during breaktime. In fact, his interactions were more than double those recorded for the student with the highest sociometric score. Contextual data is also confined to specific groupings of pupils, which is likely to omit many of their friends at school. Perhaps illustrative of this in my data is one child (Q), a girl labelled with attention deficit hyperactivity disorder, who was painfully devoid of friendships within this Year 9 class (Figure 23.3). She sat by herself and was very taxing in her dependence on me to affirm and reaffirm tasks. Attempts to gain peer assistance through moving her prompted emotional defensive reactions from her which then had to be calmed. The negative data revealed that eight classmates chose her as a peer they would choose not to sit near, thus placing her in the category 'rejected'.

Zettergren's (2003) results show that rejected children are a risk group for which schools must cater. These children are likely to experience problems over a long period of time and are integral to high drop-out statistics. Warrington and Younger (2011: 165) advance a broader perspective, claiming that "schools which are locally popular, which receive excellent reports from government inspectors, and where students have high levels of academic achievement … have a responsibility to identify and support isolated students … [to move beyond] the rhetoric of inclusivity".

In this case, no pupils selected to sit near, work with, or share a hypothetical room with Q. However, scrutiny showed that Q consistently nominated two girls (K and Z).[1] Their data responses did not reject Q. As a result, I was able to quietly inform K and Z of Q's preference and enquire whether they would be open to assisting Q periodically if she was stuck. I was then able to confidently request K or Z's help and observed Q receive them without a fuss and proceed to address the task.

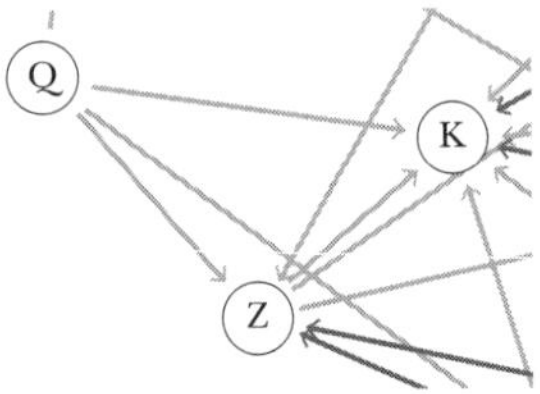

Figure 23.3. Isolate

Although space prevents me from documenting individuals' affirmative comments of our lessons, the class's evaluation of their performance in comparison to their general behaviour in other lessons is presented in Figure 23.4.

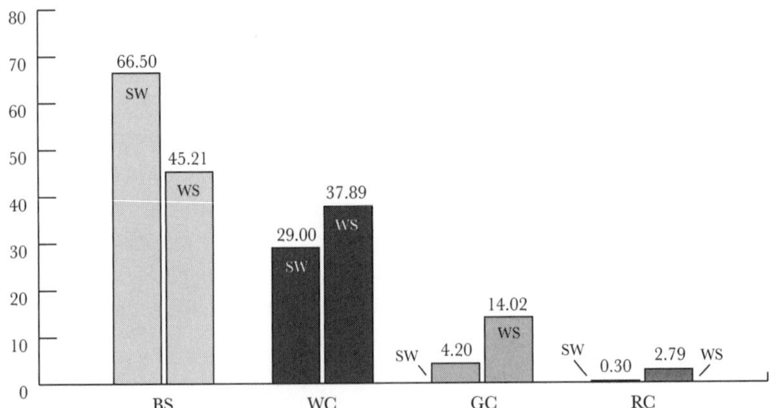

Figure 23.4. Pupils' self-assessment of their conduct in Sean Warren's (SW) class in comparison with their whole school (WS) behaviour

1 Q also chose Y, a non-attending 'rejected' boy to work with, and X to sit with but not work with.

The left hand and middle columns indicate order and show that for a significant proportion of time, order could be defined by pupils' cooperation rather than mere compliance (Blue Skies as opposed to White Clouds). The data on the right reveals that a minimal proportion of time was spent off-task, through low level disruption or wilful sabotage. The connection I made with this class is demonstrative of what Surrey (1991: 61) describes as "relationship authenticity". Here, in the midst of my research, I felt I was "seen and recognized for who [I am] … and [met] the need to see and understand the other".

My action research had, thus far, concentrated on creating a climate which minimised the possibility of disruption and demonstrated the process I would undertake to enhance my capacity to cope whilst operating according to stated values. For much of the research period there was little indication that the nature of the teaching and learning qualified for further scrutiny. The uncomfortable realisation that it should emerged from a most surprising source.

Chapter 24

The Teaching and Learning Interaction

Sean

My pedagogical approach had evolved over many years. It was an amalgamation of many strands, evolving from Accelerated Learning and on through Claxton's (2002) Building Learning Power programme, via thinking skills. During the research period, I incorporated the notion of liminal learning, which advocates the use of characterisation, and Petty's (2006) evidence-based present, apply, review (PAR) model. Affirming much of what I had intuitively recognised as good practice, my perfectionist tendencies set about reorganising schemes of work to complement this new structure.

Although I was greatly encouraged by the response from the majority of pupils, I became acutely aware that apparent order did not necessarily equate to individual cooperation; performance sometimes masqueraded as learning. Three responses to a question enquiring why pupils behave in my lessons took me completely by surprise and added a further dimension to my research. Contrary to the vast majority of responses received, a trio of Year 9 boys from the same class wrote:

> 9TH3M3: By being patronising, quite annoying. Because we don't want to really get into trouble with you.
>
> 9TH3M7: You are patronising and too controlling. Because you patronise everyone until they have no other motives (George Orwell, *1984*).[1]
>
> 9TH3M11: Quite patronising and very annoying but I behave out of respect. Because they are respectful.

The revelation shook my confidence and provoked a defensive reaction which I then had to quell. Analysis of the sociometric data revealed that the three boys had nominated each other and were clearly an established subgroup. As the three did not sit together and were not forewarned about the questionnaire, the answers confirm that pupils do discuss their learning

1 The quotation was in the pupil's original response.

experience outside of lessons. A review of their comparative 'weather' estimates (Table 24.1) confirmed substantial disengagement with my lesson.

Table 24.1. Contextual disengagement

		BS/S	WC	GC	RC
9TH3M3	My lesson	0	95	5	0
	General performance	80	15	5	0
9TH3M7	My lesson	0	80	20	0
	General performance	70	30	0	0
9TH3M11	My lesson	40	60	0	0
	General performance	90	10	0	0

Some months after I had finished teaching the group, I approached 9TH3M7 and requested an interview to better understand his use of the term 'patronise'. The self-assured and able student accepted the invitation without hesitation. The interview represented the feedback I had mentioned to the pupils when they had the option of recording their names as part of the first cohort to consider the end of unit questionnaires. The boy was not surprised that his comment represented a minority view. He was less harsh than he had been in his comment, but he eloquently explained his experience of being subjected to a subtle form of control that I had administrated through my teaching method. Over-prescription, in the form of tasks and groupings, constrained his desire to express his independence and meant that he was disengaged, though compliant. I realised I had been missing a subtle distinction: I had placed an emphasis on teaching the subject, rather than teaching the pupils.

I had long recognised that the nature and quality of the teaching and learning experience is integral to the likelihood of behaviour disruptions. (This was discussed in Chapter 11.) I also came to acknowledge that my lesson structure acted to quell the possibility of pupils being off-task. Despite consistently achieving 'outstanding' judgements, in truth, I did not trust my classes to behave if I gave them more freedom. Incongruous with my relational approach, my pedagogical method remained comparatively restrictive and conditional. I was now challenged to engage with Morrison's (2008: 20) question: "How can autonomy, creativity, and cooperative and collaborative learning be promoted in learners?" I was aware that many of my learners had learned to deal with lesson demands by being (over-)dependent on me to give clear and unambiguous directives. I was sceptical that, even with encouragement, they could cope with being more autonomous. However, in light of my research question – which asked whether my approach could "contribute towards a well-ordered class of self-disciplined pupils" – it became apparent to me that omitting study of my pedagogy would render the coverage incomplete. Subsequently, trust was identified as my standard of judgement for this aspect of the research.

McDermott (1977: 199) views trust in the teacher–student relationship as "a quality of the relations amongst people, as a product of the work they do to achieve a shared focus. Trust is achieved and managed through interaction." Tzuo (2007) acknowledges the tension between teacher control and children's freedom. I came to realise that the PAR model had lured me into formulising my creative approach. The discrepancy between what I espoused and what I did was subtle yet profound, and elucidated for me both the distinction between norming and performing (Figure 24.1; see also Figure 17.2), and between compliance and cooperation.

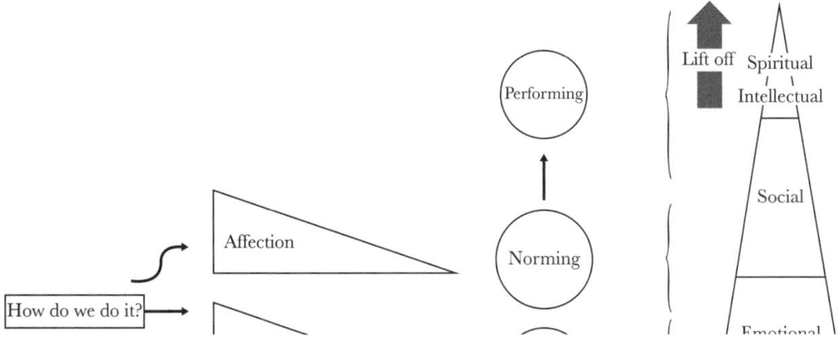

Figure 24.1. Norming and performing

Reconceptualising 'Disorder'

As a consequence of the incongruity I had uncovered, I turned again to complexity theory. Building on my coverage of emergent behaviour, Sawada and Caley (1985) argue that the prevailing view of classrooms as turbulent, messy, and disorderly should make room for the possibility that disorderliness (i.e. turbulence) can be productive. Morrison (2008: 18) cites Kauffman (1995), who suggests that "order comes for free and replaces control; internally generated, it is the antithesis of external control; [it] is not imposed; it emerges". Tosey (2002) provides the phrase 'minimal structures' which I expanded to include 'maximum choices'. This involved using different resources, choosing different tasks, adopting various forms of presentation, working with different people, and so on – if I deemed the options would enhance the learning experience.

I began to apply complexity principles to extract insights into the pedagogical interactions which were so familiar to me. I learned that complex systems have a rhythmic movement which helps to create stable structures. Rea (1997) refers to this as 'fold' and 'stretch'; I later added an interim phase I called 'flex'. These emerge from local rules as pupils self-organise. The contextual rules (derived from interactions between peers and teacher) create patterns that form the structure, which is constantly receptive to both positive and negative feedback.

If water could symbolise learning, I saw it as a tidal movement. So, having congregated on the sand, my task was now to get them to swim – to engage with the learning. If shallow water represented occasions when learners were dependent on me, conversely, deep water would symbolise the ideal of interdependence through peer collaboration. I became attracted to the concept of the 'edge of chaos' (Tosey 2002) to represent an optimum state of interdependent learning, conceiving it as being analogous to 'surfing the waves'. Rea (1997) coined the term 'serious fun' to denote the heightened learning motivation in which learners are absorbed.

However, before experiencing this optimal state, I needed to find a way for the tentative swimmer to negotiate the increasing depth in order for them to be secure and capable enough to venture deeper into the water without succumbing to distractions or being overwhelmed by overcomplicated tasks and instructions leading to cognitive overload. Thus, I created a transitional phase – flex – which recognised the intermediate steps from dependence towards independence within the zone of complexity (Stacey et al. 2000).

As illustrated in Figure 24.2, the concept of interactive fold, flex, and stretch provided a language to describe the natural ebb and flow of classroom energy, as the groups interacted with different types of tasks. I endeavoured to find a way to monitor emergent patterns to both recognise and influence classroom ambience. In terms of my psychological and operational state, I would have to account (Temple 2007), dress appropriately, and be (and appear) confident in uncertainty. Rodgers and Raider-Roth (2006: 284) argue that the climate I sought is created through "slowing down to observe students' interactions with the subject matter".

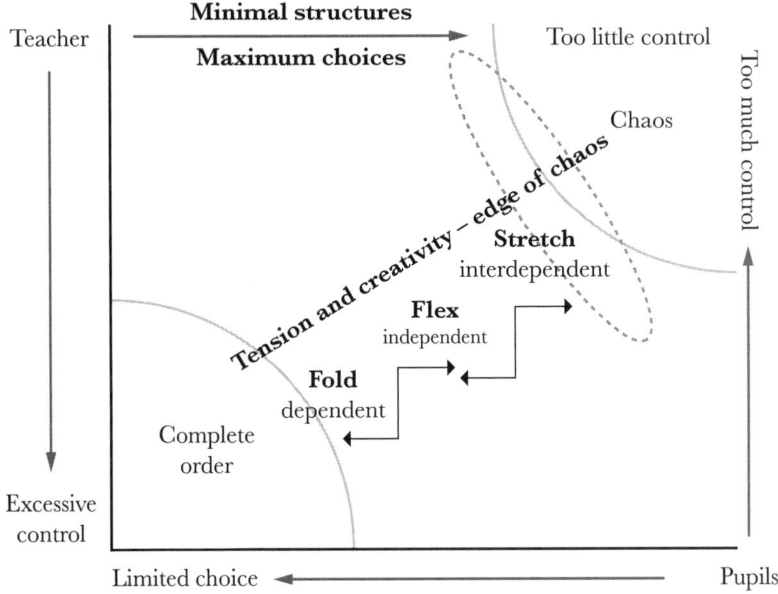

Figure 24.2. Ebb and flow

Lesson Observation Model

Illustrative of my approach is the lesson observation model which incorporated behaviourist, cognitive, constructivist, and social constructivist theoretical approaches. It recognised that all have legitimate contributions to make to the learning process. Rather than entertaining the proposed dichotomy between traditionalist and progressive, my experience suggested that there are times when pupils are best served by being dependent, whilst on other occasions their learning and development benefit from independence and opportunities for interdependence. The initial idea for the template (Figure 24.3) came from a colleague who was experimenting with a way of recording different levels of challenge.

Insights from cognitive load theory (Sweller 1994) contributed to my planning and delivery, so consideration of a pupil's prior knowledge (i.e. whether they were a comparative novice or expert) informed my approach. Expanding pupils' comprehension was further facilitated by steering them to choose from differentiated resources that would supplement whole class explanations, interactive software, and core texts. These choices were colour coded to be consistent with traffic light symbols (Figure 24.4).

Figure 24.4. Differentiated support material

The practicalities of smooth transitions remained key (Kounin 1970). To illustrate, exemplars of reflection and observation show the ebb and flow of teaching and learning interactions (see Figure 24.5). Dewey (1938) refers to 'intelligent action' to denote the process of observation and analysis, and Rodgers (2002) uses 'intelligent response' to embody the reflective process of teaching. Wiechert (2011) describes the process of pedagogical interaction as a rhythm which the adult must heed as it reveals itself through the pupils. It is the teacher's task to find equilibrium as the group 'breathe in' (think and concentrate) and 'breathe out' (engage in imaginative and creative endeavour). The familiar Bloom's taxonomy (Krathwohl 2002) offers another layer, which informed my planning of the three phases: the notion that questioning and tasks get progressively deeper as shallow, lower order tasks (knowledge and comprehension) lead to middle order tasks (application) and higher order tasks (synthesis, analysis, and evaluation).[2]

In the next few pages, I offer two applications to demonstrate the contribution that this tool made to my research aims. Figure 24.5 was recorded in response to a request from a colleague to observe a 'very disruptive' group, and Figure 24.6 captured the interactions in one of my own lessons.

2 Ritchhart et al.'s (2011: 7) critique of Bloom's taxonomy is helpful. They point out that the taxonomy is a theory, rather than being based on research about learning. Useful though it is, they find the notion of thinking being sequential or hierarchical as problematic, and conclude that comprehension or "understanding is not a precursor to application, analysis, evaluating and creating, but a result of it".

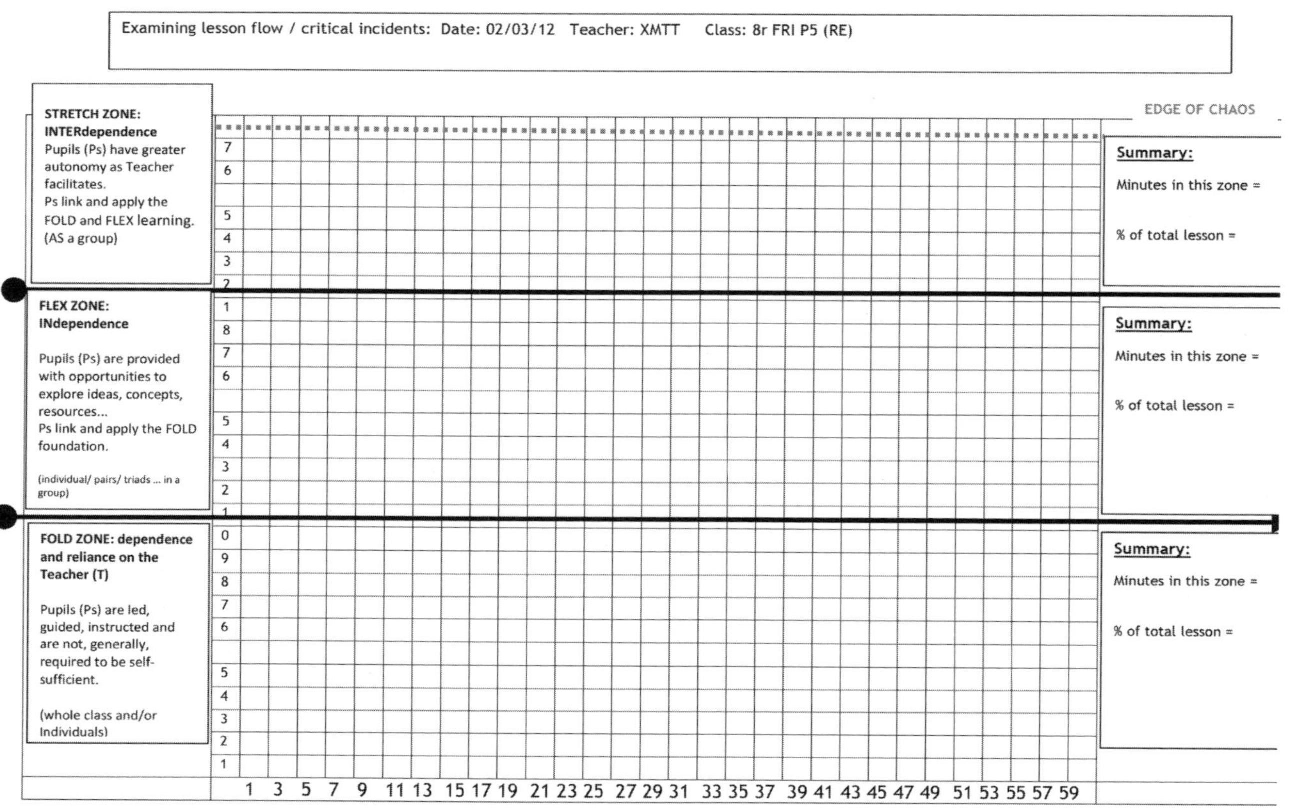

Figure 24.3. Align observation template

Archetypal Friday Period 5

The criteria enabled me to simply describe the interaction between the teaching and learning activities. There was no evaluation; I simply recorded what I saw on the grid. In complexity theory terms, we endeavour to capture something of what *is* rather than a preoccupation with *ought*. Post-observation, the teacher's instant realisation of the amount of time spent in fold (74%) revealed to him that his lack of trust in the group was a contributory factor to the constant interruptions he was experiencing. The teacher had asked me to include his learners' perspectives; the teacher chose the questions. Whilst discussing the data and the pupils' collective responses, it became apparent that he had all the right ingredients for a successful lesson, but he hadn't used them in a way which was conducive to the needs and interests of the group. The discrepancy between the content of a thorough lesson plan, which had been approved by his head of department, and the experiential delivery became self-evident for this teacher as we engaged in dialogue.

Complexity principles offered the notion of the strange attractor to describe patterns and the possibility of unpredictability. (This was described in Chapter 12 and illustrated through the attractor of excitement.) In contrast, a fixed point or constrictive attractor denotes near equilibrium, like a clock pendulum eventually settling down to become static. If the pendulum is placed in a vacuum, the swinging motion is termed a 'limit cycle'. The route is easily traceable on a computer simulation as it goes back and forth. Rea (1997) equates this with an authoritarian teacher keeping pupils strictly on-task through the enforcement of predictable routines. To illustrate further, I suggested that a prolonged period requiring the pupils' attention could quite easily turn into the attractor of boredom. During this particular observation, clues that the pupils were becoming restless or zoned out were either ignored or missed, and individuals were joined by others in finding ways to distract. On this occasion, the teacher's series of reminders and warnings were not taken seriously by the perpetrators, and so acted to amplify the system. All the while, the system's energy was being diverted from the learning task.

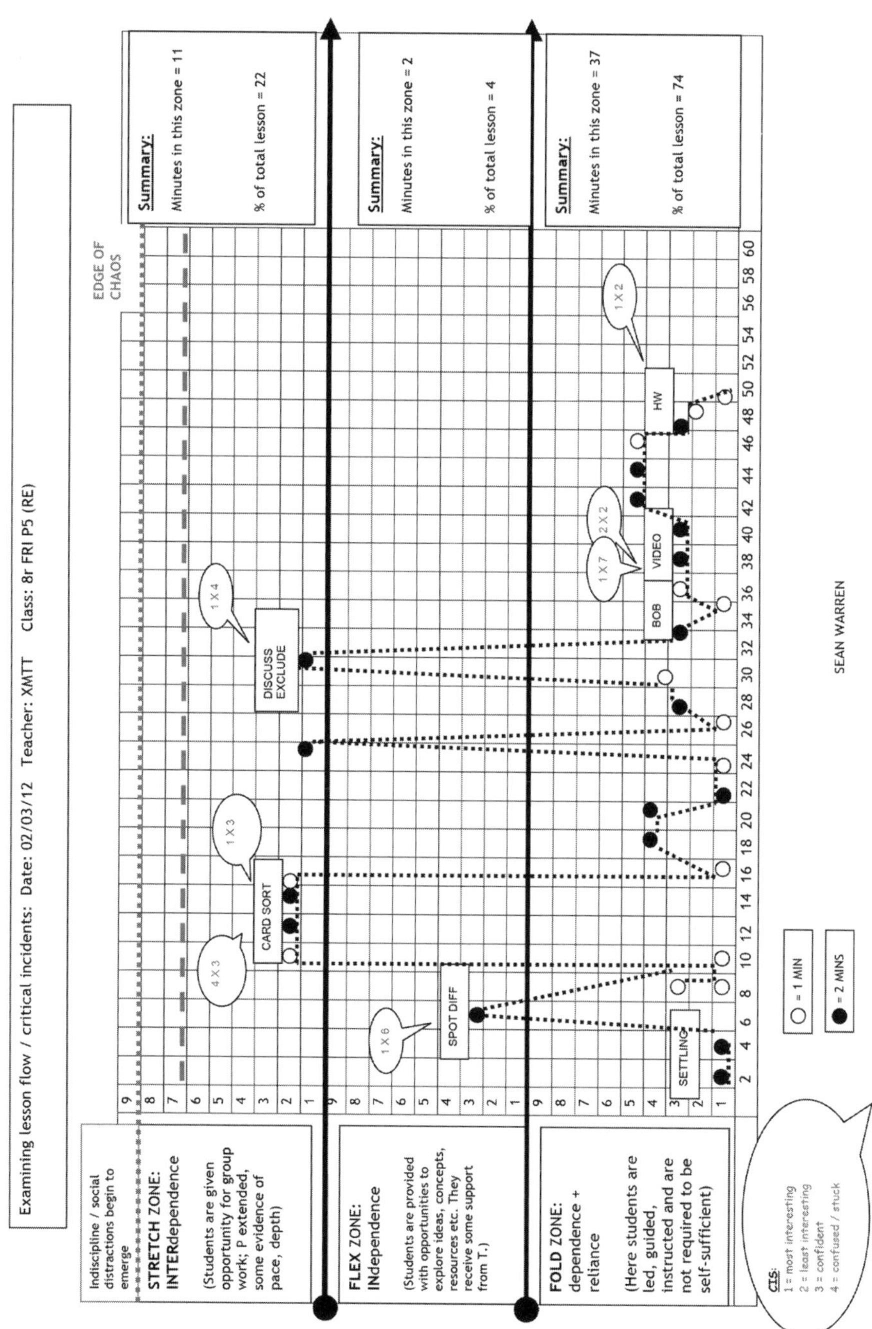

Figure 24.5. Friday period 5

Capturing the Edge of Chaos[3]

This observation of one of my lessons was recorded by a colleague. The data was initially logged onto an early prototype and has since been plotted onto this more recent template (Figure 24.6).

It shows periodic fold and flex preparation with the group before I introduce opportunities for stretch around 21 minutes into the lesson. Intervention at 30 minutes indicates that I sensed the emerging patterns were not conducive to quality learning. Some 16 minutes operating at the 'edge of chaos' then ensues, before the class is brought back to a calm place to share their findings and then to pack away. As Rodgers and Raider-Roth (2006: 271) advise: "Attention is not only on the learner but also simultaneously on the group, the environment(s) in which they all work, the directions in which the individual and group might go next, the variegated terrain of the subject matter(s) at hand."

It is important to point out that there is no ideal lesson segmentation; if it is most appropriate for a class to stay in fold for the majority of the lesson to maximise learning for a specific part of the course, then that is simply recorded for reflection and discussion – the percentages are value free.

As shown earlier (in the speech bubbles in Figure 24.5), the multi-layered template facilitated pupil voice, enabling them to be integral to the formative process – commenting on their experience of different facets of the lesson. To conclude, I wanted to provide pupils with a platform to express their summative evaluations of their learning. I asked:

> How do you feel about the way we learn the subject – do you like the open challenges or do you prefer to be told exactly what to do and led to do it? (*n.* 106)

The vast majority affirmed their preference for 'open challenges'. A selection of comments represented a rationale with common and affirmative terms (emphasis added):

> Yes, because we have *fun* but we learn a lot as well. It is very clever.
>
> I like to be left to do the task.

---

3 An important note for researchers: LET methodology enabled me to submit a video clip of my pupils learning 'at the edge of chaos' as part of my doctorate. This was discussed at my viva examination. I believe that this medium is more appropriate and effective than written forms of communication for capturing and conveying the life affirming energy in these types of encounter. The submission can be viewed at www.confidenceinuncertainty.co.uk. Permission to share was attained from all pupils and their parent(s).

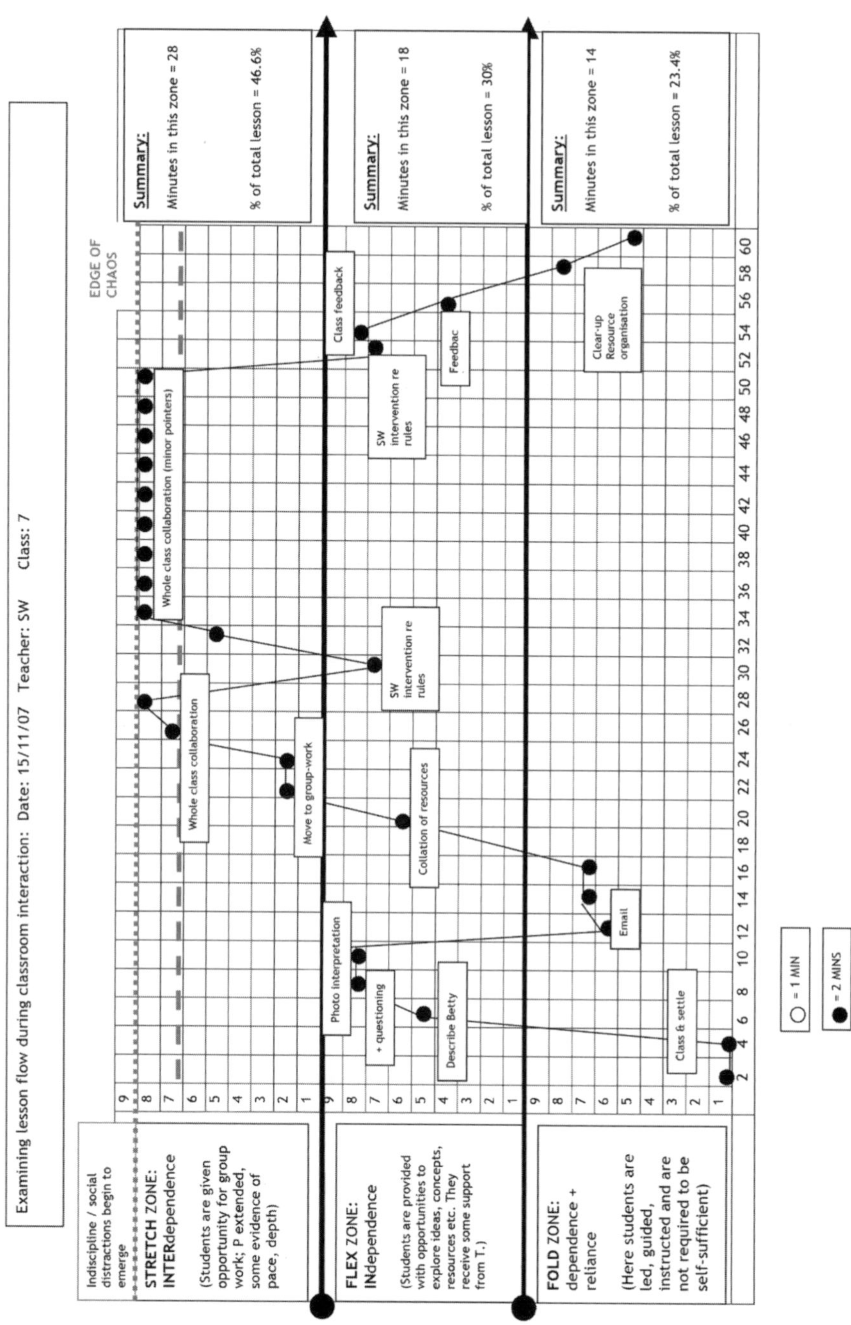

Figure 24.6. The edge of chaos

> I like the open challenges because he *trusts* us to make the right decisions whilst other teachers don't.
>
> I love that he lets us choose and lets us have *responsibility*.
>
> He tells us then we get on *independently*.
>
> Open challenges and choices most of the time I prefer, but sometimes need to be told exactly.

Whether termed open or closed, independent or dependent, the dynamic approach should address the varied educational needs of the learners. The exploration of content for a novice will need to be adapted for a more competent learner, and vice versa. Providing novices, who have limited prior knowledge or experience of the subject content, with open tasks and multiple choices is akin to asking them to eat soup with a fork. More often than not, it provides a platform for pupils to be unproductive because they exchange ignorance. Likewise, if a knowledgeable learner, such as Sarah in Chapter 1, is restrained by the teacher's planned directed coverage or spoon feeding, this prevents her from progressing appropriately from 'liquids' to 'solids'. My job was to cater for the needs of all the 'diners' and to keep those plates spinning. It seems that I didn't always achieve this. As with previous data exploring relationships, there remained a minority whose comments challenged the consensus and reminded me of the reality when diverse individuals gather as a group in a classroom:

> I hate RE and do not see the point of learning it; the lessons are taught well and he makes it fun but I don't tend to learn much. (Year 7)

Overall, however, my approach enabled many to benefit. During the research period, from September 2008 to July 2011, eight internal observations were conducted by my head of faculty using Ofsted criteria. I was intent on finding out whether my decisions to move away from authoritarian relationships, and subsequently overly directive methods of teaching, would meet the criteria deeming teaching and learning to be grade 1 or 'outstanding'. All eight performance management evaluations elicited a grade 1.

So, I have made claims that I have changed, or perhaps more accurately, that I have become more adaptable in my approach to my students and the joint endeavour we term 'teaching and learning'. Naturally, part of the validation process required me to enquire of those on the receiving end of my theories and efforts. I tentatively asked pupils in every one of the 16 research groups to independently assess whether, in their experience of me, I had changed.

Responses to the question overwhelmingly support my assertions that my performance had changed and had been increasingly consistent throughout the research period. I use amalgamated comments from the Year 8 group I taught for two consecutive years as representative of the key points:

> Has been the same, I have more respect [for] him now than at the start.
>
> He has become more relaxed and gives us more freedom.
>
> [He] has become less harsh and more trusting over the years.
>
> You trust us more now and know what we struggle with. We know your expectations and try to live up to them.
>
> We've changed toward Sir, we respect him more.
>
> I have changed to Sir because he is friendlier now than two years ago.
>
> You have become more fun to be with ... I have changed, maybe more open.
>
> We have grown to respect you and we see you as a friend.

The qualifying statements also include comments from those pupils who had known me longest and were therefore best placed to remark on whether I had changed. I have selected two Year 10s as being representative:

> You have changed because you used to be quite mean but now you're funny and you are hardly ever strict.
>
> I will be honest up until this year I absolutely hated you, I think you probably hated me too, but now I think you're ace! You treat us with respect and you are an amazing teacher.

Quantitative data in Figure 24.7 affirms that, collectively, the pupils responded positively to my relational and pedagogical approaches. Scores indicate that there was order for 95% of the time (a positive difference of more than 20% on students' estimated conduct around school), with over 15% greater cooperation defining their expression of self-control.

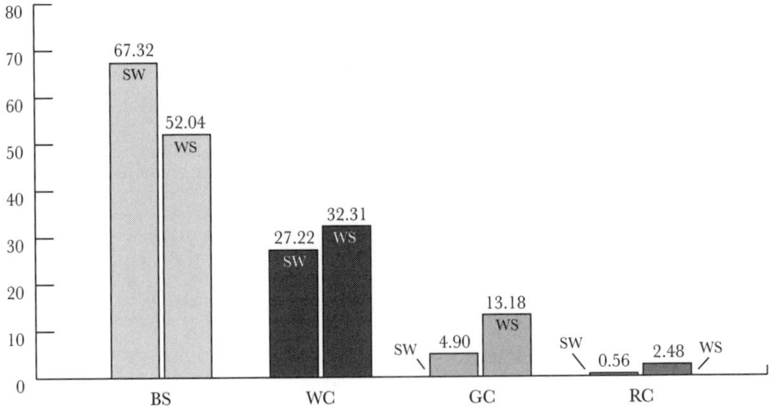

Figure 24.7. Comparison of Sean Warren's (SW) class with whole school (WS) behaviour (2009–2011)

The cumulative data indicates that my approach helped to cultivate a climate in which classes were well-ordered due to pupils being self-disciplined. However, I also acknowledge that such gatherings remain unpredictable. I believe that considering individual needs, and observing how individuals contribute to the class entity, provided me with a lens to reconceptualise how we interact. I have progressively amended my psychological default position which sought, in accordance to institutional norms, to uncritically instil order. I came to ponder the question: what is the goal of education? I concur with Ginott (1972: 10), who concludes:

> When all is said and done, we want children to grow up to be decent human beings, a 'mensch', a person with compassion, commitment, and caring … [in seeking to humanise I recognise that] the process is the method, that the ends do not justify the means, and that in our attempt to get children to behave in a way that is conducive to learning, we do not damage them psychologically.

In the final chapters, I return to a fundamental aim of my research: to deconstruct classroom interactions in order to articulate the tacit knowledge I had acquired over the years. As always, the challenge is whether I might be able to disseminate it to others. The final research cycle provided me with an opportunity to share ideas with colleagues and acted to inform my subsequent work in schools. This collaborative approach forms the basis of Part V.

Part V

Working with Colleagues

Chapter 25

Affirmation and the Potential for Continuing Professional Development

Sean

Was anything generalisable in my experiences? Beyond my personal engagement, I sought to make changes to classroom dynamics in order to make a positive contribution to shaping the whole school culture. Thus, I used aspects of my work to inform colleagues' CPD and took opportunities to contribute to teachers' initial training. Recently, viewing and reflecting on the challenges facing Teach First candidates in the BBC TV series, *Tough Young Teachers*, I believe that similar issues and trials faced colleagues finding their feet in the profession, in a new school, or even with a new class.

In the third year of my research, I worked alongside a male established teacher (ET) and two female NQTs; I then returned to the school to work with two other female NQTs. I considered them all to be competent human beings; however, each had a specific 'problem class' which challenged their conventional approach and, in the case of the NQTs, left them without confidence. Both NQT1 and NQT2 had time off during the research period due to stress. Each of the teachers engaged (to varying degrees) with the individual research blogs I had set up, and between them they contributed reams of data to accompany summative interviews, emails, and observations. The correspondence provided a rich source of material with the potential for further research. Here, I present selected extracts, as well as some longer passages, which together illustrate their collective engagement with different aspects of my approach.

Established Teacher

ET inherited a 'difficult' Year 11 class and was charged with ensuring that they achieved their predicted grades. A very competent and established teacher in his fourth year in the profession, he found the sociograms intriguing (see Chapter 23). In addition he said, "The whole weather thing put a label on my experience." ET also found Temple's (1992a) four model link-up fascinating, especially Tuckman's (1965) forming, storming, norming, and performing model, which provided assurance that the storming stage was typical and could be fleeting. 'Manners' became ET's byword for expectations with his class. This was, inexplicably, a phrase I had overlooked throughout the duration of the research. I believe it has potential to direct further research in examining the classroom climate. A less successful aspect of my work with ET was his consideration of the literature explaining hegemony. I was disappointed, as the problems he described suggested this concept would provide him with insight; however, he deemed the ideas to be too abstract.

NQTs

NQT1 was in the same department as ET. He was her mentor and so I took a subsidiary role in administering support. NQT1 initially found the socio-data of her Year 10 set 5 maths group thought-provoking. However, her evaluative interview revealed that there was too much information for her to decipher and so the impact was limited. The insight prompted a change in my methodology; subsequently, I analysed the data and fed back snippets via email, so enabling colleagues to digest snapshots to prompt further enquiry.

NQT1 left the school at the end of her induction year. I received an email in the first term of her work in a new school. It shows that many of the strategies I have described in this book are transferrable:

> In the first few weeks the students tested me and at first I felt a bit out of my depth in establishing myself again when I had worked so hard to do that at X. But I think a lot of the strategies I learned from you have become more second nature, so I think I have done a better job at establishing myself than I thought at the time …
>
> Going back to last year, as you know, I got so down about the Year 10 class and, ironically, I have a difficult Year 10 set 5 class again this year. The first few weeks were a bit of a struggle but I felt like I had lots of skills to use, and the main difference was that I didn't feel down about this class at all. I didn't dread lessons; I saw it as a challenge that I knew I would crack eventually. I found out about the relationships in the class, made a more effective seating plan, was very careful about the way I worded what I said … Now they are the most cooperative class I have!
>
> This week I carried out a survey with them on the SurveyMonkey website to see what the students thought of my behaviour management skills. They all rated me as either good or excellent. I think if I had done the same survey with last year's Year 10 class they definitely would not have said that! I didn't do a survey with them because I thought I would be upset about what they thought about me. So my perspective has also changed in that way; I felt confident to find out

> what my new students think about me. They also commented on the relaxed atmosphere and how they liked how we work together, which is really good to hear as I always bear in mind that I am aiming for cooperation not control.

NQT2 started her first year in teaching thinking that 'control is what I should be doing'. Yet, she was also desperate to be liked by the students and consequently found the pupils took advantage of her inconsistent approach. Her Year 9 'problem' class left her feeling "insignificant, worthless … useless, vulnerable … invisible". Her conception of control changed during the two terms that we worked together. She said: "Instead of trying to control or dominate everything they do, [I] concentrated on controlling the situation, to be aware, prepared for every eventuality." NQT2 sought to shape the children's expectations of her consistency by following up on every incident. I helped to establish clear avenues between her and her line managers to ensure instant communication about disruptive incidents and any ensuing support. TIFF enabled her to find an ethical balance between structuring and nurturing as she re-established herself from a firm base.

It is interesting to note that of the five colleagues who completed a TIFF profile (NQT1 was not available), a correlation is apparent. Whilst ET's profile showed his scores for 'care' outweighed his scores for 'control', each of the others (still in the midst of dealing with a 'problem' class) recorded scores which show 'control' as significantly prominent over 'care'. The results support Temple's (2012) assertion that TIFF does not measure 'type'; it provides a unique snapshot of present behaviour patterns.

NQT3's engagement with TIFF was profound. One of her emails tells of an experience which resonates with mine:

> You were the first person who was actually asking questions about me as a person, a teacher with a soul. I thought I knew myself pretty well and I'd reflect my actions fairly well, but some bits of the TIFF feedback were very surprising to me, or maybe more of an eye-opener. I was slightly shocked at how much energy I was basically 'wasting' and what sort of 'dominating, controlling' strategies I tried in the challenging classes. Instead of 'responding' I am/was 'reacting', and therefore functionally not very fluent. I realised that I could be the kind of teacher who I don't want to be and who I never really liked myself when I was a student. At the same time it made me more aware of my positive mode strengths which I should 'celebrate' or those that I should use more of.

Her colleague (NQT4) also engaged fully with many of the strategies. Their collective feedback was that they could engage more fully in exploration of their mode scores because I had already invested time in them and won their trust. This was achieved, in part, through my observation of them performing well with selected groups, rather than being seen struggling with their 'problem' classes. They considered that, if I had started with TIFF, although conceptually interesting, they would have been more guarded in their responses.

Trainee

An additional application for my study emerged unexpectedly in the third year of the research. I agreed to mentor a trainee teacher (Mr John). Hallett (2010: 435) advocates an examination of the pedagogical beliefs of teacher-educators, to expose any incongruity, by asking, "Do we practice what we preach?"

Mr John, now in his first teaching post, affirmed that many aspects of my approach had had a lasting impact on his performance as an authority figure:

> In my practice since leaving I have paid particular attention to your theory about preparedness, trying always to ensure that I am 'appropriately dressed' for the behaviour climate in my classroom. This was the area that most concerned me. Having been involved in youth work, building relationships never seems to be a problem, but managing behaviour used to scare me. My confidence in dealing with behaviour issues has grown tremendously. Whilst we received some training at university, the sessions I had with you helped me to put things in perspective, and I especially valued the comment you made regarding not being able to control the behaviours of others, rather we are only able to influence and manage.

And as an educator:

> My teaching has been completely changed. When I first started my training my feedback was quite often about a lack of creativity, but that I had a good questioning technique. Working under you, I was encouraged to take risks, to encourage students to 'go on a journey' towards independence, and to develop these aspects by ensuring lessons have a good 'flow'. My initial training was all about working within a very rigid structure – starter, main activity (with some chunking), and a plenary without much thought of anything else – if these elements were in place that would be fine. However, you encouraged me to look at the flow of the lesson – allowing students to experience episodes that were on 'the edge of chaos' and then bringing them back

> to reinforce the learning they had experienced. This was initially a frightening thought because, to an outsider (me to begin with), it was easy to view the session as being disorganised and there was also a feeling that the edge of chaos was a place where some students could 'coast' or work to their own agendas. You showed me through some simple behaviour techniques how this could be avoided, and that with the right stimulation students would use these episodes to push themselves and develop their own independent learning skills. I have to say that on seeing your lessons for the first time, I was blown away and went home thinking I could never do this! You gave me the confidence to fight against these feelings and to really begin to give it a go.
>
> In terms of my teaching now, I would say that my confidence has grown beyond measure. Instead of having to have total control the whole time, I now feel comfortable allowing students to be truly independent as I am able to look for the signs of engagement and progression. I have become aware of how I would dominate a session with unnecessary talking, thereby confusing students with too many instructions and things to think about. My instructions are now much sharper, more straightforward, and this allows the students to grow in confidence because they know they can do things rather than having to rely on me to re-explain my complicated instructions.
>
> ... recently, an [Ofsted] inspector came in and said he wanted to see me teach. I had no planned lessons that day so I volunteered to teach another person's class. I would not have done this before as I had never seen the class or had time to build up a rapport. His feedback to my training manager was that the lesson was outstanding – a copy of their observation is attached!

I consider the common strand between myself and the six participants who contributed towards this study is that we have all had our psychological and philosophical 'default settings' examined and challenged to various degrees – we moved beyond an inclination to restrict ourselves to technical answers. The experience of working alongside others has reinforced my desire to contribute to the development of those who serve in the classroom.

My research provided me with a prolonged opportunity to shine a light on the complex variables which contribute to classroom life. The process has enabled me to distil key elements which have the capacity to make a profound difference to professional development in schools. Exciting opportunities to develop a classroom observation app with the capacity to incorporate remote access video have enhanced the effectiveness and efficacy of my approach. Further information is presented in Appendix C.

Chapter 26

A Salutary Reminder: Colleagues and Pupils

Sean

If an external researcher had collated quantitative data about my contact time in school, s/he would have found a couple of apparently insignificant five minute slots covering the morning registration of tutor groups in the event of a colleague's absence. If another researcher sought to record how I established a climate for learning in the first five to ten minutes of the lesson, s/he would likely start recording when the pupils arrived and I began the process of welcoming, organising, and engaging. Sitting at the back of my room, or even viewing remotely, the researcher would be oblivious to events preceding the interaction.

I have observed many lessons, where I have waited for the teacher to arrive and take responsibility for an increasingly boisterous group congregating in the corridor. On many such occasions, I have made a snap judgement, whilst noting the teacher's late arrival on my sheet. As I will show, fragmented, decontextualised data and observation notes do not necessarily do justice to the teacher's lot, especially those on a full timetable or required to teach in different locations.

In an era of accountability, I am also mindful of the propensity for middle leaders and the SLT to arrive unannounced – to 'take the pulse', as it were, of learning in their department/school. This chapter is empathetic to the teacher and reminds observers to appreciate that their snapshot may consist of a written account, but it does not necessarily capture the whole story.

Harried

Nestled in my research notes were two snippets which I had taken the time to record only as a matter of course. In the normal school day the experiences would not have warranted much attention, and probably would have dissolved into the deep and unexamined tapestry of a teacher's career. Far, far removed from the world of civil servants, politicians, and journalists, I set down words laced with strong emotion as I conveyed my frustration at having been 'set up' for a conflict first thing in the morning:

> It was non-uniform day and there was a requirement to collect 20 or so £1 coins from a Year 11 tutor group I was told to cover. The five

> minute slot in which I also had to take the register, give out notices, etc. was sabotaged by three 'madams' who, dressed in their own clothes, had not brought any money and refused my harassed suggestion that they borrow a pound from one of their friends.

Upon uploading this account to my online research diary, it was apparent to me that the measured and reasonable response from my doctoral supervisor (Stephen) – who, quite naturally, was completely removed from the emotion, sense of injustice, and pressure of time – was nonetheless the counsel of an 'outsider', just as I had been when advising colleagues caught in their own crossfire. He responded:

> Take a long term view. Your reasonableness and apology will be remembered longer than your anger. The kids are also learning to manage anger, and you have set them an example. Give it time.

How irritating, when someone is right but you are not yet in a place to accept it! The digital platform provided me with an opportunity to grapple with my experience and articulate my apparent need to object, to protest at the unfairness of it all, and to put my case forward for those on the front line. I replied:

> The literature I have been reading recently writes about the possible discrepancy between academic theorists, who might take months, even years, to analyse the complexities of a problem, and the practical reality of teachers having to address the same complexities by making a decision over a ten minute period. This distinction must always be at the forefront of my thinking when deep contemplation of theory is offered as a factor in trying to solve a problem on the ground. Experiential reality is everything!
>
> Another example of this occurred today as I made my way across the school to cover the tutorial registration of a Year 11 group. On entering the room, the group was already established in their territory with their social allies, coats, hats, and scarves still on, and texting fingers danced over a variety of mobiles. Within two seconds, a cupboard door smashes open as the young lady, who had snapped at me previously, emerged screaming obscenities towards the boy who had leaned against the door preventing her from coming out.
>
> I stood in the classroom doorway. The group momentarily had something to distract them from their texting. "Out," I said with a clear gesture as her verbal volley subsided. Her face was like thunder. "Out," I repeated. She stormed towards me as if to barge past me in the doorway. I still had my hand on the handle. "Don't you even think

about pushing past me." She stopped. I asked her calmly who her head of house was and then quietly directed her to wait at the house office for me. She left in an orderly fashion.

"Good morning," I said. "I am taking off my coat. I have no scarf on. My mobile is not in use …" They figured it out and joined me.

The short registration and notices passed and I quickly spoke to the boy involved and then went to the house office to see the angry girl. It was being sorted, and so I hurriedly made my way over to the other side of the school where my class were waiting.

I didn't get more than 30 yards when a known Year 11 'face' came towards me drinking a can of high energy drink. This has been banned in the school because of the hyper effects it has on the students consuming it.

I had no choice but to stop him – it's my job! Initial enquiry led to me having to confiscate it. He wasn't happy. "It's my breakfast, for f***'s sake." "Sorry, what was that?" I asked. "For f***'s sake," he repeated. Great!

I have to march back to the house office to pass on the 'offensive item', I can't deal with the lad at the moment, I will have to follow-up, I'm teaching all day, and I have a club to run at lunch. Oh, and I'm covering those lovely Year 11s again this afternoon. I'm now very late for my class waiting outside my room. When I get there, they are as high as kites skidding down the icy ramp. Thankfully there was no observer waiting to record that my class were unruly and that I had arrived late!

In a later diary entry I note:

I have just described an 11 minute period.

Where would the theorists start? Do I look at the apparent reoccurring anger issues affecting the Year 11 girl? Is it to do with her home life, as blurted out the last time her anger was directed at me? What effect does relationships with parents have on her mindset – is it to do with something more troubling?

What about the research on the effects of an inadequate breakfast/neglected kids left to fill up with poor nutrient substitutes?

How about the effects of tiredness to comprehend my condition? My sick daughter had us up in the middle of the night causing me to feel like a zombie as I got out of bed to get to work, and, yes, there I have it: an email telling me to go back out into the cold, across to the other side of the school, to register this Year 11 group!

> I am immensely grateful for the reminder to never lose focus of the holistic, dynamic complexities that insistently impose themselves on the teacher situated within the moments of chaos.
>
> Decisions like these and the emotional overspills that often follow represent the site of my interest. Theoretical insights and opportunities for reflection offer signposts to colleagues, but cannot be allowed to distract or diminish from the reality of pressures exerted upon them *in situ*.
>
> I must guard against the objective theoretical perspective formed in the quiet, calm isolation of my study, luring me away from my experience working on the front line.

This exchange illustrates the distinction between the intensity of the moment and the logical remoteness of an academic or a consultant, far removed from the situation, no matter how well-intentioned. As I reread my notes, and the objective, rational comments made by my supervisor, I was reinvigorated to ensure that my research captures something of the lived reality which defined my daily experience of school life.

It is so easy to forget that my colleagues might not be in a state to see beyond the superior/reactive 'old lady' figure discussed in Chapter 1, as I wax lyrical about clever ideas representative of the composed/responsive character. The need to listen – for empathetic understanding and pragmatic short term advice rather than a theoretical model (with the potential to eventually shine a light on the troubling experience) – might be most appropriate in that instant. It is a delicate balance to negotiate: trust, experience, wisdom, and timing are paramount, but even they are not fool-proof in terms of getting it right. On occasion, a colleague has been nodding away at my advice, only to go off and complain to a line manager about what I have suggested! There is no doubt that we humans are complex and unpredictable. It is essential that, as we come alongside relative strangers, we should always be mindful of the dilemmas of teaching and be empathetic with their lot. I would love to confidently announce that I have found the solution, but that is unrealistic: schools and teachers have to find a way of operating in this contrived educational system. I can, however, present a number of tools, strategies, and a framework which may positively contribute something to classroom life.

As teachers, we hope that we have a positive impact on the young people in our charge. Often, evidence of that is reduced to the grade they receive at the end of Year 11 or 13. How often I have invested everything into helping individuals achieve the grade they needed (or the school expected), only to never see them again. It is sobering to think that the children I taught on my first teaching practice are now in their forties! How many thousands have followed them I can only guess. Sometimes, I even lose contact with children during the course of their career at the school – pupils I taught in Key Stage 3 'disappear' as timetabling and selection of subject options determine that our paths rarely converge.

My final contribution to this book, and indeed my teaching career, draws on a blessed occasion when I was afforded an opportunity to touch base once again with one such lad who I had taught many years before. The brief encounter provides a sobering reminder to those of us who come to work when we are ill or spend hours marking books religiously as testament to our commitment and effectiveness.

A Mere Contribution

Having worked in the same classroom for over a decade, it is fair to say that I had become a hoarder. In the last few weeks before leaving my room, the school, and the teaching profession, I had no choice but to venture into my resources cupboard and separate the wheat from the chaff. I filled a school skip with materials I had brought with me from my old school, all now obsolete. Within the piles I found some old exercise books from a Year 7 class who had passed my way many years before. I recognised the names but struggled to match them with faces. However, there was one lad I had no trouble identifying: Greg was still in the school and was just about to leave Year 13 to make his way in the world. I looked through his book and saw a record of our time together. I was quietly impressed by the thoroughness of my marking and comments, and Greg's presentation was immaculate. I decided it would be a nice way to finish if I passed Greg's old book on to him before we both left, and so sent a message that I had a present for him. A couple of days later he came to my room. It was great to catch up with him, now he was all grown up; even though we still shared the same campus, our paths rarely crossed. I showed him the book and watched for his reaction. It was, of course, one of appreciation and a hint of nostalgia.

However, his comments took me aback. Despite the written evidence before us showing he had clearly paid attention and understood the lesson content, he said he could remember hardly any of the lessons, let alone the subject knowledge. For me, the lessons were as clear as day, as I had taught each one countless times prior to Greg's cohort and subsequently in the intervening years. I went into overdrive trying to jog his memory: "Don't you remember when we watched the video and you had to empathise that you were the flag pole being washed during the Sikh festival of Baisakhi? How about when we learned about culture by videoing the people of Forest Mountain?" Vague recollections of the activities slowly came back to him, although the learning remained obscured.

I wondered if he had ever really learned it in the first place, despite all the correct answers he had recorded. I was feeling a little deflated, but recognised that the one hour we shared per week, six years ago, was simply sandwiched between all the other knowledge he had encountered in his 25 period week, term after term, year after year. My contribution, and my subject (RE), felt insignificant alongside the comparative importance and time given to the core subjects of maths, English, and science. And then he lifted me up: "To be honest, Sir, I don't remember writing any of this, and I don't remember much about what we learned. But I do remember that I really enjoyed your lessons, and that I liked you." We shook hands and I wished him all the best for university. He left and I was content that I had contributed something, however minor, to him becoming a fine young man.

Epilogue

Stephen

It falls to me to offer some final comments. We have come to the end of Sean's detailed account of the years in which he sought a new way of relating to the pupils he taught. His journey contains pain and heartache but ultimately opens up new horizons. The fieldwork diary using blogging technology helped with keeping a long term record, day-by-day reflections, and discussions of the issues and emotions. It took up time but it was not a chore: it seemed to me that the benefits were greater than the cost in effort. We recommend this approach to other teacher-researchers.

His account has encouraged me to look back at my own schooling. As a pupil after the age of 9, I was a bit of a Rain Cloud, though never of the worst kind. The birth of much younger siblings and the loss of older siblings to boarding school may have been the cause. I was certainly a rebel trying to sabotage the demands of adults with power. I remember putting deliberate spelling mistakes into my work in primary school and being in deep trouble for sticking random gold stars onto the star chart. I passed my eleven-plus but failed to apply myself for the first three years. The other aspect of these years was my role as an outsider – I was sociable and keen to observe but lacked close friendships.

I don't remember much about what I was taught and it is hard to pick out a teacher who taught well. I have pored over old staff lists to convince myself that this was not true, but I can sift staff into the categories of either bullies or stressed. Within these headings, I could describe only a quarter as being caring. General school behaviour in this little grammar school was far from good and I escaped into solitude. Being one of five children, that worked well at home too. When I discovered how to study in the sixth form, it was through private study (reading and note taking). I still have boxes of very busy files on my three subjects – English, Latin, and religious studies – for which I received BAA grades. I discovered at university that few students, if any, had developed this facility in private study, but it has served me well since then.

I described earlier (Chapter 5) that my entry into secondary school teaching after my PhD was a great shock, being untrained and the school in the chaos of reorganisation. A quarter of my timetable was with non-exam 15-year-olds, and I floundered without support or mentoring. Moving to a school with A level provision in RE, I found most of the staff caring but working in a system which provoked rebellion in many pupils. Moving from there into primary schools provided me with some excellent models of caring practice, though these were not universal. It was clear that some inspirational teachers tried very hard to ensure that their schools were happy, motivating, and empowering. These became role models for me, illustrating what could happen in schools when teachers are able to develop positive relationships. Since I also supervised students in secondary schools, my own teaching experience of fragmented days (as pupils moved from class to class) was equally true in other schools. Teacher stress appeared to be common.

My discussions with Sean came out of my thoughts on caring and motivating pedagogy on the one hand, and developing the potential for private study in pupils on the other.[1] Can an atmosphere of mutual caring lead to a deep respect for others, resulting in responsibility and self-discipline? And to what extent can schools empower learning? These are both challenging ideas but full of potential. Biesta and Stengel (2016) suggest six 'iconic' representations of teachers: Plato's dialogic questioner, Rousseau's responsive autonomy-seeking tutor, Dewey's community-building democratic designer, Freire's learning partner and liberator, Rancière's critical egalitarian, and Noddings' carer. These are not either/or models but interact. Dialogue aims at autonomy, encouraging debate which is a feature of consensus democracy. Energising unheard voices leads to liberation – a critique of how things are – promoting care for all rather than privilege. These are all facets of teaching, like the sides of a (numberless) dice.

Sean has taken these thoughts on positive pedagogical relationships and run with them. He arrived at a deep learning pedagogy that can be satisfying for both pupils and teachers. We have tried to show the importance of respectful relationships between teachers and pupils. That pupils can look back at their school years with affection and thanks strongly suggests that they experienced effective schooling, whilst memories which are painful and resentful raise different but important questions. Pedagogy needs both to motivate and challenge intellectually; our challenge is how to put all this positive aspiration into practice within the humdrum circumstances of a busy secondary school. This book demonstrates how Sean used his position as a practitioner-researcher to explore how this might be achieved.

Just a few comments here about what we are not saying. Authority and relationship are held in balance; they are not in opposition. Pupils need boundaries which may have to be imposed in some cases: a pupil's behaviour should not harm others physically or psychologically. This can be done through caring and with humour, but avoiding sarcasm. A child exhibiting challenging behaviour can learn to become impervious to an aggressive, confrontational response, but they may also be won over by a teacher who is willing to listen and build a relationship. Sean's comments from pupils in Parts III and IV affirm this.

1 By 'self-study' Biesta and Stengel (2016) mean autobiographical activities – studying oneself – which I discussed in Chapter 2.

Nor do we want to be embroiled in the 'no excuses' debate. Many pupils break some rules at some times. 'No excuses' might apply to serious matters, but Sean has shown that low level disruption can be tackled more positively. The context of low level disruption needs to be properly examined to ensure consistent and reasonable responses. Sean taught himself not to provoke negative reactions by knee-jerk authoritarianism and to generate a climate of cooperation and collaboration between teacher and pupils. It was sometimes hard to dig out and replace the habits of a lifetime. A libertarian free-for-all had to be avoided, and different approaches to pedagogy and learning had to be developed over a long period to secure a peaceful classroom. He found that he had to learn to 'tolerate uncertainty'. We relate this to the work of Turner (1990) who terms it 'fructile [i.e. fruitful] chaos'. This was the primary outcome of the process in which Sean reflected on his default position defined as control. He became increasingly 'confident in uncertainty', so apparent disorder and challenge were no longer automatically perceived as a threat. The aim was to replace imposed discipline with pupil self-discipline within a climate of respect and fairness – that is, a teacher smiling rather than frowning. An emotionally relaxed teacher is more likely to help a class to calm down than an uptight one. If both pupils and teachers are emotionally stressed out for most of the day, it is worth spending time and effort to consider different ways of working.

Positive pedagogy and consistent expectations will not, of course, eliminate all problems. Antisocial actions will still have consequences. But if pupils generally encounter positive relationships across schooling, rebellion and hostility have a chance to be reduced: Sean and I argue for teaching and learning approaches which reduce conflict and confrontation. If there is disruption in the classroom – a situation that is hard to escape from – it is important that the teacher is not causing or adding to this disruption. Sean uses insights from Berne's (1964) transactional analysis: the ideal classroom relationships we espouse might be described as 'adult to adult'. This means everyone, adults and pupils, treating each other as mature adults should. Mature relationships lead to learning through discussion, debate, discovery, and experimentation. Our hope is that such relationships will develop personal and social awareness which will last throughout life.

Sean changed from being an effective, hard-nosed (albeit not unfriendly) disciplinarian who could quieten most classes with a look, to becoming a more nuanced teacher whose positive relationships (for the most part) produced self-disciplined pupils. He built up the skills to cope with disruptive pupil behaviour without confrontation and to cope when hostile moods were brought from previous classes. There are pupils with attitude, sometimes because of difficult home or social circumstances. Pupils who habitually react to conflict with conflict, both at home and at school, will need patient intervention early and throughout their schooling. When these children experience only confrontation, they learn to survive through confrontation.

If this happens at school as well as home, there is little chance of transformation.

This brings us back to the purpose of schooling. In a sense it is a preparation for future life, hence the pursuit of qualifications. But it is a future life we cannot second-guess. The burst of technology over the last two decades could not have been prepared for in schools in the 1980s, and education today has no idea what will dominate life and jobs a decade or two on. Schooling is not just a preparation for future life. For pupils, the school years *are* their lives for over a decade, and how they live their lives needs to be positive and transformational.[2] The school curriculum needs to be an open intellectual journey, a combination of independent learning, understanding and challenging knowledge, and developing the ability to think clearly. It helps if the pupils are interested and motivated, and we have focused on ways to achieve this.

However, there is more to it than this. Education has a moral purpose, such as considering how people treat each other, how we interact with the environment, and how science is used for good or ill. There are underlying questions about how we (pupils and adults) make the world a better place. Schooling should help pupils to become serious contributors to the world community rather than mere consumers and onlookers. I use the word 'should' to represent my view of the purpose of education. Of course, the issue is open to debate, so my 'should' might not be yours. However, if schooling is not moral, it must be either amoral or immoral, and a defence of that position would be tricky.

The literature about school discipline describes disruptive pupils and low level disruption. There are two opposing positions on how to rectify this: removing disruptive pupils by exclusion or over time transforming them into well-balanced future citizens. In the short term, the exclusion option might promise a quieter class environment for learning (itself not unimportant), but it does nothing for disengaged pupils who need real help. These polarised outlooks may be read as a dichotomy between realism and idealism. We have argued that this need not be the case. The aspirational is achievable.

It is clearly important to get the tone right in the classroom. We expect proper behavioural boundaries, leading to self-discipline and ethical behaviour, which are monitored by the whole school community – pupil and adult. Clearly, exclusion has to be an option, but we argue that this should be a last resort and not a routine convenient option which passes the buck. School processes need to be reconceptualised so that pupils with behaviour issues are supported and transformed, rather than labelled and contained. This is the spirit of inclusion to which education has paid lip service but never really

2 Biesta and Stengel (2016) touch on similar issues in their detailed discussion of the philosophical issues around the purpose of education.

engaged with fully. The term 'pupil centred' focuses on the belief that schools should educate pupils first and pass on (and assess) knowledge second. Pupil centred does not mean what it is accused of meaning – that is, letting children do whatever they like. Its proper use coincided with the time when Carl Rogers developed person centred counselling to replace earlier, more authoritarian models (Rogers et al. 1990). Using discussion, Rogers looked for solutions to suit individuals rather than a one-size-fits-all diagnosis of people into pre-existing boxes. In a pupil centred classroom, individual needs are known by adults and other pupils, with the class climate encouraging everyone to be supportive of each other. This is the class dynamic that Sean was seeking to develop.

Critical pedagogy, discussed in Chapter 5, views relationships, including those in the classroom, as political – that is, there are power agendas at play which benefit some and disadvantage others. By being socially critical, we raise an awareness of community, pro-social behaviour, and political accountability. School communities model the wider community, for good or ill, so this needs to be explicitly thought through and not left to drift chaotically. Within critical pedagogy is the aspiration that silenced voices are heard and valued. The broad range of points of view are balanced in a search for agreement or consensus. These discussions are themselves educational. There will also be inaccurate, unethical, selfish, and opinionated views to be challenged. The discussion process will provoke thought and develop understanding and skills for reaching reasoned and informed opinions based on properly tested information. Young people who are educated in such an environment will be on the road to political astuteness and community contribution, developing skills in listening, expression, and analytical awareness.

As this is being written, the winning sides in both the US presidential election and the campaign for the UK to leave the European Union have shown little regard for truth, respect, or honesty, and disrespect for foreigners has proved a notable electoral advantage. Opinion today is increasingly knee-jerk and backed by little substance. Accepted 'truths' are often lies, or at best ideological opinions cunningly packaged and frequently repeated, producing campaign slogans and sound bites. The current generation needs to become better equipped to thoughtfully challenge dominant political ideology, unevidenced assertions, and political rhetoric. They should have the language to interrogate what is proposed in terms of natural justice (in the broadest sense), being alert to ways to make the community and the world a better place for everyone. All this is implied by critical pedagogy.

Just as Freire (2005) approaches literacy ('reading the word') as 'reading the world' (i.e. raising social and political consciousness), so the school curriculum needs to examine the world, locally and globally with a syllabus which sharpens pupils antennae for justice. Freire suggests that teachers should be constantly reflecting and adapting their strategies to achieve this, and Sean has taken this seriously. The Education Reform Act 1988 claimed spiritual, moral, social, and cultural relevance, all now in danger of becoming submerged in a prescribed, narrowed curriculum. Regardless, Sean adhered to these broader principles as he met his requirement to teach subject knowledge on a daily basis. It had profound implications for him, and hopefully for the pupils who walked with him on this part of his journey.

Overcomplicating a message is not helpful. Our advice boils down to a simple intention: fill school relationships with deep respect. This means respect by pupils for teachers, which stems from respect by teachers for pupils, and respect of managers for all school stakeholders, young and old. Respect does not come from fear. You cannot demand respect, but you can earn it by mutual caring and support. Of course, there will be pupils who resist all efforts and regard friendly attitudes as weakness, who repay goodwill with disrespect. Sean had a positive experience with one of his Rain Cloud pupils later in her life. Conversely, challenging pupils can behave similarly as adults, even years later.

Not that troubled youngsters should be written off. I worked with and evaluated the Swindon Youth Empowerment Programme, a Bahá'i project, which focused on troubled pupils for whom personal difficulties damaged their mental health as well as their school work. Some were disruptive at school, others suicidal. Seeing them turning their lives around and progressing to college, university, and employment was special. In the foreword to Viv Bartlett's (2014) description of this work, I wrote:

> Two key themes have stood the test of time – that the individual is full of potential, a 'mine rich in gems of inestimable value'; and that the best way these gems (inner positive qualities and capacities) can be developed is in service to others. These are two sides of the same coin: all of us need to recognize that we have something to offer, and then understand that we can make a huge difference in our community.
>
> The journey towards this is however not simple. The young people enter the process with various life experiences, including dysfunctional and destructive relationships. This can damage self-esteem and cause emotional pain. Such personal burdens can be left behind once they are recognized and dealt with …

I was summing up an issue that we have faced in this book: when faced with the question, 'What do we want our education system to do for our children?' having good qualifications is not at the top of my list. Rather, it is to encourage young people to be well-rounded, personally confident, helpful, and responsible members of the group – unprejudiced, intellectually curious, critical of authoritarianism, and champions of the less fortunate.

Appendix A

FIRO Theory[1]

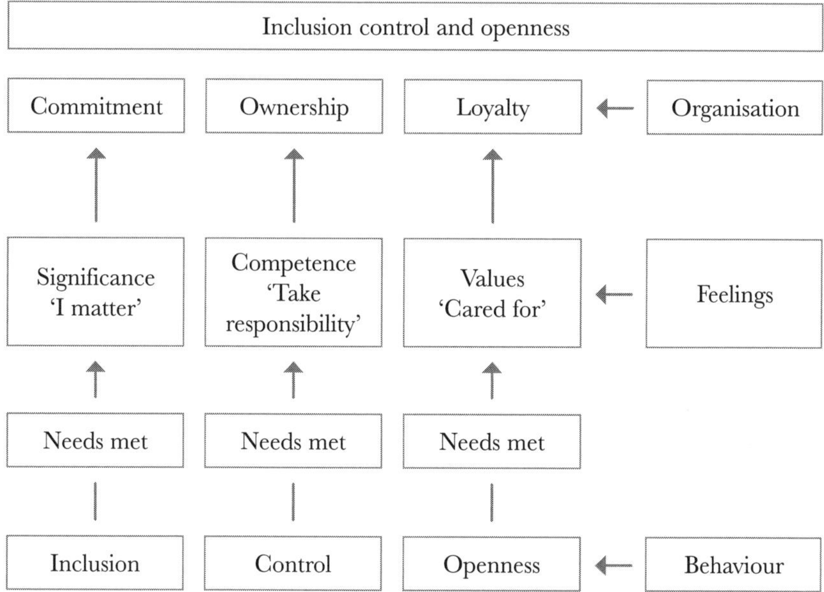

Source: Adapted from Schutz (1994)

1 For further information and training in FIRO theory I recommend contacting Dr Julie Bullen: j.bullen7@ntlworld.com.

Appendix B

Temple Index of Functional Fluency (TIFF) Descriptors[1]

The Functional Fluency Modes in Action

The TIFF questionnaire gives you scores on these nine modes of behaviour

Dominating

Using dominating mode, we focus on the negative. We believe we are right and may take an adversarial 'me or you' stance. We want obedience from others, notice mistakes, and find fault in order to improve people or situations, from a point of view of knowing better. We persuade or coerce others into compliance, including ourselves, using warnings, threats, or sometimes even punishments in order to teach a lesson. Others may indeed comply, but also react by resisting or rebelling.

Marshmallowing

Using marshmallowing mode, we confuse wants with needs and over-supply others with help, attention, and material goods, though this may not be beneficial in the long term. Over-indulgence is the result, and recipients finish up sad and angry rather than grateful, which leads to confusion and frustration on both sides. In this mode we don't realise that inappropriate assistance hinders rather than helps, and that lack of consistent limits and expectations is harmful to people's health and development.

Structuring

Using structuring mode, we actively empower others by our ways of inspiring confidence and motivation. We set appropriately firm limits and high expectations, providing the boundaries for others to feel secure enough to grow and learn. We believe in people's potential for success and offer the help and support that is needed. We focus on the positive, believing that whatever gets attention is likely to increase. In response, people tend to do their best, and develop their own competence and self-confidence.

Nurturing

Using nurturing mode, we respond empathetically to others, including ourselves, appreciating how people may be feeling and responding appropriately to their needs. We use understanding and kindness to express non-judgemental acceptance of ourselves and others, which encourages people to be more fully themselves. Being available for people in this way promotes healthy self-acceptance and the positive attitudes which support healing and building of self-esteem.

Using accounting mode, we are 'with it' and in tune with our own internal states, as well as being sensitive and receptive to stimuli from others and the environment. We take an objective attitude and keep things in proportion.

Reality Accounting mode Assessment

Accounting also means making logical sense of available data so that decision making and actions can be based on relevant and realistic assessment of the current situation. Accounting is an essential component of effective use of the four other positive modes.

1 For more on TIFF visit: www.functionalfluency.com/.

Reality Accounting mode Assessment

Cooperative

Using cooperative mode, we show assertive friendliness and consideration for others. We stand up for ourselves in socially acceptable ways, and are willing to listen and negotiate from an 'I'm OK – you're OK' standpoint. We feel confident about handling social situations because we can rely on our skills of diplomacy and assertiveness, expecting for ourselves the same respect that we show to others. Using this mode, we get on well with others and enjoy company at work and leisure.

Spontaneous

Using spontaneous mode, we often have a playful attitude which lets our creativity flow freely. We access energy and motivation to use our unique and original ideas both in response to situations and to take initiatives. Our vitality is infectious and enjoyable. We feel, and express, what we feel freely, without any inhibition or censorship, and yet also keep an age-appropriate sense of proportion. Individual temperamental style will influence our level of natural exuberance in this mode.

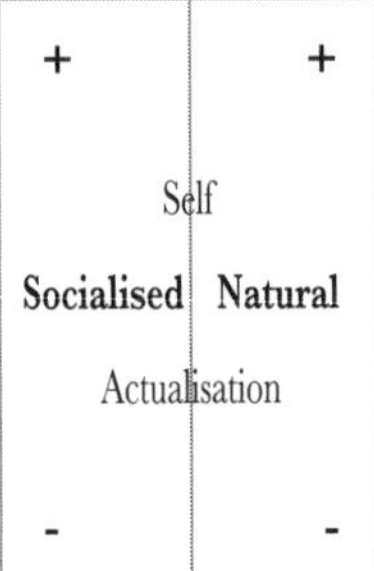

Compliant/Resistant

Using compliant/resistant mode, we often favour one of the two styles, depending on how we have learned in the past to cope with demands we have found too difficult. In the compliant style, we conform, make concessions, and try to please others. We often feel nervous about doing things, scared of making mistakes. In the resistant style, we vary between mild obstinacy and outright aggressive rebellion. Sometimes we switch from one style to the other depending on the context.

Immature

Using immature mode, we don't fully take grown-up viewpoints or responsibilities. We leave others to take precautions, do maintenance jobs, or the clearing up, unless it happens to suit us or we are made to do it. We don't enjoy sharing or taking turns, and often fail to see how our actions may be affecting others, and what the consequences of this lack of care or consideration might be. Emotional expression is sometimes out of control and may be out of proportion to the circumstances.

Appendix C

Professional Development

Sean

Sean's approach to supporting is unlike any I have come across. Don't think 'whole school staff training day', rather an ongoing bespoke intervention which is entirely tailored to address the needs of an individual teacher with a specific class. This approach has the potential for genuine impact, exactly where it is needed. He coaches colleagues in observing and analysing the dynamics within the group, considering how each child affects learning in the class. This shared understanding forms the basis of the strategies which Sean develops and supports the teacher to implement. Dialogue is maintained and practical solutions are drip-fed over an extensive time period using a dedicated blog. The colleague sees practical solutions and ongoing support, underpinned by robust educational philosophy. They also benefit from Sean's passion for helping them to develop professionally.

Mr Rob Johnston, deputy head, Hanley Castle High School, Worcestershire

---

Wiliam (2011) makes a compelling case that the key determinant in raising educational standards is teacher quality. He concludes, and I concur, that it is crucial that we invest in the teachers already working in our schools. However, in an era of initiatives, there is an apparent discrepancy between knowing about approaches deemed to be effective and implementing the principles in one's practice. Drawing on Cordingley (2009) and the Teacher Development Trust (2015), my work since attaining my PhD has been to explore a way to bridge that gap. For me, a commitment to attune to the teacher, and an appreciation of their context, is an essential prerequisite to a process I call 'alignment'.

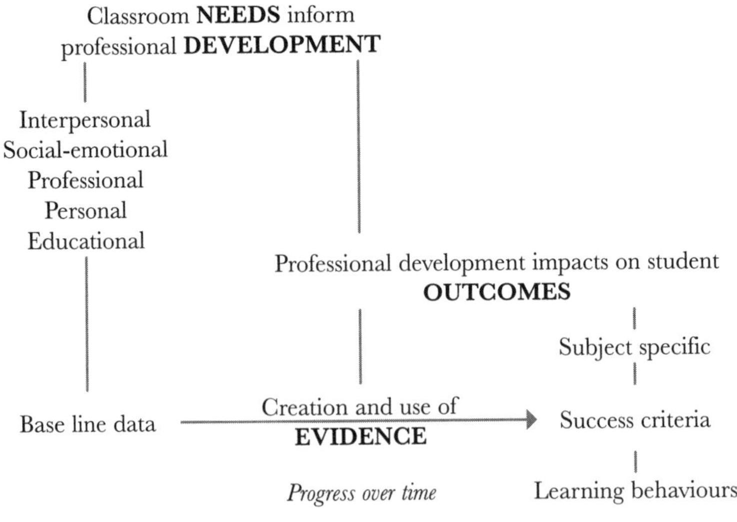

> The best teachers are those who show you where to look but don't tell you what to see.
>
> **Alexandra K. Trenfor**

Core to the notion of alignment is the challenge of implementing the principles of reputable research findings to teachers' habitual practice in order to improve student outcomes. I stated my reservations about an uncritical acceptance of 'what works' in Chapter 7.[1] Here, I use the analogy of cooking to illustrate the process I use to enable the teacher to make subtle amendments to their perspectives and subsequently their methods, routines, and manner.

Highlighting the distinction between a cook and a chef, Align provides the coach and the teacher with an array of 'pedagogical ingredients'. These are rich pickings from an array of available evidence – for example, Wiliam's *Embedded Formative Assessment* (2011) and Nuthall's *The Hidden Lives of Learners* (2007). How the teacher mixes and presents these elements in the lesson is the initial point of interest. As with a chef, insightful decisions – the sprinkling of some herbs and spices, knowing when to bring everything to a boil or when to simmer slowly – are refinements which can make all the difference. So it is with teaching and learning. The Align process enables teachers to deconstruct classroom interactions and provides them with a language to articulate that wonderful sense of knowing.

1 My methodology is consistent with the points made by Greenhalgh (2015).

Appendix C

A Focus on Impact and Outcomes

Align conceives the lesson as a meal prepared by the teacher, of course, but one that is tasted and consumed by the pupils. At the crux is the consideration of whether the 'food' brings long term health and nourishment to the learners:

Filled a gap, bit off and swallowed content, *short term* satisfaction, can regurgitate (performance), needs feeding again in no time. Equipped with steel cutlery.	Chewed and absorbed knowledge, understanding, and skills nutrients and vitamins (learning dispositions) into system for *long term* nourishment to bones and vital organs. Equipped with sharper knife to cut through steak.	Picked at and played with food, grazed, took in little sustenance, malnourished, may hide food, propensity for spoon feeding, may throw food to distract others. Equipped with plastic cutlery.

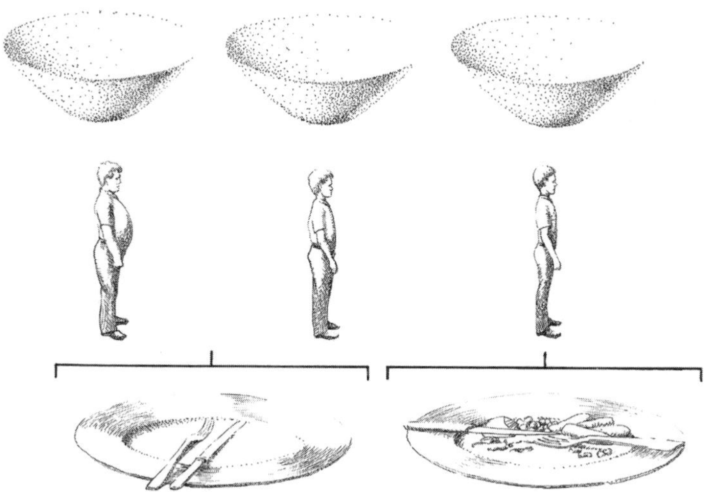

The 'diner' on the right is relatively easy for a teacher to spot; less so is the distinction between the pupil on the left and the one in the middle as they both leave the lesson with an empty plate. These two students illustrate the difference between 'performance' and 'learning' (discussed in note 3 in Chapter 7). This is the level of analysis which interests me.

The testimony at the beginning of this appendix highlights the service I offer to schools. However, the Align app and accompanying training course are available online for teachers to use as part of their professional development.

Align App

Align is a non-judgemental observational tool which informs teachers' professional development. Based on the template in Chapter 24, its descriptive data provides insights on teaching and learning exchanges, and illuminates pupils' social interactions during these activities. Instead of being graded against a predetermined set of criteria, the Align template provides a snapshot of lesson flow and illuminates critical moments to encourage reflection. A beginner's guide for observers to use basic functions and core criteria is provided.

Align Online Training Course

The online training course is comprehensive in familiarising users with the app's advanced features. Moving beyond the recording of generic 'sauces', such as questioning, explanation, and feedback, participants are equipped to recognise specific evidence informed 'ingredients' within the observed lesson. Also demonstrated, the multi-layered template provides a function which facilitates recording of the group's collective responses as the lesson unfolds. In addition, the opportunity to recognise the teacher's capacity to be 'responsive' to emerging classroom needs, is a subtle, yet powerful, option to enrich data.

The course also provides guidance for analysis of both the teacher's experience and the objective Align data. Prompts aid self-reflection for the teacher and stimulate a professional conversation. As the teacher offers their interpretations, the observer contributes the descriptive data captured on the Align template.

Satisfactory completion of the course provides the user with an accreditation certificate to qualify them as an Align Practitioner.

Align Select Remote Practitioner Service

The Align Practitioner qualification enables select individuals to use Align and Lesson VU to offer remote observation and coaching. This service provides the opportunity to support teachers' professional development, both in the UK and internationally. To ensure reliability, during workshops, applicants must demonstrate a high level of competency in applying the Align observation and feedback methodology to sample lessons.

Lesson VU

Since 2015, an exciting project to enhance the efficacy and effectiveness of Align has been ongoing. A meeting with a friend from my teacher training days has brought about an amalgamation with Lesson VU.[2] The technology now means we can sit a small digital camera (the size of a 50 pence piece) in the ceiling, which produces 360 degree coverage of the classroom and allows for remote viewing, either live or on demand. The viewer can scan the classroom from multiple viewpoints, thereby homing in on key development needs applicable to the whole class, a group, or individual 'diners'.

Trials designed to refine the Align/Lesson VU methodology have been taking place in both primary and secondary schools since January 2016.

The Align app can be downloaded from www.confidenceinuncertainty.co.uk or www.onvulearning.com, where you can also find more information about using the app and the Align Select Remote Practitioner course and vacancies.

2 See www.onvulearning.com.

References

Ahmed, S. (2004) *The Cultural Politics of Emotion*. Edinburgh: Edinburgh University Press.

Alexander, R. J. (2001) *Culture and Pedagogy: International Comparisons in Primary Education.* Oxford: Blackwell.

Alhadeff-Jones, M. (2008) Three generations of complexity theories: nuances and ambiguities. In M. Mason (ed.), *Complexity Theory and the Philosophy of Education*. Chichester: John Wiley, pp. 62–78.

Allen, J. (2004) 'Deterritorializations': putting postmodernism to work on teacher education and inclusion. *Educational Philosophy and Theory*, 36(4), 417–432.

Allison, J. (2013) Behaviour and boundaries. *Journal for Waldorf Education*, 15(1), 13–14.

Althusser, L. (1971) Ideology and ideological state apparatuses. In L. Althusser (ed.), *Lenin and Philosophy and Other Essays.* New York: Routledge Press, pp. 121–176.

Araújo, M. (2005) Disruptive or disrupted? A qualitative study on the construction of indiscipline. *International Journal of Inclusive Education,* 9(3), 241–268.

Argyris, C. and Schön, D. (1975) *Theory in Practice: Increasing Professional Effectiveness.* London: Jossey-Bass.

Asch, S. E. (1952) *Social Psychology.* Englewood Cliffs, NJ: Prentice Hall.

Asch, S. E. (1955) Opinions and social pressures. *Scientific American,* 193(5), 31–35.

Asch, S. E. (1957) An experimental investigation of group influence. In *Symposium on Preventative and Social Psychiatry: 5–17 April 1957, Walter Reed Army Institute of Research.* Washington, DC: US Government Printing Office, pp. 15–17.

Ashley, K. M. (ed.) (1990) *Victor Turner and the Construction of Cultural Criticism.* Birmingham and Indianapolis, IN: Indiana University Press.

Ashley, M. (1992) The validity of sociometric status. *Educational Research,* 34(2), 149–154.

Ball, P. (2003) *Critical Mass: How One Thing Leads to Another*. New York: Farrar, Straus and Giroux.

Ball, S. J. (1972) Self and identity in the context of deviance: the case of criminal abortion. In R. Scott and J. Douglas (eds), *Theoretical Perspectives on Deviance.* New York: Basic Books, pp. 158–186.

Ball, S. J. (2003) The teacher's soul and the terrors of performativity. *Journal of Education Policy*, 18(2), 215–228.

Ball, S. J. (2013) *Foucault, Power, and Education* [Kindle edn]. Abingdon: Routledge.

Ball, S. J. (2015) La entrevista Educativa – Stephen Ball [interview by José Weinstein] [video] (5 January). Available at: http://cedle.cl/video/la-entrevista-educativa-stephen-ball/.

Banks, M. (2001) *Visual Methods in Social Research*. London: SAGE.

Baranger, M. (2001) Chaos, complexity, and entropy: a physics talk for non-physicists. Available at: http://necsi.edu/projects/baranger/cce.pdf.

Barrow, G., Bradshaw, E., and Newton, T. (2002) *Improving Behaviour and Raising Self-Esteem in the Classroom: A Practical Guide to Using Transactional Analysis*. London: David Fulton.

Bartlett, V. (2014) *Nurturing a Healthy Human Spirit in the Young*. Welwyn: George Ronald Publishers.

Bassey, M. (1995) *Creating Education Through Research: A Global Perspective of Educational Research for the 21st Century*. Newark: Kirklington Moor Press.

BBC (2007) In full: Cameron on school discipline (31 July). Available at: http://news.bbc.co.uk/1/hi/uk_politics/6923941.stm.

BBC (2011) Gove: truancy push to tackle 'educational underclass' (1 September). Available at: http://www.bbc.co.uk/news/education-14748268.

BBC (2014) Michael Gove: stronger sanctions for truants' parents (7 June). Available at: http://www.bbc.co.uk/news/education-27741261.

Beijaard, D. (1995) Teachers' prior experiences and actual perceptions of professional identity. *Teachers and Teaching: Theory and Practice*, 1, 281–294.

Beijaard, D., Meijer, P. C., and Verloop, N. (2004) Reconsidering research on teachers' professional identity. *Teaching and Teacher Education*, 20(2), 107–128.

Berkowitz, L. (1974) Some determinants of impulsive aggression: the role of mediated associations with enforcements of aggression. *Psychological Review*, 81(2), 165–176.

Berlak, A. and Berlak, H. (2002) Dilemmas of schooling. In A. Pollard (ed.), *Readings for Reflective Teaching*. London: Continuum, pp. 8–10.

Berlin, I. (1969) *Four Essays on Liberty*. London: Oxford University Press.

Berne, E. (1964) *Games People Play: The Psychology of Human Relationships*. New York: Grove Press.

Bernstein, B. (2000) *Pedagogy, Symbolic Control and Identity* (Critical Perspectives) (2nd edn). Lanham, MD: Rowman & Littlefield.

Biddulph, S. (2003) *Raising Boys: Why Boys Are Different – And How to Help Them Become Happy and Well-Balanced Men*. London: Harper Thorsons.

Biesta, G. (2007) Why 'what works' won't work: evidence-based practice and the democratic deficit in educational research. *Educational Theory*, 57(1), 1–22.

Biesta, G. (2011) *Good Education in an Age of Measurement: Ethics, Politics, Democracy* (Interventions: Education, Philosophy, and Culture). Abingdon: Routledge.

Biesta, G. (2014) *The Beautiful Risk of Education*. Abingdon: Routledge.

Biesta, G. and Stengel, B. S. (2016) Thinking philosophically about teaching. In D. Gitomer and C. Bell (eds), *Handbook of Research on Teaching*. Washington, DC: American Educational Research Association, pp. 7–68.

Bigger, S. (1996) Post 16 Compact in Birmingham. In M. Abraham, J. Bird, and A. Stennet (eds), *Further and Higher Education Partnerships: The Future for Collaboration*. Buckingham: Open University Press, pp. 154–166.

Bigger, S. (2000) Motivating students to succeed: the work of Birmingham Compact 1988–1994. In M. Leicester, S. Mogdil, and C. Mogdil (eds), *Education, Culture and Values. Vol. 3: Classroom Issues – Practice, Pedagogy and Curriculum*. Abingdon: RoutledgeFalmer, pp. 85–95.

Bigger, S. (2009a) The potential of blogs for higher degree supervision. Available at: http://eprints.worc.ac.uk/707/1/PRABlogs.pdf.

Bigger, S. (2009b) Victor Turner, liminality and cultural performance. *Journal of Beliefs and Values*, 30(2), 209–212.

Bigger, S. (2015) Thresholds, liminality and fruitful chaos: revolutionary change in education? Available at: https://eprints.worc.ac.uk/834/.

Bigger, S. and Brown, E. (1999) *Spiritual, Moral, Social and Cultural Education: Exploring Values in the Curriculum*. London: David Fulton.

Bjork, R. (2012) *Dissociating Learning from Performance* [video] (11 July). Available at: https://www.youtube.com/watch?v=MMixjUDJVlw.

Breidenstein, G. (2007) The meaning of boredom in school lessons: participant observation in the seventh and eighth form. *Ethnography and Education*, 2(1), 93–108.

Brookfield, S. D. (1995) *Becoming a Critically Reflective Teacher*. San Francisco, CA: Jossey-Bass.

Brookfield, S. D. (2006) *The Skillful Teacher: On Technique, Trust, and Responsiveness in the Classroom.* San Francisco, CA: Jossey-Bass.

Brookfield, S. D. (2008) *The Power of Critical Theory for Adult Learning and Teaching*. Maidenhead: Open University Press.

Brooks, R. M., McCormack, M., and Bhopal, K. (2013) *Contemporary Debates in the Sociology of Education*. Basingstoke: Palgrave Macmillan.

Brown, W. E. (1983) The is and should be of assertive discipline. *Intervention in School and Clinic*, 19(2), 175–178.

Bruner, J. S. (1986) *Actual Minds, Possible Worlds* (The Jerusalem-Harvard Lectures). Cambridge, MA: Harvard University Press.

Bruner, J. S. (1996) *The Culture of Education*. Cambridge, MA: Harvard University Press.

Bruner, J. S. (2014) *How Does Teaching Influence Learning?* [video] (9 October). Available at: https://www.youtube.com/watch?v=aljvAuXqhds.

Buber, M. (1958 [1937]) *I and Thou*, tr. R. G. Smith. Edinburgh: Clark.

Bucholtz, M. and Hall, K. (2005) Identity and interaction: a sociocultural linguistic approach. *Discourse Studies*, 7(4–5), 585–614.

Bullough, R. V. Jr and Pinnegar, S. (2001) Guidelines for quality in autobiographical forms of self-study research. *Educational Researcher*, 30(3), 13–21.

Burke, P. J. (2004) Identities and social structure: the 2003 Cooley-Mead award address. *Social Psychology Quarterly*, 67(1), 5–15.

Burke, P. J. and Stets, J. E. (2009) *Identity Theory*. New York: Oxford University Press.

Burton, D. M., Bartlett, S. J., and Anderson de Cuevas, R. (2009) Are the contradictions and tensions that have characterised educational provision for young people with behavioural, emotional and social difficulties a persistent feature of current policy? *Emotional and Behavioural Difficulties*, 14(2), 141–155.

Cameron, D. (2011) PM's speech on the fightback after the riots (15 August). Available at: https://www.gov.uk/government/speeches/pms-speech-on-the-fightback-after-the-riots.

Cannella, G. S. (1999) The scientific discourse of education: predetermining the lives of others – Foucault, education and children. *Contemporary Issues in Early Childhood*, 1(1), 36–44.

Canter, L. (1988) Let the educator beware: a response to Curwin and Mendler. *Educational Leadership*, 46(2), 71–73.

Carnegie Corporation (1996) *Years of Promise: A Comprehensive Learning Strategy for America's Children: Executive Summary.* New York: Carnegie Corporation.

Chaltain, S. (2009) *American Schools: The Art of Creating a Democratic Learning Community*. Plymouth: Rowman and Littlefield Education.

Charlton, E. (2007) 'Bad' girls versus 'good' girls: contradiction in the constitution of contemporary girlhood. *Discourse: Studies in the Cultural Politics of Education*, 28(1), 121–131.

Clark, L. (2014) Should all schools be screening their pupils for weapons? Stabbing of Ann Maguire triggers national debate over security. *Mail Online* (29 April). Available at: http://www.dailymail.co.uk/news/article-2615422/Should-schools-screening-pupils-weapons-Stabbing-Ann-Maguire-triggers-national-debate-security.html#ixzz32EwiBVS6.

Claxton, G. (2002) *Building Learning Power*. Bristol: TLO.

Clough, P. and Nutbrown, C. (2012) *A Student's Guide to Methodology* (3rd edn). London: SAGE.

Coe, R. (2014) Lesson observation: it's harder than you think. *Centre for Evaluation & Monitoring* (13 January). Available at: http://cem.org/blog/414.

Cohen, L., Manion, L., and Morrison, K. (2007) *Research Methods in Education* (6th edn). Abingdon: Routledge.

Cohen, S. (1972) *Folk Devils and Moral Panics: The Creation of Mods and Rockers*. London: MacGibbon & Kee.

Cole, T. and Visser, J. (2005) Review of literature on SEBD definitions and 'good practice', accompanying the *Managing Challenging Behaviour* report published by Ofsted.

Conroy, J. C. and de Ruyter, D. J. (2008) Contest, contradiction, and security: the moral possibilities of liminal education. *Journal of Educational Change*, 10(1), 1–12.

Cooper, K. and Olson, M. (1996) The multiple 'I's' of teacher identity. In M. Kompf, T. Boak, W. R. Bond and D. Dworet (eds), *Changing Research and Practice: Teachers' Professionalism, Identities and Knowledge*. London: Falmer Press, pp. 78–89.

Cordingley, P. (2009) Using research and evidence as a lever for change at classroom level. AERA paper. Available at: http://www.curee.co.uk/files/publication/1240997413/AERA%20Paper%2031March2009%20final.pdf.

Cornell, D. G. and Mayer, M. J. (2010) Why do school order and safety matter? *Educational Researcher*, 39(1), 7–15.

Cowley, S. (2010) *Getting the Buggers to Behave* (4th rev. edn). London: Continuum.

Dadds, M. and Hart, S. (2001) *Doing Practitioner Research Differently*. Abingdon: RoutledgeFalmer.

Darder, A., Baltodano, M. P., and Torres, R. D. (eds) (2009) *The Critical Pedagogy Reader* (2nd edn). Abingdon: Routledge.

Datta, L. (1994) Paradigm wars: a basis for peaceful coexistence and beyond. In C. S. Reichardt and S. Rallis (eds), *The Qualitative-Quantitative Debate: New Perspectives*. San Francisco, CA: Jossey-Bass, pp. 53–70.

Day, C., Kington, A., Stobart, G., and Sammons, P. (2006) The personal and professional selves of teachers: stable and unstable identities. *British Educational Research Journal*, 32(4), 601–616.

de Waal, A. (2009) Are Sir Dexter's four rules the key to school success? *The Express* (28 August).

Delgado, R. (1989) Storytelling for oppositionist and others: a plea for narrative. *Harvard Law Review*, 87(2), 2411–2441.

Delgado, R. (1995) *The Rodrigo Chronicles: Conversations About Race and Class*. New York: New York University Press.

Denzin, N. K. (2013) *Interpretive Autoethnography* (Qualitative Research Methods 17). Thousand Oaks, CA: SAGE.

Department for Children, Schools and Families (DCSF) (2009) *Statistical First Release: Special Educational Needs in England, January 2009*. SFR 14/2009. Available at: http://webarchive.nationalarchives.gov.uk/20110906154653/http://www.education.gov.uk/rsgateway/DB/SFR/s000852/index.shtml.

Department for Education (DfE) (2009) *Permanent and Fixed Period Exclusions from Schools and Exclusion Appeals in England, 2007/08*. Ref: 18/2009. Available at: http://webarchive.nationalarchives.gov.uk/20120504203418/http:/education.gov.uk/rsgateway/DB/SFR/s000860/index.shtml.

Department for Education (DfE) (2010) *The Importance of Teaching: The Schools White Paper 2010*. Cm 7980. Available at: https://www.gov.uk/government/publications/the-importance-of-teaching-the-schools-white-paper-2010.

Department for Education (DfE) (2011a) Getting the simple things right: Charlie Taylor's behaviour checklists. Available at: https://www.gov.uk/government/uploads/system/uploads/attachment_data/file/571640/Getting_the_simple_things_right_Charlie_Taylor_s_behaviour_checklists.pdf.

Department for Education (DfE) (2011b) *Permanent and Fixed Period Exclusions from Schools and Exclusion Appeals in England, 2009/10*. Ref: 17/2011. Available at: http://www.education.gov.uk/rsgateway/DB/SFR/s001016/sfr17-2011.pdf.

Department for Education (DfE) (2011c) *Support and Aspiration: A New Approach to Special Educational Needs and Disability: A Consultation*. Cm 8027. Available at: http://www.education.gov.uk/consultations/downloadableDocs/SEND%20Green%20Paper.pdf.

Department for Education (DfE) (2011d) Behaviour and discipline in schools: memorandum submitted by Department for Education. House of Commons Education Select Committees Session 2010/11. Available at: http://www.publications.parliament.uk/pa/cm201011/cmselect/cmeduc/writev/behaviour/we39.htm.

Department for Education (DfE) (2012) *Pupil Behaviour in Schools in England*. Research Report DFE-RR218. Available at: https://www.gov.uk/government/uploads/system/uploads/attachment_data/file/184078/DFE-RR218.pdf.

Department for Education (DfE) (2016a) *Educational Excellence Everywhere*. Cm 9230. Available at: https://www.gov.uk/government/uploads/system/uploads/attachment_data/file/508447/Educational_Excellence_Everywhere.pdf.

Department for Education (DfE) (2016b) *Permanent and Fixed Period Exclusions from Schools and Exclusion Appeals in England, 2014/15*. Ref: SFR 26/2016. Available at: https://www.gov.uk/government/uploads/system/uploads/attachment_data/file/539704/SFR_26_2016_text.pdf.

Department for Education and Employment (DfEE) (1997) *Excellence in Schools*. Cm 3681. London: HMSO.

Department for Education and Skills (DfES) (2001) *Special Educational Needs Code of Practice*. Ref: DfES/581/2001. London: HMSO. Available at: http://webarchive.nationalarchives.gov.uk/20130401151715/https://www.education.gov.uk/publications/eorderingdownload/dfes%200581%20200mig2228.pdf.

Department for Education and Skills (DfES) (2003) *Key Stage 3 National Strategy Behaviour and Attendance Strand*. DfES 0391/2003. London: HMSO.

DeRosier, M. E. and Thomas, J. M. (2003) Strengthening of sociometric prediction: scientific advances in the assessment of children's peer relations. *Child Development*, 74(5), 1379–1392.

Dewey, J. (1938) *Experience and Education*. New York: Macmillan.

Docking, J. W. (1980) *Control and Discipline in Schools*. London: Harper and Row.

Doerr, N. M. (2009) Introduction: knowledge, ignorance, and relations of dominance. *Critical Studies in Education*, 50(3), 289–294.

Doll, W. E. (2008) Complexity and the culture of curriculum. In M. Mason (ed.), *Complexity Theory and the Philosophy of Education*. Chichester: John Wiley, pp. 181–203.

Dollard, J., Doob, L. W., Miller, N. E., Mowrer, O. H., and Sears, R. T. (1939) *Frustration and Aggression*. New Haven, CT: Yale University Press.

Dottori, R. (2009) The concept of phronesis by Aristotle and the beginning of hermeneutic philosophy. In *Ethics and Politics*, XI/1. Trieste: University of Trieste, pp. 301–310.

Downes, D. M. and Rock, P. (2011) *Understanding Deviance: A Guide to the Sociology of Crime and Rule-Breaking* (6th edn). Oxford: Oxford University Press.

Dreikurs, R., Cassel, P., and Dreikurs Ferguson, E. (2004) *Discipline Without Tears*. New York: John Wiley.

Durmer, J. S. and Dinges, D. F. (2005) Neurocognitive consequences of sleep deprivation. *Seminars in Neurology*, 25(1), 117–129.

Dweck, C. S. (2000) *Self-Theories: Their Role in Motivation, Personality and Development*. Philadelphia, PA: Psychology Press/Taylor & Francis.

Dweck, C. S. (2006) *Mindset: How You Can Fulfil Your Potential*. New York: Ballantine.

Dyer, W. (2005) *Mercury's Child: Behaviour Change System* [ebook]. Available from: http://www.booklocker.com/p/books/1982.html?s=pdf.

Elliott, J. (2004) Worst pupils in the world. *TES* (16 January). Available at: http://www.tes.co.uk/article.aspx?storycode=389350.

Elliott, J. (2006) Educational research as a form of democratic rationality. *Journal of Philosophy of Education*, 40(2), 169–185.

Elliott, J. (2007) Assessing the quality of action research. *Research Papers in Education*, 22(2), 229–246.

Elton, Lord (1989) *Discipline in Schools. Report of the Committee of Enquiry Chaired by Lord Elton* [Elton Report]. London: HMSO.

Feingold Association (2007) *Behaviour, Learning and Health: The Dietary Connection*, ed. S. Edelkind. Available at: http://www.feingold.org/BLUEBOOK.pdf.

Fiedler, F. E. (1978) The contingency model and the dynamics of the leadership process. In L. Berkowitz (ed.), *Advances in Experimental Social Psychology*. New York: Academic Press, pp. 59–112.

Finnigan, L. (2016) Police called to parent protest outside school after 50 children sent home for wearing wrong uniform. *The Telegraph* (6 September). Available at: http://www.telegraph.co.uk/news/2016/09/06/police-called-to-parent-protest-outside-school-after-50-children/.

Forsyth, D. R. (1983) *Group Dynamics* (2nd edn). Monterey, CA: Brooks/Cole Publishing.

Foucault, M. (1977) *Discipline and Punish: The Birth of the Prison*. New York: Vintage Books.

Foucault, M. (1979) Governmentality. *Ideology and Consciousness*, 1979(6), 5–21.

Foucault, M. (1980) *Power/Knowledge; Selected Interviews and Other Writings 1972–77*. Brighton: Harvester Press.

Francis, B. (1999) Lads, lasses and (New) Labour: 14–16-year-old students' responses to the 'laddish behaviour and boys' underachievement' debate. *British Journal of Sociology of Education*, 20(3), 355–371.

Francis, B., Skelton, C., and Read, B. (2010) The simultaneous production of educational achievement and popularity: how do some pupils accomplish it? *British Educational Research Journal*, 36(2), 317–340.

Freedman, S., Lipson, B., and Hargreaves, D. (2008) *More Good Teachers*. London: Policy Exchange. Available at: https://policyexchange.org.uk/wp-content/uploads/2016/09/more-good-teachers-apr-08.pdf.

Freire, A. M. A. and Macedo, D. (2000) *The Paulo Freire Reader*. New York: Continuum.

Freire, P. (2005) *Teachers as Cultural Workers: Letters to Those Who Dare to Teach*, tr. D. Macedo, D. Koike, and A. Oliveira. Boulder, CO: Westview Press.

Freire, P. (2014) *Pedagogy of Hope*. New York: Continuum.

Fromm, E. (1941) *Escape from Freedom*. New York: Holt, Rinehart and Winston.

Garland, D. (1999) Durkheim's sociology of punishment and punishment today. In M. S. Cladis (ed.), *Durkheim and Foucault: Perspectives on Education and Punishment.* Oxford: Durkheim Press, pp. 19–35.

Gavron, K. (2009) Foreword. In K. P. Sveinsson (ed.), *Who Cares About the White Working Class?* London: Runnymede Trust, pp. 1–72.

Gee, J. and Crawford, V. (1998) Two kinds of teenagers: language, identity, and social class. In D. Alvermann, K. Hinchman, D. Moore, S. Phelps, and D. Waff (eds), *Reconceptualizing the Literacies in Adolescents' Lives*. Mahwah, NJ: Erlbaum, pp. 225–245.

Gerlach, L. and Bird, J. (2006) Feel the difference: learning in an emotionally literate school. Paper presented at Rotherham EiC Action Zone conference, Creating a Climate for Learning, 3 November.

Gibb, J. R. (1978) *Trust: A New View of Personality and Organisational Development.* Los Angeles, CA: Guild of Tutors Press.

Gilbert, I. (2015) *Meet the Renegades* [video]. Available at: https://www.youtube.com/watch?v=hZthsIqQq5w.

Gillborn, D. (2008) *Racism and Education: Coincidence or Conspiracy?* Abingdon: Routledge.

Ginott, H. G. (1972) *Teacher and Child: A Book for Parents and Teachers*. New York: Macmillan.

Giroux, H. (2011) *On Critical Pedagogy*. New York: Continuum International Publishing Group.

Giroux, H. (2015) *Dangerous Thinking in the Age of the New Authoritarianism*. Abingdon: Routledge.

Giroux, H. (2016) Radical politics in the age of American authoritarianism: connecting the dots. *Truthout* (10 April). Available at: http://www.truth-out.org/news/item/35573-radical-politics-in-the-age-of-american-authoritarianism-connecting-the-dots.

Glaser, B. and Strauss, A. (1967) *The Discovery of Grounded Theory*. New Brunswick, NJ: Aldine Transaction.

Gleick, J. (1987) *Chaos: Making a New Science*. New York: Penguin.

Goldstein, D. (2014) *The Teacher Wars: A History of America's Most Embattled Profession*. New York: Doubleday.

Goleman, D. (1996) *Emotional Intelligence: Why It Can Matter More Than IQ*. London: Bloomsbury.

Goodman, J. (2006) School discipline in moral disarray. *Journal of Moral Education*, 35(2), 213–230.

Goodson, I. F. and Cole, A. L. (1994) Exploring the teacher's professional knowledge: constructing identity and community. *Teacher Education Quarterly*, 21(1), 85–105.

Gramsci, A. (1971) *Selections from the Prison Notebooks*, eds D. Forgacs and G. Nowell-Smith. London: Lawrence & Wishart.

Greenhalgh, T. (2015) *Real vs. Rubbish EBM: What is the State of Evidence-Based Medicine, and is it Broken?* [video]. Available at: https://www.youtube.com/watch?v=qYvdhA697jI.

Gudmundsdottir, S. (1997) Introduction to the theme issue of 'narrative perspectives on research on teaching and teacher education'. *Teaching and Teacher Education*, 13(1), 1–3.

Haggis, T. (2008) 'Knowledge must be conceptual': some possible implications for complexity and dynamic systems theories for educational research. In M. Mason (ed.), *Complexity Theory and the Philosophy of Education.* Chichester: John Wiley, pp. 150–168.

Hallett, F. (2010) Do we practice what we preach? An examination of the pedagogical beliefs of teacher educators. *Teaching in Higher Education*, 15(4), 435–448.

Haney, C., Banks, W. C., and Zimbardo, P. G. (1973) Interpersonal dynamics in a simulated prison. *International Journal of Criminology and Penology*, 1(1), 69–97.

Hargreaves, A. (1994) *Changing Teachers, Changing Times: Teachers' Work and Culture in the Postmodern Age*. New York: Teachers College Press.

Hargreaves, D. H., Hester, S., and Mellor, F. (1975) *Deviance in Classrooms*. Abingdon: Routledge & Kegan Paul.

Harris, A. and Ranson, S. (2005) The contradictions of education policy: disadvantage and achievement. *British Educational Research Journal*, 31(5), 571–587.

Harris, T. A. (1995) *I'm OK – You're OK*. London: Arrow Books.

Hart, R. (2010) Classroom behaviour management: educational psychologists' views on effective practice. *Emotional and Behavioural Difficulties*, 15(4), 353–371.

Hastings, E. C., Karas, T. L., Winsler, A., Way, E., Madigan, A., and Tyler, S. (2009) Young children's video/computer game use: relations with school performance and behaviour. *Issues in Mental Health Nursing*, 30(10), 638–649.

Hattie, J. A. C. (2009) *Visible Learning: A Synthesis of Over 800 Meta-Analyses Relating to Achievement*. Abingdon: Routledge.

Hay McBer (2000) *Research Into Teacher Effectiveness: A Model of Teacher Effectiveness*. Report no. 216. Norwich: DfEE/HMSO.

Hayden, C. (2011) Crime, anti-social behaviour and schools in Britain – are all schools 'at risk'? Inaugural lecture at the Crime, Anti-Social Behaviour and Schools conference, University of Portsmouth, 26 January.

Hayden, C. and Martin, D. (2011) *Crime, Anti-Social Behaviour and Schools*. Basingstoke: Palgrave Macmillan.

Haydn, T. (2012) *Managing Pupil Behaviour: Working to Improve Classroom Climate*. Abingdon: Routledge.

Haydn, T. (2014) To what extent is behaviour a problem in English schools? Exploring the scale and prevalence of deficits in classroom climate. *Review of Education*, 2(1), 31–64. Available at: http://onlinelibrary.wiley.com/doi/10.1002/rev3.3025/pdf.

Hempel-Jorgensen, A. (2009) The construction of the 'ideal pupil' and pupils' perceptions of 'misbehaviour' and discipline: contrasting experiences from a low-socio-economic and a high-socio-economic primary school. *British Journal of Sociology of Education*, 30(4), 435–448.

Hirst, E. and Cooper, M. (2008) Keeping them in line: choreographing classroom spaces. *Teachers and Teaching: Theory and Practice*, 14(5–6), 431–445.

Hitlin, S. (2003) Values as the core of personal identity: drawing links between two theories of self. *Social Psychology Quarterly*, 66(2), 118–137.

Hogg, M. A. and Abrams, D. (1988) *Social Identifications: A Social Psychology of Intergroup Relations and Group Processes*. Abingdon: Routledge.

Hogg, M. A., Terry, D. J., and White, K. M. (1995) A tale of two theories: a critical comparison of identity theory with social identity theory. *Social Psychology Quarterly*, 58(4), 225–269.

Hollander, E. P. (1981) *Principles and Methods of Social Psychology*. New York: Oxford University Press.

Holman Jones, S., Adams, T. E., and Ellis, C. (2013) *Handbook of Autoethnography*. Abingdon: Routledge.

Holt, J. (1972) *Freedom and Beyond*. Harmondsworth: Penguin.

Holt, J. (1982 [1964]) *How Children Fail*. Harmondsworth: Penguin.

Home Office (2011) *An Overview of Recorded Crimes and Arrests Resulting from Disorder Events in August 2011*. Available at: https://www.gov.uk/government/publications/an-overview-of-recorded-crimes-and-arrests-resulting-from-disorder-events-in-august-2011.

Horn, J. (2008) Human research and complexity theory. In M. Mason (ed.), *Complexity Theory and the Philosophy of Education*. Chichester: John Wiley, pp. 124–136.

House of Commons Education Committee (HCEC) (2011) *Behaviour and Discipline in Schools. First Report of Session 2010–11. Vol. 1: Report, Together with Formal Minutes*. HC 156-1. Available at: http://www.publications.parliament.uk/pa/cm201011/cmselect/cmeduc/516/516i.pdf.

Human-Vogel, S. (2008) Complexity in education: does chaos and complexity require a different way of learning and teaching? *Educational Research Review*, 3, 77–100.

Huuki, T., Manninen, S., and Sunnari, V. (2010) Humour as a resource and strategy for boys to gain status in the field of informal school. *Gender and Education*, 22(4), 369–383.

Illsley Clarke, J. and Dawson, C. (1998) *Growing Up Again: Parenting Ourselves, Parenting Our Children* (2nd edn). Minnesota, MN: Hazelden.

Jackson, C. (2006) 'Wild' girls? An exploration of 'ladette' cultures in secondary schools. *Gender and Education*, 18(4), 339–360.

Jackson, C. (2010) Fear in education. *Educational Review*, 62(1), 39–52.

Jacobson, E. (2003) *Metaphysics of the Profane: The Political Theology of Walter Benjamin and Gershom Scholem*. New York: Columbia University Press.

Juvonen, J. and Cadigan, R. J. (2002) Social determinants of public behaviour of middle school youth perceived peer norms and need to be accepted. In F. Pajares and T. Urdan (eds), *Academic Motivation of Adolescents*. Greenwich, CT: Information Age Publishing, pp. 277–298.

Kanpol, B. (1999) *Critical Pedagogy: An Introduction* (2nd edn). Westport, CT: Bergin and Garvey.

Karpman, S. (1968) Fairy tales and script drama analysis. *Transactional Analysis Bulletin*, 7(26), 39–43.

Kauffman, S. A. (1995) *At Home in the Universe: The Search for the Laws of Self-Organization and Complexity*. Harmondsworth: Penguin.

Kelling, G. L. and Coles, C. M. (1996) *Fixing Broken Windows*. New York: Touchstone.

Kelman, H. C. (1958) Compliance, identification, and internalization: three processes of attitude change. *Journal of Conflict Resolution*, 2, 51–60.

Kershaw, A. (2012) Teachers 'in the firing line', says Michael Gove. *The Independent* (13 January). Available at: http://www.independent.co.uk/news/education/education-news/teachers-in-the-firing-line-says-michael-gove-6289108.html.

Kidd, D. (2014) *Teaching: Notes from the Front Line*. Carmarthen: Independent Thinking Press.

Kitching, K. (2009) Teachers' negative experiences and expressions of emotion: being true to yourself or keeping you in your place? *Irish Educational Studies*, 28(2), 141–154.

Košir, K. and Pečjak, S. (2005) Sociometry as a method for investigating peer relationships: what does it actually measure? *Educational Research*, 47(1), 127–144.

Kounin, J. S. (1970) *Discipline and Group Management in Classrooms*. Austin, TX: Holt, Rinehart and Winston.

Krathwohl, D. R. (2002) A revision of Bloom's taxonomy: an overview. *Theory Into Practice*, 41(4), 212–218.

Kuhn, L. (2008) Complexity and educational research: a critical reflection. In M. Mason (ed.), *Complexity Theory and the Philosophy of Education*. Chichester: John Wiley, pp. 169–180.

Kuhn, T. S. (1970) *The Structure of Scientific Revolutions* (2nd enlarged edn). Chicago, IL: University of Chicago Press.

Laevers, F. and Heylen, L. (2008) How a new era for a science of learning and education has commenced. Reflections on the position paper 'Towards a new, complexity science of learning and education'. *Educational Research Review*. Position paper 3, 87–91.

Langer, E. J., Blank, A., and Chanowitz, B. (1978) The mindlessness of ostensibly thoughtful action. *Journal of Personality and Social Psychology*, 36(6), 635–642.

Le Bon, G. (1910 [1895]) *The Crowd: A Study of the Popular Mind* [Psychologie des Foules]. London: Fisher Unwin.

Lewin, K. (1951) *Field Theory and Social Science*. New York: Harper & Brothers.

Lincoln, Y. S. (1995) Emerging criteria for quality in qualitative and interpretive research. *Qualitative Inquiry*, 1(3), 275–289.

Lipman, P. (2009) Beyond accountability: towards schools that create new people for a new way of life. In A. Darder, M. P. Baltodano, and R. D. Torres (eds), *The Critical Pedagogy Reader* (2nd edn). Abingdon: Routledge, pp. 364–383.

Little, S. G. and Akin-Little, A. (2003) Classroom management. In W. O'Donohue, J. Fisher, and S. Hayes (eds), *Cognitive Behavior Therapy: Applying Empirically Supported Techniques In Your Practice*. Hoboken, NJ: Wiley, pp. 65–70.

Lodge, C. (2001) An Investigation Into Discourses of Learning in Schools. Unpublished EdD thesis, University of London, Institute of Education.

Lührmann, T. and Eberl, P. (2007) Leadership and identity construction: reframing the leader-follower interaction from an identity theory perspective. *Leadership*, 3(1), 115–127.

Mann, L. (1981) The baiting crowd in episodes of threatened suicide. *Journal of Personality and Social Psychology*, 41(4), 703–709.

Marzano, R. J., Marzano, J. S., and Pickering, D. (2003) *Classroom Management that Works*. Alexandria, VA: ASCD.

Maslow, A. (1950) *Motivation and Personality*. New York: Ronald.

Mason, M. (2008) Complexity theory and the philosophy of education. In M. Mason (ed.), *Complexity Theory and the Philosophy of Education*. Chichester: John Wiley, pp. 1–15.

Mayes, P. (2010) The discursive construction of identity and power in the critical classroom: implications for applied critical theories. *Discourse Society*, 21(2), 189–210.

McCormack, S. (1989) Response to Render, Padilla, and Krank: but practitioners say it works! *Educational Leadership*, 46(6), 77–79.

McDermott, J. (1981) *The Philosophy of John Dewey*. Vol. 2: *The Lived Experience*. Chicago, IL and London: University of Chicago Press.

McDermott, R. P. (1977) Social relations as contexts for learning in school. *Harvard Educational Review*, 47(2), 198–213.

McLaren, P. L. (1986) *Schooling as a Ritual Performance: Towards a Political Economy of Educational Symbols and Gestures*. Abingdon: Routledge & Kegan Paul.

McLaren, P. L. (2002 [1989]) *Life in Schools: An Introduction to Critical Pedagogy in the Foundations of Education* (4th edn). London: Longman.

McLaren, P. L. (2009) Critical pedagogy: a look at the major concepts. In A. Darder, M. P. Baltodano, and R. D. Torres (eds), *The Critical Pedagogy Reader* (2nd edn). Abingdon: Routledge, pp. 61–83.

McNiff, J., Lomax, P., and Whitehead, J. (2003) *You and Your Action Research Project* (2nd edn). London: Hyde Publications.

Meeus, W. and Mahieu, P. (2009) You can see the funny side, can't you? Pupil humour with the teacher as target. *Educational Studies*, 35(5), 553–560.

Merei, F. (1958) Group leadership and institutionalization. In E. E. Maccoby, T. M. Newcomb, and E. L. Hartley (eds), *Readings in Social Psychology* (3rd edn). New York: Holt, Rinehart and Winston, pp. 522–531.

Milgram, S. (1963) Behavioral study of obedience. *Journal of Abnormal and Social Psychology*, 67(4), 371–378.

Milgram, S. (1974) *Obedience to Authority*. New York: Harper & Row.

Mills, C. W. (1959) *The Sociological Imagination*. New York: Oxford University Press.

Ministry of Justice (2011) Statistical Bulletin on the Public Disorder of 6th to 9th August 2011 – October Update (24 October). Ministry of Justice Statistics Bulletin. Available at: https://www.gov.uk/government/uploads/system/uploads/attachment_data/file/217807/august-public-disorder-stats-bulletin-241011.pdf.

Mishler, E. G. (1999) *Storylines: Craft Artists' Narratives of Identity*. Cambridge, MA: Harvard University Press.

Moreno, J. L. (1934) *Who Shall Survive? A New Approach to the Problem of Human Inter-Relations*. Washington, DC: Nervous and Mental Disease Publishing.

Morgan, M., Ludlow, L., Kitching, K., O'Leary, M., and Clarke, A. (2010) What makes teachers tick? Sustaining events in new teachers' lives. *British Educational Research Journal*, 36(2), 191–208.

Morrison, K. (2008) Educational philosophy and the challenge of complexity theory. In M. Mason (ed.), *Complexity Theory and the Philosophy of Education*. Chichester: John Wiley, pp. 16–31.

Moscovici, S. (1985) Social influence and conformity. In G. Lindzey and E. Aronson (eds), *Handbook of Social Psychology* (3rd edn). New York: Random House, pp. 347–412.

Mullen, B. (1986) Atrocity as a function of lynch mob composition: self-attention perspective. *Personality and Social Psychology Bulletin*, 12(2), 187–197.

Myhill, D. (2002) Bad boys and good girls? Patterns of interaction and response in whole class teaching. *British Educational Research Journal*, 28(3), 339–352.

Myhill, D. and Jones, S. (2006) 'She doesn't shout at no girls': pupils' perceptions of gender equity in the classroom. *Cambridge Journal of Education*, 36(1), 99–113.

National Union of Teachers (NUT) (2017) *What Happens to School Land and Buildings When a School Becomes an Academy?* London: NUT.

Newell, C. (2008) The class as a learning entity (complex adaptive system): an idea from complexity science and educational research. *SFU Educational Review*, 2(1), 5–17.

Nias, J. (1989) *Primary Teachers Talking: A Study of Teaching As Work*. Abingdon: Routledge.

Nias, J. (1996) Thinking about feeling: the emotions in teaching. *Cambridge Journal of Education*, 26(3), 293–306.

Noddings, N. (2003) *Caring: A Feminine Approach to Ethics and Moral Education* (2nd edn). Berkeley, CA: University of California Press.

Nouwen, H. J. M. (1975) *Reaching Out: The Three Movements of the Spiritual Life*. Garden City, NY: Doubleday.

Nuthall, G. (2002) The cultural myths and the realities of teaching and learning. *New Zealand Annual Review of Education*, 11, 5–11.

Nuthall, G. (2007) *The Hidden Lives of Learners*. Wellington: NZCER Press.

O'Farrell, C. (2005) *Michel Foucault*. London: SAGE.

O'Leary, M. (2013) *Classroom Observation*. Abingdon: Routledge.

Ofsted (2000) *Inspection Report: Ninestiles Secondary School, Birmingham, UK*. Ref: 224013.

Ofsted (2005) *The Annual Report of Her Majesty's Chief Inspector of Schools, 2003/04*. HC195. Available at: https://www.gov.uk/government/publications/ofsted-the-annual-report-of-her-majestys-chief-inspector-of-schools-2003-04.

Ofsted (2012) *The Framework for School Inspection*. Ref: 090019. Available at: https://www.aaia.org.uk/content/uploads/2011/03/The-framework-for-school-inspection-January-2012.pdf.

Ofsted (2013) *The Annual Report of Her Majesty's Chief Inspector of Education, Children's Services and Skills 2012/13*. HC 855. Available at: https://www.gov.uk/government/uploads/system/uploads/attachment_data/file/274262/0855.pdf.

Ofsted (2014) *Below the Radar: Low-Level Disruption in the Country's Classrooms*. Ref: 140157. Available at: http://www.gov.uk/government/publications/below-the-radar-low-level-disruption-in-the-countrys-classrooms.

Olsen, B. (2008) *Teaching What They Learn, Learning What They Live*. Boulder, CO: Paradigm Publishers.

Olweus, D. (1993) *Bullying At School: What We Know and What We Can Do*. Oxford: Blackwell.

Palmer, P. J. (1997) The heart of a teacher identity and integrity in teaching. *Change: The Magazine of Higher Learning*, 29(6), 14–21.

Paul, J. L. and Epanchin, B. C. (1991) *Educating Emotionally Disturbed Children and Youth: Theory and Practice for Teachers*. New York: Merrill.

Petty, G. (2006) *Evidenced-Based Teaching: A Practical Approach*. Cheltenham: Nelson Thornes.

Phelps, R. and Hase, S. (2002) Complexity and action research: exploring the theoretical and methodological connection. *Educational Action Research*, 10(3), 507–524.

Phelvin, P. (2007) David Cameron outlines school discipline plan. *The Telegraph* (31 July). Available at: http://www.telegraph.co.uk/news/uknews/1559034/David-Cameron-outlines-school-discipline-plan.html.

Polanyi, M. (1958) *Personal Knowledge*. Abingdon: Routledge & Kegan Paul.

Pople, L., Rees, G., Main, G., and Bradshaw, J. (2015) *Good Childhood Report 2015*. The Children's Society and the University of York. Available at: http://www.childrenssociety.org.uk/what-we-do/resources-and-publications/the-good-childhood-report-2015.

Porter, L. (2006) *Behaviour in Schools: Theory and Practice for Teachers* (2nd edn). Maidenhead: Open University Press.

Qualley, D. (1997) *Turns of Thought: Teaching Composition as Reflexive Inquiry*. Portsmouth, NH: Heinemann.

Quantz, R. A., O'Connor, T., and Magolda, P. (2011) *Rituals and Student Identity in Education*. New York: Palgrave Macmillan.

Radford, M. (2008) Complexity and truth in educational research. In M. Mason (ed.), *Complexity Theory and the Philosophy of Education*. Chichester: John Wiley, pp. 137–149.

Raz, J. (2003) *The Practice of Value*. Oxford: Oxford University Press.

Rea, D. (1997) Achievement motivation as a dynamical system: dancing on the 'edge of chaos' with 'serious fun'. Paper presented at the annual meeting of the American Educational Research Association, Chicago, 24–28 March.

Reddy, W. M. (1997) Against constructionist: the historical ethnography of emotions. *Current Anthropology*, 38(3), 327–340.

Reddy, W. M. (2001) *The Navigation of Feeling: A Framework for the History of Emotions*. Cambridge: Cambridge University Press.

Reid, A. and Deaux, K. (1996) Relationship between social and personal identities: segregation or integration? *Journal of Personality and Social Psychology*, 71(6), 1084–1091.

Remer, R. (1998) Values Orientations: Cultural Strange Attractors. Unpublished manuscript, University of Kentucky.

Reynolds, C. (1996) Cultural scripts for teachers: identities and their relation to workplace landscapes. In M. Kompf, T. Boak, W. R. Bond, and D. Dworet (eds), *Changing Research and Practice: Teachers' Professionalism, Identities and Knowledge*. London: Falmer Press, pp. 66–71.

Rigoni, D. and Walford, G. (1998) Questioning the quick fix: Assertive Discipline and the 1997 Education White Paper. *Journal of Education Policy*, 13(3), 443–452.

Riley, D. (2007) Anti-social behaviour: children, schools and parents. *Education and the Law*, 19(3–4), 221–236.

Ritchhart, R., Church, M., and Morrison, K. (2011) *Making Thinking Visible: How to Promote Engagement, Understanding, and Independence for All Learners.* San Francisco, CA: Jossey-Bass.

Robin, C. (2004) *Fear: The History of a Political Idea.* Oxford: Oxford University Press.

Rodgers, C. R. (2002) Seeing student learning: teacher change and the role of reflection. *Harvard Educational Review*, 72(2), 230–253.

Rodgers, C. R. and Raider-Roth, M. B. (2006) Presence in teaching. *Teachers and Teaching: Theory and Practice*, 12(3), 265–287.

Rogers, B. (1994) *The Language of Discipline: A Practical Approach to Effective Classroom Management.* Plymouth: Northcote House.

Rogers, B. (2002) *Classroom Behaviour: A Practical Guide to Teaching, Behaviour Management and Colleague Support.* London: Paul Chapman.

Rogers, B. (2006) *Cracking the Hard Class: Strategies for Managing the Harder Than Average Class* (2nd rev. edn). London: Paul Chapman/SAGE.

Rogers, C. R., Kirschenbaum, H., and Henderson, V. L. (1990) *The Carl Rogers Reader*. London: Constable.

Rose, N. (1999) *Powers of Freedom: Reframing Political Thought.* Cambridge: Cambridge University Press.

Ross, A. (2009) *Disengagement from Education Among 14–16 Year Olds* [Research report]. Reference: DCSF-RR178. London: National Centre for Social Research/ Department for Children, Schools and Families.

Rud Jr, A. G. (1995) Learning in comfort: developing an ethos of hospitality in education. In J. W. Garrison and A. G. Rud Jr (eds), *The Educational Conversation: Closing the Gap*. Albany, NY: SUNY Press, pp. 119–128.

St John, G. (ed.) (2008) *Victor Turner and Contemporary Cultural Performance.* New York and Oxford: Berghahn Books.

Sawada, D. and Caley, M. T. (1985) Dissipative structures: new metaphors for becoming in education. *Educational Researcher*, 14(4), 13–19.

Schön, D. A. (1983) *The Reflective Practitioner: How Professionals Think in Action.* New York: Basic Books.

Schön, D. A. (2010) Reflection-in-action. In A. Pollard (ed.), *Readings for Reflective Teaching*. London: Bloomsbury, pp. 70–72.

Schutz, W. (1979) *Profound Simplicity*. London: Turnstone Books.

Schutz, W. (1994) *The Human Element: Productivity, Self-Esteem and the Bottom Line.* San Francisco, CA: Jossey-Bass.

Sellgren, K. (2016) Harassment: girls 'wear shorts under school skirts'. *BBC News* (7 June). Available at: http://www.bbc.co.uk/news/education-36468984.

Sherif, C. W. (1976) *Orientation in Social Psychology*. New York: Harper & Row.

Sherif, M. (1936) *The Psychology of Social Norms*. New York: Harper & Row.

Sherif, M. (1966) *In Common Predicament: Social Psychology of Intergroup Conflict and Cooperation*. Boston, MA: Houghton Mifflin.

Shirlow, P. and Pain, R. (2003) The geographies and politics of fear. *Capital and Class*, 27(2), 15–26.

Shrogren, K. A., Faggella-Luby, M. N., Bae, S. J., and Wehmeyer, M. L. (2004) The effect of choice-making as an intervention for problem behaviour: a meta-analysis. *Journal of Positive Behaviour Interventions*, 6(4), 228–237.

Siegel, D. J. (2014) *Brainstorm: The Power and Purpose of the Teenage Brain*. London: Scribe.

. F. (1953) *Science and Human* New York: Macmillan.

., A. (1996) *Accelerated Learning in the* *sroom*. Stafford: Network Educational .ess.

Smith, A. (2002) *The Brain's Behind it: New Knowledge About the Brain and Learning*. Stafford: Network Educational Press.

Sommer, R. (1967) Small group ecology. *Psychological Bulletin*, 67(2), 145–152.

Stacey, R. D., Griffin, D., and Shaw, P. (2000) *Complexity and Management: Fad or Radical Challenge to Systems Thinking?* Abingdon: Routledge.

Stake, R. E. and Schwandt, T. A. (2006) On discerning quality in evaluation. In I. Shaw, M. Mark, and J. Greene (eds), *Handbook of Evaluation*. New York: SAGE, pp. 404–418.

Steer, Sir A. (chair) (2005) *Learning Behaviour: The Report of the Practitioners' Group on School Behaviour and Discipline*. Ref: DFES-1950-2005. Nottingham: Department for Education and Skills. Available at: http://www.educationengland.org.uk/documents/pdfs/2005-steer-report-learning-behaviour.pdf.

Steer, Sir A. (2009) *Learning Behaviour: Lessons Learned. A Review of Behaviour Standards and Practices in Our Schools*. Ref: DCSF-00453-2009. Nottingham: Department for Education and Skills. Available at: http://www.educationengland.org.uk/documents/pdfs/2009-steer-report-lessons-learned.pdf.

Steer, Sir A. (2010) *Behaviour and the Role of Home–School Agreement*. Ref: DCSF-00350-2010. Nottingham: Department for Education and Skills. Available at: http://www.educationengland.org.uk/documents/pdfs/2010-steer-behaviour-home-school.pdf.

Stets, J. E. and Burke, P. J. (2000) Identity theory and social identity theory. *Social Psychology Quarterly*, 63(3), 224–237.

Stets, J. E. and Carter, M. J. (2011) The moral self: applying identity theory. *Social Psychology Quarterly*, 74(2), 192–215.

Stets, J. E. and Tsushima, T. M. (2001) Negative emotion and coping responses within identity control theory. *Social Psychology Quarterly*, 64(3), 283–295.

Steutel, J. and Spiecker, B. (2000) Authority in educational relationships. *Journal of Moral Education*, 29(3), 323–337.

Stewart, I. and Jones, V. (1987) *TA Today: A New Introduction to Transactional Analysis*. Nottingham: Lifespace Publishing.

Strodtbeck, F. L., James, R. M., and Hawkins, C. (1957) Social status in jury deliberations. *American Sociological Review*, 22(6), 713–719.

Stryker, S. (1968) Identity salience and role performance. *Journal of Marriage and the Family*, 30(4), 558–564.

Stryker, S. (1980) *Symbolic Interactionism: A Social Structure Version*. Menlo Park, CA: Benjamin Cummings.

Stryker, S. (1987) *The Interplay of Affect and Identity: Exploring the Relationships of Social Structure, Social Interaction, Self, and Emotion*. Chicago, IL: American Sociological Association.

Stryker, S. and Serpe, R. T. (1982) Commitment identity salience, role behaviour: a theory and research example. In W. Ickes and E. S. Knowles (eds), *Personality, Roles, and Social Behaviour*. New York: Springer-Verlag, pp. 199–218.

Sugden, J. (2009) Waltham Forest pioneers random weapon checks in all schools. *The Times* (29 April). Available at: http://www.thetimes.co.uk/tto/education/article1800809.ece.

Súilleabháin, S. V. O. (1983) The concept of authority: an essential personal dimension for the professional teacher. *Irish Educational Studies*, 3(1), 9–20.

Sunderland, M. (2006) *The Science of Parenting: How Today's Brain Research Can Help You Raise Happy, Emotionally Balanced Children*. London: DK Publishing.

Surrey, J. L. (1991) The 'self-in-relation': a theory of women's development. In J. Jordan, A. Kaplan, J. B. Miller, I. Stiver, and J. Surrey (eds), *Women's Growth in Connection: Writings from the Stone Center*. New York: Guilford Press, pp. 51–66.

Sutton, R. E., Mudrey-Camino, R., and Knight, C. C. (2009) Teachers' emotion regulation and classroom management. *Theory Into Practice*, 48(2), 130–137.

Sutton Trust (2001) *Education Apartheid: A Practical Way Forward*. Available at: http://www.suttontrust.com/researcharchive/educational-apartheid-practical-way-forward/.

Swann Jr, W. B., Stein-Seroussi, A., and Giesler, R. B. (1992) Why people self-verify. *Journal of Personality and Social Psychology*, 62, 392–401.

Sweller, J. (1994) Cognitive load theory, learning difficulty and instructional design. *Learning and Instruction*, 4, 295–312.

Swinson, J. (1990) Improving behaviour: a whole-class approach, using pupil perceptions and social skills training. *Educational Psychology in Practice*, 6(2), 82–89.

Sylvester, R. (2011) Teacher as bully: knowingly or unintentionally harming students. *Delta Kappa Gamma Bulletin*, 77(2), 42–45.

Teacher Development Trust (2015) *Developing Great Teaching: Lessons from the International Reviews into Effective Professional Development*. Available at: http://tdtrust.org/wp-content/uploads/2015/10/DGT-Summary.pdf.

Temple, S. (1992a) Group process: the growing group's four model link-up. Unpublished coursework material.

Temple, S. (1992b) Stages of group development adapted from Tuckman. Unpublished coursework material.

Temple, S. (1999) Functional Fluency for educational transactional analysts. *Transactional Analysis Journal*, 29(3), 164–174.

Temple, S. (2004) Update on the Functional Fluency model in education. *Transactional Analysis Journal*, 34(3), 197–204. Available at: https://westtownapps.com/modx2/assets/pdfs/TAJ_34_3_Functional_Fluency.pdf.

Temple, S. (2005) Teachers are young people's leaders. *Antidote's Emotional Literacy Update*, 20, 10–11. Available at: https://westtownapps.com/modx2/assets/pdfs/Teachers_as_Leaders_ELU_20_09_05.pdf.

Temple, S. (2007) Accounting – the core of the concepts: what is the difference between 'accounting' in adult and 'accounting' from parent or child? Paper for the Institute of Developmental Transactional Analysis annual conference, Glasgow, 9–10 November.

Temple, S. (2008) Bringing up the child: the importance of functionally fluent parents, carers and educators. In K. Tudor (ed.), *The Adult is Parent to the Child: TA with Children and Young People*. Lyme Regis: Russell House Publishing, pp. 217–227.

Temple, S. (2009) The Functional Fluency modes in action. Available at: https://westtownapps.com/modx2/assets/pdfs/The_FF_Model_has_Come_of_Age_EATA_2003_update_2009.pdf.

Temple, S. (2012) Lifecycle of a research project TIFF – ten years on. *The Transactional Analyst* (autumn). Available at: https://westtownapps.com/modx2/assets/pdfs/TIFF_10_Years_on.pdf.

Theramin Trees (2010) *Transactional Analysis 2: Games* [video] (17 June). Available at: https://www.youtube.com/watch?v=YOqJ4sc9TAc.

Thompson, G. (2010) Acting, accidents and performativity: challenging the hegemonic good student in secondary schools. *British Journal of Sociology of Education*, 31(4), 413–430.

Todes, D. P. (2014) *Ivan Pavlov: A Russian Life in Science*. Oxford: Oxford University Press.

Tosey, P. (2002) Teaching on the edge of chaos. Complexity theory, learning systems and enhancement. Working paper. Available at: http://epubs.surrey.ac.uk/1195/.

Tuckman, B. W. (1965) Developmental sequence in small groups. *Psychological Bulletin*, 63(6), 384–399.

Turner, J. C. (1985) Social categorization and the self-concept: a social cognitive theory of group behaviour. In E. J. Lawler (ed.), *Advances in Group Processes: Theory and Research.* Greenwich, CT: JAI Press, pp. 77–121.

Turner, J. C. (1991) *Social Influence.* Milton Keynes: Open University Press.

Turner, J. C., Hogg, M. A., Oakes, P. J., Reicher, S. D., and Wetherell, M. S. (1987) *Rediscovering the Social Group: A Self-Categorization Theory.* Oxford: Blackwell.

Turner, V. W. (1969) *The Ritual Process: Structure and Anti-Structure.* Abingdon: Routledge.

Turner, V. W. (1990) Are there universals of performance in myth, ritual and drama? In R. Schechner and W. Appel (eds), *By Means of Performance: Intercultural Studies of Theatre and Ritual.* Cambridge: Cambridge University Press, pp. 8–18.

Tzuo, P. W. (2007) The tension between teacher control and children's freedom in a child-centered classroom: resolving the practical dilemma through a closer look at the related theories. *Early Childhood Education Journal*, 35(1), 33–39.

Usher, R. (1996) A critique of the neglected epistemological assumptions of educational research. In R. Usher and D. Scott (eds), *Understanding Educational Research.* Abingdon: Routledge, pp. 9–32.

Usher, R. and Edwards, R. (2004) *Postmodernism and Education: Different Voices, Different Worlds.* Abingdon: Routledge.

Varenne, H. (2007) Difficult collective deliberations: anthropological notes toward a theory of education. *Teachers College Record*, 109(7), 1559–1588.

Verkuyten, M. (2002) Making teachers accountable for students' disruptive classroom behaviour. *British Journal of Sociology of Education*, 23(1), 107–122.

Walls, R. T., Sperling, R. A., and Weber, K. D. (2001) Autobiographical memory of school. *Journal of Educational Research*, 95(2), 116–127.

Walton, S. (2001) *Scared of the Kids? Curfews, Crime and the Regulation of Young People.* Leicester: Perpetuity Press.

Warnock, M. (1989) The authority of the teacher. *Westminster Studies in Education*, 12, 73–81.

Warrington, M. and Younger, M. (2011) 'Life is a tightrope': reflections on peer group inclusion and exclusion amongst adolescent girls and boys. *Gender and Education*, 23(2), 153–168.

Waterhouse, S. (2004) Deviant and non-deviant identities in the classroom: patrolling the boundaries of the normal social world. *European Journal of Special Needs Education*, 19(1), 69–84.

Watson, J. B. (1924) *Behaviorism.* New York: People's Institute.

Watson, J. B. and Rayner, R. (1920) Conditioned emotional reactions. *Journal of Experimental Psychology*, 3(1), 1–14.

Whitehead, J. (1989) Creating a living educational theory from questions of the kind, 'How do I improve my practice?' *Cambridge Journal of Education*, 19(1), 41–52.

Whitehead, J. (1998) Educational action researchers creating their own living educational theories. Paper presented to the American Educational Research Association's annual conference, San Diego, 13–17 April.

Whitehead, J. (2006) Notes to help with constructing a doctoral thesis for examination. Available at: http://www.jackwhitehead.com/PhD/jwphdnotes081206.htm.

Whitehead, J. (2008) Using a living theory methodology in improving practice and generating knowledge. Presentation at Zhejiang University, China, 13 June.

Whitehead, J. and McNiff, J. (2006) *Action Research: Living Theory*. London: SAGE.

Widdowson, M. (2010) *Transactional Analysis: 100 Key Points & Techniques*. London: Taylor Francis.

Wiechert, C. (2011) On the question of the three-fold structure of the main lesson: a stimulus for discussion. *Journal for Waldorf Education*, 13(1), 24–29.

Wightman, A. (2010) *The Poor Had No Lawyers: Who Owns Scotland (And How They Got It)*. Edinburgh: Birlinn.

Wiliam, D. (2009) *Assessment for Learning: Why, What and How? Inaugural Professorial Lecture by Dylan Wiliam*. London: Institute of Education, University of London.

Wiliam, D. (2011) *Embedded Formative Assessment*. Bloomington: Solution Free Press.

Williams, R. (1977) *Marxism and Literature*. New York: Oxford University Press.

Willis, P. (1977) *Learning to Labor: How Working Class Kids Get Working Class Jobs*. New York: Columbia University Press.

Wolfe, S. and Alexander, R. J. (2008) *Argumentation and Dialogic Teaching: Alternative Pedagogies for a Changing World*. London: Futurelab. Available at: http://www.robinalexander.org.uk/wp-content/uploads/2012/05/wolfealexander.pdf.

Woods, P. and Carlyle, D. (2002) Teacher identities under stress: the emotions of separation and renewal. *International Studies in Sociology of Education*, 12(2), 169–190.

Wright, A. (2009) Every Child Matters: discourses of challenging behaviour. *Pastoral Care in Education: An International Journal of Personal, Social and Emotional Development*, 27(4), 279–290.

Yilmaz, K. (2009) Primary school teachers' views about pupil control ideologies and classroom management styles. *Cypriot Journal of Educational Sciences*, 4(3), 157–167.

Youdell, D. (2011) *School Trouble: Identity, Power and Politics in Education*. Abingdon: Routledge.

Young, M. E. (1992) *Counseling Methods and Techniques: An Eclectic Approach*. New York: Merrill.

Zembylas, M. (2003) Emotions and teacher identity: a post-structural perspective. *Teachers and Teaching: Theory and Practice*, 9(3), 213–238.

Zembylas, M. (2009) Global economies of fear: affect, politics and pedagogical implications. *Critical Studies in Education*, 50(2), 187–199.

Zettergren, P. (2003) School adjustment in adolescence for previously rejected, average and popular children. *British Journal of Educational Psychology*, 73(2), 207–221.

Zhang, M. (2004) Time to change the truancy laws? Compulsory education: its origin and modern dilemma. *Pastoral Care in Education: An International Journal of Personal, Social and Emotional Development*, 22(2), 27–33.

Zimbardo, P. G. (1970) The human choice: individuation, reason, and order versus deindividuation, impulse, and chaos. In W. J. Arnold and D. Levine (eds), *Nebraska Symposium on Motivation*. Lincoln, NE: University of Nebraska Press, pp. 237–307.

Zimbardo, P. G. (2007) *The Lucifer Effect: How Good People Turn Evil*. Reading: Random House Group.

Zimbardo, P. G. and Boyd, J. (2008) *The Time Paradox: Using the New Psychology of Time to Your Advantage*. Reading: Rider.

Zimbardo, P. G., Maslach, C., and Haney, C. (2000) Reflections on the Stanford Prison Experiment: genesis, transformations, consequences. In T. Blass (ed.), *Obedience to Authority: Current Perspectives on the Milgram Paradigm*. Mahwah, NJ: Erlbaum, pp. 193–237.

When the Adults Change, Everything Changes

Seismic Shifts in School Behaviour

Paul Dix

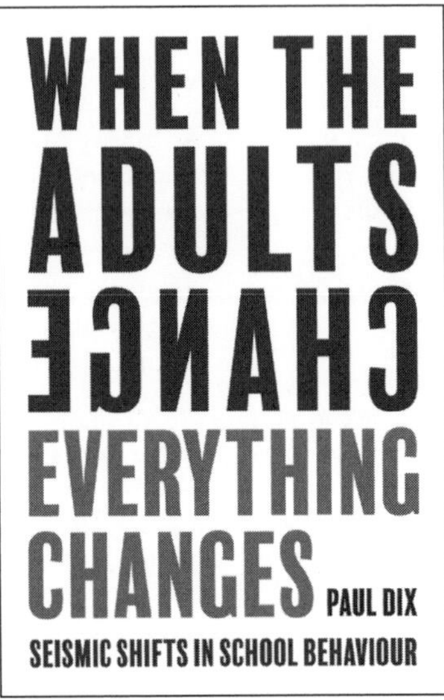

ISBN: 978-178135273-1

This book is a must-read for anyone who works with children or young people.

Seamus Oates, CBE, CEO, TBAP Multi-Academy Trust

If you want to create an inclusive school where children's behaviour is not only managed, but is changed as well, you should not miss out on reading this book.

Sue Cowley, teacher and education author

I have learnt much from this book that will shape and amend my future practice and whole-heartedly recommend it to even the most experienced teacher.

Phil Beadle, teacher and author

This book is a game changer. Your students need you to read *When the Adults Change, Everything Changes*.

Jaz Ampaw-Farr, speaker, author and 'Resilience Ninja'

Far from being just another book on behaviour, this is a blueprint for how behaviour should be in schools.

Russell J. Ingleby, Head Teacher, Hightown Junior, Infant and Nursery School

Paul Dix gets it. After reading this book, you will too.

Jarlath O'Brien, Head Teacher, Carwarden House Community School